JOHN DEWEY AND CONTINENTAL PHILOSOPHY

John Dewey and Continental Philosophy

Edited by Paul Fairfield

Southern Illinois University Press
Carbondale

Paperback edition 2013

Printed in the United States of America

16 15 14 13 4 3 2 1

The Library of Congress cataloging data for the hardcover edition is as follows:
John Dewey and Continental philosophy / edited by Paul Fairfield.
p. cm.
Includes bibliographical references and index.
ISBN-13: 978-0-8093-2987-8 (alk. paper)
ISBN-10: 0-8093-2987-5 (alk. paper)
ISBN-13: 978-0-8093-8585-0 (ebook)
ISBN-10: 0-8093-8585-6 (ebook)
1. Dewey, John 1859–1952. 2. Continental philosophy.
I. Fairfield, Paul, 1966.
B945.D44J54 2010
191—dc22 2009043157

The international standard book numbers for the paperback edition are as follows:
ISBN-13: 978-0-8093-3304-2 (paperback : alk. paper)
ISBN-10: 0-8093-3304-X (paperback : alk. paper)

The paper used in this publication meets the minimum requirements of American National Standard for Information Sciences—Permanence of Paper for Printed Library Materials, ANSI Z39.48-1992. ♾

For Gwyneth Fairfield

Contents

Introduction: Overdue Conversations

Paul Fairfield

It is a surprise to no one well versed in both classical pragmatism and philosophy in any of the continental European traditions to hear that opportunities for fruitful conversation are plentiful across this particular boundary of thought, especially in the case of the greatest of American pragmatists, John Dewey. Dewey made no secret of his profound and lifelong indebtedness to the thought of G. W. F. Hegel in particular, and not only during his early period when he was working under the heavy influence of Anglo-American idealism.[1] Whether we are speaking of Dewey in the context of late-nineteenth- and early-twentieth-century America or of phenomenology, hermeneutics, critical theory, or poststructuralism in twentieth-century continental philosophy, we find a common trajectory, or trajectories, of thought all arising from post-Kantian idealism and continuing efforts to come to terms with issues bequeathed to us primarily by Immanuel Kant and Hegel. It is this conversation into which Dewey was initiated during his doctoral studies at Johns Hopkins University in the 1880s, under the direction of George Sylvester Morris, and which provided a basic orientation to his thought throughout a long and extraordinarily productive writing career. Hegel's thought, together with an equally profound indebtedness to Darwinian biology, informed Dewey's contributions quite obviously in the fields of metaphysics and epistemology but also in various other branches of philosophical inquiry that equally concerned him, from ethics and politics to education and aesthetics. Despite the simplistic misreadings to which his works were often subject during his lifetime and which remain unfortunately common today, Dewey was an original, subtle, and fundamentally dialectical thinker. Despite waning interest in his works in the middle to latter decades of the past century—an eclipse, it seems, that was temporary and owing not to any actual refutations of his thought but to the popularity of analytic philosophy with which Dewey's thought is somewhat uncongenial—Dewey's writings remain as relevant today as any philosopher of his era (1859–1952) and have enjoyed new life since the publication of his complete works and correspondence.[2]

Widespread misunderstanding and ungenerous dismissals regularly greeted early pragmatist thought in both Anglo-American and continental philosophical circles. To early analytic critics such as Bertrand Russell and G. E. Moore, the writings of Charles Sanders Peirce, William James, and John Dewey alike seemed like so much superficiality and crass Americanism, an apologia for New World optimism that appeared to overlook dimensions of thought that philosophy in the rationalist and empiricist traditions had better grasped. These figures received an equally dismissive hearing on the Continent, aided and abetted no doubt by two world wars in the case of Germany, effectively causing pragmatism and continental philosophy to develop as separate traditions on separate continents, barely on speaking terms with each other in spite of numerous and obvious affinities between them. The nondialogue was fully reciprocated. Despite his facility with the French and German languages, his unmistakable Hegelian leanings, and a deeply phenomenological sensibility, Dewey lacked more than a passing knowledge of the writings of Søren Kierkegaard, Friedrich Nietzsche, Wilhelm Dilthey, Edmund Husserl, Martin Heidegger, Jean-Paul Sartre, and other major figures in continental philosophy after Hegel but for Karl Marx, whose works he knew and held in low regard. The thirty-eight thick volumes that make up Dewey's complete works contain either no references or only a small handful to each of these figures, again with the exception of Marx. We can only speculate about what an exchange between Dewey and Husserl or Heidegger might have looked like and the themes upon which it might have turned, the possibilities being many. Dewey's private correspondence contains a similar dearth of references to such figures, confirming his thorough lack of acquaintance with and interest in them. A letter from Dewey to Arthur Bentley from May 1941, for instance, reads in part: "I never followed Husserl; I got the impression that he was trying to say things that should be said empirically in some circuitous language that would keep up some connection with the Teutonic tradition in philosophy. But I've nothing in the way of knowledge to go on." Another letter to Bentley, from February 1942, reads: "I hope in the long run the influx of German refugees will contribute something but meantime a lot of them are committed to advertising the goods they brought over with them—intellectual carpetbaggers—and those who have 'phenomenology'[—] whatever this is—to sell seem the worst." One from January 1947 to Adelbert Ames states: "I have never read anything of Kierkegaard's—what I've read about him hasn't attracted me, but I really haven't enough to go on. The so-called 'existentialist' development in Germany and France claims to follow him, but judging from other things they don't know what they are about anyway." Yet another, from November 1947, reads:

> I have to confess—or perhaps boast—that I haven't read either Toynbee or Existentialism. . . . [T]he reviews of Nouy, [in] spite of his being a best seller closed him off entirely for me. And much the same for existentialism. I think they are the reactions of people who are scared and haven't got the guts to face life. . . . A friend and former student of mine . . . has been reading Reinhold Neibuhr, and is writing a review, . . . the publisher of which says it is devastating. Well I have the impression that both he and Kiekaagard—excuse spelling—have both completely lost faith in traditional statements of Christianity, haven't got any modern substitute and so are making up, off the bat, something which supplies to them the gist of Christianity—what they find significant in it and what they approve of in modern thought—as when two newspapers are joined, the new organ always says "retaining the best features of both." De Sartre, I take it, is typical or symbolic of the present state of Europe; has to have some refuge from its terrible state—a kind of new-stoicism in which existence reduces pretty well to what the individual, giving up everything else as hopeless, can make out of it on his own hook. As I haven't read a word of him, you don't need to bother with what I say.[3]

It is unfortunate indeed that the many opportunities for dialogue between Dewey and his continental contemporaries were so entirely missed and that these two traditions (if, for simplicity's sake, we can speak of continental philosophy as a singular tradition—which, more strictly speaking, it is not) took shape largely in ignorance of the other. It would fall therefore to later philosophers to take up this conversation on Dewey's or pragmatism's behalf—an overdue conversation, to be sure, and one that includes the present volume. The contributors to this volume are not beginning this conversation from scratch, of course. The philosopher best known for his attempt to bring Deweyan pragmatism, or something resembling it, to bear on certain themes in continental thought is undoubtedly Richard Rorty, whose efforts in this connection have met with decidedly mixed reviews. *Philosophy and the Mirror of Nature* in particular is often credited with initiating a renewed interest in pragmatist thought in general, including Dewey, while on the same basis many analysts have found cause to confirm yet again their refusal to read the pragmatists and continental figures alike or to dismiss it all as "not philosophy" (a phrase one hears rather often these days).[4] Others have made important contributions as well, including many of the authors in this volume. I shall not provide an inventory of these contributions here, nor attempt to name all those who have played a role in getting this belated conversation started, many of whom are noted in the essays that follow.

The purpose of this collection is to bring into conversation the philosophy of John Dewey and several continental philosophical traditions, from post-Kantian idealism and Nietzsche's thought to twentieth-century phenomenology, hermeneutics, and poststructuralism. Many possibilities for constructive engagement of this kind undoubtedly exist, possibilities that have been too seldom realized. This volume goes some way toward correcting this while of course making no claim to have exhausted the possibilities for meaningful exchange. The essays here assembled are by necessity somewhat selective in their focus. A few essays seek to locate Dewey's thought in the context of German philosophy, from Kant to Hegel, while others interpret the relation between the former and specific themes in the work of Nietzsche, Heidegger, Hans-Georg Gadamer, Michel Foucault, Jacques Derrida, and Gilles Deleuze. Other themes and figures might well have been chosen—Maurice Merleau-Ponty or Paul Ricoeur, for example, or perhaps Jürgen Habermas or Sartre—but the essays presented here provide a rich sample of the kind of exchange that might have taken place decades or a century ago yet, for reasons good or bad, did not.

Some of the major themes that the following chapters take up include naturalism, organicism, and contextualism, which Dewey critically appropriated from post-Kantian idealism. They further include the question of whether we can identify traces of *Bildung* in Dewey's writings on education. Whether pragmatism is a gay science in Nietzsche's sense and, beyond this, what these two figures shared in terms of the basic task and self-understanding of philosophy are further questions that are explored here. Pragmatism's complex relation to twentieth-century phenomenology and hermeneutics, including the vexed question of whether Heidegger was a pragmatist in any meaningful sense, and how Dewey and Gadamer regarded the status of poetry among the arts receive explicit treatment as well. Additionally, several essays investigate a series of connections between Dewey and contemporary French philosophy, including the notions of subjectivity, education, and the critique of modernity in Foucault, language and politics in Derrida, and the concept of experience in Deleuze.

Dewey provided a compelling and properly phenomenological case for regarding thinking as essentially the practice of inquiry, or what he often termed "experimental intelligence." It is in this spirit of experimental inquiry, as well as sound scholarship, that the essays that follow are written. Philosophy of a somewhat hybrid and boundary-crossing kind is precisely what Dewey himself often advanced in his inquiries, investigations that reveal interesting and often surprising connections. If no attempt is made in this volume to deny important differences that do separate the spirit and substance of Dewey's thought from philosophy in the continental traditions, it remains that the affinities run deep and on a variety of topics of which these studies provide an important but far from exhaustive treatment.

Notes

1. See James A. Good's fine study, *A Search for Unity in Diversity: The "Permanent Hegelian Deposit" in the Philosophy of John Dewey* (Lanham: Lexington Books, 2006).

2. John Dewey's collected writings are divided into the early, middle, and later works, all of which are edited by Jo Ann Boydston and published by Southern Illinois University Press. See as well The Correspondence of John Dewey, 1871–1952, gen. ed. Larry A. Hickman (Carbondale, Ill.: Center for Dewey Studies, 2005).

3. Correspondence of John Dewey. Dates are given in text.

4. Richard Rorty, *Philosophy and the Mirror of Nature* (Princeton: Princeton University Press, 1979).

1] German Post-Kantian Idealism and Dewey's Metaphysics: Mutual Themes

James Scott Johnston

The purpose of this essay is to note two mutual themes in post-Kantian idealism (hereafter, PKI) and Dewey's early and early-middle metaphysics (roughly 1882–1912). These themes are (a) the turn away from subjectivism and (b) naturalism. Two "waves" of each of these are discernible: the first occurred in Germany circa 1790, the second in England and the United States circa 1890. These waves were generated by the shocks of what was perceived as an *over-subjectivization* of knowledge, experience, and consciousness in German philosophy and Anglo-American philosophy. The "solution" for each was the turn toward an understanding of body/mind/spirit/world that is anti-subjective, naturalistic, and organic.

I shall demonstrate that a number of thinkers attempted to get out from under the subjectivist spell in Germany, Great Britain, and America. I discuss J. G. Fichte, J. F. C. Hölderlin, and F. W. J. Schelling in regard to PKI and (early and early-middle period) John Dewey in regard to Anglo-American neo-idealism (AANI) and experimental idealism.[1] As Dewey self-consciously identified with AANI (from 1882 to 1893), he shared many of the convictions of his contemporaries in their turn to PKI to combat materialism, crude realism, and positivism. After his "break" with AANI, he continued his quest for an anti-subjectivist, naturalistic philosophy. Crudely put, Dewey took PKI's notions of self and social relations and naturalized them and took the notion of dialectic and rendered it an experimental set of methods, which, in Dewey's terminology, is scientific inquiry. I wish to investigate Dewey's early and early-middle metaphysics in the context of his commitment to the central theses of PKI, anti-subjectivism and naturalism.

Historical Background

I shall begin with brief historical remarks on PKI. Distinguishing characteristics of PKI include a response to *skepticism* regarding claims of knowledge;

the centrality of the *self* (and particularly *self-consciousness)* that is absent from prior schools of thought, including rationalism; the turn away from *subjectivity* and *subjectivist* accounts of knowing and being; and the development of a *naturalist* account of nature/mind or mind/world.[2] I shall deal with these briefly and in turn; we shall see the latter two themes reemerge as important elements of the response to AANI in the late nineteenth century. Skepticism is best understood as a reaction to the rationalism of the period leading up to (and, in some accounts, including) Immanuel Kant.[3] Kant, it is said, "destroys" metaphysics by creating a gulf between what we can know (science) and what we can believe (faith). There is no turning back to Cartesian certainties; Kant effectively demonstrates that Descartes's understanding of the self is premised on a viciously circular appeal to a transcendental ideal that is unavailable to cognition (Kant, *Critique*, A379). Kant's solution is a seemingly dualistic one: transcendental idealism. Here, the phenomenal realm corresponds to our knowledge of the world and the noumenal realm to our thinking things in themselves. "I understand by the transcendental idealism of all appearances the doctrine that they are all together to be regarded as mere representations and not as things in themselves, and accordingly that space and time are only sensible forms of our intuition, but not determinations given for themselves or conditions of objects as things in themselves" (A369). Did Kant solve the problem? Without an overarching law or principle to connect these, the ability to ground knowledge claims seemed imperiled. This state of affairs was unacceptable to those who followed Kant; much labor was invested in closing the gap by accounts of mind and world that attempt to derive a first principle from which all further knowledge claims are possible. The way forward for PKI was to retreat from subjectivism toward a non-question-begging ground that incorporated both mind and world. Important in this movement was a "theory of the subject," as Dieter Henrich has called it.[4] This meant a robust understanding of the self, the nature of self-reflexivity, and the role the self plays in the formation or development of epistemological matters such as perceptions and representations.

The other significant development that had to occur to avoid a question-begging ground was a movement toward nature and the natural. This was not an "objectivist" move (though G. W. F. Hegel did call his objective idealism). There was no question of a fully materialist philosophy being promulgated. Rather, an organic conception of mind and world, in which one is folded into the other, was proffered. For Schelling and Hegel, this was the rejoinder to subjectivism. This account has the advantage of avoiding the skeptical results of subjectivity (the problem of "other minds," the problem of foundations, the problem of the mind/nature duality, the loss or question of the absolute/God), and it makes nature and spirit one. This required a new "method" to replace the Cartesian isolation of first principles and the postulation of God and nature from these. Fichte introduced what would become the predominant method of German idealism—dialectic. Not only is dialectic (in this case, the dialectic of subject and object) the "new" method of philosophy, but dialectic arises "organically" from the self. The world follows from the self, positing itself as other—the not-self. This is a fundamental insight that post-Kantian idealists make much of in their respective philosophies: the "I" posits itself as other.

As I have noted, naturalism for PKI was not materialistic: rather, it was the consequence of a fusion of ideal and real. The rational-ideal (*spirit* or *mind*) suffused nature. It was in this way Schelling and Hegel could say that nature is spirit-filled and has intrinsic totality or purpose. Kant first began the project of combining naturalistic and idealistic elements in his *Critique of Pure Reason*; this naturalistic philosophy he labeled "empirical realism" (Kant, *Critique*, A370–73). Nevertheless, nature and idea or spirit were not brought to an organic and complete whole until Schelling's and, later, Hegel's philosophies of nature were produced. It was in Schelling's *First Outline of a System of the Philosophy of Nature* and his *System of Transcendental Philosophy*, in particular, that naturalism stood side by side with idealism.[5]

By contrast, the dominant streams of Anglo-American philosophy by mid-nineteenth century were empiricism, one or another variant of utilitarianism (J. S. Mill's being the most popular), and positivist and realist-inspired accounts of social philosophy, especially of Auguste Comte and Herbert Spencer. Logic was generally inductive; Mill's *Logic*, published in 1843, had a pronounced effect on British science, and British science gave pride of place to inductive techniques. In the United States, professional philosophy was in its infancy: the so-called St. Louis Hegelians—most notably William Torrey Harris—had yet to arrive. What passed for philosophy was largely theology and religious doctrine dressed up as theories of morals. University students seldom had the opportunity to study philosophy per se, and when they did encounter (moral) philosophy, it was often fulsome Protestant rhetoric from the president of the university, given as the capstone course of the undergraduate program.

This state of affairs changed by the time Dewey attended Johns Hopkins (1882–84). Beyond the transformation of the universities, several powerful criticisms of the prevailing empirical philosophy are extant. To begin with, the discipline of psychology was beginning to assert itself; thinkers such as

Wilhelm Wundt in Germany blended idealist thinking with the new "discoveries" of empirical psychology. A reaction to behaviorism in science was underway: William James famously criticized Gustav Fechner and Hermann Helmholtz for their blatant materialism, mechanism, and positivism in his *Principles of Psychology* (1890). The prevalence of "mentalism" was also beginning to assert itself in psychology, and though James abhorred this as much as he did materialism, he nevertheless fought for a view that integrated the mental together with the physical in the experiential.

By 1882, AANI was competing with Mill and Spencer for the educated public's attention. AANI had a critique of positivism, mechanism, empiricism, and utilitarianism, as well as a robust theoretic base of its own. AANI owed its debt to Hegel; certainly, the St. Louis Hegelians, as well as the Scottish philosophers Edward and John Caird, Thomas Hill Green, and John Watson (all of whom were operative in 1884), drew heavily from Hegel. Yet, AANI is in some respects distinguishable from Hegel. To begin with, the focus shifted from systematic philosophy to social ethics and philosophy of religion: sensing the "demise" of arguments in favor of the existence of God and the wane of theological anthropologies, these thinkers attempted to discern the relationship of God in and to the ethical absolute.

The lines between German and American philosophers were strong in the 1880s. James, of course, famously spent many months in Germany, both as a child and on several occasions recuperating from various psychological maladies. G. S. Morris, John Dewey's teacher at the University of Vermont, studied under Adolph Trendelenburg. G. Stanley Hall, who later became famous as the author of *Adolescence*, also studied in Germany (with Wilhelm Wundt). Dewey took classes with not only Morris but Hall as well. Hall and Morris disliked each other, but this did not stop Dewey from learning from each. Hall taught Dewey experimental and physiologic psychology and, most important, introduced him to the works of Wundt. Wundt taught Dewey what became two central themes in Dewey's subsequent work: (a) behavior is rooted in a biological matrix, and (b) physiology, behavior, and mental activity combine in an organic whole (Shook 80–81).[6] Wundt himself was a philosopher of great repute and self-consciously drew from German idealism in his own works.

Beyond this, Dewey was in close contact with proponents of AANI at the time, particularly Thomas Hill Green, Edward Caird, and John Watson. Dewey's early criticisms of Kant were largely inspired by these thinkers as well as by his reading of Hegel. It was not until approximately 1891 that he began to steer away from the seeming absolutist conclusions of AANI, and this voyage was a gradual one. Dewey, as the story goes, began his philosophic career as an absolute idealist, abandoned this for "instrumentalism," and then adopted what he came to call "experimentalism" (Dewey, "From Absolutism"). This is detailed in Dewey's essay "From Absolutism to Experimentalism" and in the many standard biographies of Dewey extant, including that of Dewey's daughter Jane.

In fact, Dewey fought two tensions in his early thought. The tensions—AANI on the one hand and Wundtian (and Jamesian) empirical psychology on the other—were ultimately solidified into an organic view that considered behavior and mental activity as dynamic events and as functions rather than static faculties, concepts, or entities. In fact, it was Dewey's fortune to see the themes of evolvement, adjustment, and adaptation (important naturalist themes) as central, for he was able to bring together the AANI of his early thought with the scientific understandings of the day and fold them into a comprehensive account. The "elements" of empirical psychology and AANI were already in place in many of Dewey's earliest writings.

After 1893, Dewey effectively stopped talking in AANI terms. By this time, he began to use fully naturalist notions of logic and experience and turned to biology and biological metaphors. Indeed, he was quite suspicious of any metaphysical pronouncements. Dewey's quest for unification persisted, despite the "turn." Inquiry took center stage as the means with which to investigate and understand natural and social phenomena. The results of inquiry took the place of much of the older metaphysical apparatus: objects, knowledge, thoughts, and thinking. These results were no more important than the means by which they were obtained. Though there was never any question of Dewey accepting a fully *dialectical* understanding of mind and world, the accent on process, on method, and on transformation and continuity remained in the turn. Idealism existed in Dewey's philosophy, but it was no longer the philosophy of the absolute. This was now an *experimental idealism*, to use James Good's valuable tag.

Fichte: The Retreat from Subjectivism

As I alluded to earlier, it is a common but false assumption that PKI espoused a strong form of subjectivism.[7] All of the German idealists (as well as Kant) thought the Cartesian "subjectivist" solution to the problem of skepticism—the dualism of mind and matter—was untenable. All of them worked to overcome this dualism while aware of the need for a non-question-begging, noncircular, and nonregressive foundation for the claims of knowledge. Kant's "solution" lay in the "I think that accompanies all my representations" (Kant, *Critique*,

B131–32). That is to say, the possibility of a combination of our intuitions in one consciousness is the crucial ground for self, for self-consciousness, and for appearances and objects. Fichte "modified" this based on early criticisms of Kant's first *Critique.* I offer Fichte's conclusions on the matter. The self is originally aware only of its other—its not-self—or that which is external to it. This is the other that it has before it. It brings this other into its purview, and in so doing, it becomes aware of itself. However, this self becoming aware of itself can be recognized only as an act of the self; that is to say, self-reflection can be thought of only if the self conceives itself as a *unity* of self and other. This *negation*, Fichte claimed, is prior to the awareness that the self is a unity. In other words, negation precedes the awareness of this unity, and the two (self and not-self) subsequently combined are necessary for the determination of the object. Fichte thus added another element, a prior element, to Kant's combination: the self is self-aware only when it *posits* itself as not self, and this "posit" occurs prior to the unity that results in our cognition of the external world. Fichte developed (for the first time) a rudimentary dialectic.[8]

This unity of self and other is (with Kant) a rule we give ourselves; in Fichte's language, it is "freedom" or "spontaneity." The rule of freedom is the very first rule we formulate. We think a concept of necessity freely; when we do this, we discover that we do think freely and that the discovery of necessity is conditioned in its discovery by freedom. This necessity is the fundamental law of all reason and must be proved by a deduction. This is done as follows: The fundamental law "shows that what is first set up as fundamental principle and directly demonstrated in consciousness, is impossible unless something else occurs along with it, and that this something else is impossible unless a third something also takes place, and so on until the condition of what was first exhibited is completely exhausted, and this latter is, with respect to its possibility, fully intelligible" (Fichte, *Science*, 25). In other words, we follow the regress. And if we do, we are led to the following: The basic norm from which all other norms proceed is "I = I"—pure identity. Statements of identity such as "A = A" are contingent upon this prior norm. All analytic statements, therefore, require as their ground the norm "I = I." This means that the self is *prior* to all judgments because it is the self that is doing the judging and what is being judged is an aspect of the self. Fichte avoided the vicious circularity of "I = I" = "A = A" by claiming that all further statements of identity are actually hypotheticals (if A, then A), that a more basic norm is therefore needed for these, and that this norm is the self's own self-reflexive activity, abstracted as the necessary law of freedom.[9] We can have knowledge, strictly speaking, only of ourselves because it is only the self that is reflected back to us. Objects, of course, are cognized, but this means only that they are "taken up" by the self such that they are part of the self. Questions of sensations that plague empiricism, for example, are forestalled by the objection that we have absolutely no insight into these. We cannot posit a thing-in-itself that mysteriously lies behind the object, nor can we reduce the object to a set of sensory data or *qualia*. We simply have nothing to say about what lies outside the self. Though the question of the external world seems to be (for realists at least) begged, the relation of self-consciousness to thought is displayed. For the self must appear to itself as a self: in other words, as a self-reflexive thought. As puzzling as it might seem, Fichte saw his understanding of the self-positing I as the solution to the problem of subjectivism. This is because this first principle of all philosophy is the ground of the self and of all objects, thereby. Unlike Kant, Fichte did not "invent" a transcendentally reflected account of self-consciousness; as such, he could claim that his account of self-consciousness is authentic. The self-positing I is the possibility, through further posits, of appearances and objects, inclusive of nature. The first principle makes the natural world a possibility for us, and this is how Fichte could claim that, unlike Kant, his *Science of Knowledge* avoids the problem of subjectivism.

Hölderlin, Schelling, and Hegel: Toward a Philosophy of Nature

Both Hölderlin and Schelling were admirers of Fichte's *Science of Knowledge*, though they would come to disagree with this work.[10] Hölderlin asks, "But how is self-consciousness possible? Only in that I oppose myself to myself, separate myself from myself, while still cognizing myself as the same (I) notwithstanding this separation. But, to what extent as the same? I can, I must so ask; for from another point of view, it is opposed to itself. Thus identity is no unification of subject and object that has purely and simply taken place, thus identity is not = to absolute being" (Hölderlin, "Urteil und Sein," 147). Hölderlin's way out is ultimately not philosophical but poetic, and (in a move that anticipates Heidegger) Hölderlin argues that metaphor must substitute for identity in understanding this pre-reflective knowledge. We are to get behind language through language that conceives the very idea of pre-reflective being.

Schelling's debt to Hölderlin is immense (Frank, *Philosophical Foundations*, 113–14). In Hölderlin, Schelling saw a profound criticism not only of Fichte's identity claim but of his own arguments. Up to this point, Schelling had earlier written a manuscript that claimed, "My I contains a being which precedes all thinking and imagining. It *is* by being thought, and it is being thought because it is [note the circularity]; and all for only one reason—that is only and is being thought only inasmuch as its thinking is its own. Thus, it is because it alone is what does the thinking, and it thinks only itself because it is. It produces itself by its own thinking—out of absolute causality" (Schelling, "On the I"). This claim, that being produces itself by thinking itself, is criticized by Hölderlin in *Judgment and Being*. Schelling understood the problem with his approach only after reading Hölderlin. Being cannot be posited out of its own thinking and still be absolute. It must stand beyond even original thought. Being cannot be deduced from, or posited in, consciousness (subjectivity) because being is primordial (absolute). Schelling claimed that being resides in every unity of intuition and object such that everything that is, is being.

The PKI turn to naturalism requires further qualification. The turn is not to be thought of in a materialist sense; these thinkers did not embrace one or another of the variants that made matter the central feature of philosophy. Naturalism *was a move away from subjectivism* toward an integrated view of nature, a view in which mind or spirit suffused nature. Fichte did not develop a naturalistic account of nature; it would be Schelling and later Hegel who would do so. Nevertheless, Fichte set the stage for such an account. Fichte's first principle, "I = I," led both Hölderlin and Schelling to conclude that Fichte shrank the world, and they set about to re-integrate nature. Both admitted that Fichte began this re-integration with his first principle: the "I = I" in Fichte's estimation enfolds the world. This, however, was unacceptable to Hölderlin and Schelling, who saw in this understanding the primacy of the principle over the actual. What gets lost here is not only nature but also any sense of the absolute: the "concrete universal" (Hegel's term) that is nature and spirit fused in unity.

Schelling claimed that space and time are *reciprocal*: that is, space and time (the *forms* of intuition) require one another for the construction of objects. Together, there is unity (Kant offers a similar sentiment in the "Refutation of Idealism" of the B edition in the first *Critique).* As Schelling puts it, "If this formula [that the object is not given to us from outside but rather in intuition] had been understood, the chimera that has tormented our philosophers for so long—viz., the things in themselves (things in addition to the actual things that are also already supposed to exist, to affect us always, and to lend the substance to our representations)—this chimera would have disappeared like mists of the night dispelled by the light of the sun. It would have been recognized that nothing can be real unless there is a spirit to know it" (Schelling, "Treatise," 72; see also p. 75 footnote).

The quest for the absolute took Schelling on a different path—a path leading to "oneness" of philosophy (spirit) and nature. Matter (at least organic matter or "life") in its totality (*Zweckmäßigkeit*) is one with self-consciousness, and self-consciousness is one with this. This unity is absolute. The enmeshment of matter and spirit leads to this, as spirit "is to intuit not animated matter as such but rather itself within the animated matter. . . . Every representation of the spirit will quasi paint itself in the body (the external object is painted in the eye by virtue of light, [and] movement is formed by the ear through the medium of air, etc.); the body must imitate and portray as it were every inward movement" (Schelling, "Treatise," 94).

Schelling's point is that spirit must necessarily see itself as body to be self-complete. By the time of his 1797 *First Outline of a System of the Philosophy of Nature,* Schelling claimed that nature was "Being itself" (Schelling, *First Outline*, 13), and in his later *System of Transcendental Idealism* (1800), he claimed that philosophy must *begin* with nature. Nature, the natural world, is existentially prior to consciousness. Only when nature "returns to herself" in consciousness (that is, in a being's awareness of it) does it thereby become identical with thought. The two, in unity, are absolute. We recognize ourselves as having both thought and nature (Schelling, *System*, 6). Schelling's "nature" is dynamic all the way down: following an insight first explicated by Kant in the *Metaphysical First Principles of Science*, Schelling contends that since all matter is potentially infinitely divisible, and since we know that matter does not remain inert (it changes form—solid, liquid, gas), we must conclude that matter is ever-changing. Schelling is criticizing the mechanistic view of matter—that matter is static. Schelling concludes that we necessarily see ourselves as "embodied" (spirit *in* matter; matter *in* spirit) via the "common point [the so-called indifference point] of contact between the I and its opposite" (Schelling, *System*, 65). This "indifference point" is common to all organic matter; it is the unity of spirit and matter such that spirit has returned to itself. Indeed, the fusion of objective (world) and subjective (mind) is *constitutive*, not regulative, as it is with Kant and Fichte. We "produce" the world and our selves as we develop concepts (through limitation and discrimination of ourselves from objects) out of our self-worlds.

Despite variations in the dynamics of being (ever-growing or expanding unities), Schelling *always* insisted on being's *primordial* nature. Categories or rules for understanding nature develop through subsequent limitations and extensions of spirit to object (other): this "consciousness of" expands to include "more" unity of self and others. Spirit is itself transformed in the process. Consciousness—the will of spirit—in other words "grows" as more and further limitations and extensions form and further concepts and objects are developed. This central understanding of nature as a *rational totality*, and absolute being as dynamic and becoming, is continued by Hegel, though on a much grander scale.

By 1802, Schelling's philosophy of nature was fully embedded in his philosophy of identity. This philosophy, begun in earnest in 1800, seeks a thorough enmeshment of spirit and nature. "Absolute identity must necessarily appear as two distinct though correlated points, one of which actualizes the ideal through the real [and this is nature], the other of which actualizes the real as such by means of the ideal [and this is the domain of consciousness]" (Schelling, *Bruno*, 155). Here, consciousness is equated with the ideal or spirit. The absolute (identity) is consciousness, which is to say, "the principle of consciousness thus turns out to be 'absolute consciousness,' while the factual identity of thought and intuition is 'derivative' or 'grounded consciousness" (153). Nature and spirit are two points of the same absolute, their separation an abstraction of thought. Brought together in a common point, these are God. God is present in every derivative unity. Each ideal is enmeshed in the real and each real enmeshed with the ideal. Each real and ideal in unity is enfolded in a greater unity, and this is the absolute—which is to say, God. "In God, no concept of any individual is excluded from the concept of all things that are, or were, or will be, for these temporal distinctions we make have no intrinsic [absolute] meaning" (151).

Schelling labels the unity of nature and spirit "absolute idealism." "It is not because the Philosophy of Nature asserts an antithesis between nature and the Ego (a being of nature outside the Ego), but because it asserts an absolute identity between the two in which *both* are submerged together—hence because the Philosophy of Nature does not (re)cognize any true bound either in the [alleged] incomprehensible impact or in the [alleged] incomprehensible bounds. In a word, it is *absolute idealism*" (Schelling, *Bruno*, 370). Philosophy of nature asserts an *absolute identity* between the ego (I) and nature. Nature is *not* subordinated ideal, and neither is spirit.[11] Nature is spirit and spirit is nature, together in the absolute.

All of the themes listed here (the move away from subjectivity; the move toward nature and organicism) are present in Hegel's work, from the time of the Jena manuscripts onward. In 1801, Hegel penned his first publication, *The Difference between Fichte's and Schelling's System of Philosophy*, also known as the *Differenzschrift*. Hegel carefully constructed the arguments of both thinkers, ultimately preferring Schelling, who had an organic conception of philosophy, encompassing *both* spirit *and* nature in unity. Hegel claims: "For absolute identity [Fichte's principle] to be the principle of an entire system it is necessary that both subject and object be posited as Subject-Object. In

Fichte's system, identity constitutes itself only as subjective Subject-Object. [But] this subjective Subject-Object needs an objective Subject-Object to complete it, so that the Absolute presents itself in each of the two Subject-Objects, and finds itself perfected only in both together as the highest synthesis that nullifies both insofar as they are opposed. As their point of absolute indifference, the Absolute encloses both, gives birth to both and is born of both" (Hegel, *Difference*, 155).

Dewey: Absolute Idealism and Anti-Subjectivism

Dewey's criticism of subjectivism (subjective idealism) is featured in several early articles but most prominently in one written in 1886, "The Psychological Standpoint." Here, Dewey evaluates several distinct approaches to psychology with subjective idealism being one. He criticizes one species of subjective idealism (Alexander Bain's) and in so doing sums up his problems with subjectivisms in general. I quote the relevant passages. "The essence of Subjective Idealism is that the subject consciousness or mind, which remains after the 'object world has been abstracted,' is that for which after all this object world exists. Were this not so—were it admitted that this subject, mind, and the object, matter, are both but elements within, and both exist only for, consciousness—we should be in the sphere of an eternal absolute consciousness, whose partial realization both the individual 'subject' and the 'external object' are" (135). The problem with subjective idealism is that it is ultimately self-contradictory. Dewey continues, "Is it not a self-contradiction to declare that 'the scope of mental science' is subject consciousness or mind, and at the same time to declare that 'both subject and object are parts of our being,' are but 'two kinds' of consciousness? Surely Psychology ought to be the science of our whole being, and of the whole consciousness" (136). Here we see a demonstration (if admittedly rhetorical) of anti-subjectivism at work. Unless consciousness includes both mind and object, the mental as well as the natural, it is doomed to positing two rival consciousnesses and having to construct a bridge to connect them. This obviates the possibility that there can be unity, however. Only an "Absolute Idealism" (Dewey, "Psychological Standpoint," 135) can offer this solution. As with Schelling and Hegel, we are to develop a better model that can *integrate* these and thereby obviate the dualism, the turn to question-begging unknowns, and the paucity of the resultant experience.

Prior to the early 1890s, Dewey's "self" is an "absolute" amalgam of experiences and interactions with the world, an amalgam out of which distinctions, categories, concepts, judgments, and abstractions form. Dewey *never* invests the absolute self with religious *content*, though he does suggest that *the spiritual nature of the self* owes much to its absolute nature. For Dewey, the self is the *composite* of experiences, *not* the unifier. What unifies an experience in Dewey's early works is unclear: on occasion, Dewey gestures toward self-consciousness. At other times, he falls upon the decidedly ambiguous term "real experience." It is only later that Dewey recognizes the import of *experimental inquiry* in settling indeterminate situations. This settling—this "resolution"—results in an experiential, "unified" whole. In one place, Dewey sees the final unification of experience as the will: "The unity of the self is the will. The will is the man, psychologically speaking. Knowledge we have seen to be in its essence a process of the realization of the universal self-consciousness; feeling to be the accompaniment of self-realization; and its specific quality to be dependent upon the definite form of self-realization accomplished. Will we have just seen to be the self realizing itself. This is involved throughout in physical and prudential control, and it is explicitly developed when we study moral control. Here the will is seen to be self-determination. The will, in short, constitutes the meaning of knowledge and of feeling; and moral will constitutes the meaning of will" (Dewey, *Psychology*, 357). Will encapsulates all that is a person—knowledge, feeling, psychomotor activity, impulse and instinct, dreams and imagination, and social action: "All natural, healthy feeling never has an independent existence in consciousness. Even sense-feelings are absorbed: The pleasure of eating an orange seems a part of the orange" (276). Another example is, "Feelings of knowledge are normally lost in the objects known; aesthetic feelings, in the beautiful object created or contemplated; moral feelings, in the outgoing activity which the affection for them induces. Normal feelings, in short, are regarded as real values in the objects which excite them, or exist only as springs to action; they subserve conduct" (251). The organic nature of feeling and mental activity, together with the claim that there can be feelings of knowledge, is already on display in his earliest work. These would subsequently become themes in *Experience and Nature* and *Art as Experience*. The debt to AANI, to say nothing of Schelling and Hegel, is evident: Dewey's "unity of self as will" encapsulates what it is to be human. This is an organic account of the self. An all-encompassing self that embeds morals, knowledge, and feeling within, it is a foreshadowing of the unified organism that Dewey discusses after making the "instrumental" turn. Nevertheless, this naturalism, too, is notable for its all-embracing characteristic.

Dewey: From Absolute Idealism to Experimental Idealism

Though Dewey *seems* anti-idealist in those works published after 1893, he in fact argues for a conjoining of the reflective (thought, inquiry) and natural.

Dewey's idealism is a *transformed* idealism, with attention not on consciousness and self-consciousness (as with PKI) but rather on experience, reflection, and inquiry. A number of consequences arise from this. First, the construction of entities (objects, concepts, ideas) turns on the presence of the continuity of existence. Second, this trait of existence is thoroughgoing: it does not "begin" with perception. It is already present in any and every "doing and undergoing." We may say that it exists irrespective of our particular perceptive or cognitive biases. Third, continuity directs knowledge and not the converse. To know is to reflect upon a (continuous) experience, not to inaugurate one. Experience, not knowledge, is primary. Fourth, and most controversial, there is a reality out there. Dewey's realism is realism regardless of its propensity to accord cognitive processes with standing. It assumes that the reality of a brute world, by way of traits and qualities of existence, impresses itself upon the organism.

A good example of Dewey's thinking at the beginning of his naturalist "turn" is found in his 1893 article "The Theory of Emotions." Here, Dewey stresses the *behavioral and physiological* nature of emotions. "Emotion in its entirety is a mode of behavior which is purposive, or has an intellectual content, and which also reflects itself into feeling or Affects, as the subjective valuation of that which is objectively expressed in the idea or purpose" (171). Further, "The emotion is always 'about' or 'toward' something; it is 'at' or 'on account of' something, and this prepositional reference is an integral phase of the single pulse of emotion; for emotion, as well as the idea, comes as a whole carrying its distinctions of value within it" (173). The stress over all, as opposed to the parts, a central theme of Dewey's later and famous "Reflex Arc Concept in Psychology," published in 1896, is already present here. The point here is that Dewey has committed himself to a view of emotions integrated with values and behaviors. This is a central "move" toward a fully naturalized view (a functional view) of human behavior.

Dewey's biological-behavioral accounting of the fully unified human organism comes in "The Reflex Arc Concept in Psychology." Here, Dewey presents his telling criticism of the reflex arc: the idea that behavior (Dewey speaks of a child holding her hand to a candle) is limited to neurological action and reaction. Instead, Dewey famously argues, the child "learns" not to touch an open flame, and this presents grave difficulties for a one-sided explanation of what occurs. Dewey then puts forth an alternate explanation: the best account of what is occurring is circular, that is to say, a loop or circuit in which stimulus begets not only an automatic response but a change—a transformation—in the organism. This transformation is evidenced by the subsequent behavior of the child. No longer will she place her hand over an open flame (Dewey, "Theory of Emotion," 102). Dewey's point is to argue that behavior (even "reflex" behavior) is always already part of a larger context, situated in an environment, taking place against the backdrop of other learned behaviors. Distinguishing the reflex activity is acceptable, but only if it is remembered that it is properly part of a larger whole. To conceive of it otherwise is to commit the "psychologistic fallacy," of mistaking a part for the whole.

It will do to dig a little deeper and see how Dewey uses the terms "reality" and "realism." "Naïve realism" is Dewey's description for the direct realism developed in his middle period and represents his strongest epistemological claim for the argument that *continuity* is the central trait of a full experience.[12] It has its genesis in Dewey's early, instrumentally characterized works, such as his "Essays on the New Empiricism." Dewey foregrounds the natural trait of continuity in these early-middle works. Dewey locates continuity in an experience—a continuity that distinguishes his realism from both (objective) idealism and (what Dewey calls "presentative") realism. This continuity of experience *immerses the knowledge-object within*; that is to say, there is no existential separation of object and experience or of cognition and reality in this reckoning. Consider Dewey's criticism of objective idealism—the idealism Dewey claims is held by Kant.[13] "Thought is here conceived as *a priori*, not in the sense of particular innate ideas, but of a function that constitutes the very possibility of any objective experience, any experience involving reference beyond its own mere subjective happening. . . . It is taken to mean both the organized, the regulated, the informed, established character of an experience, an order immanent and constitutional; and an agency which organizes, regulates, forms, synthesizes, a power operative and constructive" (Dewey, "Experience," 132–33). Thought for Kant (and neo-idealists such as Green) orders and controls an experience such that the final product is knowledge. Though Dewey agrees that "organization of some sort exists in every experience," nevertheless, what Kant takes to be the fact of the matter, "the bringing to bear of the categories of the mind on the matter of perception, does not unfold as he claims" (134).

> For, be it noted, this organization, first, is not the work of reason or thought, unless "reason" be stretched beyond all identification; and secondly, it has no sacrosanct or finally valid and worthwhile character. . . . Experience always carries with it and within it certain systematized arrangements, certain classifications (using the term without intellectualistic prejudice), coexistent and serial. . . . [We may think of continuity.] Now it is one thing

> to say that thought has played a part in the origin and development of such organizations, and continues to have a role in their judicious employment and application; it is another to say that these organizations *are* thought, or are its exclusive product. Thought that functions in these ways is distinctively *reflective* thought, thought as practical, volitional, deliberately exercised for specific aims—thought as an act, an art of skilled mediation. . . . As organizations, as established, effectively controlling arrangements of objects in experience, their mark is that they are not thoughts, but habits, customs of actions. (134–35)

Not only does objective idealism mistake innate rules of organization for what is custom and habit, it also confers an ontological warrant on the conditions of thought. "No final or ultimate validity attaches to these original arrangements and institutionalizations in any case. Their value is teleological and experimental, not fixedly ontological. . . . Organization as already effected is always in danger of becoming a *mortmain*; it may be a way of sacrificing novelty, flexibility, freedom, creation to static standards" (136).[14]

A priori thought of the sort that objective idealism espouses pays no heed to biological and vital impulses. In opposition to this, psychomotor habits, ungrounded apperception, routines of behavior, *all* constitute the material for thinking. "Objective idealism depends not only upon ignoring the existence and capacity of vital functions, but upon a profound confusion of the constitutional *a priori*, the unconsciously dominant, with empirically reflective thought. . . . Plain, ordinary, everyday empirical reflections, operating as centres of inquiry, of suggestion, of experimentation, exercise the valuable function of regulation, in an auspicious direction, of subsequent experience" (Dewey, "Experience," 136). Dewey has in rudimentary form what he would later and more fully claim of an experience: that it is *had, not made*, that it is a *qualitative* activity, that qualities of an experience had can be regulated, and that this constitutes the proper task of reflective thought.

Dewey is equally critical of crude ("presentative") realism. The claim that reality exists outside of our experience and that it—or, in any event, a bit of it—presents itself is, for Dewey, anathema. "To assume that, because from the *standpoint of the knowledge experience* things are what they are known to be, therefore, metaphysically, absolutely, without qualification, everything in its reality . . . is what a knower would find it to be, is, from the immediate standpoint, if not the root of all philosophic evil, at least one of its main roots. For this leaves out of account what the knowledge standpoint is itself *experienced as*" (Dewey, "Postulate," 160). If objective idealism is too enthralled with the subject, the self, and the mind that is conferring knowledge on sense-matter, presentative realism is ignorant or dismissive of the task of empirical reflection. For to assume that reality is given to one as it is, is to confer upon it necessity, constancy, and permanence. In fact, Dewey claims, the immediate qualities of the experience that confirm the natural continuity of an experience itself are shifting and amorphous. Reality is not given; rather, it is experienced as if it was a given. The "best" proof of this is that experiences are unique.

> Experience is always of *thats*; and the most comprehensive and inclusive experience of the universe that the philosopher himself can obtain is the experience of a characteristic *that*. From the empiricist's point of view, this is as true of the exhaustive and complete insight of a hypothetical all-knower as of the vague, blind experience of the awakened sleeper. As reals [*sic*], they stand on the same level. As trues [*sic*], the latter has by definition the better of it; but if this insight is in any way the truth of the blind awakening, it is because the latter has, in its *own* determinate *quale*, elements of real continuity with the former; it is *ex hypothesi*, transformable through a series of experienced reals without break of continuity, into the absolute thought-experience. *There is no need of logical manipulation to effect the transformation, it is just by immediate experiences, each of which is just as real (no more, no less) as either of the two terms between which they lie.* (164–65, italics mine)

We have another early mention of the natural traits of an experience here, traits that are central to Dewey's later *Experience and Nature* and *Art as Experience*. In fact, Dewey's realism, though downplayed in these later texts, nevertheless constitutes the basis for his talk of qualitative wholes and immediacy. Dewey's realism is grounded in the "natural" traits of existence. These are the proper starting point for an account of experience, reflection, and inquiry. Dewey's movement away from subjectivism and toward naturalism with a strong place for inquiry and reflection mirrors at least two of the movements of PKI. Dewey's insistence on the immediacy of experience, the qualitative aspects of experience, and the presence of traits and characteristics of experience that are then investigated, reflected upon, and reproduced is an experimentalist account of an organism and world in thoroughgoing transaction with one another. As with PKI, though in a fully naturalized manner, Dewey's account of experience fuses mind (as thought or inquiry) and world together, in one organic whole.

Conclusion

It is ironic that Dewey poured so much frustration into the 1915 wartime screed *German Philosophy and Politics*, given the legacy of PKI evident in his experimental idealism. Dewey owed much of his early philosophic thought to the questions PKI poses and AANI, in particular, reflects on. Despite his later aversion to metaphysical pronouncements regarding the self, self-consciousness, and the absolute, Dewey's distrust of subjectivity, his naturalism, and his tendency to an organic conception of experience are all legacies of PKI. The question of Dewey's relationship to Hegel is particularly intriguing, and further chapters in this volume will explore this in detail. Here, I am happy to suggest that the central project is a *shared* one. If we care to look closely, we can see that the edifice Dewey developed is constructed of materials from PKI.

Notes

1. This term belongs to James Good (2006). I think it is an apt description of what Dewey tried to accomplish with philosophy after his break from AANI.

2. These characteristics are certainly not meant to be exhaustive; rather, they are pronounced in each of the thinkers discussed here.

3. For example, Paul Franks saw the history of German idealism as a response to Kant's response to the skepticism engendered by the question of causality. According to this thesis, Kant attempted to respond to skepticism by self-consciously taking up Hume's gauntlet. I shall not deal with skepticism as a possible theme in Dewey's early metaphysics. It is possible to tease such a theme out, but doing so would require far more space than allotted.

4. Henrich claims that it was Karl Reinhold and particularly Fichte who saw the need for, and began to develop, a theory of the subject. See Henrich, "Origins of the Theory of the Subject."

5. Hegel's naturalism is also evident, both in period of the Jena manuscripts and in *The Philosophy of Nature.* Of course, his philosophy of nature is differently construed in each; however, the desire to fold nature and spirit into one another is a continuous project of Hegel's.

6. Shook claims that Dewey's "Reflex Arc Concept in Psychology" article represents the pinnacle of Wundtian insight. One of the reasons most scholars of Dewey choose James over Wundt as a primary influence is Dewey's self-described indebtedness toward James as found in the former's "From Absolutism to Experimentalism." Here, Wundt is barely mentioned, while Dewey discusses James for several pages (157–59). The same is true of Jane Dewey's biography of her father that appears in *The Philosophy of John Dewey.*

7. The claim that Kant was a subjective idealist, although appearing almost immediately upon the reception of the first *Critique*, is a view *unsupported* by Kant

scholarship. Kant, whatever else he was doing, was attempting to *rescue* philosophy from subjectivism. To the degree that he did, Schelling and Hegel praised him. To the degree that he did not, they consciously worked to improve upon him. See Beiser, *German Idealism*, 601.

8. "All determination is negation," according to Spinoza. All of the German idealists (after Kant) to some degree followed Spinoza on this. Spinoza's monism, the claim that all attributes follow from one substance, finds corollaries in Fichte's notion of (transcendental) freedom and Hölderlin's, Schelling's, and Hegel's absolute. In this way, they avoided the nagging question of a consciousness that was substantive yet nonmaterialistic. None of the German idealists, however, considered their philosophies "monistic."

9. Fichte claimed that his system was the proper working out of Kant's self-consciousness. In the second introduction to his *Science of Knowledge* (1797), Fichte summarizes the disputes regarding Kant's thing-in-itself, transcendental idealism, and his own systematic "improvements" of transcendental idealism. He claims that Kant's system and his are in fundamental agreement, but Kant does not pursue a theory of self-consciousness. If he had pursued this, he would be led to Fichte's solution to the problem of the thing-in-itself.

10. Terry Pinkard talks at length about Hölderlin's influence on both Schelling and Hegel. All three were students at the Tübingen Stift and were good friends. When Hegel left to become a *Hofmeister* in Berne, he kept in touch with Hölderlin, and Hölderlin sent him his manuscripts. When Hegel returned to Frankfurt (Hölderlin was living there as well) for a new position as *Hofmeister*, he and Hölderlin renewed their bonds. Frederick Beiser also discusses the "hold" that Hölderlin had on both Schelling and Hegel: it was Hölderlin who first criticized Fichte for "subjectivizing" nature. See Pinkard, *Hegel*; and Beiser, *German Idealism*.

11. Some make the claim that Schelling (and to a lesser extent, Hegel) promoted a "naturalized" metaphysics. I think there is truth to this. This is certainly true of Schelling, 1797–1800. It is not so much that Schelling discovered a priori structures and then forced natural events and conclusions into a metaphysical mode; it is rather that natural events led to the formation of structures that are a priori and these structures foreground our understandings of natural events. The a priori *still* plays a strong role here, but it is a function of understanding nature as much as nature is a product of it. For an opposing view, see Stone, *Petrified Intelligence*.

12. Naïve realists believe that there are objects that are independent of our perceptions of them. But they differ from presentative realists in that they do not believe there are mental intermediaries such as sense-perceptions that bridge external objects and mind. They do believe, though, that "mind" does not "construct" objects. Dewey fully embraced this position from the period 1911–17; John Shook talks about this at length in *Dewey's Empirical Theory of Knowledge and Reality*.

13. Beiser perceptively notes that Dewey considered Kant to be an *objective* idealist, not a *subjective* idealist. Was Dewey mistaken? Dewey was closer to German idealists in his ascription to Kant than he was to late-twentieth-century critics. In

the earlier article "The Psychological Standpoint," it is not Kant who is singled out as an example of subjectivism but Alexander Bain.

14. This is very close to Schelling's criticism of Fichte's notion of the self. Far from being a *terminus a quo*, the self is a *terminus ad quem* that is the product of myriad syntheses. Thought is dynamic and ever-evolving, not static and rule-bound. The question of whether Dewey got Schelling and Hegel's objective idealism right is one I cannot broach. However, it seems to me that both Schelling and Hegel would admit much of Dewey's criticism of "objective" realism. Both Schelling and Hegel, for example, had strong roles for the biological to play in philosophy, and Hegel, in particular, grounded rules of social organization *in* society, *not* solely abstract thought.

References

Beiser, F. *German Idealism: The Struggle Against Subjectivism, 1781–1801*. Cambridge: Cambridge University Press, 2002.

Dewey, Jane. "Biography of John Dewey." In *The Philosophy of John Dewey*, edited by P. A. Schilpp and L. Hahn, 3–46. La Salle, Ill.: Open Court Press, 1939.

Dewey, John. "Beliefs and Existences." In *The Middle Works of John Dewey, 1899–1924*, edited by J. Boydston. Vol. 3, *1903–1906*, 83–100. Carbondale: Southern Illinois University Press, 1977.

———. "Brief Studies in Realism." In *The Middle Works of John Dewey, 1899–1924*, edited by J. Boydston. Vol. 6, *1912–1914*, 103–22. Carbondale: Southern Illinois University Press, 1979.

———. "Experience and Objective Idealism." In *The Middle Works of John Dewey, 1899–1924*, edited by J. Boydston. Vol. 3, *1903–1906*, 128–44. Carbondale: Southern Illinois University Press, 1977.

———. "From Absolutism to Experimentalism." In *The Later Works of John Dewey, 1925–1952*, edited by J. Boydston. Vol. 5, *1929–1930*, 47–160. Carbondale: Southern Illinois University Press, 1984.

———. "The Postulate of Immediate Empiricism." In *The Middle Works of John Dewey, 1899–1924*, edited by J. Boydston. Vol. 3, *1903–1906*, 158–67. Carbondale: Southern Illinois University Press, 1977.

———. "The Psychological Standpoint." In *The Early Works of John Dewey, 1882–1898*, edited by J. Boydston. Vol. 1, *1882–1888*, 122–43. Carbondale: Southern Illinois University Press, 1969.

———. *Psychology*. In *The Early Works of John Dewey, 1882–1898*, edited by J. Boydston. Vol. 2, *1887*. Carbondale: Southern Illinois University Press, 1969.

———. "Reality as Experience." In *The Middle Works of John Dewey, 1899–1924*, edited by J. Boydston. Vol. 3, *1903–1906*, 101–6. Carbondale: Southern Illinois University Press, 1977.

———. "The Theory of Emotion." In *The Early Works of John Dewey, 1882–1898*, edited by J. Boydston. Vol. 4, *1893–1894*, 152–88. Carbondale: Southern Illinois University Press, 1971.

Fichte, J. G. *Gesamstausgabe der Bayerischen Akademie der Wissenchaften*. Edited by R. Lauth, H. Jacob, and H. Gliwitzky. Stuttgart: Frommann, 1964.

———. *Science of Knowledge*. Edited and translated by P. Heath and J. Lachs. Cambridge: Cambridge University Press, 1982.

Frank, M. *The Philosophical Foundations of Early German Romanticism*. Translated by Elisabeth Millán-Zaibert. Albany: State University of New York Press, 2004.

Franks, P. *All or Nothing: Skepticism and Systematicity in German Idealism*. Cambridge: Harvard University Press, 2005.

Good, J. *A Search for Unity in Diversity: The "Permanent Hegelian Deposit" in the Philosophy of John Dewey*. Lanham, Md.: Rowman and Littlefield, 2006.

Hegel, G. W. F. *The Difference between Fichte's and Schelling's System of Philosophy*. Translated by H. S. Harris and W. Cerf. Albany: State University of New York Press, 1977.

Henrich, D. "The Origins of the Theory of the Subject." In *Philosophical Interventions in the Unfinished Project of Enlightenment*, edited by A. Honneth, T. McCarthy, C. Offe, and A. Wellmer, 27–80. Cambridge: MIT Press, 1992.

Hölderlin, F. "Urteil und Sein." In *Sämtliche Werke*, edited by D. E. Sattler, M. Franz, and H. G. Steimer. Basel: Roter Stern, 1991–.

Kant, I. *Critique of Pure Reason*. In *The Cambridge Edition of the Works of Immanuel Kant*, translated by P. Guyer and A. Wood. Cambridge: Cambridge University Press, 1998.

Pinkard, T. *Hegel: A Biography*. Cambridge: Cambridge University Press, 2000.

Schelling, F. W. J. *Bruno, or, On the Natural and the Divine Principle of Things*. Edited and translated by M. Vater. Albany: State University of New York Press, 1984.

———. *First Outline of a System of the Philosophy of Nature*. Translated by K. Peterson. Albany: State University of New York Press, 2004.

———. "On the I as Principle of Philosophy, or On the Unconditional in Human Knowledge." In *The Unconditional in Human Knowledge: Four Early Essays (1794–1796)*, translated by F. Marti, 63–129. London: Associated University Presses, 1980.

———. *Schellings Werke*. Edited by M. Schröter. Munich: C. H. Beck und Oldenburg, 1927.

———. *System of Transcendental Idealism*. Translated by P. Heath. Charlottesville: University Press of Virginia, 1978.

———. "Treatise Explicatory of the Idealism in the Science of Knowledge." In *Idealism and the Endgame of Theory: Three Essays by F. W. J. Schelling*, translated by T. Pfau, 61–139. Albany: State University of New York Press, 1994.

Shook, J. *Dewey's Empirical Theory of Knowledge and Reality*. Nashville: Vanderbilt University Press, 2000.

Stone, A. *Petrified Intelligence: Nature in Hegel's Philosophy*. Albany: State University of New York Press, 2005.

2] Dewey, Hegel, and Knowledge after Kant

Tom Rockmore

The relation between American pragmatism and German idealism remains to be studied in depth. This chapter will focus more narrowly on some common themes in John Dewey and G. W. F. Hegel. There are obviously various ways to compare and contrast their two positions. In a recent paper, Richard Rorty stresses Dewey's commitment to Darwinism in distinction to Hegel's pre-Darwinian interest in historicism.[1] Yet this is a little like comparing apples and oranges since the basis of the comparison is never made clear in the development of the problems and theories. A perhaps useful way to do this is to see both Hegel and Dewey against the background of the Kantian tradition, to which both loosely belong and of which both are strongly critical.

Immanuel Kant's influence can scarcely be overestimated. In different ways, all the later philosophical tendencies arose in reaction to the critical philosophy. Kant was a transcendental thinker, concerned with the conditions of the possibility of knowledge whatsoever with universality and necessity on the a priori plane on the basis of a cognitive subject reduced to its function within the overall theory. In reaction to Kant's transcendental philosophy, the main post-Kantian tendencies continued Kantian themes while rejecting Kantian a priorism for an a posteriori approach in moving toward a finite human conception of the cognitive subject and away from claims for universality and necessity. The result was a "naturalization" of the Kantian approach that already began in Johann Gottlieb Fichte, who loudly proclaimed his seamless Kantianism—a claim rejected by the author of the critical philosophy—and continued in post-Kantian German idealism, including Karl Marx, as well as in different ways in all the American pragmatists.[1]

Pragmatism and German Idealism

Hegel is uniformly understood in terms of German idealism. Though far removed from Charles Sanders Peirce and William James, Dewey nonetheless is generally considered to belong to the first generation of American pragmatism.

There is no idealism as such or idealism in general. There are only idealists, including those who subscribe to the term or who are regarded by others as idealist. Idealism can be understood in many different ways that have only the term in common. The philosophical term "idealist" seems to have been invented by Gottfried Leibniz. In responding to Pierre Bayle, he objects to "those who, like Epicurus and Hobbes, believe that the soul is material" and adds that in his own position, "whatever of good there is in the hypotheses of Epicurus and Plato, of the great materialists and the great idealists, is combined here."[2]

By German idealism, I will understand the tendency begun by Kant and continued by such later figures as Fichte, Friedrich Schelling, Hegel, and perhaps Marx. Each of these thinkers reacted to Kant and the other post-Kantian German idealists. With the exception of Marx, one way to understand the post-Kantian German idealism is as an effort by different hands to interpret, criticize, and reformulate the critical philosophy according to its letter while disregarding its spirit.

"Pragmatism" is currently difficult to describe. There is controversy about when it began and about its main figures. While some observers start with Peirce and James, others see pragmatism as starting to emerge in R. W. Emerson[3] or even earlier. Still others include among the pragmatists such figures as Rudolf Carnap and Nelson Goodman.[4] Rorty is one of the inventors of what can be called neo-analytic pragmatism, a tendency mainly composed of former analytic philosophers who have become disenchanted by the traditional analytic emphasis on a formal solution to the semantic problem of reference. The growing roster of neo-analytic pragmatists includes such names as Otto Neurath, Carnap, C. I. Lewis, W. V. O. Quine, Hilary Putnam, and most recently Robert Brandom. For purposes of this discussion, I will be focusing on three main members of the golden age of American pragmatism: Peirce, James, and Dewey.

The relation of American pragmatism to German idealism in general is very diverse. Peirce, the founder of the movement, was attracted both to idealism and to German idealism. He wrote on George Berkeley and claimed to know the *Critique of Pure Reason* almost by heart. After a period in which he was very critical of Hegel, he later came to believe that the differences between them were mainly terminological. Significantly, Peirce's interest in Hegel even included the latter's phenomenology. Peirce distinguished the three normative sciences (ethics, aesthetics, and logic) from a science concerned, as in Hegel's *Phenomenology*, merely to describe phenomena.[5] He considered phenomenology, much as Edmund Husserl later did, as a basic science.[6] He distinguished between phenomenology, which depended in his view on mathematics, and the other sciences.[7] And under the heading of "phaneroscopy," he began to work out his own version of phenomenology.[8]

This careful attention to Hegel and German idealism in general changed almost immediately in James. James thought ill of Kant, whose writings he did not know, and had nothing positive to say about Hegel, whose position he also did not know. The same cannot be said for Dewey. Though he later turned to experimentalism and Darwinism,[9] he had a deep grasp of Hegel. His interaction with German idealism always remained one of the important determinants of his position.

Kant was an epistemologist whose position turned on the formulation of a theory of knowledge in the critical philosophy. In virtue of the close relation among the post-Kantian German idealists, each of them reacted not only to Kant but also to each other. The result was an unusually cohesive series of interactions that imparted an extremely focused character to German idealism. Though each of the main idealists had other interests as well, the epistemological thread was strong and continuous, including Marx's position.

The later debate on knowledge was strongly determined by the critical philosophy. Kant's *Critique of Pure Reason* features two disparate strategies for knowledge: epistemological representationalism, or the representation of mind-independent objects, featuring a commitment to what is now called metaphysical realism; and epistemological constructivism, roughly the view that we can know only what we in some sense "construct." Discussion of knowledge after Kant turns on the contest between these two approaches. On the one hand, there is the steady commitment to causal theory of perception, which has never been stronger than at present. On the other, there is the conviction that representationalism fails and constructivism is a viable alternative. This latter view is featured in such writers as Kant himself as well as Fichte, Schelling, Hegel, Marx, Ernst Cassirer, and others.

Kant's influence remained strong in the later debate. Philosophy in the twentieth century can be described in terms of four main tendencies, each of which reacted to Kant: Marxism, Anglo-American analytic philosophy, so-called continental philosophy (that is, the form of phenomenology beginning in Husserl to which later thinkers reacted), and American pragmatism.[10]

The three main thinkers in the golden age of American pragmatism were about as different as any three thinkers could be and still belong to a single identifiable tendency or movement. American pragmatism, which is the only indigenous form of American philosophy, flourished after the later 1870s, when Peirce invented it. But it was already on the decline when Dewey died in the early 1950s. It was later nearly moribund when it was "rescued," so to speak, by Richard Rorty at the end of the 1970s. Rorty is a genuine crossover figure, with roots in both the analytic and later the pragmatic tradition. In *Philosophy and the Mirror of Nature*, he calls attention to three disparate figures—Martin Heidegger, Ludwig Wittgenstein, and Dewey—thereby instituting a dialogue of sorts between isolated tendencies, each of which functioned as a self-enclosed, semi-autonomous tendency, whose members took notice of each other while virtually ignoring everyone else.[11] Rorty later increasingly turned away from continental philosophy and analytic philosophy while turning increasingly toward Dewey, whom he continued to read arbitrarily. Yet since Rorty is an epistemological skeptic, he did not focus attention on Peirce but rather on James. The latter believed that pragmatism, which he interpreted idiosyncratically, had been discovered by his friend Peirce.

Rorty's approach to pragmatism was every bit as idiosyncratic as James's. Yet the result was very different. James was concerned to call attention to his friend Peirce. He did this, according to Peirce, by misinterpreting the latter's thought in a way that later caused Peirce to abandon the term "pragmatism" for "pragmaticism." Rorty was uninterested in Peirce, whom he seems not to know well, but more interested in James, whose importance he arguably overstates in *Philosophy and the Mirror of Nature*, and centrally concerned with Dewey. The result was to call attention to pragmatism while projecting an image of it as beginning in James, with scant attention to Peirce, arguably the stronger figure, perhaps the strongest pragmatist, even the strongest American philosopher, and while focusing on an idiosyncratic, even distorted reading of Dewey. In this he was only following Bertrand Russell. The latter, despite his well-known antipathy to James, accorded him vastly more attention than he paid to Peirce. In *A History of Western Philosophy*, there is a chapter devoted to James and another on Dewey but no more than two references to Peirce, one each to his influence on James and on Dewey.[12]

Peirce was not well known to James, who arguably misread him. He was also not well known to Dewey. Dewey's position, which belongs to the general rubric of pragmatism, was not strongly influenced by such pragmatic thinkers as Peirce and James. It arose mainly out of his initial interest in Hegelianism, his dissertation on Kant, and then his later turn toward experimentalism and Darwin. In part for that reason, Peirce criticized Dewey,[13] who was himself more generous in commending Peirce.[14]

On Dewey, Hegel, and German Idealism

John Dewey was initially linked to the St. Louis Hegelians. This link came about when he sent two essays to W. T. Harris, a Hegelian who was editor of the *Journal of Speculative Philosophy*. When Harris accepted the essays, Dewey was encouraged to apply to the graduate program in philosophy at Johns Hopkins University. The three young lecturers there were G. Stanley Hall, later an important child psychologist; Peirce, who was hired through James's intervention; and G. S. Morris, a Hegelian. While there, Dewey wrote a dissertation on Kantian psychology under Morris's direction, which further strengthened his awareness of Kant and Hegel.

Dewey's relation to German idealism was different depending on the particular figure. In simplest terms, Dewey was critical of Kant, who influenced him positively. He said little about Fichte, and he was generally critical of Hegel, who influenced him both positively and negatively. After graduation, in 1879, Dewey went to work teaching in public high schools, first in Pennsylvania. While working there, he wrote a Kantian article, "The Metaphysical Assumptions of Materialism," which was published in the *Journal of Speculative Philosophy*. Dewey's dissertation, "The Psychology of Kant," was completed in 1884. It was never published, and the manuscript was lost. "Kant and Philosophic Method," published in the *Journal of Speculative Philosophy* in April 1884, probably covers some of the same material as the dissertation. Dewey, who was exposed to two conflicting strains in graduate school, experimental psychology and neo-Hegelianism, probably criticized Kant from a Hegelian point of view.

Dewey's critique of Kant is well known.[15] The relation between Dewey and Fichte is practically unknown. Edmund Montgomery calls attention to a link between Dewey's early conception of psychical monism and Fichte.[16] I do not know if Dewey was himself ever interested in Fichte. Yet the fact remains that Dewey followed Fichte in understanding philosophy as a basically theoretical response to practical problems. For both thinkers, philosophy arose out of what Dewey later called the stresses and strains of social existence.[17] This means that philosophy deals not with the kind of philosophical questions that Wittgenstein thought needed to be exorcised. It rather deals with practical difficulties that require theoretical answers. The difference is that Fichte, writing closely after Kant, reconfigured philosophy as arising out of practical concerns while maintaining a version of Kant's transcendentalism. Yet Dewey, writing after Hegel, defended a weaker, non-transcendental view.

Dewey's relation to Hegel is very complex. According to James A. Good, there is "a permanent Hegelian deposit" in Dewey's thought.[18] Good is following Dewey's own testimony on this point. Dewey writes that "acquaintance with Hegel has left a permanent deposit on my thinking."[19] I take that to mean that Dewey, who criticized Hegel, also incorporated Hegelian themes and ideas in his position. Already in the discussion of Darwin, Dewey called for philosophy to turn away from eternal concerns in dealing with pressing temporal issues. He suggests that "philosophy must in time become a method of locating and interpreting the more serious of the conflicts that occur in life, and a method of projecting ways for dealing with them."[20] Taking his cue from experimental science, Dewey proposed an experimental view of philosophy that yields no more than experimental results. According to Dewey, there is not and cannot be a single philosophy true in all times and places since philosophy is merely a secondary enterprise arising within and limited to different situations in different historical moments. As in his study of certainty,[21] so in his account of philosophical reconstruction[22] Dewey sketches a view of philosophy as intrinsically experimental.

Yet to be clarified is precisely how Hegel influenced Dewey. Dewey's texts suggest various possibilities, and commentators have also made suggestions. One obvious point, with many ramifications, is the contextualism that broke out in post-Kantian German idealism, which was developed in Hegel and which carried over into American pragmatism. This contextualism divides into a number of areas. One of them, which Dewey favored, is the social formation of mental life. In this respect, Dewey was attracted to Hegel's idea of what Dewey called cultural institutions as objective mind, that is, as the concretion, so to speak, of human activities, aims, and purposes.[23]

The contextualism Dewey discerned in Hegel's account of spirit was important for his rejection of Kant's view as well as his own turn to social psychology. The Enlightenment idea of reason as entirely independent of the surroundings reached its peak in Kant. Dewey rejected this view. In Hegel's wake, he accepted a quasi-Hegelian view of the relation between culture and the making of minds, a view of reason that is not always already there, so to speak, but that is a product or result of the interaction between individuals, groups, and the surroundings. His acceptance of a Hegelian approach is, as he says, "a factor in producing my belief that the not uncommon [Enlightenment] assumption in both psychology and philosophy of a ready-made mind over against a physical world as an object has no empirical support."[24] This same idea led him to reject dualism and toward social psychology: "The only possible psychology, as distinct from a biological account of behavior, is a social psychology."[25]

The general commitment to contextualism led to a shared commitment to what Hegel called *Bildung*, or education. Good suggests that "in *Democracy and Education*, Dewey demonstrates a continuing commitment to *Bildung*, or education, particularly in the fourth chapter of the book, 'Education as

Growth.'"[26] The penultimate sentence of this chapter states: "Since growth is the characteristic of life, education is all one with growing; it has no end beyond itself."[27] This bold claim depends on something even bolder, which is Dewey's rejection of almost the entirety of Western metaphysics.

Yet there is an unbridgeable difference in the two views of contextualism. Both Hegel and Dewey insisted on the importance of context, which, for Dewey, was obviously different from that of his German predecessor in the German restoration period. "American philosophy must be born out of and must respond to the demands of democracy, as democracy strives to voice and to achieve itself on a vaster scale, and in a more thorough and final way than history has previously witnessed. And democracy is something at once too subtle and too complex and too aspiring to be caught in the midst of a single philosophical school or sect. It is, then, to the needs of democracy in America that we turn to find the fundamental problems of philosophy; and to its tendencies, its working forces, that we look for the points of view and the terms in which philosophy will envisage these problems."[28]

Hegel on Knowledge

To compare Dewey's view of knowledge to Hegel's, we need to say something about the latter's view. Hegel has an undeserved reputation of being uninterested in knowledge. There is a widespread but mistaken view in the debate that Hegel does not offer a theory of knowledge. This point is made in various ways: for instance, in the claim that he was disinterested in skepticism.[29] It is further suggested that Hegel was even disinterested in epistemology. For instance, J. B. Baillie, a qualified observer, asserts that Hegel justified philosophy in a way that no one in other cognitive disciplines would accept[30] and adds that Hegel was simply unconcerned with whether thought can grasp being.[31] Yet on consideration, we see that Hegel provided a sophisticated epistemological analysis that bears comparison with any other modern theories.

It has already been noted that Hegel's theory of knowledge arose in the reaction to Kant's as part of the ongoing effort to interpret, criticize, reformulate, and complete the critical philosophy on a constructivist basis. In the Second Attitude of Thought with respect to Objectivity in the *Encyclopedia Logic*, Hegel formulates a general critique of empiricism, including the critical philosophy, as unavailing efforts to know what Kant calls noumena, or the mind-independent world as it is. He focuses this critique in the *Phenomenology of Spirit* in examining the three levels of sense-certainty, or sensation, perception, and force and understanding. Hegel's argument presupposes that a necessary condition of cognition is that the cognitive object be a unity. The argument, which is very complex, consists in claiming that a representational approach to knowledge fails. Sensation yields at most that an object is but not what it is. Perception tells us what the object is at the cost of a dualism between its existence as a single object and as a multiplicity of qualities. Theoretical efforts to overcome this dualism are unavailing. They fail to grasp the object as it is since, as Hegel says, when we withdraw the curtain, we find there only ourselves.

This suggests that, as Kant famously proposes in his Copernican revolution, we know only what we in some sense "construct."[32] The key difficulty is how to understand the term "construct." Kant's approach is based on mathematical construction. Since antiquity, geometry has been based on the construction of geometrical figures with a straightedge and compass. Kant initially turned to a representationalist approach to knowledge, which failed. It failed for the reason that, as he later realized, there is no reliable way to assert knowledge of a mind-independent external object. If it is independent, then there is no cognitive link to it. Hence, it cannot be represented or otherwise known. Kant's solution is the constructivist suggestion that we know what we construct. Yet Kant was unable to describe the activity of construction, which he famously claimed is hidden in the human soul.[33]

Post-Kantian German idealism can be regarded as a series of efforts by different hands—including Fichte, Schelling, Hegel, and Marx—to reformulate the conception of epistemological construction. Hegel's effort, which is central to his view of idealism, is arguably best described in the introduction to the *Phenomenology.* In the introduction, Hegel sketches the outlines of an empirical approach to knowledge of cognitive objects in terms of theories, or categorial frameworks, in which both frameworks and objects are variables. There is a difference between knowledge and truth.

Knowledge arises out of a process of interaction including experience as well as theories about it. An experience is followed by the formulation of a theory, which is then tested against further experience. The terminus ad quem, or final goal, is a theory that agrees in all respects with further experience. Knowledge differs from and by definition falls short of truth. Knowledge arises in the course of a process in which claims to know are formulated and compared with experience. If a given theory fails the test of experience, it must be reformulated. At a minimum, the successor theory should do all the things the initial theory did plus a least one further thing it failed to do but which "agrees" with the intent with which it was formulated.

Theory is not formulated about a mind-independent external object, which lies outside experience and knowledge. It is rather formulated about the contents of experience, as distinguished from the way the world really is. In some epistemological approaches, the world is held to be a constant, independent of theories about it. On the contrary, in Hegel's approach, the cognitive object is not independent of but rather "dependent" on the theory formulated to explain it. As the theory changes, the cognitive object also changes. A trivial example is the difference between a theory formulated about water we experience in myriad ways and a different theory that from the chemical perspective concerns H_2O.

Though little known, Hegel's theory of knowledge is sophisticated and surprisingly modern. Experience constitutes the limit of knowledge. Hegel's theory is naturalistic, based on the cognitive activities of finite human beings. It is fallibilistic since at any moment new information could arise that, as Peirce might say, could transform belief into doubt and hence create the need for a successor theory. Claims for knowledge are formulated on the basis of prior experience and justified in terms of their ability to explain future experience.

Dewey on Knowledge

Dewey's suggestion that philosophy should concern itself with problems drawn from the American experience was certainly an important motivation in his position. Yet this suggests a local approach that does not do justice to the breadth of his thinking about traditional figures and problems that he transformed from his own perspective. Though not as deeply grounded as Peirce in the history of philosophy, he was certainly better than James about dealing with traditional figures. James wanted to break with the German tradition, which he did not know well, throughout his career. Yet even after his interests changed from idealism to Darwinism, Dewey remained under the influence of his early grounding in German philosophy. This background is apparent in his critical comments on Kant, his general description of his own position as objective idealism, and his general stress on practice in distinction to theory.

Dewey's interest in, and contribution to, epistemology has often been passed over for two reasons. On the one hand, it is sometimes thought he was uninterested in the problem of knowledge. While he was mainly concerned with particular problems of knowledge, he devoted a series of important works, including the *Quest for Certainty*, *Reconstruction in Philosophy*, and *Experience and Nature* to describing and criticizing the mainline philosophical conception of knowledge as well as to working out his own version of the pragmatic alternative in the form of empirical naturalism, or naturalistic empiricism. His general attraction to the Darwinian biological model should not distract attention from his interest in epistemological issues.

Like Kant and Hegel, Dewey's most important concept is his concept of experience, whose most important statement is *Experience and Nature.* In this book, Dewey favors empirical naturalism, or, as he also says, naturalistic empiricism, and again naturalistic humanism. By "naturalism," he has in mind an account based on and limited to the natural world or nature, an approach very different from naturalizing epistemology in analytic thinkers. For Dewey, as for such German idealist thinkers as Fichte and Hegel, knowledge is human knowledge, knowledge resulting from the actions of finite human beings. By "empiricism," Dewey means that whatever claims philosophy raises about the world must be traced back to experience. General conclusions must be brought into line with experience. In accordance with Dewey's experimental approach to philosophy, naturalism is intended to reveal the inconsistency of old accounts with the nature of things. Dewey's whole effort is intended to overcome the supposed separation of human beings and nature in formulating a philosophic method that reveals human beings within nature and nature as cognitively accessible to us.[34] His account denies the transcendent status accorded to reflection by Kant and many of his followers. As a natural event, reflection occurs within nature.[35] "These commonplaces," he writes, "prove that experience is of as well as *in* nature."[36] For Dewey, when used intelligently, an experiential approach to nature progressively reveals it. Unlike many scientists and too many philosophers, he is not claiming to know nature in itself or to grasp metaphysical reality. What is revealed is not nature in itself but rather nature as it occurs in human experience. In taking an instrumental approach, he claims no more than that physical science discovers how to appropriate nature for human purposes, that is, as he says in the preface added in the second edition, "those properties and relations of things in virtue of which they are capable of being used as instrumentalities."[37]

Dewey, who was born in the year that Darwin published *On the Origin of Species* (1859), was attracted to evolution. For Dewey, Darwinism was useful in helping us to abandon the idea of species as tending toward the realization of a fixed *telos,* or *eidos,* an idea that goes back in the tradition to Aristotle. The Darwinian insight that life depends on transition eliminates the idea of a designer, hence intelligent design, while suggesting the need for a new logic. "The influence of Darwin upon philosophy," Dewey writes, "resides in his having conquered the phenomena of life for the principle of transition, and thereby freed the new logic for application to mind and morals and life."[38]

Dewey, who was not a logician, here uses "logic" in a nonstandard sense. By "logic," he does not mean methods of formal reasoning but rather the logic of inquiry. In this respect, Dewey overlapped with Peirce. Peirce, of course, was a formidable logician, whose insights, had Dewey known them better, would have enabled him to sharpen his own account. There is a further difference in the scope of their respective approaches to logic. The logic of scientific inquiry, Peirce's field of predilection, is only a subset within Dewey's much wider concern with inquiry in general.

Dewey studies what he calls the pattern of inquiry in *Logic: The Theory of Inquiry.* Inquiry is a process in which what initially appears unformed and inchoate is transformed into a determinate situation. "Inquiry," he writes, "is the directed or controlled transformation of an indeterminate situation into a determinately unified one."[39] This may include introducing hypotheses that are tested in determining claims that provide what Dewey, in a rare arresting turn of phrase, calls "warranted assertibility."[40] He has in mind conclusions roughly defensible in terms of a particular pattern of inquiry, as ascertained through testing different possible solutions, as distinguished from traditional claims for apodictic knowledge.

Traditional claims for knowledge are often directed toward grasping the mind-independent real. Warranted assertibility, on the contrary, denotes claims for knowledge based on meeting a set of criteria introduced prior to a constative determination. Dewey's view has attracted attention from many angles of vision. Dewey's concept led to skeptical criticism, above all from Russell.[41] The latter followed up his criticism of James's so-called transatlantic theory of truth by complaining that Dewey conflated truth and warranted assertibility. In response, Dewey stated that "warranted assertibility" is intended as a definition of knowledge in the sense that "only true beliefs are knowledge."[42]

Dewey's view of logic as experimental inquiry turned him against the traditional philosophical approach to knowledge and in the direction of philosophical reconstruction. His most extended discussion of the traditional philosophical approach to knowledge occurs in *The Quest for Certainty.* Typically for Dewey, he is not concerned with the question of knowledge as such but rather its social function. For Peirce, the problem of knowledge oscillates between the two poles of belief and doubt.[43] Dewey generalizes a version of this thesis to the history of the problem of knowledge.

Dewey's related thesis is that insecurity generates the quest for certainty in both philosophy and religion. "The quest for certainty is a quest for a peace which is assured."[44] The interest in certainty leads to an emphasis on stability, in which science in the true sense meant grasping the real that, as Dewey says, traditionally "glorified the invariant at the expense of change."[45] The success in providing certainty was earlier guaranteed by religion through a synthesis between belief and authority that came undone through the rise of modern science. This synthesis, which cannot be restored either by holding to religion or through returning to ancient philosophical views, can be restored only by abandoning certainty and adopting an experimental or operational view in practice.

Dewey, Hegel, and Knowledge after Kant

Kant, who did many things, was above all an epistemologist. The author of the critical philosophy believed he both began philosophy worthy of the name as well as brought it to an end. This opinion remains influential. It is sometimes believed that epistemology ended with Kant. It follows that neither Hegel nor Dewey was concerned with the problem of knowledge. It is often held that Hegel had nothing to contribute to the problem of knowledge, which was not even a concern for Dewey. If we think of the recent debate, one of the reasons why Rorty was interested in Dewey and not Peirce was because it was easier to suggest that Dewey was concerned with social issues but not epistemology, but this was simply implausible for Peirce.

Yet when we go beyond the misconceptions in the literature, we easily detect a considerable degree of overlap. This begins with a transformation of the concept of experience from the a priori to the a posteriori plane, from the possibility for every representation to be accompanied by an "I think," or abstract concept of subjectivity, to the consciousness or self-consciousness of finite human beings in the role of the real cognitive subject. The change in the view of experience leads to abandoning transcendental argument in favor of a naturalistic approach to knowledge broadly conceived, a related shift to the practical over the theoretical, an emphasis on fallibilism,[46] and warranted assertibility or its functional equivalent instead of familiar but unworkable claims to apodicticity.

It was noted above that in each case, the respective position was determined by a reaction against the hugely influential critical philosophy. Dewey and Hegel both were working broadly in Kant's wake, hence within the conceptual matrix he proposed as well as the debate to which it gave rise. Kant's concern to formulate a critical approach to knowledge was widely influential. Yet many aspects of his position, including his conception of critique, met fierce opposition. The debate set in motion by the critical philosophy includes the acceptance or rejection of specific doctrines, such as the thing in itself, about which F. H. Jacobi famously said he could not enter into the system without it nor remain in the system with it;[47] the effort, following Kant's own suggestion, to distinguish between the letter and the spirit of the critical philosophy; the concern, begun by K. L. Reinhold in his *Letters on the Kantian Philosophy*, to formulate the conception of system on which Kant insisted but that he allegedly did not provide;[48] the concern to carry forward and complete his Copernican turn that engaged all the post-Kantian German idealists, which took the form of a reformulation of the conception of epistemological construction; and so on.

Within the larger framework of the reaction to Kant, there are a number of important similarities between Hegel's and then later Dewey's views of knowledge. Hegel and then later Dewey both belonged to the anti-Kantian reaction that rejected Kant's a priori approach to knowledge in favor of an a posteriori epistemological strategy. Both of them also belonged to the subsequent trend away from efforts to know the mind-independent world as it is, efforts that go back to early Greek philosophy and continue in Descartes and Kant, hence to the rejection of what is now called metaphysical realism in favor of what Kant labeled empirical realism.

The convergence between Dewey, the American pragmatist, and Hegel, the German idealist, is not unexpected but expected—in fact, easy to foresee—if one thinks about their respective conceptual contexts in which each worked out his position. It confirms Josiah Royce's insight that early in the twentieth century, pragmatism was what observers were calling idealism. This insight is further illustrated by the work of Nicholas Rescher.[49]

Yet, though there is an important degree of overlap, there are also significant differences between American pragmatism and German idealism. Dewey is not Hegel, and the former's position should not be conflated with the latter's. This chapter has focused on their respective approaches to the problem of knowledge. I have insisted that in his own way, each made an often unrecognized but significant contribution to this theme. Yet as concerns knowledge, there are at least two differences.

One difference concerns the respective views of constructivism. This was an epistemological approach that came into modern philosophy through Thomas Hobbes and Giambattista Vico and was discovered independently by Kant. There is a tendency to regard all forms of constructivism as the same.[50] Yet constructivism is developed in different ways by different observers. Hobbes was interested in political science and Vico in human history. Kant was concerned with theory of knowledge. This concern was further worked out in Hegel's a posteriori transformation of Kant's a priori form of constructivism. Though very different, Kant and Hegel shared a view of the construction of the cognitive object as a phenomenon, hence a shift toward phenomenology. Dewey, however, was less interested in the general problem of knowledge than in educational theory and practice. His particular form of constructivism was concerned with the relation of knowledge and action in the field of education.[51]

A second difference relates to the historical shift in the conception of knowledge after Kant. The critical philosophy was rigorously ahistorical. The post-Kantian evolution toward a historical conception of knowledge passed through various stages, culminating in a deeply historical approach in Hegel and Marx. A historical approach to knowledge runs throughout Hegel's position. It began with Hegel's general interest in historical phenomena, especially the French Revolution. It was carried further in his philosophy of history. It was basic to his conception of the history of philosophy. And it was worked out in Hegel's view of the relation of knowledge and history that offers a historical analysis of the epistemological process. This culminates in the suggestion, which was central to Hegel's conception of the process of knowledge as itself historical, that, since each of us belongs to our own historical period, knowledge claims are literally indexed to the historical moment.[52]

In order to understand the significance of this difference, it is necessary to return to naturalism. This term, which is currently widespread after Quine's seminal article,[53] is presently used in many different ways without a precise meaning. It seems to have originally been used in philosophy by a series of "naturalists" (Dewey, Ernest Nagel, Sidney Hook, and Roy Wood Sellars) to proclaim the interest of bringing philosophy closer to science. In this sense, it is often taken to include the idea that nature is all reality and the scientific method is the best way to study it.[54]

If, for present purposes, we provisionally adopt the view of naturalism as the idea that nature is all reality and should be investigated through scientific methods, an important difference between Dewey and Hegel becomes apparent. The point can be made with respect to the knowing subject. Dewey and Hegel both approached knowledge from the perspective of finite human beings, rooted in social context. Dewey further turned to evolution in considering human beings as biological and cultural. Hegel, a pre-evolutionary figure, understood the subject as cultural and historical. The difference is that Hegel brought in the historical dimension but lacked the biological dimension in the evolutionary sense. Dewey insisted on the evolutionary dimension but lacked the historical dimension. Human beings are not only cultural but also biological and historical beings. In Kant's wake, a fully naturalistic account needs to include at least these three dimensions. I conclude that in this respect, the views of Hegel and Dewey diverge in ways that are complementary. Each focuses on an aspect of what we need in order to work out a complete view, but neither tells the whole story of how to shift to a full-blown naturalism in Kant's wake.

Notes

1. See Richard Rorty, "Dewey between Hegel and Darwin," in *Philosophical Papers*, vol. 3, *Truth and Progress* (New York: Cambridge University Press, 1998), 290–307.

2. G. W. Leibniz, *Philosophische Schriften*, ed. C. I. Gerhardt (Berlin: Weidmann, 1875–90), 4:559–60.

3. See Cornel West, *The American Evasion of Philosophy: A Genealogy of Pragmatism* (Madison: University of Wisconsin Press, 1989).

4. See Nicholas Rescher, *Realistic Pragmatism: an Introduction to Pragmatic Philosophy* (Albany: SUNY Press, 2000).

5. According to Peirce:

> [B]efore we can attack any normative science, any science which proposes to separate the sheep from the goats here [Peirce "names three normative sciences: Ethics, Esthetics, and Logic, 'the three doctrines that distinguish good and bad' representations of truth, . . . efforts of will, . . . (and) objects considered simply in their presentation"], it is plain that there must be a preliminary inquiry which shall justify the attempt to establish such dualism. This must be a science that does not draw any distinction of good or bad in any sense whatever, but just contemplates phenomena as they are, simply opens its eyes and describes what it sees; not what it sees in the real as distinguished from figment—not regarding any such dichotomy—but simply describing the object, as a phenomenon, and stating what it finds in all phenomena alike. [Hegel, Peirce says, made this his "starting-point" in the *Phenomenology*,] although he considers it in a fatally narrow spirit, since he [Hegel] restricted himself to what *actually* forces itself on the mind. . . . I will so far follow Hegel as to call this science *phenomenology* although I will not restrict it to the observation and analysis of *experience* but extend it to describing all the features that are common to whatever is *experienced* or might conceivably be experienced or become an object of study in any way direct or indirect.

C. S. Peirce, *Collected Papers of Charles Sanders Peirce*, ed. Charles Hartshorne and Paul Weiss (Cambridge: Harvard University Press, 1960–66), 5:37.

6. "The science of Phenomenology is in my view the most primal of all the positive sciences. That is, it is not based, as to its principles, upon any other *positive science*. By a *positive science* I mean an inquiry which seeks for positive knowledge, that is, for such knowledge as may conveniently be expressed in a categorical proposition." Ibid., 5:39.

7. Ibid., 5:238: "Phenomenology, which does not depend upon any other positive science, nevertheless must, if it is to be properly grounded, be made to depend upon the Conditional or Hypothetical Science of *Pure mathematics*."

8. Ibid., 1:284: "Phaneroscopy is the description of the *phaneron*; and by the *phaneron* I mean the collective total of all that is in any way or in any sense present to the mind, quite regardless of whether it corresponds to any real thing or not. If you ask present *when*, and to *whose* mind, I reply that leave these questions unanswered, never having entertained a doubt that these features of the *phaneron* that I have found in my mind are present at all times and to all minds."

9. For Hegel's influence on Dewey, see John Dewey, "From Absolutism to Experimentalism," in *The Later Works of John Dewey, 1925–1953*, 17 vols., ed. Jo Ann Boydston (Carbondale: Southern Illinois University Press, 1981–90), 5:147–60.

10. See Tom Rockmore, *In Kant's Wake: Philosophy in the Twentieth Century* (Oxford: Blackwell, 2006).

11. See Richard Rorty, *Philosophy and the Mirror of Nature* (Princeton: Princeton University Press, 1979).

12. See Bertrand Russell, *A History of Western Philosophy* (New York: Simon and Schuster, 1945), 816, 824.

13. See Peirce's review of *Studies in Logical Theory* in *Collected Papers*, 8:188–90.

14. See, e.g., John Dewey, "The Pragmatism of Peirce," in *The Middle Works of John Dewey, 1899–1924*, ed. Jo Ann Boydston (Carbondale: Southern Illinois University Press, 1976–83), 10:71–78; "Peirce's Theory of Quality," in *Later Works*, 11:86–94; and "Peirce's Theory of Linguistic Signs, Thought and Meaning," in *Later Works*, 15:141–52.

15. See James Scott Johnston, "Dewey's Critique of Kant," *Transactions of the Charles S. Peirce Society* 42, no. 4 (Fall 2006): 518–51.

16. See Edmund Montgomery, "Psychical Monism," *Monist* 2 (1891–92): 338–56.

17. See Dewey, *Middle Works*, 11:94.

18. See James A. Good, *A Search for Unity in Diversity: The "Permanent Hegelian Deposit" in the Philosophy of John Dewey* (Lanham, Md.: Lexington Books, 2006).

19. Dewey, *Later Works*, 5:254.

20. John Dewey, "The Influence of Darwin on Philosophy," in *The Influence of Darwin on Philosophy and Other Essays* (Amherst: Prometheus Books, 1997), 17.

21. See John Dewey, *The Quest For Certainty: A Study of the Relation of Knowledge and Action* (New York: Putnam, 1960).

22. See John Dewey, *Reconstruction in Philosophy* (Boston: Beacon Press, 1960).

23. "Hegel's idea of cultural institutions as an 'objective mind' upon which individuals were dependent in the formation of their mental life fell in with [other influences]. . . . The metaphysical idea that an absolute mind is manifested in social institutions dropped out; the idea upon an empirical basis, of the power exercised by cultural environment in shaping the ideas, beliefs, and intellectual attitudes of individuals remained." John Dewey cited in Jane M. Dewey, *The Philosophy of John Dewey*, ed. Paul Arthur Schilpp and Lewis Edwin Hahn (La Salle, Ill.: Open Court, 1939), 17.

24. Ibid., 17–18.

25. Ibid., 18.

26. Good, *Search for Unity*, 44.

27. Dewey, *Middle Works*, 9:58.

28. Dewey, "Philosophy and the American Way of Life," in ibid., 3:73–74.

29. Solomon claims that Hegel refuses to take skepticism seriously. See Robert Solomon, *In the Spirit of Hegel* (Oxford: Oxford University Press, 1983), 184–85. Vieweg shows, on the contrary, that Hegel is deeply concerned with and knowledgeable about contemporary skeptics. See Klaus Vieweg, *Philosophie des Remis: Der Junge Hegel und das Gespenst des Skepticismus* (Munich: Fink Verlag, 1998). Forster argues that Hegel is deeply concerned to come to grips with the problem of skepticism. See Michael N. Forster, *Hegel and Skepticism* (Cambridge: Harvard University Press, 1989).

30. Baillie writes that "it is a justification in terms of and satisfactory to philosophy itself, not one that any other form of knowledge would accept." J. B. Baillie, trans., *The Phenomenology of Mind,* (London: Allen and Unwin, 1931), 33.

31. "Whether thought is able to know, or how far it can know being at all, is a problem which from the start [Hegel] never seems to have considered." J. B. Baillie, *The Origin and Significance of Hegel's Logic* (London: Macmillan, 1901), 42.

32. See Immanuel Kant, *Critique of Pure Reason,* trans. Paul Guyer and Allen Wood (New York: Cambridge University Press, 1998), B xiii, 109.

33. See ibid., B 181, 273.

34. The first chapter of his book is devoted to making this point. See John Dewey, "Experience and Philosophic Method," in *Experience and Nature* (La Salle: Open Court, 1971), 1–36.

35. Ibid., 59.

36. Ibid., 4.

37. Ibid., xvi.

38. Dewey, "Influence of Darwin on Philosophy," 8–9.

39. John Dewey, "The Pattern of Inquiry," in *Later Works*, 12:122.

40. Dewey formulated the concept of warranted assertibility in *Logic: The Theory of Inquiry* (New York: Holt, Reinhart and Winston, 1938). Russell responded in his contribution to the Dewey volume in the Library of Living Philosophers series (1939), then in a chapter in *An Inquiry into Meaning and Truth* (1940), and in the chapter on Dewey in *A History of Western Philosophy* (New York: Simon and Schuster, 1945). Dewey answered Russell in his general reply in the volume in the Library of Living Philosophers and in an article in the *Journal of Philosophy* in response to the chapter in Russell's *An Inquiry into Meaning and Truth.* See John Dewey, "Propositions, Warranted Assertibility, and Truth," *Journal of Philosophy* 38, no. 7 (1941): 169–86, reprinted in *Dewey and His Critics: Essays from the "Journal of Philosophy,"* selected and with an introduction by Sidney Morgenbesser (New York: Journal of Philosophy, 1977), 265–82. See, for discussion, Tom Burke, *Dewey's New Logic: A Reply to Russell* (Chicago: University of Chicago Press, 1994).

41. "On the Very Idea of a Third Dogma," in W. V. O. Quine, *Theories and Things* (Cambridge: Harvard University Press, 1985), 39: "The proper role of experience or surface irritation is as a basis not for truth but for warranted belief."

42. Dewey, "Propositions, Warranted Assertibility, and Truth," 169.

43. See, for a summary of Peirce's view of pragmatic inquiry, T. L. Short, *Peirce's Theory of Signs* (New York: Cambridge University Press, 2007), 347: "We have no knowledge a priori of how to inquire—there can never be a time when we will know, for sure, that we are proceeding in the right way or even that there is a right way to proceed. We can only go by the evidence we have so far acquired, in faith that there is an impersonal truth, that is, a final opinion toward which an ideal inquiry would tend. The evidence that supports that faith is extensive and compelling and yet conceivably erroneous. It is shot through with uncertainty, unanswered questions, unresolved problems, and vague formulations."

44. Dewey, *Quest for Certainty*, 8.

45. See ibid., 17.

46. Fallibilism of different kinds is invoked by many writers, including Peirce and Popper. It is sometimes thought that fallibilism is central Peirce. See Joseph Margolis, "Rethinking Peirce's Fallibilism," *Transactions of the Charles S. Peirce Society* 43, no. 2 (Spring 2007): 229–49.

47. See F. H. Jacobi, *David Hume über den Glauben, oder Idealismus und Realismus. Ein Gespräch* (Breslau: Gottlieb Löwe, 1787), 223.

48. See Karl Leonhard Reinhold, *Letters on the Kantian Philosophy*, trans. James Hebbeler (Cambridge: Cambridge University Press, 2006).

49. See Nicholas Rescher, *A System of Pragmatic Idealism* (Princeton: Princeton University Press, 1992–93), 3 vols.

50. See Arthur Child, *Making and Knowing in Hobbes, Vico, and Dewey*, University of California Publications in Philosophy, 16, no. 13 (Berkeley and Los Angeles: University of California Press, 1953).

51. Dewey's view of education has been extensively discussed. See, e.g., Jim Garrison, "Deweyan Pragmatism and the Epistemology of Contemporary Social Constructivism," *American Educational Research Journal* 32, no. 4 (Winter 1995): 716–40.

52. "As for the individual, every one is a son of his time; so philosophy also is its time apprehended in thoughts. It is just as foolish to fancy that any philosophy can transcend its present world, as that an individual could leap out of his time or jump over Rhodes." G. W. F. Hegel, *Philosophy of Right*, trans. T. M. Knox (New York: Oxford University Press, 1977), 11.

53. See W. V. O. Quine, "Epistemology Naturalized," in *Ontological Relativity and Other Essays* (New York: Columbia University Press, 1969), 69–90.

54. This is different from the type of naturalism associated with analytic figures like Carnap, who favor such forms of reduction as physicalism. See, e.g., Rudolf Carnap, "Psychology in Physical Language," in *Logical Positivism*, ed. A. J. Ayer (Glencoe, Ill.: Free Press, 1959), 165–98.

3] Traces of Hegelian *Bildung* in Dewey's Philosophy

James A. Good and Jim Garrison

Our research on John Dewey's debt to G. W. F. Hegel convinces us that we can fruitfully view his philosophy of education as a development of the German *Bildung* tradition.[1] In the first section of this chapter, we focus primarily on *Bildung* in the writings of Johann Herder, Johann Goethe, and Hegel. For these thinkers, *Bildung* was an organic model of education. More precisely, they viewed education as the developmental formation of an individual's unique potential through participation in the social practices and institutions of their culture (that is, family, school, university, civil institutions, and such). These thinkers envisioned an endlessly actualizing self that is both willing and able to make unique cultural contributions through immanent critique and creative reconstruction of cultural norms, beliefs, and values, positively affecting their subsequent self-development and the education of future generations.

The second and third sections exposit Dewey as a philosopher of *Bildung*, showing that rather than a substance with an essence, he theorized the self as a complex function developing through a rhythm of equilibrium–disequalibrium–restoration of equilibrium, a biologically based version of Hegel's dialectic. We demonstrate how Hegel's dialectical theory of *Bildung* showed Dewey ways to combine a social theory of the self with a theory of immanent critique that provides individual freedom through right relationship with others and continual reconstruction of cultural institutions. Stated in another way, the individual can achieve a self capable of understanding the conditions that formed it and transform itself by transforming those conditions. We conclude that Dewey deployed Hegel's concept of identity in difference in his defense of a democratic society emphasizing diversity of socially coordinated interaction as crucial to self-realization, individual freedom, and continuous learning.

Hegel and the German *Bildung* Tradition

Sixteenth-century German pietists initiated the *Bildung* tradition in an effort to substitute a focus on the Christian life for contentious theological disputes, encouraging the devout to seek cultivation (*Bildung*) of their individual talents in the image of God innate in their souls.[2] By the end of the eighteenth century, however, *Bildung* had spiritual, philosophical, and political overtones and was associated with liberation of the mind from tradition and superstition—and also liberation of the German people from a premodern political system of small feudal states.

Herder used *Bildung* in the sense of individual formation but also to connote the development of a people (*Volk*); *Bildung* became the totality of experiences that provide a people's coherent sense of identity and common destiny. Although Herder is rightfully associated with late-eighteenth-century German nationalism, he conceived the German *Volk* as a classless society. Accordingly, his nationalism required promoting social unity from the bottom up, in contrast to the top-down political nationalism to which many historians attribute the subsequent rise of German militarism. Moreover, Herder's cultural nationalism did not include the idea of uniting the German principalities into an all-encompassing political and administrative nation-state.[3]

Herder's importance to Western intellectual history is immense. Largely as a result of his 1770 encounter with Herder, Goethe developed from a good but lackluster poet into the seminal artist remembered today. Herder conceived fundamental ideas about the dependence of thought on language we now take for granted and that inspired Wilhelm von Humboldt's foundational work in modern linguistics. Herder developed the methodological foundations of hermeneutics that Friedrich Schleiermacher built on and that culminated in nineteenth-century German classical scholarship and modern biblical scholarship. Herder's writings also established the modern discipline of anthropology. Additionally, Herder profoundly influenced intellectuals as diverse as Hegel, J. S. Mill, Friedrich Nietzsche, and Wilhelm Dilthey.

In a series of writings, Herder articulated the conception of philosophy at the heart of the German *Bildung* tradition. The titles of some of his works are revealing: *How Philosophy Can Become More Universal and Useful for the Benefit of the People*, *Ideas for the Philosophy of History of Humanity*, and *Letters for the Advancement of Humanity*. As these titles suggest, Herder believed philosophy must promote human growth and that we must understand philosophical ideas within their social and historical context. Similar to the Renaissance humanists, he believed the proper study of man is man and sought to displace academic philosophy with philosophical anthropology. For Herder, philosophy is the theory of *Bildung*, the theory of how individuals develop into the sort of organic unity that unceasingly works toward the full development of their talents and abilities, driving social *Bildung* as well.

John H. Zammito accurately asserts that Herder's conception of philosophy carried "forward from Herder to Wilhelm von Humboldt and G. W. F. Hegel, to Friedrich Schleiermacher . . . to the Left Hegelians . . . and Wilhelm Dilthey: the tradition of hermeneutics and historicism."[4]

Herder and Goethe's *On German Nature and Art* was a manifesto of the pre-romantic Sturm und Drang movement in literature, emphasizing the unpredictable emotional life of the individual in contrast to the French Enlightenment. Thus, in Goethe's *Sorrows of Young Werther*, despair over a romantic infatuation drives the protagonist to suicide. By the end of the 1780s, however, Goethe and Friedrich Schiller responded to the excesses of romanticism by endorsing a recovery of the organic wholeness of the Greek polis through harmonization of passionate feeling with the clarity of Enlightenment reason. Weimar Classicism, as the movement became known, sought the liberation of man through organic unification and harmonization of thought and feeling, mind and body.[5] Although in some ways he broke with Herder, Goethe continued to embrace Herder's emphasis on immanent reason and truth in contradistinction to the romantic notion that an individual apprehends transcendent truth by intuitively tapping into his or her genius as well as to the Enlightenment model of reason as a transcendent power.

Goethe's *Wilhelm Meister's Apprenticeship* inaugurated the tradition of the *Bildungsroman* by depicting its protagonist in a journey of self-formation. The only transcendence Wilhelm seeks is to rise above the soulless life of a bourgeois businessman by harmonizing his particular interests in service to a universal social good. W. H. Bruford accurately describes the novel as representing "the very essence of German humanism," the formation of individuals whose conduct is governed by a highly developed inner character rather than by imitation of others.[6] Goethe's vision of character formation requires the identification and molding of one's unique talents and inclinations through wise education and life experience. This education teaches Wilhelm that the individual must find his vocation, a calling to which he is well suited and that contributes to the maturation of the culture in which he lives. In so doing, the individual harmonizes not only mind and body but also self and society. In both dichotomies, mind/body and self/society, neither term is the cause of the other because they are reciprocal. Consider Elizabeth M. Wilkinson's discussion of the nonessentialist theory of form in Goethe's scientific writings: "A living thing, [Goethe] says in the preface to his *Morphology*, is not a single unit but a plurality. Some of its elements are already joined together when it comes into being. But growth consists of constant interchange of its own elements with elements of the environment, a taking-in and a giving-out, an incessant rearrangement of patterns in all directions. What is formed is immediately broken down and reformed. Stable identity derives not from the unchanging elements, but from the pattern which survives all their changes."[7]

Herder and Goethe had launched a neo-humanist tradition that stressed the individual's unique talents as well as the need to live in a society in which the talents of others complement their own. Hence, a well-developed society is one that allows wide scope for the unique development of individuals. Individual diversity is the very engine of social development. Rather than depict the individual as at odds with social unity, German neo-humanism champions a harmony of self and society through the development of individual uniqueness and acceptance of social responsibility as the avenue toward self-development. Self-realization is unattainable for those who wallow in their own narrow emotions or self-interest. Satisfaction is not found in a romantic transcendence of social bonds but in the activities of concrete social life. Goethe further developed these ideas in *Wilhelm Meister's Travels*. As Bruford explains, "We learn here better than anywhere else what kind of 'Bildung' Goethe . . . held to be essential for his countrymen in the post-revolutionary world. It is a process which, while allowing for the free development of the individual's natures and capacities, does not fail to make him aware of the debt he owes to the past, of his duty to society in the present and of the dependence of all men on immeasurable, imperfectly known forces."[8]

Since the 1960s, a growing body of scholarship has emphasized the extent to which Hegel was influenced by German neo-humanism, eschewing transcendent realities and timeless truths and championing a philosophy that deals with the world of human experience rather than a transcendent noumenal realm. On this reading, Hegel's logic is not a theory of the categories of reality but a post-Kantian theory of the categories according to which we cognize reality.[9] Most important, Hegel was concerned with *Bildung*, the self-development of the individual human spirit and of the human species. As Josiah Royce and others have noted, the *Phenomenology of Spirit* can be read as a *Bildungsroman*. Hegel shows the reader the development of an open and intelligent mind in a complex society lacking universally accepted values as the main character encounters a wide variety of experiences. The center of interest is the links between the main character's successive experiences and his gradual achievement of a fully rounded personality and well-tested philosophy of life.[10]

Early in the *Phenomenology*, Hegel makes the crucial claim that "self-consciousness is *Desire* in general."[11] Thus, all self-conscious activity is goal- or project-oriented, which has profound ramifications for epistemology. As

Robert Pippin notes, Hegel envisioned the philosophical search for truth as intimately connected to the satisfaction of desire: "The 'truth' is wholly relativized to pragmatic ends. . . . [W]hat counts as a successful explanation depends on what practical problem we want solved." Pippin continues, "*Which* desires a subject determines to pursue, which ends to satisfy, and indeed what counts as true satisfaction . . . are *results* of the collective, historical, social subject's self-determination and have no natural status."[12] Although Hegel agreed with Kant that we seek norms for our behavior that all rational agents would embrace, he added a social dimension to explain how we apprehend those norms. Hegel averred that we confirm the value of our norms by receiving recognition of their worth from self-conscious agents like ourselves.

In Hegel's discussion of the master/slave dialectic, it is apparent the self possesses certain natural desires that compel it to seek specific goals. Those desires, however, cannot fully determine the norms by which they are judged. Because of insecurity about their norms, when one self encounters another, they each seek recognition that their norms are worthy. In so doing, each self recognizes that its own self-conceived project for life determines its hierarchy of norms. The self becomes aware of its "negativity" as it realizes that its projects are never fully determined by any particular desire but are the result of a host of competing desires.[13] When a person decides his desire for recognition is more important than life itself, he willingly enters into a "trial by death."[14] When one person surrenders to the other out of fear for his life, he submits to a master/slave relationship, and the master imposes his norms upon the slave. But the master/slave relationship is unsustainable, as the slave comes to see the master's norms and authority as socially contingent. Conversely, the master realizes the slave cannot give the recognition he sought because it is not freely given. Nonetheless, this struggle for recognition is the "formative activity" that gives birth to self-consciousness because it teaches individuals that they actively shape their world.[15] Hence, rather than a natural or divinely imparted endowment, for Hegel, the mind emerges through social struggle.

Subsequently, Hegel contends, Western man sought other avenues for self-mastery and independence (for example, Stoicism and skepticism) that also ran their course. Throughout the medieval period, which he depicts as an era of universal servitude, Christianity prepared the way for the assertion of self-activity (*Selbsttätigkeit*), realized in the Protestant Reformation. The gradual rejection of serfdom, slavery, and feudalism were manifestations of the ongoing development of self-consciousness, ultimately apparent in the emergence of modern subjectivity. In the section of the *Phenomenology* titled "Reason," Hegel paints a succession of obscure portraits of different ways early modern European culture tried to ground its normative commitments and how each undermined itself on its own terms. The conclusion of this section is that reason gains authority only when we see that its norms are embedded in a worthy way of life. This realization comes through education as *Bildung.*

In his reflections on the history of moral thought, Hegel distinguishes between *Moralität* and *Sittlichkeit*, the former being individual morality arrived at by one's own reasoning and the latter being ethical norms embodied in the customs and institutions of one's society. This is not a rigid distinction, however, because he sees *Moralität* and *Sittlichkeit* as systematically related. Hegel depicts *Sittlichkeit*, embodied in the Greek polis, as historically prior to *Moralität*, which emerged in the modern nation-state. Describing a complete harmony between the individual and the community in the early Greek polis, Hegel provides a variety of historical reasons to explain why the accord collapsed.[16] The crux of the problem, for Hegel, was that the Greek polis provided objective freedom but made no room for subjective freedom, a distinctly modern achievement. He sees subjective freedom as a genuine advance over the polis but maintains that modern *Moralität* depends on *Sittlichkeit.* In order to reason for themselves about morality, individuals must live in a context of social norms that give content to abstract moral concepts. Moreover, people of *Bildung* do not accept social norms unreflectively; they accept norms only for which they can see rational justification. To the extent that the actual practices of their society are inconsistent with the rational basis of its social norms, they seek to reform their society. Only by working to harmonize *Moralität* and *Sittlichkeit* can the person of *Bildung* possess wisdom and virtue, because "wisdom and virtue consist in living in accordance with the customs of one's nation."[17]

Dewey's connection to Hegel is apparent when we look specifically at Hegel's account of human cognition. Not only do the two philosophers share the view that the self is always engaged in a project, they also agree that the self ordinarily proceeds in a state of harmony with its environment (Hegel's "natural consciousness").[18] In this state, there is no subject/object dualism because the self is at one with its environment. Precisely because it is always engaged in a project, the self inevitably encounters obstacles, which Hegel terms "negations."[19] This occurrence renders consciousness asunder, identifying an object over and against the self (*Gegenstand*), the obstacle that disrupted its project. After analysis of the negation in the stage of understanding (*Verstand*), the self formulates solutions that alter both its project and the object, achieving a reunification of consciousness that allows the self to resume its project. Upon reunification, the self eliminates the otherness of the object, regaining a holistic vision of its place in the world (the stage of reason or *Vernunft*). For Hegel, the culmination of this process is *Aufhebung*, which preserves the truth and individual diversity of both subject and object in the emergent unity, creating an identity in difference. The negation is transformed into a "determinate negation," one that leads to progress and growth. The self emerges from the process unified and enlarged because it has gained valuable experience. Rather than a metaphysical dualism, subject/object are moments within experience that serve a particular function. Although this process is Hegel's dialectic, it is also *Bildung*. Accordingly, rather than a theory of knowledge, Hegel developed a theory of learning, and philosophy became the philosophy of education.

It is simplistic to describe Hegel's concept of negation as contradiction, because negation diminishes the existential angst that results from any negation's disruption of the self's overall life project. Rather than a contradiction of propositions, negation is a disorientation that causes the self to lose "its truth on this path. The road can therefore be regarded as the pathway of doubt, or more precisely as the way of despair. For what happens on it is not what is ordinarily understood when the word 'doubt' is used: shilly-shallying about this or that presumed truth, followed by a return to that truth again, after the doubt has been appropriately dispelled—so that at the end of the process the matter is taken to be what it was in the first place."[20] The self presumes to have knowledge until it encounters negation, which leads it into a state of doubt or despair. When the self successfully resolves the problem that initiated the process, it gains knowledge that is has tested for itself. The self literally gains self-determination.

Hegel's account of self-consciousness includes awareness of oneself in contrast to objects, but it also includes a realization that one's consciousness makes the world its own by permeating it. Thus, as seen in the master/slave dialectic, rather than a given mental state, self-consciousness is an achievement that accompanies and promotes a sense of self-confidence and assurance. As the slave recognizes the contingency of his master's norms, he gains confidence that he can assert equally valid norms himself. Consciousness and object are mutually related, implying and complementing one another. Neither is consciousness an unchanging medium that presents various objects to reason; the character of its objects shapes consciousness as consciousness removes the alien otherness of objects and gains objectivity.

This is relevant to Hegel's conception of truth: "Consciousness provides its own criterion from within itself, so that the investigation becomes a comparison of consciousness with itself."[21] For Hegel, truth cannot be a static correspondence of subject and object because they are functional distinctions rather than markers of discrete metaphysical realms. Truth is a conceptual activity through which we comprehend the world together with a realization that our concepts contour it. Truth is experience conceived through *Begriff*. Although *Begriff* is often rendered as "concept" or "notion," its relationship to the verb *greifen*, "to grasp or seize," is revealing. Hegel's *Begriff* is more than a concept or a notion because it entails that mind is activity, rather than substance, engaged in capturing and embracing its object within consciousness. The object actualizes the concept, while *Idee*, as Hegel uses the term, is the unification of the concept and its object. Neither is *Begriff* a representation or empirical conception, for which Hegel uses *Vorstellung*.[22] Rather than intellectual entities existing within a mental realm, these terms denote functional moments that occur as we dialectically navigate through our world.

Hegel's concept of *Bildung* dovetails with his view that knowledge is gained only from experience and that we must seek, like the protagonist of a *Bildungsroman*, the widest variety of experience.[23] Furthermore, he rejected John Locke's passive spectator theory of the mind, according to which we should restrain our passions in order to gain objective knowledge. For Hegel, learning required a passionate search for truth; it is a matter of conscious self-development requiring arduous individual effort and responsibility. Thus, fulfillment must come in the activities of real life. Finally, his emphasis on self-knowledge, an accurate perception of one's talents, interests, and abilities, explains his charge that the Enlightenment's conception of knowledge as a search for indubitable truth is too narrow. Hegel believed the French Revolution had turned to terror because revolutionaries thought they possessed the eternally correct blueprint for human society.[24] The result of such certainty is inflexible dogmatism that not only foreshortens inquiry but leads to fanatical ideological devotion.

Because of his emphasis on self-knowledge, as rector of the Nuremburg *Gymnasium*, Hegel followed Goethe's lead by claiming each person must find his or her vocation and, at the same time, by arguing that education should prepare students for life rather than merely for narrowly defined jobs. Education is a dialectical process of alienation and return, according to Hegel, in which the mind continually stretches beyond its ordinary point of view. He sought to accomplish this by alienating the child's mind from its received point of view through the study of the ancient world and its languages. Ancient civilizations are sufficiently alien, he claimed, to separate children from their natural state but sufficiently close to their own language and world for them to return to themselves enlarged and transformed. The goal of education was to help students realize the ideal of modernity, which is for the individual to become a self-directed, self-formed person.[25]

Thus Hegel preserved and expanded on the German *Bildung* tradition's emphasis on education that liberates one from blind obedience to superstition, tradition, or transcendent realities. Hegel was also consistent with past proponents of *Bildung* in emphasizing the social nature of the self. Although persons of *Bildung* learn to think critically about their society, they cannot transcend it. This brings us to Hegel's primary development of the *Bildung* tradition. Rather than the unfolding of a form immanent in an individual, or in a people, as James Schmidt has noted, Hegel "presents Bildung as a process of relentless self-estrangement."[26] Hegel writes that consciousness "suffers . . . violence at its own hands" because it must confront its own naive certainty to go beyond itself and experience growth.[27] *Bildung* is not an autonomous activity, nor is it divorced from one's desires. On the contrary, *Bildung* requires self-knowledge, discerning one's own talents by discovering activities that bring satisfaction and a sense of fulfillment. And the greatest sort of fulfillment for Hegel was activity that promotes social *Bildung*.

Viewing the dialectic as a process of alienation and return reveals why Hegel's conception of *Bildung* is more than naive acquiescence to prevailing social norms. The person of *Bildung* advances cultural progress through the same process, which Steven B. Smith aptly describes as a method of immanent cultural critique because it criticizes society according to its own standards.[28] Because of the dialogical character of the dialectic, it does not occur within an internal, private mind but is always a conversation between past, contemporaneous, and future interlocutors. For Hegel, the intellectual tradition within which we live and work mediates all thinking. The mind actively categorizes sense data, à la Kant, but our conceptual structure is historically and culturally relative.[29]

Bildung is also a central motif of Hegel's *Elements of the Philosophy of Right*, in which he illuminates the concept by repeating the advice of a Pythagorean philosopher to a father about the best way to educate his son: "Make him the citizen of a state with good laws."[30] *Bildung* requires a well-ordered society that provides sufficient individual freedom for the development of each person's unique talents and abilities. The modern state must permit individuals to seek their own self-satisfaction by determining their own identities.[31] Among other rights, the state must protect individuals' right to their own bodies and their right to hold private property as well as the freedom of religion and conscience.[32] These rights are necessary because *Bildung* requires a society in which there is scope for all kinds of complementary individuals and activities. Exposure to different kinds of people and experimentation with different types of lives is crucial to moral development. Hegel contends that *Bildung* should begin in the family, continue more systematically in school, and be taken to a higher level in the university. After completing formal schooling, civil society provides the third stage of *Bildung*, wherein individuals recognize the rational basis of their society's institutions. In the third stage of *Bildung*, individuals are capable of independent thought and well prepared to engage in immanent critique of their society's practices.

The accusation that Hegel eschewed individual natural rights as the sure foundation of a just society is correct in that he rejected the essentialism of traditional natural rights theory, according to which humans are born with rights. Hegel claimed individual rights apart from a social context are empty, even detrimental, abstractions because a social order founded on abstract individual rights could not protect rights. As individuals insist on abstract rights, they alienate themselves from the community in which they seek to exercise them. An alienated individual's options may be vast outside of society, but they lose their meaning because society gives them content. The British liberal tradition's atomistic conception of "man" depicts the state as an abstraction in opposition to the individual, reducing its function to nothing more than the supervision and regulation of the actions of individuals through coercive force. For Hegel, only a well-constituted ethical life, a *Sittlichkeit*, could assure individual freedom by integrating individual rights into a system of institutions and customs that provide them with concretely fulfilling life options. The state has a responsibility toward its members to provide social environments that facilitate *Bildung*.

To conclude, in the *Bildung* tradition, philosophy and education are virtually synonymous terms that designate an ongoing process of both personal and cultural maturation. A harmonization of the individual's mind and heart and a unification of society evidence this maturation. Harmonization of the self is achieved through a wide variety of experiences that challenge the individual's accepted beliefs; in Hegel's writings, these challenges entail agonizing alienation from one's "natural consciousness" that leads to a reunification and development of the self. Similarly, although social unity requires well-formed institutions, it also requires a diversity of individuals with the freedom to develop a wide variety of talents and abilities. Rather than an end state, both individual and social unification is a process driven by an unrelenting succession of determinate negations. Most systematically in Hegel's writings, the *Bildung* tradition rejects the pre-Kantian metaphysics of being for a metaphysics of experience that disdains speculation about timeless realities. Learning requires a passionate search for continual growth tempered by reason that is developed through intense study of one's cultural history. Fulfillment comes through practical activity that promotes the development of one's talents and abilities as well as the development of one's society. Rather than acceptance of the sociopolitical status quo, *Bildung* requires the ability to engage in immanent critique of one's society, challenging it to actualize its own highest ideals.

Deweyan *Bildung*: The Biological Matrix

Dewey concedes: "I should never think of ignoring, much less denying . . . that acquaintance with Hegel has left a permanent deposit on my thinking."[33] Traces of this deposit are evident in a puzzling passage from *Democracy and Education*: "If we are willing to conceive education as the process of forming fundamental dispositions, intellectual and emotional, toward nature and fellow-men, philosophy may even be defined as the general theory of education."[34] Viewing philosophy and education as *Bildung* clarifies this claim. Dispositions are habits and attitudes formed (*Bild*) primarily by participating in the norms, beliefs, and values of institutionalized social practices (*Sittlichkeit*). For Dewey, habits are "social functions," and individual habits persist because "individuals form their personal habits under conditions set by prior customs."[35]

Although acquired, Dewey claims habits are "as potent and urgent" as involuntary physiological functions. His thinking about habits resembles Aristotle's, who coined the word for "function" (*ergon*) and used it to refer to what a thing characteristically *does* and what *use* that activity serves in preserving itself or something else. For Dewey, habits serve as the biological matrix for development. If habits are functions, the mind and self are also functions rather than fixed metaphysical forms. As cognitive functions, acquired habits help us realize long-term goals by structuring innate impulses and disciplining desires. As habits take root, they become "second nature," universal responses to classes of stimuli. Thus, for Dewey, "the universal is not primarily logic, but is factual, habitual. Control of knowing requires that it be noted so as to function logically."[36]

For Hegel, habit is the self's "abstract universal being" that yields "a universal mode of action," which is "rightly called a second nature." Thought depends on habits, which both free and constrain us. Habits provide skilled ability; even if one has "a decided talent," it must be "technically trained" to develop skill at the art. As with Dewey, for Hegel a habit is a cognitive, universal mode of action.[37]

Dewey concludes that habits "constitute the self" and in "any intelligible sense of the word will, they *are* will." Habits "form [*Bild*] our effective desires," "furnish us with our working capacities," and "rule our thoughts." Even reason "is not an antecedent force that serves as a panacea. It is a laborious achievement of habit needing to be continually worked over."[38] Rather than an atomistic individual with innate capacities, Dewey's self, like Hegel's, achieves reason, free will, and mind through struggle within a biological matrix. Like H_2O, which forms in the physical matrix of hydrogen and oxygen but is not reducible to either, Dewey's self is the product of habits but is not reducible to its constituent parts; it is Hegelian *Aufhebung*.

Dewey confesses Hegel "supplied a demand for unification that was doubtless an intense emotional craving . . . that only an intellectualized subject matter could satisfy." Hegel's theory of organically evolving universals (the *Begriff*) allowed him to overcome Kantian dualism, which is why Dewey acknowledges that "Hegel's synthesis of subject and object, matter and spirit, the divine and the human . . . operated as an immense release, a liberation."[39] Dewey's reliance on modern biological functionalism retains Hegel's notion of identity in difference as emergent functional coordination.

Dewey remarks that he preserved "the Hegelian emphasis upon continuity and the function of conflict . . . after my earlier confidence in dialectic had given way to skepticism."[40] In "Hegel's Philosophy of Spirit," Dewey emphasizes the importance of Hegel's concept of negation, which he ultimately translates into the Peircian language of the doubt-inquiry process. Hegel's great insight, according to Dewey, is that negation is neither "a mere unreality" nor "something aside of and apart from the positive." Negation "was the moving spring by which the positive first really made itself positive."[41] When consciousness doubts how to achieve its ends, it inquires to overcome creatively the disruption. Dewey understood that Hegel's dialectic is the pattern of a universal (for example, the self) breaking itself up (particularization) through alienation and estrangement when it encounters obstacles to action that are sublated (*Aufhebung*) by an emergent universal habit as a unity in diversity. The basic biological and psychological pattern is a movement from functional coordination (equilibrium) to disruption of coordination (disequalibrium) to restoration of coordination (equilibrium).

Dewey describes life as "a continual rhythm of disequilibrations and recoveries of equilibrium. . . . The state of disturbed equilibration constitutes *need*. The movement towards its restoration is search and exploration. The recovery is fulfillment or satisfaction." He insists that the restoration of equilibrium does not return the organism to its original state, asserting that "the *form* of the relationship, of the interaction, is reinstated, not the identical conditions."[42] The resemblance to Goethe's morphology is striking. In *Art as Experience*, Dewey constructs a definition of "form" out of his definition of "rhythm" as an "ordered variation of changes." He contends that "the existence of rhythms in nature" is the condition "of form in experience." The moment of functional coordination balances "antagonistic forces." Indeed, "polarity, or opposition of energies, is everywhere necessary to the definition, the delimitation, that resolves an otherwise uniform mass and expanse into individual forms." He concludes: "There is unity only when the resistances create a suspense that is resolved through cooperative interaction of the opposed energies."[43] Dewey conceives "form" as a Hegelian unity in diversity. Moreover, in his *Logic*, Dewey refers specifically to the passages on form in *Art as Experience* and states they "can be carried over, *mutatis mutandis*, to logical forms."[44]

There are also strong resonances of Hegel's dialectic in Dewey's theory of unique potentiality, development, change (including growth), and creativity: "Individuality itself is originally a potentiality and is realized only in interaction with surrounding conditions. In this process of intercourse, native capacities, which contain an element of uniqueness, are transformed and become a self. Moreover, through resistances encountered, the nature of the self is discovered. The self is both formed and brought to consciousness through interaction with environment. . . . [T]he self is created in the creation of objects, a creation that demands active adaptation to external materials, including a modification of the self so as to utilize and thereby overcome external necessities by incorporating them in an individual vision and expression."[45] This is a pregnant passage.[46] First, note that individuality is primordially a potential concretely actualized through interactions with already actualized surrounding conditions. The actual in one of the subfunctions of the transaction actualizes the potential in the other subfunction, and conversely. With each transaction, the unique potential of the self undergoes ever-evolving transformation.

Second, note there is "an element of uniqueness" to these native potentials. Third, because potentials set limits to development, freedom is never absolute; it is always contextualized and constrained. Fourth, interaction is necessary to actualize unique potentials. Fifth, freedom depends on already actualized otherness and difference. Sixth, awareness of "objective" environmental conditions, especially alienating differences, are critical to self-realization. Seventh, note that, for Dewey, self-development requires determinate negation: "The only way [the self] can become aware of its nature and its goal is by obstacles surmounted and means employed. . . . Nor without resistance from surroundings would the self become aware of itself; it would have neither feeling nor interest, neither fear nor hope, neither disappointment nor elation. Mere opposition that completely thwarts, creates irritation and rage. But resistance that calls out thought generates curiosity and solicitous care, and, when it is overcome and utilized, eventuates in elation."[47] Self-consciousness emerges when goal-directed activity reflects back upon the unconsciously desiring subject, which only occurs when the impulsion to act meets "objective" resistance from the environment. The self must functionally coordinate the situation to achieve its ends. If the self acquires new habits of action, its *Bild* morphs.

Eighth, observe that the self is created in the creation of objects used to achieve the ends it desires. In creative action, we not only express the present self but also form the future self in reciprocally transformative transactions. Finally, like Hegel, Dewey rejects latent potentiality, making otherness and difference necessary to potential and its actualization: "[P]otentialities cannot be *known* till *after* the interactions have occurred. There are at a given time unactualized potentialities in an individual because and in as far as there are in existence other things with which it has not as yet interacted."[48] Uniquely individual potentiality always depends on mutually modifying transactions with other existences. Pluralistic diversity, interaction, unique potentiality, and change are as critical to Dewey as to Hegel, Herder, or Goethe.

Deweyan *Bildung*: The Social Matrix

Dewey specifically mentions the importance of Hegel's notion of the social construction of mind: "Hegel's idea of cultural institutions as an 'objective mind' upon which individuals were dependent in the formation of their mental life fell in with [other influences]. . . . The metaphysical idea that an absolute mind is manifested in social institutions dropped out; the idea upon an empirical basis, of the power exercised by cultural environment in shaping the ideas, beliefs, and intellectual attitudes of individuals remained."[49] He further claims Hegel's depiction of the mind as a cultural artifact nurtured his belief that the common "assumption in both psychology and philosophy of a ready-made mind over against a physical world as an object has no empirical support." Hegel "was a factor," Dewey affirms, "in producing my belief that the only possible psychology . . . is a social psychology."[50]

Traces of *Bildung* are evident in Dewey's social matrix when we view Hegel's concept of spirit as the concrete actualization of cultural consciousness: "Spirit, being the *substance* and the universal, self-identical, and abiding essence, is the unmoved solid *ground* and *starting-point* for the action of all. . . . [T]his substance is equally the universal *work* produced by the action of all and each as their unity and identity."[51] Rather than an antecedently existing metaphysical substance, Hegel's spirit is the sum of human work in cultural history.[52] Hegel's doctrine of essence can be interpreted similarly. He claims the successful resolution of a problem takes us to "the real essence of the things" because, like Aristotle, Hegel held that the real essence is in the world rather than in a transcendent realm. Nonetheless, he speaks of "the real essence" of what "is an object to us" because, unlike Aristotle, he believed that the object of experience is constructed in the knowing process. Hegel asserts, "Though the categories, such as unity, or cause and effect, are strictly the property of thought, it by no means follows that they must be ours merely and not also characteristics of the objects."[53] As noted above, for Hegel, the mind/body dichotomy is a moment within the dialectic rather than a fixed metaphysical gulf. By resisting any temptation to reduce the object to a mere effect of experience, Hegel avoids subjective idealism.[54] Object and consciousness are both causes and effects of each other.

Consequently, for Hegel, essence emerges from the history of an object's effects in the world. Hegel argues that painting is limited in its ability to convey truth because it is restricted to "a specific space" and moment of "temporal development." Truth comprises "a unity of essential distinctions," but those essential distinctions "develop in their appearance not only as juxtaposed in space, but in a temporal succession as a history, the course of which painting can only present graphically in an inappropriate way. Even every blade of grass, every tree has in this sense its history, alteration, process, and a complete totality of different situations. This is still more the case in the sphere of the spirit; as actual spirit in its appearance, it can only be portrayed exhaustively if it is brought before our minds as such a course of history."[55] Essence is a product of the process by which the knower overcomes the otherness of the object. We apprehend the essence of an object by observing its actual effects in the world thus far. Their history defines objects and selves; thus, rather than an inner, transcendent reality, essence is a public, social reality.

We believe Dewey gradually developed this non-metaphysical reading of Hegel during the 1890s.[56] Thus, when he claims "the social" is "The Inclusive Philosophic Idea," Dewey affirms his debt to Hegel.[57] We will follow the inclusive philosophical idea through Dewey's theory of labor, tools, and language.

For Hegel, work, acquiring an occupation, was critical to the ethical life of *Bildung*. Alexandre Kojève notes: "Work is *Bildung* in the double sense of the word: on the one hand, it forms [*Bild*], transforms the world, humanizes it by making it more adapted to Man; on the other, it transforms, forms, educates man, it humanizes him by bringing him into greater conformity with the idea that he has of himself."[58] Socially organized work provides individuals with creative self-expression, but in the objective neo-humanist sense rather than the subjective, idiosyncratic romantic sense. As Smith notes, "Labor is for Hegel an 'expressive' activity where we not only interact with a world of material objects (*Gegenstände*) in a causal way but in the course of that interaction develop our own distinctive capacities, skills, and dispositions. Labor is primarily a means of self-realization."[59] In creating objects that satisfy desire, we create and come to know ourselves self-consciously.

Dewey remarks that for many years, his philosophy was "most fully expounded" in *Democracy and Education* and speculates that his "philosophical critics" fail to examine it because they do not believe "any rational person could actually think it possible that philosophizing should focus about education as the supreme human interest in which . . . other problems, cosmological, moral, logical, come to a head."[60] This perspective comes readily to the philosopher of *Bildung*.

Dewey maintains that we use available cultural tools (including hammers, scientific laws, and such), in our *work* to make meaningful connections; in so doing, we create both the world and ourselves.[61] He declares: "Education *through* occupations consequently combines within itself more of the factors conducive to learning than any other method."[62] Dewey agrees with Hegel that it is important to have a socially fulfilling calling but that vocational training alone is too narrow. Learning by structured doing, by working, is crucial to the developmental formation of mind and self, to the education of fundamental intellectual and emotional dispositions, to *Bildung*.

When taken up into an occupational context controlled by universal norms of the practice, the ability to use tools and to communicate (for example, shop talk) sublates (*Aufhebung*) universal habits of action: "Meanings acquired in connection with the use of tools and of language exercise a profound influence upon organic feelings. In the reckoning of this account, are included the changes effected by all the consequences of attitude and habit due to *all* the consequences of tools and language."[63] For Dewey, "every meaning is generic or universal." Additionally, "the invention and use of tools have played a large part in consolidating meanings."[64]

For Hegel, self-development depends on fulfilling the universal norms of a determinate social function, thereby achieving social recognition: "[A] human being must be *somebody* [*etwas*] . . . he must belong to a particular estate [*Stand*, a place, a standing in society]; for being somebody means that he has substantial being. A human being with no estate [*Stand*] is merely a private person, and does not possess actual universality."[65] We seek confirmation of our self worth through the recognition of other self-conscious agents like ourselves. If we completely comply with every cultural norm to achieve recognition, however, we sacrifice unique self-expression.

For Dewey, too, work is creative self-development: "Occupation is a concrete term for continuity. It includes the development of artistic capacity of any kind, of special scientific ability, of effective citizenship, as well as professional and business occupations, to say nothing of mechanical labor or engagement in gainful pursuits."[66] Recall that for Dewey, "the self is created in the creation of objects."[67] This explains Dewey's claim that "spirit quickens; it is not only alive, but spirit gives life. Animals are spirited, but man is a living spirit. He lives in his works and his works do follow him."[68]

Tools are the permanency of labor and extensions of human functioning. With linguistic animals, tools become abstract-meaning functions. Language, in its instrumental use, is a special instance of means-ends relationship, a more pervasive and powerful tool. Dewey describes language as "the tool of tools . . . the cherishing mother of all significance."[69] Tools are means to desired ends, an extension of self-consciousness as desire in general, which is why Dewey states, "Yet till we understand operations of the self as the tool of tools, *the* means in all use of means . . . science is incomplete."[70]

Mind and self emerge through the give and take of community, communication, and mutual recognition in shared social practices. For Dewey, the "interaction of human beings, namely, association, is not different in origin from other modes of interaction." Language itself is "a natural function of human association," and "its consequences react upon other events, physical and human, giving them meaning or significance."[71] Linguistic functions involve diversity, interaction, and change while resembling biological functions in many ways. Most fundamentally, a linguistic function involves two or more emergent "body-minds" that must functionally coordinate their action with regard to a third emergent "stimulus-object." Meaning emerges (*Aufhebung*) when the potential of natural events is functionally coordinated in an appropriate way because "meaning is not . . . a psychic existence; it is primarily a property of behavior [action], and secondly a property of objects." But for meaning to emerge, the behavior must include cooperative "response to another's act."[72] Human beings have the ability to acquire language because they are able to take the attitude of another organism in a cooperative interaction: "The motion of A attracts his gaze to the thing pointed to; then, instead of just transferring his response from A's movement to the native reaction he might make to the thing as stimulus, he responds in a way which is a function of A's relationship, actual and potential, to the thing. The characteristic thing about B's understanding of A's movement and sounds is that he responds to the thing from the standpoint of A. . . . Something is literally made common in at least two different centres of behavior [action]."[73] Here A, B, and the object are emergent subfunctions of a single linguistic functional coordination.

For Dewey, the self projects an identity through speech that allows "a person [to] dramatically identify[y] himself with potential acts and deeds. . . . Thus mind emerges." Indeed, to have a mind is to have meaning because "mind denotes the whole system of meanings as they are embodied in the workings of organic life." Dewey concludes that mind "is an added property assumed by a feeling creature, when it reaches that organized interaction with other living creatures which is language, communication."[74]

Similarly, Hegel writes that "self-consciousness exists in and for itself when, and by the fact that, it so exists for another; that is, it exists only in being acknowledged."[75] The self grows through alienation from itself in other things and persons, followed by a return as the self incorporates otherness and difference into itself. Initially, objects, persons, social institutions, cultural customs, and such are external to our existence, but the person of *Bildung* makes them internal to their emergent functioning. For both philosophers, the linguistic reference that leads to the emergence (*Aufhebung*) of minds requires social recognition.

Hegel's reflections on language are remarkably similar to Dewey's: "Language is self-consciousness existing *for others*, self-consciousness which *as such* is immediately *present*, and as *this* self-consciousness is universal. . . . It perceived itself just as it is perceived by others, and the perceiving is just *existence which has become a self*."[76] For Hegel, without interactions with others, we have no potential for the development of personal identity. Dewey worked out this theory of mind and self with his friend and colleague George Herbert Mead in their years together at Michigan and Chicago. According to Mead, "We are in possession of selves just insofar as we can and do take the attitude of others toward ourselves and respond to those attitudes. We approve of ourselves and condemn ourselves." A fully developed self must assume "the generalized attitude of the group" and respond to "the generalized other" (an especially extensive, concrete universal) in order to achieve abstract thought and objectivity.[77] Dewey and Mead affirm the importance of recognition.

Without socialization, abstract, indeterminate individuals cannot actualize their potential to grasp linguistic universals (meanings) and develop mental functioning. The young must learn to coordinate their action with others by grasping universal norms, rules, and laws of action (stop at red lights, vote intelligently, the Golden Rule, and so on). Socialization is always somewhat restrictive; you cannot give reasons for something until you have acquired enough structured social meaning to engage in ordered discourse. Socialization can become tyrannical when twisted toward the interests of dogmatic groups. How to socialize the young is the crucial issue: "Any education given by a group tends to socialize its members, but the quality and value of the socialization depends upon the habits and aims of the group."[78] Dewey wished to instill universal habits of democratic citizenship aimed at social melioration.

Dewey insists on "social control," which he defines as "the formation of a certain mental disposition; a way of *understanding* objects, events, and acts which enables one to participate effectively in associated activities."[79] Human beings do not even have a mind or self until their actions come under the control of shared meanings, and they do not have ethical status until their actions come under the control of ethical universals. This does not mean these meanings and canons of ethical conduct are necessarily good.

Dewey goes so far as to insist on "social efficiency." Rather than bureaucratic rationality, however, "social efficiency is nothing less than the socialization of *mind* which is actively concerned in making experiences more communicable; in breaking down the barriers of social stratification which make individuals impervious to the interests of others." For him, democracy was far more than a form of government because it was chiefly about "conjoint communicated experience" wherein "each has to refer his own action to that of others."[80] Given Dewey's theory of the emergence of mind and self, communication becomes critical in personal identity formation, so pluralistic communication is critical to democratic *Bildung*.

Dewey advanced two criteria for democracy. The first calls for "not only more numerous and more varied points of shared common interest, but greater reliance upon the recognition of mutual interests as a factor in social control." The second "means not only freer interaction between social groups but change in social habit—its continuous readjustment through meeting the new situations produced by varied intercourse."[81] Dewey's version of social efficiency contributes to meeting both criteria. In "Creative Democracy—The Task Before Us," he declares: "To cooperate by giving differences a chance to show themselves because of the belief that the expression of difference is not only a right of the other persons but is a means [to the end] of enriching one's own life-experience, is inherent in the democratic personal way of life."[82] If we wish to grow, we must interact cooperatively with otherness and difference, not just tolerate them.

Hegel states that "in point of fact self-consciousness is the reflecting out of the being of the world of sense and perception, and is essentially the return from otherness."[83] For Dewey also, human beings learn and grow by incorporating otherness and differences. Initially, other persons, social institutions, cultural customs, and such are external to our existence but later may become internal to our emergent functioning. For instance, food, water, and mates are desirable instances of external otherness and difference necessary for our sustenance and growth. Philip Kain highlights this point in Hegel: "If we desire food, we want to consume it. . . . We transform otherness into oneness, difference into identity. Only in negating the object—its independent otherness or difference—do we affirm ourselves."[84] Consciousness eventually learns not to eradicate otherness because it requires it.

The ideal of pluralistic democracy is that everyone interacts to advance reciprocal self-development. Like Hegel, Dewey believes persons must have standing in a community of practice to fully actualize their unique potential: "An occupation is the only thing which balances the distinctive capacity of an individual with his social service. To find out what one is fitted to do and to secure an opportunity to do it is the key to happiness. Nothing is more tragic than failure to discover one's true business in life, or to find that one has drifted or been forced by circumstance into an uncongenial calling."[85] Moreover, Dewey preferred social self-development to atomistic self-creation: "The kind of self which is formed through action which is faithful to relations with others will be a fuller and broader self than one which is cultivated in isolation from or in opposition to the purposes and needs of others. In contrast, the kind of self which results from generous breadth of interest may be said alone to constitute a development and fulfillment of self, while the other way of life stunts and starves selfhood by cutting it off from the connections necessary to its growth."[86] Dewey's affirmation of democratic society builds on the pluralism of the German *Bildung* tradition. We get beyond positive and negative freedom when we embrace relationships of reciprocal connection, care, and conversation with others who are conducive to our growth.

Once we recognize that self-consciousness requires socialization, we accept its inevitability while acknowledging its dangers. The kind of *Bildung* envisioned by Herder, Hegel, and Dewey is destroyed when it becomes what Theodor W. Adorno called "*Halbbildung*" (Half-*Bildung*). Adorno worries about how education socializes citizens to become compliant to the needs of the self-regulating system of "late capitalism."[87] *Halbbildung* socializes while ignoring the development of unique human potential for immanent critique and self-expression.

By contrast, Dewey takes us beyond customary morality by advocating *Vollbildung*: "The intellectual distinction between customary and reflective morality is clearly marked. The former places the standard and rules of conduct in ancestral habit; the latter appeals to conscience, reason, or to some principle which includes thought. The distinction is as important as it is definite, for it shifts the centre of gravity in morality. Nevertheless the distinction is relative rather than absolute."[88] Kain notes that Hegel's concept of *Sittlichkeit* is "grounded in custom and tradition and developed through habit and imitation in accordance with the laws and practices of the community." In a sense, this richness of content makes *Sittlichkeit* superior to *Moralität*. However, "traditional *Sittlichkeit* is inferior to *Moralität*" because "reflection is minimal and individual freedom is undeveloped." Hegel "combines the rational and reflective side of *Moralität*" with traditional *Sittlichkeit* to attain a reflective theory of custom and tradition in the formation of habit.[89] Reflective morality enables immanent critique of cultural customs, beliefs, and values that form our self-constituting habits.

Dewey's reliance on intelligent critique offers a creative alternative to traditional liberal rationality and an alternative comprehension of freedom as creativity: "If [customary] habit fails, the sole alternative to caprice and random action is reflection. . . . Thinking has to operate creatively to form new ends."[90] He describes deliberation as "a dramatic rehearsal (in imagination) of various competing possible lines of action"; imagination creates its own alternative possibilities. For Dewey, "intelligence is the key to freedom in act."[91]

Dewey concedes that many individuals are unreflectively indoctrinated into the "system of belief, recognitions, and ignorances" prescribed by customary morality. They achieve recognition, self-consciousness, and mind, thereby actualizing their potential as a "rational being," but sacrifice their unique potential in the process. There are others, however, who, while also socialized into the universal norms of cultural practice, realize themselves in a diverse democratic community that preserves and cultivates their unique potential. *Vollbildung* helps solve the "problem involved of breaking loose from the weight of tradition and custom" by cultivating creative intelligence as the key to freedom and eventually exercising that intelligence to fully realize themselves through contribution to the larger community.[92] This is Hegel democratized for the twenty-first century.

Notes

1. James A. Good, *A Search for Unity in Diversity: The "Permanent Hegelian Deposit" in the Philosophy of John Dewey* (Lanham, Md.: Lexington Books, 2006); Jim

Garrison, "Dewey's Philosophy and the Experience of Working: Labor, Tools and Language," *Synthese* 105.5 (1995): 87–114.

2. Laurence Dickey, *Hegel: Religion, Economics, and the Politics of Spirit, 1770–1807* (Cambridge: Cambridge University Press, 1987), 69.

3. On the complexity of Herder's cultural nationalism, see Harold Mau, *Enlightenment Phantasies: Cultural Identity in France and Germany, 1750–1914* (Ithaca: Cornell University Press, 2003), 15–44.

4. John H. Zammito, *Kant, Herder, and the Birth of Anthropology* (Chicago: University of Chicago Press, 2002), 7–9. Cf. Michael N. Forster, *Hegel's Idea of a* Phenomenology of Spirit (Chicago: University of Chicago Press, 1998).

5. For a standard account of "Weimar Classicism," see T. K. Reed, *The Classical Center: Goethe and Weimar, 1775–1832* (London and New York: Croom Helm and Barnes & Noble, 1980).

6. W. H. Bruford, *The German Tradition of Self-Cultivation:* Bildung *from Humboldt to Thomas Mann* (London: Cambridge University Press, 1975), 55.

7. Elizabeth M. Wilkinson, "Goethe's Conception of Forms," in *Goethe: A Collection of Critical Essays,* ed. Victor Lange (Englewood Cliffs, N.J.: Prentice-Hall, 1968), 121.

8. Bruford, *German Tradition*, 104.

9. The emphasis on Hegel's position with the German neo-humanist tradition and the non-metaphysical reading of his philosophy developed simultaneously as the work of intellectual historians has converged with the work of scholars engaged in more traditional philosophical exposition. For a recent example of both, see Terry Pinkard, *Hegel: A Biography* (Cambridge: Cambridge University Press, 2000).

10. Josiah Royce is generally credited as the first English-speaking scholar to articulate this reading of the *Phenomenology* in his *Lectures on Modern Idealism* (1919). Cf. John H. Smith, *The Spirit and Its Letter: Traces of Rhetoric in Hegel's Philosophy of* Bildung (Ithaca: Cornell University Press, 1988), 174–238.

11. Georg W. F. Hegel, *Phenomenology of Spirit*, trans. A. V. Miller (Oxford: Oxford University Press, 1977), §167.

12. Robert Pippin, *Hegel's Idealism: The Satisfactions of Self-Consciousness* (Cambridge: Cambridge University Press, 1989), 148–49.

13. Hegel, *Phenomenology of Sprit*, §22.

14. Ibid., §188.

15. Ibid., §§191–96.

16. See, for example, Hegel's discussion of the conflict between the law of the gods and the public law in Sophocles' *Antigone. Phenomenology of Spirit,* §470.

17. Hegel, *Phenomenology of Spirit,* §352.

18. Ibid., §78.

19. William Maker, "Hegel and Rorty, or, How Hegel Saves Pragmatism from Itself," *Owl of Minerva* 37, no. 2 (Spring/Summer 2006): 105.

20. Hegel, *Phenomenology of Spirit*, §78.

21. Ibid., §84.

22. Ibid., §37.

23. Ibid., §802. The original title of the *Phenomenology* was "Science of the *Experience* of Consciousness" (emphasis in original).

24. See Hegel, *Phenomenology of Spirit*, "Absolute Freedom and Terror," §§582–95; and relevant sections of his *Elements of the Philosophy of Right* (trans. H. B. Nisbet, ed. Allen W. Wood [Cambridge: Cambridge University Press, 1991]), such as "Abstract Right," §§34–40.

25. Pinkard, *Hegel*, 269.

26. James Schmidt, "The Fool's Truth: Diterot, Goethe, and Hegel," *Journal of the History of Ideas* 57, no. 4 (1996): 630.

27. Hegel, *Phenomenology of Spirit*, §80.

28. Steven B. Smith, *Hegel's Critique of Liberalism: Rights in Context* (Chicago: University of Chicago Press, 1989), 10, 167–68.

29. Cf. Lewis Hinchman, *Hegel's Critique of the Enlightenment* (Gainesville and Tampa: University Presses of Florida, 1984); William Maker, "The Science of Freedom: Hegel's Critical Theory," *Bulletin of the Hegel Society of Great Britain* 41–42 (2000): 1–17; and Georg W. F. Hegel, *Hegel's Science of Logic*, trans. A. V. Miller (Atlantic Highlands, N.J.: 1969), 580–81.

30. Hegel, *Elements of the Philosophy of Right*, §153. Cf. Hegel, *Natural Law: The Scientific Ways of Treating Natural Law, Its Place in Moral Philosophy, and Its Relation to the Positive Sciences of Law*, trans. T. M. Knox (Philadelphia: University of Pennsylvania Press, 1975), 115.

31. Hegel, *Philosophy of Right*, §185, 187.

32. Ibid., §§57, 45–49, 66, 137.

33. John Dewey, *The Later Works of John Dewey, 1925–1953*, 17 vols. (hereafter *LW*), ed. Jo Ann Boydston (Carbondale: Southern Illinois University Press, 1981–90), 5:154.

34. John Dewey, *The Middle Works of John Dewey, 1899–1924*, 15 vols. (hereafter *MW*), ed. Jo Ann Boydston (Carbondale: Southern Illinois University Press, 1976–83), 9:338; cf. *MW* 9:342. For an interpretation of Dewey's criticisms of Hegel in *Democracy and Education* and *German Philosophy and Politics*, see Good, *Search for Unity*, 239–45.

35. *MW* 14:43.

36. Ibid., 14:15 (cf. *LW* 13:108); *MW* 13:389.

37. Georg W. F. Hegel, *Philosophy of Mind*, trans. William Wallace and A. V. Miller (Oxford: Clarendon Press, 1971), §410.

38. *MW* 14:20, 137.

39. *LW* 5:153.

40. Ibid.

41. John Dewey, "Hegel's Philosophy of Spirit: Lectures by John Dewey," University of Chicago, 1897. Unpublished manuscript, John Dewey Papers, Collection 102, Special Collections, Morris Library, Southern Illinois University, Carbondale, p. 17.

42. *LW* 12:34, 35.

43. Ibid., 10:158, 167, 159, 161, 166.

44. Ibid., 12:372.

45. Ibid., 10:286–87.

46. The next few paragraphs are indebted to Craig Cunningham (1994).

47. *LW* 10:65–66

48. Ibid., 14:109.

49. Quoted in Jane Dewey, "Biography of John Dewey," in *The Philosophy of John Dewey*, ed. Paul Arthur Schilpp and Lewis Hahn (La Salle, Ill.: Open Court, 1939), 17.

50. Ibid., 17–18.

51. Hegel, *Phenomenology Of Sprit*, §439.

52. Philip Kain, *Hegel and the Other* (Albany, N.Y.: State University of New York Press, 2005), 137.

53. Georg W. F. Hegel, *The Logic of Hegel*, trans. W. Wallace (Oxford: Clarendon Press, 1975), §42.

54. Kenneth R. Westphal, *Hegel's Epistemological Realism: A Study of the Aim and Method of Hegel's* Phenomenology of Spirit (Dordrecht: Kluwer Academic Publishers, 1989), 140.

55. Georg W. F. Hegel, *Hegel's Aesthetics: Lectures on Fine Art*, trans. T. M. Knox (Oxford: Oxford University Press, 1975), 2:961–62.

56. Good, *Search for Unity*, chapters 4 and 5.

57. *LW* 3:41–54.

58. Alexandre Kojève, *Introduction to the Reading of Hegel* (Ithaca: Cornell University Press 1969), 52.

59. S. Smith, *Hegel's Critique of Liberalism*, 120.

60. *LW* 5:156.

61. *MW* 9:316. Cf. MW 2:43–43.

62. Ibid., 9:319.

63. *LW* 1:227–28.

64. Ibid., 1:147, 146.

65. Hegel, *Philosophy of Right*, §207.

66. *MW* 9:317.

67. *LW* 10:286.

68. Ibid., 1:224.

69. Ibid., 1:146.

70. Ibid., 1:189.

71. Ibid., 1:138, 137.

72. Ibid., 1:141.

73. Ibid., 1:140–41.

74. Ibid., 1:135, 230, 198.

75. Hegel, *Phenomenology of Spirit*, §178.

76. Ibid., §652.

77. George Herbert Mead, "The Genesis of the Self and Social Control," in *Selected Writings: George Herbert Mead*, ed. A. J. Reck (Chicago: University of Chicago Press, 1964), 288.

78. *MW* 9:88.

79. Ibid., 9:41.

80. Ibid., 9:127, 92.

81. Ibid., 9:92.

82. *LW* 14:228.

83. Hegel, *Phenomenology of Spirit*, §167.

84. Kain, *Hegel and the Other*, 45.

85. *MW* 9:318.

86. *LW* 7:302.

87. Theodor W. Adorno, "Theorie der Halbbildung," in *Gesammelte Schriften*, ed. Rolf Tiedemann (Frankfurt: M. Suhrkamp, 1972), 8:93–121.

88. *LW* 7:162.

89. Kain, *Hegel and the Other*, 89, 90.

90. *LW* 7:185.

91. *MW* 14:132, 210.

92. *LW* 1:169, 170.

4] Pragmatism and Gay Science: Comparing Dewey and Nietzsche

Barry Allen

It is seldom appreciated that all the first critics of the "Correspondence Theory of Truth," especially Friedrich Nietzsche, William James, and John Dewey, were Darwinists. In epistemology, postmodernism begins as post-Darwinism, which explains similarities in the arguments of these otherwise different thinkers. Darwin did not elaborate on the epistemological implications of evolution and may not have thought them through. He was reluctant to appear radical in philosophy even when he was.[1] His theory had enough trouble without a reputation for innovation in the philosophy of science. He left epistemology to the experts, and Nietzsche, shortly followed by James and Dewey, was the first to take him up. All the thinkers one might today call "postmodern" concur on one point, albeit a negative one: the metaphysical idea of truth as a correspondence or mimesis is hopeless. Like the idea of God, it can no longer be taken seriously. This thought belongs to Nietzsche's legacy. The simplest, least controversial, most helpful sense of the elusive term "postmodern" is to describe philosophers who take Nietzsche seriously.

The beginning of the postmodern critique of "correspondence" is Nietzsche's essay of 1873, "On Truth and Lying in a Nonmoral Sense," unpublished in his lifetime.[2] He developed his arguments in *The Gay Science* (1882), *Beyond Good and Evil* (1886), and the magnificent closing sections of *On the Genealogy of Morals* (1888). By 1906, James was on the same path, thinking about the pragmatic meaning of "truth." There seems to be no influence. James heard of Nietzsche and apparently read something, but not much, and probably never studied Nietzsche's arguments concerning truth. Dewey may have read more but still didn't perceive the similarity between Nietzsche's rather outlandish writings and what the pragmatists were saying about "truth."

Plato first formulated Western philosophy's idea of truth, working with hints from Parmenides. Aristotle reduced it to a formula: "to say of what is that it is, is true"; and the idea passed without criticism into even the most "critical" modern philosophy.[3] More striking even than the metaphysical extravagance of the idea is how the philosophers, never reluctant to quarrel, found so little to quarrel with, so little to doubt about it. The most interesting and important of the new questions Nietzsche raised about truth concern not its epistemological unavailability or metaphysical impossibility. They concern its value, truth's claim to a place among the highest values, especially if you are a philosopher. Mulling over this history, he says, "it . . . looks to us as if the problem has never been raised until now." He had a keen sense of being on his own in this question: "Let us thus define our own task—the value of truth must for once be experimentally called into question." He was also convinced that the questions were not going away.[4] Hence the dramatic closing words of *On the Genealogy of Morals*: "All great things bring about their own destruction through an act of self-overcoming. . . . In this way Christianity *as a dogma* was destroyed by its morality; in the same way Christianity *as morality* must perish too: we stand on the threshold of *this* event. After Christian truthfulness has drawn one inference after another, it must end by drawing its *most striking inference*, its inference *against* itself; this will happen . . . when it poses the question '*what is the meaning of all will to truth?*' And here again I touch on my problem, on *our* problem, my *unknown* friends (for as yet I *know* of no friend): What meaning would our whole being possess if it were not this, that in us the will to truth becomes conscious of itself *as a problem*?"[5]

Nietzsche has lots of friends now. They are the postmoderns. Is Dewey a friend? Is pragmatism a gay science?

Unknown Friends

Nietzsche raised doubts of two sorts against classical truth, metaphysical and moral. Metaphysically, the envisioned correspondence is impossible and absurd. No medium is innocent; perception and cognition are adaptations, not transcendental faculties. According to the classical theory, truth is an adequation or congruence, some very precise objective sameness between *what is* (fact or being) and *what is said*. But no two things are the same unless we more or less willfully overlook their differences. In speaking, or even thinking of speaking, we form a designation—a word or concept; but even the most painstaking analysis cannot untangle the "object" of perception from the instrumentality of our body or the contingency of our evolution. Contemplative metaphysical disinterestedness is not an option for us. We have no godly part and differ from the beasts only by degree, as Darwin inferred. The test cognition is "designed" (by mindless natural selection) to pass is survival, not the transcendence of disinterested objectivity. People lack sharp teeth and claws. We are really not formidable at all compared to bears or tigers. In compensation, we have knowledge. We are clever beasts, we invented cognition—Nietzsche's way to say what Darwin said: cognition is a contingent adaptation, not a transcendental faculty; intellect is not divine, nor human beings unique in nature. Our intelligence and everything that comes with it is an outcome of evolution, arising by accidental causes and surviving by a contribution to adaptation or "fitness." Nietzsche drew the conclusion (which looks even better today) that nothing we think, see, or say, no matter how fanatical the methodology, is simply *true* in the way that classical truth expected.

The value of cognition, including perception, reference, and memory, is as an adaptive response to stimuli. We see and hear (and think) in terms of our body. There is nothing contemplative about it. To perceive and interpret, to think, speak, "know," is to impose simplification, assimilate old to new, chase novelty, disregard the inconsistent, and arbitrarily select what of the "external world" to stress or overlook.[6] Everything we say falsifies something, sacrificed to overriding interests or limited perspective. Some of these "errors" prove useful, promoting survival. They become humanity's erroneous articles of faith and include the belief in things, in identity, in bodies, in free will, and in an appearance different from reality—most of what Immanuel Kant supposedly "deduced" as inevitable, timeless transcendental categories of understanding.

What, then, is truth "from a nonmoral standpoint"? A metaphor, a blatant falsehood (A is B) that proves useful in thinking through conduct so that people forget its outrageous falsity (how could A be B? If it were B, it would not be A) and treat it instead as an evident truth. What we call "the truth" is the current sum of such metaphors. A truthful person is one who uses the usual metaphors in the usual way. Truthfulness is a matter of abiding by conventions of usage, not transcendental logic. To be careful with the truth is to use words as others do. To tell the truth is to lie with the herd, a lie in a nonmoral sense, meaning a useful fiction, an artifact of the intellect, something fabricated and unconsciously imposed.

Nietzsche's genealogy of truthfulness discovers a conformity not of thought and reality but of speech and convention. We love the truth because we hate the usual effects of being lied to, despite our also having a formidable talent and kind of instinct for deception. That is the dilemma of the clever beasts who invented cognition. The most potent weapon of individual survival is cunning, yet cunning undermines the trust required of a social existence to which we as a species are committed. The solitary life of a panther or bear is not an option for us. It is only in a social context, decked out with tools, language, and other people willing to cooperate, that the full adaptive value of cunning emerges—and right beside it the most potent threat to social life. In this early unpublished work, Nietzsche apparently thinks the brute force of the herd disposes of the dilemma by extracting, in return for herd protection, a promise to keep promises, which includes abiding by the conventions of language, and that is our "truthfulness."

With Nietzsche, the theory of knowledge enters the post-Darwin age. Evolutionary thinking provides a way out of the fruitless argument between the a priori and the a posteriori. What looks like an a priori condition on possible knowledge is an a posteriori effect of material process on a geological timescale. Yes, we project causation onto events that are not intrinsically, necessarily related. No, that's not a transcendentally necessary, a priori form of possible perception, as Kant said. It's a contingent effect of accidental evolution on an improbable planet orbiting an inconspicuous star. We have to accept irrational limitations on knowledge and turn them to advantage. We cannot have certainty. Very well, let us make successful action despite uncertainty a virtue and goal of a "knowledge" that does not presume certainty. We cannot set aside perspective and look around our own corner. Very well, let us value knowledge for what it does, its service to life, and forget about disinterested contemplation.

It is easy to imagine James agreeing with all of this. He makes many of the same points in his *Pragmatism* lectures and the notorious chapter "Pragmatism's Idea of Truth." It is also easy to imagine Dewey agreeing, and for the same reason, namely, Darwin and evolution against "truth" and "essence." Dewey tosses out the whole idea of a "knower" and an "object," the classical model for correspondence. Knowledge is a state of the organism, the condition of a situation, distinct from the opposite condition (not knowing) in its felicity and greater purposiveness. A "knower" is one who is stimulated to act by the anticipation of future consequences. Knowing is action that successfully increases one's power to direct consequences. As for the value of that, it is the good of effectiveness, efficiency, practicality, a good instrument or tool. Dewey says knowledge "is a mode of experiencing things which facilitates control of objects for purposes of non-cognitive experiences."[7] As for telling the truth, it has, he says, "always been a matter of adaptation to a social audience." "To think of things rightly or wrongly is to think of them according to or contrary to social demands." "Either there is *no* rule about observation and judging, and correctness and incorrectness have no application, or else *Nomos* and *Ethos are* the rule."[8] The only difference from Nietzsche is that

Dewey thought in terms of a community with which he identified, while for Nietzsche the "social audience" was a contemptible herd.

In part 2 of "On Truth and Lying in a Nonmoral Sense," Nietzsche describes two types of human beings. One is rational but inartistic, the other artistic but irrational—the philosopher and the poet, Socrates and Homer, reprising the opposition between artistic and theoretical in *The Birth of Tragedy*.[9] Artists love appearances, veils, coincidences, stories, and details and don't worry about a truth behind appearances. Theorists love unveiling, unmasking, ferreting out assumptions, discovering hidden truth. One appeals to rationality and prudence, the other to pleasure and beauty. The poet's use of language flagrantly violates convention. People ought to be outraged; Plato apparently was. No one told more lies than Homer, yet none are deceived and we love his impossible stories. He makes us love life, even though what he tells us about it is untrue. Theory can't give such pleasure. But the pleasure of art doesn't last, and pleasant as it is, it's no remedy against the ills of life. Reason may be prosaic, but it promises to master misfortune.

Nietzsche saw European society as having chosen the path of rationalism and theoretical knowledge over art. It was a choice with terrible if unforeseen consequences, nothing short of nihilism. This civilization has perfected science. The world has never been better understood or more predictable. Knowledge has made people more powerful, a greater danger to other species, to the earth, and to themselves. But it has not made them happier, wiser, or better, contradicting the great promise of "philosophy" in the Western tradition. Socrates taught that vice and evil are no more than ignorance. The perfection of knowledge must therefore be the perfection of humanity and even the world, overcoming evil at its source. That is what philosophy promised to do. Its concepts of knowledge, truth, being, reason, and so on were designed to make this vision plausible. And though it may have seemed like a good idea at the time, historical experience has obviously failed to confirm the speculative hypothesis that the perfection of knowledge is equally the perfection of morality and humanity. Knowledge cannot be the panacea Socrates thought. It can be taken too far, and then it becomes demoralizing and may even undermine the seriousness knowledge and truth require. We need an antidote to this pessimism of knowledge, this nihilism of science and research, and Nietzsche thought it might be art. "Art alone can re-direct those repulsive thoughts about the terrible or absurd nature of existence into representations with which man can live."[10]

I think Dewey might reply that science fuels demoralization and nihilism only because it is limited, immature, incomplete science. Science creates social problems because society is not yet completely scientific. A society more enthusiastically pursuing its scientific reconstruction would not be unnerved by doubts about a few old moral truisms. This view is clearly suggested in *Reconstruction in Philosophy* (1920):

> While the evils resulting at present from the entrance of "science" into our common ways of living are undeniable they are due to the fact that no systematic efforts have as yet been made to subject the "morals" underlying old institutional customs to scientific inquiry and criticism.
>
> The science that has so far found its way deeply and widely into the actual affairs of human life is partial and incomplete science: competent in respect to physical . . . conditions, but nonexistent with respect to matters of supreme significance to man.
>
> What is called "modern" is as yet unformed, inchoate. Its confused strife and unstable uncertainties reflect the mixture of old and new that are incompatible. The genuinely modern has still to be brought into existence.[11]

The first passage proves how little Dewey knew of Nietzsche's work or its ambition. A systematic effort to subject the morals underlying old institutions to scientific inquiry and criticism is exactly Nietzsche's project for a "genealogy of morals." Dewey would be unlikely to disagree when Nietzsche says that the traditional morality of European civilization is on par with astrology and alchemy or that it should be "mercilessly taken to court and made to account for [itself]."[12] To Nietzsche, the objectionable thing about this morality is its claim to universality. What is immoral is bad and wrong for anyone, for everyone, always and everywhere. There is one Moral Law and all must obey, regardless of differences among us. That is "the law of every morality. There [is] only one norm: '*the* human being.'"[13] Nietzsche scorned this idea. It was thinking of it that he called himself an "immoralist."[14] He thought some deeds could be gross immorality when committed by one person and the bounden duty of another. What a person must do or must not do flows from what or who that person is, from self-mastery and nobility of spirit. There is a rank order of humanity, and some must do (or be allowed to do) what is forbidden to others.

I think Dewey would gladly dispense with "*the* good," that is, a unique highest value, but not follow Nietzsche in his anti-egalitarian conclusion. The idea of one law for all is an obstacle to experimentation in the reconstruction of social life and its "morality." Dewey says, "The abolition of *the* final goal and *the* single motive power and *the* separate and infallible faculty in morals, will quicken inquiry into the diversity of specific goods of experience."[15] We have to experiment on morality as much as nature. Indeed, that's how Dewey reads Nietzsche, whom he describes as "brandish[ing] in rude ecstasy the banner of brute survival as a happy omen of the final victory of nobility of mind."[16] Rather than dismiss this as unphilosophical, he insightfully aligns Nietzsche with a wider European movement of thought (to which he subscribes pragmatism), transforming ideas of moral theory away from the logic of a highest end and *summum bonum*.

It seems obvious that Dewey "believed" in things Nietzsche did not. Nietzsche may have thought that he didn't "believe" in anything—he called himself a nihilist—but we'll see it's not quite true. For instance, he appears to believe in an a spontaneous order of rank. Yet he certainly didn't "believe" in the things Dewey believed in most: democracy, science, and America. Each of these is worth a closer look.

Science

Dewey talks a lot about it. He "believed" in science in a way few philosophers do any more, partly because of Nietzsche, partly because of the post-positivist philosophy of science associated with T. S. Kuhn, Paul Feyerabend, and others. Dewey's faith in science may give some "the feeling of listening to a Strauss waltz, a melody from the time when the world was young."[17] Yet he never conceived of science as the positivists Ernst Mach, Moritz Schlick, or Rudolf Carnap did. So when their ideas withered under the post-positivist critique, Dewey was unscathed. Pragmatism always was an alternative to logical positivism, even before disappointed positivists started calling for one.[18]

"Science" for Dewey is not a hyper-formal discipline culminating in the apprehension of Truth. It is the formal fruition of a long-cultivated, highly adaptive human norm whose effects are visible in the continuous accumulation of *techne* since the Stone Age. Science is an activity, a practice, a kind of work, a business, the business of inquiry, which is not the disinterested pursuit of pure theoretical truth but really no less than the experimental life of practical reason. He describes "scientific method" as the "systematic, extensive, and carefully controlled use of alert and unprejudiced observation and experimentation in collecting, arranging and testing facts to serve as evidence."[19] Appeal to "unprejudiced" observation may suggest a questionable expectation of objectivity, but Dewey would probably find nothing wrong with Hans-Georg Gadamer's defense of "prejudice" as a medium of observation and a condition of understanding.

Yes, Dewey might say, fact is fabricated. Facts are not "out there" like fruit to pick from a tree. Knowledge is instrumental interaction, not contemplative mimesis. An "unprejudiced" observation is not the metaphysical adequation of thought and idea. Prejudice is a kind of injustice, an unfairness in judgment, unfairness to others who rely on one's judgment. An unprejudiced observation is one that really essays observation and does not manipulate others. What standards, what criteria, what agreement there is concerning justice are all matters of particular communities and histories, which is where hermeneutical prejudice returns, appropriately, to the pragmatics of science.

What the sciences accomplish is not the epistemic miracle some philosophers have expected—not an intuition of being, a corresponding truth, or an adequate idea. Science means experiments, inquiry; knowledge means instruments, technologies of power. Dewey was, after all, a pragmatist. Science, he says, does not reach the really real; it reaches "objects which are better, because reached by method which controls them and which adds greater control to life itself."[20] "The office of physical science is to discover those properties and relations of things in virtue of which they are capable of being used as instrumentalities; physical science makes claim to disclose not the inner nature of things but only those connections of things that determine outcomes and hence can be used as means."[21] This idea is as old as Bacon (knowledge is power) and as new, as postmodern, as Nietzsche (the *will to* knowledge is a will to *power*).

The difference between gay and normal science is a lifestyle choice. Normal work in the sciences is routine, a job. Normal research is institutionalized, and the institution has a herd instinct for mediocrity. Gay science begins as an existential choice to reinvest research with the romance it was stripped of by thinkers like Francis Bacon and Robert Boyle, who desacralized and democratized experiments as the price of acceptability in a world wary of heresy or magic.[22] A beautiful passage from *The Gay Science* concerns this romantic reinvestment in research. Entitled "In media vita," in mid-life, Nietzsche was about thirty-eight when he wrote it: "No, life has not disappointed me. On the contrary, I find it truer, more desirable and mysterious every year—ever since the day when the great liberator came to me: the idea that life could be an experiment of the seeker for knowledge—and not a duty, not a calamity, not trickery.—And knowledge itself: let it be something else for others; for example, a bed to rest on, or the way to such a bed, or a diversion, or a form of leisure—for me it is a world of dangers and victories in which heroic feelings, too, find places to dance and play. '*Life as a means to knowledge*'—with this principle in one's heart one can live not only boldly but even gaily, and laugh gaily, too."[23] In a passage that recalls Bacon's emblem of ships bound for the New World, Nietzsche writes of the "daring of the lover of knowledge": "We philosophers and 'free spirits' feel, when we hear the news that 'the old god is dead,' as if a new dawn shone on us; our heart overflows with gratitude, amazement, premonitions, expectations. At long last the horizon appears free to us again, even if it should not be bright; at long last our ships may venture out again, venture out to face any danger; all the daring of the lover of knowledge is permitted again; the sea, our sea, lies open again; perhaps there has never been such an 'open sea.'"[24]

Knowledge, science, takes daring, meaning daring to experiment. There cannot be enough experiments, nor can experimentation go too far. Dewey's canons of "unprejudiced observation" and "experimentation in collecting, arranging and testing facts" are unspoken matters of conscience among such experimentalists, simple good taste, second nature. Gay science is *pragmatic* science with an existential twist, partially echoed in Dewey's concurrence that experiments take courage. He describes "the experimental method" as "the foe of every belief that permits habit and wont to dominate invention and discovery." You cannot be afraid of change, afraid to destroy a favorite theory, even a sacred temple. "The mind that is hampered by fear lest something old and precious be destroyed is the mind that experiences fear of science." "Surrender of what is possessed, disowning of what supports one in secure ease, is involved in all inquiry and discovery."[25]

Possibly Dewey's most antithetical argument, comparing him with Nietzsche, is that scientific inquiry can fill the vacuum of authority scientific knowledge creates. "Take science . . . for what it is, and we shall begin to envisage it as a potential creator of new values and ends. We shall have an intimation, on a wide and generous scale, of the release, the increased initiate, independence and inventiveness, which science now brings in its own specialized fields."[26] That's what Nietzsche was looking for, a form of the scientific, experimental life of knowledge that somehow generates new values, rather than merely subverting old ones, as science historically has in the West. It was not science inadequate, incomplete, or incompetent that killed the Christian God, Nietzsche might argue. It was science triumphant. The more we know, the more science, the less value in the world, until we are outright nihilists.

Gay science is an existential choice, a brotherhood rather than an institution. It refers to how one lives institutional identities. Nietzsche seemed to give up on institutional science, imbued with a love of Truth he traced back to Plato and Christianity, making "Science" a kind of Christianity by other means. He may have thought that most "men of science" in his day held a

Platonic-Christian self-conception as lovers of disinterested truth and were going to be fiercely disappointed to see it discredited. In Europe, perhaps, but not in America, about which Nietzsche knew nothing. What made American pragmatism at once disreputable and seductive was how it took truth off the mantel, urging that the value of knowledge and science is not the purity of its Truth but its powerful instruments of action. To these pragmatists, obviously including Dewey, the subversion of Platonic and Christian assumptions about "the Truth" was not a crisis but a joyful relief, motivating a critique of metaphysics and epistemology paralleling Nietzsche's, though independently inspired.

Democracy

For Dewey, "the future of democracy is allied with the spread of the scientific attitude."[27] His argument is not the hopeless one of Herbert Spencer, that democracy is scientifically "proven" to be the proper political organization. Dewey's point is that democracy (on what he will call the "American" theory of it) is *analogous* to science, *analogous* to the economy of authority in a scientific community, and can be expected to participate in the rationality of scientific inquiry.[28] One sees the experimental rationality of democracy in its norms of free debate, fallibility, the preference for evidence over other authority, and a willingness to test ideas by their fruits, experimentally, not dogmatically ruling things out in advance.

Dewey was annoyed by critics who equated democracy with "mass rule" or "majority rule." It was also incorrectly equated with universal suffrage and the election of officials. He says the deep philosophical meaning of democracy is "faith in individuality, in uniquely distinctive qualities in each normal human being; faith in corresponding unique modes of activity that create new ends, and willing acceptance of modifications of the established order entailed by the release of individualized capacities."[29] Toward elections, voting, and so on, however, one should take an experimental attitude; they are worth talking about only as means to the end of individuality (itself a great experiment), and Dewey says they do "not work very satisfactorily."[30]

We need but treat the plainest man *as* an individual to find that *he becomes* one. Presumably Nietzsche would mock this idea, mock its sentiment, denounce it, reverse it, or perhaps merely ignore it. He certainly would not "believe" it—not because he believed in nothing but because he had an opposite belief of his own, belief in an "order of rank." The "Free Spirit," Nietzsche's philosophical alter ego, rejected the requirement of one Moral Law for all. Some people are spontaneously, physically, instinctively naturally higher, better specimens than others. There is noble and base among human beings, an inbred order of rank. Civilization, Nietzsche sort of argued, should recognize the natural superiority of the few and the natural inferiority of the many and rule itself accordingly.

He appreciated how repellent that is to ears like ours. His "belief" in it put him "at the other end of all modern ideology and herd desires."[31] So why insist on it? What is wrong with democracy? I think the best texts on this question are in *Beyond Good and Evil*, where I find three lines of argument.

1. Every enhancement of humanity has been the work of an aristocracy, and this pattern must continue into the future if humanity is to develop and not stagnate or reverse. Only an aristocratic society believes in and institutes rank order and value distinctions among people, which Nietzsche claims is required for "the development of states that are increasingly high, rare, distant, tautly drawn and comprehensive"—the source of all cultural advance.[32] Or so he says, though he does not give examples of cultural advance, nor does he explain how an aristocratic pathos of distance lies behind them. (Was Benjamin Franklin's lightning rod a cultural advance? Was it created from a pathos of social distance?)

2. Respect and equality cannot be the fundamental principles of society, because they are contrary to the principle of life, which is the principle of the will to power. "Life itself is *essentially* a process of appropriating, injuring, overpowering the alien and the weaker, oppressing, being harsh, imposing your own form, incorporating, and at the very least exploiting." For humanity to flourish, society must fall in with the ways of the will to power—"*must,*" he explains, "not out of any morality or immorality, but because it is *alive*, and because life *is* precisely will to power." "'Exploitation' does not belong to a corrupted or imperfect primitive society: it belongs to the *essence* of being alive . . . it is a result of genuine will to power, which is just the will of life."[33] From a pragmatic point of view, however, this is not a convincing argument. Does life really have an essence—a good, old-fashioned *essence*? Surely not. Essences are relative constructions; what we call "essential" reflects our interests, not the intrinsic constitution of a thing in itself. Elsewhere, Nietzsche says as much himself. So what is *his* interest in so emphatically privileging the "will to power" as the "essence" of life? Despite provoking a great deal of commentary, some of it disappointingly dogmatic, "will to power" remains among Nietzsche's most poorly worked out ideas, and its invocation against the ethics of democracy is more conviction than convincing.[34]

3. "We . . . consider the democratic movement to be not merely an abased form of political organization, but rather an abased (more specifically a dimin-

ished) form of humanity, a mediocritization and depreciation of humanity in value."[35] He apparently thinks that a herd of cattle provides a better image of human social life than a troop of chimpanzees. It's unlikely, but that's what he says. We are like herd animals, anxious on our own, always watching others carefully, desiring what they desire, doing what they do. What we call "morality" is a ranking of drives and actions based on the survival of a herd. To be moral is to act with the herd. Conscience is the voice of the herd, and so is "truth." The first principle of herd morality is: don't be dangerous. That means don't be independent; don't be obviously intelligent; don't stand out. Herd values "praise what is familiar and harmless, loathe what is different and unexpected." The motive is security. "'We want the day to come when there is *nothing more to fear*!' The day to come—the will and way *to that day* is now called 'progress' everywhere in Europe."[36]

Modern political institutions like democracy, liberalism, equality, and human rights come down to the same thing: "*herd-animalization*," unloosing our most herd-like instincts against everything individual.[37] These "progressive" social movements "are one and all united in thorough and instinctive hostility toward all forms of society besides that of the *autonomous* herd . . . united in their dogged opposition to any special claims, special rights, or privileges." In the name of this "ideal," modern reformers wage "war on everything rare, strange, privileged, on the higher man, higher soul, higher duty, higher responsibility, on creative power and mastery."[38] Anything hostile, evil, or untrustworthy is repressed and bred out. Remember what Zarathustra said about chaos? "You must have chaos in you to give birth to a dancing star."[39] The more democracy and equality, the weaker all institutions must become, bringing the decay of discipline, the mediocritization of the arts and sciences, the elimination of the marginal, the dominance of routine and normality—the banal utopia of the "last men."

The differences among people somehow argue their different freedoms and duties. But it's not just difference. Some are suited for higher responsibility and greater power than others. Obstacles to the rule of rank, including especially the noisy politics of democracy and blather about equality, should not prevent the superior few from rendering their higher service to humanity. They are nature's nobles, profound individuals, compelled to make something of themselves (and us) or die trying. Nietzsche seems to think they are literally driven to their creativity, precisely because they are exceptional, therefore shunned. "The individual is left standing there, forced to give himself laws, forced to rely on his own arts and wiles of self- preservation, self-enhancement, self-redemption."[40] Nature's nobles require the shelter of aristocratic birth to survive. That's why a form of aristocracy must emerge if humanity is not to decline. The trouble is that the weak are more adaptable than the strong. There is therefore a tendency to breed the strong out of existence, unless the order of rank is enforced. So the herd should be disciplined by an extra-moral, übermoral, *immoral* order of rank. The exceptional and superior are not bound by the morality of the herd. They are beyond good and evil. Their only duty is to themselves. They must do what they have to do to become who they are. *Not* to make them exceptions to morality would be immoral.

We can imagine Dewey's response especially to this last argument by looking at what he says about Plato, who held the same view. He says Plato's *Republic* offers "the most perfect picture of the aristocratic ideal." The multitude is incapable of governing itself, of formulating an ideal and reaching it. "The few best, the aristoi; these know and are fitted for rule. . . . [A]ll will go wrong, until the few who know and are strong, are put in power, while others, foregoing the assertion of their individuality, submit to superior wisdom and goodness."[41] That's Nietzsche, too, in a nutshell. Dewey doesn't favor the idea. Why not?

Because he is a pragmatist, and the idea doesn't work. Aristocracy has been tried. We don't need more experiments to draw a conclusion. The approach fails. It fails, Dewey says, "because it is found that the practical consequence of giving the few wise and good power is that they cease to be wise and good."[42] Nothing in Plato and nothing in Nietzsche is a credible challenge to this plain lesson of historical experience. In the words of a critic friendly to Nietzsche, "the violent men who are assigned their specific historical task" so differ from the wise "that it remains incomprehensible how the two types, who raise themselves to the superhuman level and are expected to coalesce in such extreme elevation, can be thought of as compatible."[43] Nietzsche may have "believed" that an Übermensch would find a brilliant solution, but that's his *Glaube*, faith, belief, and a skeptic is free to ignore it.

Dewey calls aristocracy "blasphemy against personality." That is presumably why it didn't work when tried. Democracy is better suited to the willful individuality of the human primate, who is much more clever and dangerous than Nietzsche's image of the herd suggests. The point of democracy is not just to reach a certain desirable social condition. How the end is achieved, the process, matters. Key is that it not "be put into man from without." People have to work it out for themselves, not just be spectators to the glory. According to Dewey, the aristocratic idea "implies that the mass of men are to be inserted by wisdom or, if necessary, thrust by force, into their proper positions in the social organism." By contrast, "personal responsibility" and "individual initiation" are "the notes of democracy," which, he says, "is a form of government only because it is a form of moral and spiritual association." What form? He refers to "the theory . . . that every citizen is a sovereign, the American theory." With aristocracy, the end, the ideal, is to be gained "by means of special institutions or organizations within society," while democracy "holds that the ideal is already at work in every personality, and must be trusted to care for itself." "There is," he says, "an individualism in democracy which there is not in aristocracy; but it is an ethical, not a numerical, individualism; it is an individualism of freedom, of responsibility, of initiative." Dewey describes the democrat's conviction that "personality is the one thing of permanent and abiding worth, and that in every human individual there lies personality" as "the highest ethical idea which humanity has yet reached."[44]

To this bald statement of principle he adds some philosophical qualifications. First, he admits "that the full significance of personality can be learned by the individual only as it is already presented to him in objective form in society." There are no "personalities" in a state of nature, awaiting the first encounter with another. He also admits "that the chief stimuli and encouragements to the realization of personality come from society." Nevertheless, "personality cannot be procured for any one, however degraded and feeble, by any one else, however wise and strong." What makes "personality" special? How is it different from *nous* or *Wille zur Macht*? Dewey explains that personality is valued for potentiality. No one of us has an intrinsic greatness waiting to express itself. Each of us is, *in potentia*, as great as a human being ever has been. "In every individual there lives an infinite and universal possibility," "a chance to which no possible limits can be put, a chance which is truly infinite, a chance to become a person."[45]

Such is Dewey's belief, against Nietzsche's belief in an order of rank. Unlike Nietzsche's, it is a belief that has not repeatedly failed historical experiment. It is not clear why Nietzsche should have opposed or devalued "personality." He observed how the modern experiment with democracy made Europeans more various, different, chaotic, and that's a good thing. He says he feels "compelled to locate the greatness of humanity . . . in the very scope and variety of humanity, in its unity in multiplicity."[46] That's a deep insight of Darwinism, a kind of biological nominalism. The individual comes first, not the species. Individuals are primary; essences do not exist.[47] Nietzsche drew all of these conclusions. So why did he not draw Dewey's conclusion about democracy? Why did he take the view that there is not merely difference but a natural, spontaneous order of rank? And why did Dewey detest this idea and believe in democracy? The answer reduces to geography, which brings me to America.

America

Beware of Antinomianism.
—R. W. Emerson

In *The Puritan Origins of the American Self*, Sacvan Bercovitch draws a contrast between Emerson and Nietzsche that is very apropos. "If Emerson differs from the chauvinist by his Romantic self-reliance, he differs equally from the Romantic Antinomian by his reliance on a national mission. The natural habitat of the Übermensch is the sublime, anywhere; Emerson's is America." Nietzsche's thought of the Übermensch "may hold out grand prospects for mankind, but it locates the divine center in the individual. The self-reliant American may [like Thoreau] declare his whim superior to the entire legal code, but he remains by definition the hero as guide and national benefactor."[48]

Dewey belongs to this tradition, too, after Emerson and Thoreau (and James). Like theirs, his work is a politically nuanced public discourse, as Nietzsche's is not, and this public is implicitly American. Being American is mainly an ideological rather than an ethnic condition, a conviction about the "American theory" of the sovereign individual. Charles Frankel, Dewey's long-time colleague at Columbia University, observes, "Dewey took it for granted that America had set the terms for the achievement of a form of human excellence that would represent a distinct advance morally and spiritually in the career of mankind."[49] It is democracy's American theory, the sovereignty of the individual, extending the greatest possible freedom to the endless expansion of "personality."

That can work only if sovereign individuals agree and cooperate. To take the individual beyond cooperation—beyond good and evil, if you like—is what Emerson castigates as antinomian and what Nietzsche calls nihilism. A sovereign individual is a law unto himself or herself, which is still to be under law. To be against the law because it is the law sets you beyond law; you're not even a law unto yourself. This "liberation" from law turns out to be an infinite void.[50] Purpose disappears; there is nothing left to prefer except not-preferring—the Buddhism for Europeans Nietzsche called nihilism. He may have thought he had passed through the ordeal of the modern will and emerged on the other side, a postmodern "completion" of nihilism that suggested to Nietzsche a way through it to the other side of modernity. Dewey, however, followed Emerson and recoiled from antinomianism—the "blasphemous" thought that some are more individual than others. In placing oneself outside the law, one is setting a higher value on oneself than anyone else, according oneself the privilege of not being bound by the law of the "herd"—blasphemy against the sovereign singularity of the individual.

Nietzsche might have smiled at the accusation of blasphemy. Dewey seemed likely to agree, though, that "God is dead," even if he refrained from so melodramatic an epitome. The question is what to make of this "problematic situation." Nietzsche's suggestion was to "complete" nihilism by subverting everything Europeans still believed in. That called for radical individuals who set themselves beyond the law. Dewey might have found the tactics far-fetched. Certainly his is the more optimistic scenario, implying that we can ignore "nihilism" and concentrate on the intelligent reconstruction of social life, a project equally of the sciences and political democracy. His optimism was alien to Nietzsche, or to his voice, or to the spirit we read into his books. But it is not clear that Dewey missed some great insight of Nietzsche's. He's just not so broody or melodramatic. That may be because unlike Nietzsche, who had nothing to lose, Dewey did not feel so alone. He was read, he cared about readers, addressed them sincerely, with reasonable arguments—marks of a public discourse, a discourse that appeals to and solicits a public for something more responsible than a rant.

Yes, Nietzsche mocks this "responsibility," but the question is whether that's wise. Does belief in democracy or the sciences invariably imply Platonic-Christian dogmatism and "metaphysics"? Apparently not, as Dewey's work demonstrates. Democracy means the sovereignty of the individual; science means practical, pragmatic, experimental rationality. America is the ideal synthesis of the two, of democracy and science, knowledge and liberty, individuality and cooperation. The promise of the country is to overcome these oppositions and dualisms, to unite experimental logic with democratic norms, and to create a powerful engine for reconstructing modern civilization. This argument is virtually antipodean to everything in Nietzsche, yet there is not really any uncritical presupposition of Dewey's argument that Nietzsche can be said to have made problematic. So why should Dewey give up? America is a day-after-tomorrow kind of place, where the future, with its possibilities, is more important than the past, with its traditions, resentments, and failed hope.

It's unlikely Nietzsche would be moved to rethink his assumptions by Dewey's confidence that America still has something to say to the world after the death of God. But was Dewey naive? It's a hard charge to make stick. What was he supposed to be naive in not grasping? Unlike the European nihilist, he believed in the sciences and democracy, but he also had rather nuanced ideas of both, a long way from the antique assumptions of "Platonism for the people." He was no more "metaphysical" than Nietzsche was. Dewey's hopefulness was not the Socratic optimism Nietzsche criticized, especially in *The Birth of Tragedy*, according to which the universe is somehow on our side and the triumph of good a metaphysically foregone conclusion. Like James, Dewey saw the universe as an evolving, unfinished, really changeable place, "a wide open universe, a universe without bounds in space or time, without final limits of origin or destiny, a universe with the lid off." James said much the same, and so did Nietzsche.[51] Between Dewey and Nietzsche, then, especially on the issue of democracy versus aristocracy, we have a difference that probably cannot be adjudicated. Neither can be said to have decisively discredited the other. Instead, we seem to be at the point where, as James wrote, "temperaments with their cravings and refusals do determine men in their philosophies and always will."[52]

Dewey says "there is no trace by which one personality may be distinguished from another so as to be set above or below."[53] Biology does not rationalize one over another form of political organization, but it is clear that all the people on the earth today are at exactly the same evolutionary level, with exactly the same evolutionary potential. For all that biology can tell, no human being today is more or less "evolved" than any other. Darwin had a strong presentiment of this evolutionary unity and assembled the evidence available to him in support of it, attaching significance to the evidence of "psychical unity" in universals of emotional expression.[54] Today, evidence comes from many directions without serious disagreement. There are no human subspecies, no "races," no Übermenschen and no Untermenschen.[55] Herd is an unhelpful image for humanity. It discounts (except in the most melodramatic, often self-destructive instances) one of our greatest resources as a species, which is our diversity or individual difference. Dewey thought that individuality can and should more commonly become a matter of everyday life, the ethos of a polity or civilization that practices democracy on American theory.

Nietzsche did not do justice to the deep causes of why and how human beings live social lives, which seemed to lead him to underestimate the objection to antinomianism. Human beings (psychopaths aside) are *adapted* for social life. Caring for the opinion of others, feeling sympathy and solidarity, and expecting reciprocity are not merely the resentful fantasies of instinct-denying Christians. They are social adaptations, instinctive human behaviors, evolved ways of negotiating the social life we can never wholly abdicate. These patterns and preferences cannot be changed without terrible violence to what Darwin calls our social instincts. What makes *this* violence against instinct acceptable and not that of Socrates or St. Paul? Nietzsche's immorality requires as much violence against instincts ("decadence") as he deplores in Christianity and Platonism.[56]

Cooperation and coordination are among humanity's most valuable resources. Without them there is no survival, to say nothing of prosperity or greatness. To despise, devalue, and subvert morality, including democracy and human rights, is to despise, devalue, and subvert a necessary condition on future human existence. Perhaps that makes it a kind of nihilism. Dewey expected that democracy properly understood is the culture most amenable to that luxuriant growth of individuals which Nietzsche seemed to admire. The best milieu in which to cultivate individuality is where the sovereignty of each, the equality of each as a unique potential, is respected by all. Let that be the experiment. One cannot say it's been tried. Aristocracy has been tried. In favoring it, Nietzsche showed a reluctance to learn from experiments, contrary to his own best sense of *gay science*.

Notes

1. On Darwin's influence on epistemology, see Robert J. Richards, *Darwin and the Emergence of Evolutionary Theories of Mind and Behavior* (Chicago: University of Chicago Press, 1987). I discuss Darwin's quietly revolutionary philosophy of science in "The Abyss of Contingency: Contingency and Purposiveness in Darwin and Kant," *History of Philosophy Quarterly* 20 (2003): 373–91. Thanks to Colin Koopman and David Rondel for comments on a draft.

2. Friedrich Nietzsche, "On Truth and Lying in a Nonmoral Sense," in *The Birth of Tragedy and Other Writings*, ed. Raymond Geuss and Ronald Speirs, trans. Ronald Speirs (Cambridge: Cambridge University Press, 1999), 141–53.

3. Aristotle, *Metaphysics*, in *The Basic Works of Aristotle*, ed. R. McKeon (New York: Random House, 1941), 1011b. Compare Plato, *Cratylus* 385b. On all this history, see my *Truth in Philosophy* (Cambridge, Mass.: Harvard University Press, 1993).

4. Friedrich Nietzsche, *Beyond Good and Evil: Prelude to a Philosophy of the Future*, ed. Rolf-Peter Horstmann and Judith Norman, trans. Judith Norman (Cambridge: Cambridge University Press, 2002), §1, p. 5; and *On the Genealogy of Morals*, trans. Walter Kaufmann (New York: Vintage, 1967), Third Essay, §24.

5. Nietzsche, *Genealogy of Morals*, Third Essay, §27. I discuss Nietzsche's question about truth in *Truth in Philosophy*, chap. 3.

6. Nietzsche, *Beyond Good and Evil*, §4.

7. John Dewey, *The Quest for Certainty* (New York: G. P. Putnam's Sons, 1929), 98.

8. John Dewey, "The Problem of Truth" (1911), in *Political Writings*, ed. Debra Morris and Ian Shapiro (Indianapolis: Hackett, 1993), 12, 14.

9. Nietzsche, *Birth of Tragedy*, §15.

10. Ibid., p. 40.

11. John Dewey, *Reconstruction in Philosophy* (Boston: Beacon, 1957), xxiii, xxviii, xxxv.

12. Nietzsche, *Beyond Good and Evil*, 33.

13. Friedrich Nietzsche, *The Gay Science*, ed. Bernard Williams, trans. Josefine Nauckhoff (Cambridge: Cambridge University Press, 2001), §143, p. 127.

14. Friedrich Nietzsche, *Daybreak: Thoughts on the Prejudices of Morality*, trans. R. J. Hollingdale (Cambridge: Cambridge University Press, 1982), §103.

15. Dewey, *Intelligence and Morals* (1908), in *Political Writings*, 74.

16. Dewey, "Individuality in Our Day" (1930), in *Political Writings*, 72–73.

17. Charles Frankel, "John Dewey's Social Philosophy," in *New Studies in the Philosophy of John Dewey*, ed. Steven M. Cahn (Hanover, N.H.: University Press of New England, 1977), 10–11.

18. See C. S. Peirce, "Critique of Positivism," in *Writings of Charles S. Peirce: A Chronological Edition*, vol. 2 (1867–71), ed. E. C. Moore (Bloomington: Indiana University Press, 1984).

19. Dewey, *Political Writings*, 28.

20. John Dewey, *Experience and Nature*, 2nd ed. (La Salle, Ill.: Open Court, 1929), 60.

21. Ibid., xvi.

22. On Boyle, see Steven Shapin, *A Social History of Truth: Civility and Science in Seventeenth-Century England* (Chicago: University of Chicago Press, 1994); and Steven Shapin and Simon Schaffer, *Leviathan and the Air Pump* (Princeton, N.J.: Princeton University Press, 1985). On Bacon, see Paolo Rossi, *Francis Bacon: From Magic to Science*, trans. S. Rabinovitch (London: Routledge and Kegan Paul, 1968); and "Truth and Utility in the Science of Francis Bacon," in *Philosophy, Technology, and the Arts in the Early Modern Era*, trans. S. Attanasio (New York: Harper and Row, 1970). I discuss Nietzsche's relation to this tradition in "'All the Daring of the Lover of Knowledge is Permitted Again,'" in *Nietzsche, Epistemology, and Philosophy of Science*, ed. Babette Babich (Lancaster: Kluwer, 1999); and *Knowledge and Civilization* (Boulder, Colo.: Westview Press, 2004), chap. 3.

23. Nietzsche, *Gay Science*, §324.

24. Ibid., §343.

25. Dewey, *Political Writings*, 83, 84; and *Experience and Nature*, 201.

26. Dewey, "Individuality in Our Day"; *Political Writings*, 84.

27. Dewey, "Science and Free Culture" (1939), in *Political Writings*, 57.

28. I draw from Frankel, "Dewey's Social Philosophy," 16–18. See also James Kloppenberg, *Uncertain Victory* (Oxford: Oxford University Press, 1986), 383–85.

29. Dewey, "Individuality, Equality, and Superiority" (1922), in *Political Writings*, 77.

30. Dewey, *Political Writings*, 77. I don't mean to suggest Dewey is original in explaining the value of democracy in terms of individuality or personality, which is usual in liberalism. Thus, for instance, J. S. Mill: "Having said . . . [i]ndividuality is the same thing with development, and that it is . . . the cultivation of individuality which produces . . . well-developed human beings, I might here close the argument:

for what more or better can be said of any condition of human affairs, than that it brings human beings themselves nearer to the best thing they can be?" J. S. Mill, *On Liberty and Other Writings*, ed. Stefan Collini (Cambridge: Cambridge University Press, 1989), 64. Dewey's originality, in the essay from which I quote, is to derive this liberal value from a Hegelian conception of organic society, which is usually thought to smother personality rather than be its natal matrix, as Dewey says.

31. Nietzsche, *Beyond Good and Evil*, §41.

32. Ibid., §257.

33. Ibid., §259.

34. I develop this criticism of "will to power" in a chapter on Nietzsche in *Knowledge and Civilization*.

35. Nietzsche, *Beyond Good and Evil*, §203.

36. Ibid., §§202, 201.

37. Friedrich Nietzsche, *Twilight of the Idols*, trans. Richard Polt (Indianapolis: Hackett, 1997), 74.

38. Nietzsche, *Beyond Good and Evil*, §§202, 212.

39. Friedrich Nietzsche, *Thus Spoke Zarathustra*, trans. Walter Kaufmann (New York: Modern Library, 1995), 15.

40. Nietzsche, *Beyond Good and Evil*, §262.

41. John Dewey, "The Ethics of Democracy" (1888), in *The Early Works of John Dewey, 1882–1898*, ed. Jo Ann Boydston, vol. 1 (Carbondale: Southern Illinois University Press, 1969), 242.

42. Ibid.

43. Wolfgang Müller-Lauter, *Nietzsche: His Philosophy of Contradiction and the Contradictions of His Philosophy*, trans. David Parent (Urbana: University of Illinois Press, 1999), 98.

44. Dewey, "Ethics of Democracy," 242, 240, 237, 243–44.

45. Ibid., 245–46.

46. Nietzsche, *Beyond Good and Evil*, 106.

47. On Darwin's anti-essentialism, see Steven Jay Gould, *Full House* (New York: Three Rivers Press, 1996), 41–42; and Ernst Mayr, *What Evolution Is* (New York: Basic Books, 2001).

48. Sacvan Bercovitch, *The Puritan Origins of the American Self* (New Haven, Conn.: Yale University Press, 1975), 174–76. On the Puritans' struggle with antinomianism in New England, see Perry Miller, *Orthodoxy in Massachusetts* (Cambridge, Mass.: Harvard University Press, 1933). On Puritanism and pragmatism, see my "Truth in America," *Cohesion and Dissent in America*, ed. C. Colatrella and J. Alkana (Albany: SUNY Press, 1994); and *Truth in Philosophy*, chap. 4.

49. Frankel, "Dewey's Social Philosophy," 23.

50. Nietzsche, *Gay Science*, §347.

51. Dewey, *Political Writings*, 74. I am thinking of this passage from Nietzsche's unpublished notebook. "Do you know what the 'world' is to me? . . . [A] monster of energy, without beginning, without end; a firm, iron magnitude of force that does

not grow bigger or smaller, that does not expend itself but only transforms itself . . . a play of forces and waves of forces, at the same time one and many. . . . This world is the will to power—and nothing besides!" In Friedrich Nietzsche, *The Will to Power,* trans. Walter Kaufmann and R. J. Hollingdale (New York: Vintage Books, 1967), §1065.

52. William James, *Pragmatism* (1907) (Cambridge: Harvard University Press, 1978), 24.

53. Dewey, "Ethics of Democracy," 245.

54. See Charles Darwin, *The Expression of the Emotions in Man and Animals* (1872), 3rd ed. (Oxford: Oxford University Press, 1998).

55. See Richard Lewontin, *Human Diversity,* 2nd ed. (New York: Scientific American Library, 1995).

56. See Charles Darwin, *The Descent of Man* (New York: Modern Library, 1936), chap. 4; and Howard E. Gruber, *Darwin on Man* (New York: E. P. Dutton, 1974). On decadence as having to fight against instincts, see Nietzsche, *Twilight of the Idols,* I. §11. Elsewhere in that work, he says, "Everything good is instinct—and consequently easy, necessary, free" (31). But social life, cooperation, association, and sympathy are like that, for all of us, as an outcome of species evolution.

5] Dewey, Nietzsche, and the Self-Image of Philosophy

Paul Fairfield

John Dewey was an uncommonly gentle critic. Whether correcting common misinterpretations of his writings, replying to criticisms both charitable and uncharitable, or contesting philosophical positions not his own, Dewey was invariably measured in his criticism and a singularly mild-mannered philosopher. On the subject of the state of philosophy during his day, however, his penchant for charity was rather less evident. The condition of philosophy and the role of the thinker were major preoccupations of Dewey, and the assessment he offered from some of his earliest writings to his last was harsh by contemporary standards and far more by his own. As he wrote in an essay published in 1952, the final year of his life, "It is perhaps too extreme to say that philosophy today is in a state of doldrums. . . . But only optimists, who at best are not numerous, would say that philosophy is making great headway at present." Philosophy was "becoming a form of Busy-work for a few professionals," a kind of "intellectual gymnastics" utterly removed from human life, "aloof," "scholastic," and marked by "a hateful division of theory and practise."[1] One of Dewey's chapters from *Knowing and the Known*, a book coauthored with Arthur F. Bentley and Dewey's last extant book (1949), includes the following remarks: "It is, I submit, the growing tendency of 'philosophy' to get so far away from vital issues which render its problems not only technical (to some extent a necessity) but such that the more they are discussed the more controversial are they and the further apart are philosophers among themselves:—a pretty sure sign that somewhere on the route a compass has been lost and a chart thrown away."[2] Dewey would offer countless remarks to this effect throughout his career, and it is an assessment that exhibits interesting similarities to a philosopher whose name is rarely mentioned in the same breath as Dewey and with whose works it appears Dewey had at most a passing acquaintance: Friedrich Nietzsche.

The latter figure was, of course, equally harsh in his opinion of his contemporaries. This is unsurprising given Nietzsche's love of criticism both moderate and immoderate, yet what is surprising is the similar note on which both the American and the German thinker pronounced their critiques of the philosophy of their day. Clearly, the differences between their philosophical positions run deep, yet on the question that is before us, the diagnoses they pronounced show an interesting affinity. I wish to return to these critiques and to ask a few slightly awkward questions about their relevance today. What is the self-image under which philosophy has labored from Nietzsche's time to our own? What ultimately is the role of the philosopher in a culture, and is it possible in an age of academic professionalism to take Dewey's or Nietzsche's now decidedly unfashionable opinions on the subject seriously?

Dewey's Critique of Philosophy

Before venturing to answer this last question ever so cautiously in the affirmative, let us examine exactly what Dewey's and Nietzsche's critiques consisted of and what both figures considered the philosopher's role in a society to be. Among the many criticisms that he advanced, Dewey objected above all to the disconnection between philosophy and the actual course of human experience. As it was being practiced by the university professors of his day, philosophy had largely lost contact with social practices, common sense, social issues in general and the condition of democracy in particular, and the overall state of the culture in which philosophers found themselves. The vital context in which philosophical problems arise had been lost sight of, transforming an important field of inquiry into a kind of parlor game with few implications for human life. The problems of philosophy had become so many technical puzzles for philosophical professionals alone and were at best distant cousins of "the problems of men." Thought had become divorced from action and had "torn the intellectual, the emotional, and the practical asunder, erecting each into an entity, and thereby creating the artificial problem of getting them back into working terms with one another." Distinctions between subjectivity and the world, fact and value, theory and practice, and so on had become "*absolute* separations" that effectively compartmentalized thought while severing it from life.[3] Most fundamentally, it was the "neglect of context"—the vital business of human experience outside of the philosopher's study—that constituted "the most pervasive fallacy of philosophic thinking."[4]

A consequence of this disconnection is the transformation of the ancient love of wisdom into a branch of the academic profession whose problems no longer arise from human life and its "problematic situations" but are manufactured as purely formal, technical, and conceptual analyses. Philosophy had withdrawn from the world and become a "merely technical skill," a "search for forms simply as forms . . . forms that are comprehensive only because they are so abstract as to have no connection with any specific subject whatever, human or otherwise."[5] Extravagant in its technicality and jargonizing, philosophy had been "reduced . . . to a show of elaborate terminology, a hair-splitting logic, and a fictitious devotion to the mere external forms of comprehensive and minute demonstration."[6] Its exaggerated and wholly unrealizable aspirations of certainty and systematicity had caused it to lose touch with the probable and the reasonable, with common sense and all ways of thinking that are worldly and without absolute foundations. Philosophical formalism had encouraged a love of forms for their own sake, quite apart from the tangible particulars they ostensibly govern. Genuine problems that had their origins in experience had been transformed into purely formal issues, the relevance of which was apparent to philosophical professionals alone, causing the general public to look upon philosophical discourse as a perfect irrelevance, and with some justification. Whereas for Dewey "[a]ctual thinking . . . always has reference to some context" and is the process by which experienced difficulties are resolved experimentally, formalist thought is acontextual while the forms with which it deals, in logic for instance, are asserted to be "constant, unchanging, indifferent to the subject matter with which they are filled. . . . Because forms are uniform and hospitable to any subject matter whatever, they pay no attention to context."[7] Not unlike the forms of Plato, such forms had cut-and-dried definitions and belonged to a world of thought wholly removed from the world of ordinary life.

Another major worry of Dewey's was the trend toward specialization, which was having a dramatic effect on philosophical and indeed all forms of humanistic and scientific inquiry during his lifetime. No specialist himself, Dewey categorically rejected the view that progress in philosophy requires a narrowing of horizon on the part of individual philosophers or the kind and degree of specialization that had become the norm. While a degree of specialization, he maintained, is "indispensable" to scholarly life (although he himself managed to dispense with it and made major contributions to nearly every subdiscipline of philosophy), it was its excess that was a frequent object of his criticism. Overspecialization, Dewey argued, "contributes to decline of liberality of mind"; it confines the mind within an unduly narrow horizon, inclines one toward pedantry and excessive technicality, and removes the conditions—including especially breadth of knowledge—that make creativity possible.[8] This trend exacerbates the problems alluded to above, in particular the habit of specialists to retreat from the world since the opportunities for engaging it with some claim to knowledge grow fewer.

When one's expertise as a philosopher consists in a specialized knowledge of Spinoza or some minute issue in the philosophy of language, all other matters fall outside one's area and are none of one's concern. Specialists who do venture an opinion outside their field are often "gullible," "inept and ill-advised" in so doing, their judgment and facility with concepts having long since been restricted to a narrow range of issues.[9] "One may be an authority in a particular field and yet of more than usually poor judgment in matters not closely allied, *unless* the training in the special field has been of a kind to ramify into the subject matter of the other fields."[10] Dewey would speak of overspecialization as "the great enemy" of inquiry since, in a word, it "means withdrawal. It means preoccupation with a comparatively remote field in relatively minute detail."[11] Were specialization to realize in practice what it aspires to in theory—that researchers divide the labor which the pursuit of knowledge requires while also, and importantly, sharing their knowledge with and demonstrating its implications for specialists in other fields in a spirit of cooperative inquiry rather than addressing their arguments exclusively to colleagues in their own field—then all would perhaps be well, but as Dewey noted and as we today can hardly deny, this is far from the case. As discourses become increasingly technical, distinctions ever more fine, and vocabularies more formalistic, specialties and subspecialties became ever narrower and uncommunicative with outsiders.

As researchers' focus narrows in scope, circles of specialists increase in number while decreasing in size and in the process, by a seemingly inescapable logic, lose contact with researchers in even closely related fields and with the surrounding culture still more. Dewey would frequently remark upon the aloofness and social irresponsibility of philosopher-specialists, and again in uncharacteristically strident terms. Philosophy from its ancient origins had aspired after a wisdom that was socially useful, intelligible to ordinary humanity, and of profound human importance, yet by the twentieth century, philosophers were speaking only to each other and had become indifferent to larger human interests. The increasing departmentalization of thought and unconcern for the wider implications of one's expertise had created a class of "socially isolated and socially irresponsible scholar[s], specialist[s], esthete[s] and religionist[s]," a class that pursued a life of leisure and culture while appearing to pride itself on its disconnection from the world.[12] The remoteness of philosophy was by this time not an unfortunate necessity of the division of investigative labor but a choice and a mark of intellectual distinction. By 1949, Dewey felt obliged to counter the charge increasingly heard that human interests and worldly issues are not proper objects of philosophical inquiry at all: "Those philosophers who are now subjected to criticism from their fellow professionals on the ground that concern with the needs, troubles, and problems of man is not 'philosophical,' may, if they feel it necessary, draw support and courage from the fact that they are following, however imperfectly, in the path initiated by the man to whom is due the very term *philosophy*."[13]

An additional object of Dewey's criticism was the conservatism that, he believed, had taken hold of the philosophy profession. Philosophers now clung to the problems of old and transformed the questions that had preoccupied their forebears into ahistorical, perennial issues that ostensibly beset the human mind whenever it troubles itself to think. What calls for thinking can only be the questions that René Descartes posed, or Immanuel Kant, or another of the venerable personages of our philosophical tradition, not any merely worldly problems of the present. Philosophy's "intrinsic conservatism," Dewey wrote, is due in part to its absorption within the university and association with the teaching profession: "Scholastic philosophy persisted in universities after men's thoughts outside of the walls of colleges had moved in other directions. In the last hundred years intellectual advances of science and politics have in like fashion been crystallized into material of instruction and now resist further change. I would not say that the spirit of teaching is hostile to that of liberal inquiry, but a philosophy which exists largely as something to be taught rather than wholly as something to be reflected upon is conducive to discussion of views held by others rather than to immediate response. Philosophy when taught inevitably magnifies the history of past thought, and leads professional philosophers to approach their subject-matter through its formulation in received systems." As philosophy clings to traditional problems and remains within the orbit of old theoretical schools, the problems themselves lose something of their genuineness and take on the appearance of blackboard exercises while the theoretical alternatives themselves become restricted to a few polarized and well-fortified camps between which we are obliged to choose. As philosophers continue to replow old ground, "[d]irect preoccupation with contemporary difficulties is left to literature and politics."[14] It was the traditional solutions and the traditional problems still more that needed to be transcended, Dewey fervently believed, and the institutional conservatism of the philosophy profession was presenting a large obstacle to this coming to pass.

A further consequence of philosophy's remoteness and conservatism was the ethos of old-world aristocracy that had affected the university department of philosophy and its self-image, an ethos and a self-image that constituted the very antithesis of philosophical and all other forms of rational investigation as Dewey conceived of it. When philosophers draw a sharp line between knowing and doing and insist upon the prestige of the theoretical over the pragmatic, they embrace a logic whose social implication is profoundly antithetical to democracy. Dewey would often remark upon the tendency of intellectual culture in general "to be sterile, to be turned back to feed on itself; their art becomes a showy display and artificial; their wealth luxurious; their knowledge over-specialized; their manners fastidious rather than humane."[15] Philosophical culture is particularly susceptible to this, he believed, separating purely intellectual studies from the pragmatic while creating an unmistakable hierarchy between the two. "Philosophers," Dewey wrote, "are not a separate and monopolistic priesthood set apart to guard, and, under certain conditions, to reveal, an isolated treasury of truths."[16] Yet a priesthood of sorts is exactly what they had become, a class of personages remote, scholastic, and otherworldly. In a lecture that Dewey delivered in Peking in 1920, for instance, he directed this criticism at the philosophy of his sometime friend and frequent critic Bertrand Russell. What Dewey found "strange" in Russell's work was the discordance between its somewhat radical and democratic political stance, of which Dewey largely approved, and the remainder of his philosophy—a theoretical stance that "smacks of authoritarianism appropriate to an aristocracy." These may be mild words by Russell's standards, but they are harsh indeed by Dewey's. "Why do we compare this attitude with that of the aristocracy? It is simply that some people are impatient with the practical affairs of life, and seek to raise themselves above mundane considerations and enter a sphere of pure reflection. Such people feel that they are 'artistic,' and that they belong to a higher order of being than the run of common man. It is not difficult to see that the theoretical aspects of Russell's philosophy are characterized by this tendency."[17] It was Russell's arid brand of rationalism and his idolatry of mathematics and of a reason that soared above the empirical order to which Dewey objected in the strongest terms. Russell's inability to reconcile the world of pure reason with the concrete order of experience and politics was to Dewey an error as fatal to philosophy as it was common.

By 1941, Dewey would cite with qualified approval remarks from R. G. Collingwood's autobiography concerning some of his Oxford colleagues, remarks that left no doubt of Collingwood's disdain both for their philosophies and for the aristocratic pretensions inherent to them. As Collingwood wrote, "They were proud to have excogitated a philosophy so pure from the sordid taint of utility that they could lay their hands on their hearts and say it was of no use at all, a philosophy so scientific that no one whose life was not a life of pure research could appreciate it, and so abstruse that only a whole-time student, and a very clever one at that, could understand it."[18] Dewey's approval of Collingwood's remarks was qualified only by pointing out the somewhat emotional tone in which the remarks were expressed.

We find Dewey arguing along these lines not only in his later and middle works but as far back as 1891, in a very intriguing essay titled "The Scholastic and the Speculator." This seldom noted essay finds Dewey asking what has become of philosophical scholasticism. Did it disappear, as the received wisdom had it, along with the schoolmen of the Middle Ages, or perhaps carry on as a marginalized minority within a rational and post-scholastic university environment? It had done neither, Dewey asserted, but merely became transformed while preserving its "inner habit and tendency"—a habit and tendency Dewey illustrated with reference to the scholastic's treatment of Aristotle: "First he transferred Aristotle from the pellucid atmosphere of living Greece to his own stuffy cell. He subtracted Aristotle from life; from the circumstances of time, of place, of social and intellectual life which gave him his meaning, and regarded him *in abstracto*; in the air, that is to say." In the hands of the scholastics, the texts of Aristotle represented no longer the search for wisdom of a mortal man profoundly connected to the social conditions of his time and place but the worldless ratiocinations of a "philosophical pope." Questioning and hypothesizing were replaced by authoritative pronouncements that the scholastics themselves could interpret and analyze but not challenge. Rigidity and deference to authority characterize the scholastics' way of thinking, along with a propensity for abstraction in the sense not only of reflection but of "carrying something off," secreting it away to a location of one's choosing. Philosophical abstraction in their hands meant "taking a thing [the works of Aristotle in this case] not out of its apparent relations in order to get it into its real relations, but taking a thing out of relations and keeping it out."[19] Divested of context, Aristotle's writings were available to be absorbed into the scholastics' own system, preserved and stored away for whatever purpose that system required.

But the scholastics did not merely remove Aristotle from the larger context of Greek life; they also "proceeded to dismember the remains": "Even the miser, I suppose, has to do something with his gold, or else he wouldn't know he had it. He must count it over, he must jingle it together, he must bury his fingers in it and roll the coin about. So the Scholastic had to use his learning in some way. He pulled it this way and pulled it that until he pulled it all to pieces. When anything is abstracted, when it is taken off by itself, having lost its connections, all that remains is to go over and over the same thing, dissecting, dividing, analyzing, and then sorting out and piling up the fragments." The scholastics' habit is to draw increasingly fine distinctions, to systematize, pick apart, collect and shuffle about, to place carefully under glass but not to question or to understand contextually. It is the dead thing that is the object of the scholastics' concern, an object or its parts viewed in no relation to the context that gave it meaning but in a rational vacuum. In the modern period, this object was no longer limited to the texts of Aristotle or the scriptures but came to include nature itself and the entire domain of human affairs, politics, and of course philosophy. The writings of all the great thinkers became available to the scholastic, multiplying the opportunities for distinction-making and jargonizing many times over. The cloister had metamorphosed into the study and lecture hall, while the commentaries on Aristotle were succeeded by commentaries on every major thinker and issue and by an endless array of commentaries on commentaries. The scholastic of the twentieth century no less than the thirteenth "criticises the criticisms with which some other Scholastic has criticised other criticisms, and the writing upon writings goes on till the substructure of reality is long obscured."[20]

Dewey would never withdraw these early criticisms—on the contrary, he repeated and elaborated upon them throughout a seventy-year writing career. If anything, his criticisms of his philosophical contemporaries became more strident with time rather than less and were regularly brought to bear on the analytic philosophy that was then emerging in the English-speaking world.

Nietzsche's Critique

For his part, Nietzsche would cast his net still wider than Dewey, applying his critique of philosophy and philosophers not only to his contemporaries but to the entire tradition stemming from Socrates, in the process anticipating both the substance and tone of Dewey's critique. Nietzsche, of course, did not witness the advent of analytic philosophy as Dewey later would, yet there can be no doubt of the opinion he would have formed of it had he lived a few decades longer. The philosophers of the nineteenth century and prior, Nietzsche held, had committed errors so numerous and profound that documenting their full extent is a daunting and perhaps impossible task. I shall focus therefore on several of the major critiques from which many of the smaller and more specific criticisms are derived, beginning with the general enervation of philosophy that he believed to be something of an epidemic by his time.

The roots of this phenomenon, Nietzsche maintained, extend many centuries prior to the nineteenth, in the philosophical systems of Plato and Aristotle as well as in the person of Socrates. What this period represents, for Nietzsche, is not a transition from *mythos* to *logos* but "a decline of the instincts" and the decisive triumph of the Apollonian over the Dionysian.[21] Philosophical thinking invariably constitutes an instinctive activity of sorts, a form of self-expression not unlike the artistic. If Greek tragedy represented, in Nietzsche's view, the supreme achievement of ancient culture, it was because of its power to synthesize the rational spirit of the Apollonian with the instinctive drive of the Dionysian, a synthesis that would not be duplicated by the greatest of the Greek philosophers or by any who would follow. Philosophy from this point forward would be dominated by dichotomies of reason or passion, theory or practice, reality or appearance, necessity or contingency, and so on, all of which both Nietzsche and Dewey would decisively reject.

The enervation of philosophy of which Nietzsche spoke was a symptom of this ancient decline of the instincts and along with them the only ground on which philosophy could stand. "The history of philosophy" then became "a secret raging against the preconditions of life, against the value feelings of life, against partisanship in favor of life."[22] With Socrates began the renunciation of the instincts, of the body and the senses, of appearance and experience in favor of the rational and otherworldly, creating a trajectory that would orient all later philosophers in one way or another. The loss of the Dionysian instincts in philosophy led directly to its decline or perhaps its stillbirth, since for Nietzsche there was no time either prior to Socrates or later in which philosophy would synthesize the Apollonian and Dionysian in the manner of the ancient tragedians.

By Nietzsche's own time, philosophers had become very much as Dewey later described them: university men, scholastics, specialists, decidedly not what Nietzsche or Dewey regarded as the philosopher's proper calling. As Nietzsche would write in *Beyond Good and Evil*, "I insist that people should finally stop confounding philosophical laborers, and scientific men generally, with philosophers; precisely at this point we should be strict about giving 'each his due,' and not far too much to those and far too little to these."[23] Nietzsche would often demarcate rather carefully philosophers from a range of academic professionals that included scholars, critics, historians, scientists, and philosophical laborers, all of whom far outnumbered the former. A typical expression of this point from the notes to *The Will to Power* reads as follows: "Superstition about philosophers: confusion with scholars and scientists. As if values were inherent in things and all one had to do was grasp them! To what extent they study under the direction of given values (their hatred of appearance, the body, etc.). . . . At last, confusion goes so far that one regards Darwinism as philosophy: and now the scholars and scientists dominate."[24]

The philosopher, for Nietzsche, is a fundamentally creative and free spirit, beholden to no values or judgments that are not of one's own explicit fashioning. The academics from whom he distinguished the philosopher follow a trajectory of someone else's design and values that they neither created nor chose. Of scholars and specialists Nietzsche would write with palpable disdain: "[T]hey are all losers who have been *brought back* under the hegemony of science, after having desired *more* of themselves at some time without having had the right to this 'more' and its responsibilities—and who now represent, in word and deed, honorably, resentfully, and vengefully, the *unbelief* in the masterly task and masterfulness of philosophy."[25] Countless such remarks may be found in Nietzsche's works, and what they clearly signify is a lament for philosophy itself and the disappearance of an ideal among those who were calling themselves philosophers. The note of contempt in such remarks is consistent and unmistakable: "For this is the truth [says Zarathustra]: I have left the house of scholars and slammed the door behind me."[26] Why this note of contempt, we might ask? Is this merely symptomatic of an unusually cantankerous personality, or is there a properly philosophical point to this?

To answer this, we must understand Nietzsche's rather elevated conception of philosophy and the philosopher and how the thought of his day quite obviously fell short not only of this ideal but of philosophy's original self-understanding as the love of wisdom. I shall discuss Nietzsche's positive conception of the philosopher in more detail in the following section. For now it will suffice to note that its principal themes include value-creation, inventiveness, critical questioning, depth of understanding, breadth of vision, and responsibility for one's culture. The academic laborer of the nineteenth century lacked not one but all of these qualities, Nietzsche fervently believed; their business required a narrowing of vision, a focused and limited range of knowledge, and a self-restraint that is antithetical to free-spirited questioning. Fundamentally, they were servants of received thought: analysts and systematizers, commentators, followers and managers of ideas not their own. "It is for these investigators to make everything that has happened and been esteemed so far easy to look over, easy to think over, intelligible and manageable, to abbreviate everything long, even 'time,' and to *overcome* the entire past." He continues: "*Genuine philosophers, however, are commanders and legislators*: they say, '*thus* it *shall* be!' They first determine the Whither and For What of man, and in so doing have at their disposal the preliminary labor of all philosophical laborers, all who have overcome the past."[27]

The philosophers of Nietzsche's time were scholastic in Dewey's sense, "mere spectators in everything," as Zarathustra put it: "Like those who stand in the street and stare at the people passing by, so they too wait and stare at thoughts that others have thought." Such scholars "crack knowledge as one cracks nuts"—again not a complimentary description, even while Nietzsche would occasionally qualify this by suggesting that the philosopher's education must include a certain quantity of scholarly labor as a precondition for thought.[28] Yet a precondition is all that it is, and it is this fact of which the philosophers of Nietzsche's time had lost sight. For this advocate of perspectivism, it was necessary to a philosopher's development that they master the skills of the scholar, critic, historian, and what have you, "to be *able* to see with many different eyes and consciences, from a height and into every distance."[29] Creative thought undoubtedly requires that we stand on others' shoulders, but as a means of finding a voice of our own, not in order to become lifelong scribes and disciples. For Nietzsche, even the greatest of German thinkers—Kant and G. V. F. Hegel—had been but great critics and schematizers, not philosophers in this sense. Anyone following their lead could at best remain at their level, while a vast majority of their number would of course fall far below. One implication of this is that "the philosopher should be a *rare* plant," above all not one to be confused with the academics of the nineteenth-century university.[30]

The failure of the professors to rise above the condition of laborer creates further problems when the judgments and evaluations of the past are adopted as a kind of faith. This is a faith, of course, that does not realize it is a faith and that indeed regards itself as at the furthest remove from this: it represents a call to rational order, to certain truth and justice. It is a rejection of appearances and uncertainty, of unreasoning faith and prejudice of any kind. Nietzsche's rejoinder is that the philosophers are one and all believers in "*the faith in opposite values,*" in an endless series of dichotomies whose values are hierarchically ordered and unquestioned.[31] Reality and appearance, truth and falsehood, objectivity and subjectivity, good and evil, and so on remain incontrovertible polarities between which we are compelled to choose and where there is no choice to be made but for how to articulate the meaning of the former in each of these pairings. In failing to question the dichotomies themselves, philosophers fall victim to historical forgetfulness and transform evaluations and interpretations into an orthodoxy. Concepts that are historical contingencies, symbols, and expressions of a particular form of life or will to power become transcendental deliverances to be analyzed and systematized but not questioned. Here we arrive at the heart of Nietzsche's critique: "You ask me about the idiosyncrasies of philosophers? . . . There is their lack of historical sense, their hatred of even the idea of becoming, their Egyptianism. They think they are doing a thing *honour* when they dehistoricize it, *sub specie aeterni*—when they make a mummy of it. All that philosophers have handled for millennia has been conceptual mummies; nothing actual has escaped from their hands alive." Such philosophers are "conceptual idolaters"; "they have trusted in concepts as completely as they have mistrusted the senses: they have not stopped to consider that concepts and words are our inheritance from ages in which thinking was very modest and unclear."[32]

It is the tendency toward historical forgetfulness above all that causes philosophy to deteriorate into scholasticism and idolatry. If the classical love of wisdom had by Nietzsche's time been transformed into an orthodoxy of received concepts and values, it was the thinker's task to philosophize with a hammer—which always means not to demolish such values but to question them in a radically undogmatic way. Yet this is precisely what his contemporaries had failed to do, leaving philosophy with an altogether false objectivism of reified symbols and unquestioned values. This lack of historical consciousness contributed to philosophy's reduction in the modern period to the theory of knowledge, with its erroneous notions of objectivity, certainty, and epistemic foundations. Philosophical thought that conceived of itself as a quest for incontrovertible grounds amounted, as Nietzsche put it, to a "doctrine of abstinence—a philosophy that never gets beyond the threshold and takes pains to *deny* itself the right to enter—that is philosophy in its last throes."[33] A thinking that was free-spirited and questioning had no quarter under these conditions and on the pretense of objective reason succumbed to what Zarathustra would call the "spirit of gravity." A philosophy that was beholden to science and that idolized received concepts was a solemn business indeed; it required from the scholar a painstaking sobriety and a seriousness of purpose not unlike the priests of old to whom Nietzsche would compare modern philosophers. It required as well an increasingly minute division of intellectual labor that again had the effect of narrowing vision and hemming thought within ever smaller specialties.

Nietzsche's critique of his contemporaries, again like Dewey's, did not exclude the personal foibles of philosophers. Ever the psychologist, Nietzsche would often remark upon "the self-glorification and self-exaltation of scholars [which] now stand in full bloom, in their finest spring, everywhere." If philosophy during the long period of the Middle Ages had been the handmaid of theology, forcing the thinker to adopt the ways of the scholastic, its modern transformation into the handmaid of science changed nothing essential and left entirely intact the "Jesuitism of mediocrity" that prevailed among scholars prior to the Enlightenment, including its characteristic preoccupations and ostensible virtues. Respectability and reputation remain uppermost here, whether we are speaking of the medieval schoolmen or modern philosophers, scholars, or scientists: "Let us look more closely: what is the scientific man? To begin with, a type of man that is not noble, with the virtues of a type of man that is not noble, which is to say, a type that does not dominate and is neither authoritative nor self-sufficient: he has industriousness, patient acceptance of his place in rank and file, evenness and moderation in his abilities and needs, an instinct for his equals and for what they need; for example, that bit of independence and green pasture without which there is no quiet work, that claim to honor and recognition . . . , that sunshine of a good name, that constant attestation of his value and utility which is needed to overcome again and again the internal *mistrust* which is the sediment in the hearts of all dependent men and herd animals."[34] The personal vanity of scholars was a frequent object of his criticism. No modest man himself, of course, Nietzsche's own brand of immodesty was of a rather different and somehow more forgivable kind than what he so often diagnosed among his contemporaries: a petty egotism rooted in mediocrity and envy of superiors. The psychology of the scholar was one of *ressentiment* and respectable ordinariness, a character not without ambition and skill in satisfying the requirements of professional life, but uncreative and uninspired. The nineteenth-century philosopher–cum–university professor desired above all the "dignities and respectabilities" that Zarathustra contrasted with the "freedom and the air over fresh soil" that were the conditions of his own proper existence.[35] Little can be expected when the comforts of position and reputation had thoroughly supplanted the free-spirited urgency and untimeliness of the Nietzschean philosopher.

What Are Philosophers For?

The question sounds odd to us today, in this era of academic professionalism, unless of course it were to be posed by a non-philosopher or perhaps an anti-intellectual, in which case it would likely be summarily dismissed. Yet it is a question that throughout their writing careers Dewey and Nietzsche regarded as of the highest importance, as did numerous other philosophers of the nineteenth and early twentieth centuries when large questions of this nature seemed somehow more answerable than to most today. The answers that these two figures offered, moreover, had far more in common with the Greeks than with the philosophers of their own day or ours. The philosopher's reason for being must still be understood in terms of the classical love of wisdom, where this means neither the division of knowledge into an endless array of specialties nor its altogether secure possession but rather its unending pursuit. For both figures, philosophy's proper object is not any merely formal or technical knowledge but a knowledge of what is of ultimate importance to human beings as individuals and as a culture. For this reason, the self-image of philosophy must not be what for so many it is today: that of a science or quasi-science, a technical specialty of logical and linguistic analysis or deductive formalism. Philosophy, Dewey and Nietzsche both believed, must retain something of its original self-understanding while aspiring to something rather more difficult and experimental than the norm of their time and, still more, our own.

In speaking of the question that is before us, Dewey and Nietzsche both emphasized the great responsibility of the philosopher, one that expands far beyond the obligations of the scholar or professional and that takes upon itself a wider responsibility for the culture of which one is a part. Nietzsche's philosopher, as he would say of himself, is a psychologist of sorts and "cultural physician," responsible for the detection of maladies such as the nihilism that he himself diagnosed as a widespread condition of modern Europe. It is a responsibility that includes pronouncing a verdict on how the general culture is faring and indeed on the value of human life itself. Philosophy does not shy from such questions but takes them up in the boldest spirit possible, contestable though any judgment we form will inevitably be. Dewey as well would speak of philosophy as an examination of the roots of one's culture and an interpretation of its undercurrents as they manifest themselves in the arts, religion, politics, language, and so on. "The principal task of philosophy," as he expressed it, "is to get below the turmoil that is particularly conspicuous in times of rapid cultural change, to get behind what appears on the surface, to get to the soil in which a given culture has its roots."[36] Though Dewey would not be given to Nietzschean excess on this point, or any other, their positions here are substantially the same: philosophy properly concerns itself with cultural problems whose scope and depth transcend all specialized inquiry. No mere technicians, philosophers "derive their substance from the stream of culture" and remain tied to the traditions in which they invariably stand and which supply them with a fundamental orientation.[37] They are charged not only with interpreting culture but with getting out in front of it and if need be supplying it with a new direction. Philosophy, Dewey would write, "is a language in which the deepest social problems and aspirations of a given time and a given people are expressed in intellectual and impersonal symbols. It has been well said that philosophy is a reflective self-consciousness of what first exists spontaneously, effectively, in the feelings, deeds, ideas of a people."[38] Dewey would always speak of philosophical reflection on the model of problem-solving—albeit a model far more complex than is often thought—however, he would also speak in a more Hegelian and perhaps Nietzschean vein of a depth dimension of culture, which it is the task of philosophy to understand in explicit terms. Philosophy so conceived "is a conversion of such culture as exists into consciousness," a translation of its symbols and aspirations into a coherent way of thinking.[39]

For related reasons, both figures would also emphasize the difficulty of philosophical thinking. Owing to its broad-ranging responsibility, its necessarily creative dimension, and other factors, such thinking "is the most difficult occupation in which man engages," as Dewey put it.[40] For Nietzsche, the untimeliness of the thinker, his standing as "*of necessity* a man of tomorrow and the day after tomorrow," adds to the difficulty of the task. Such a thinker invariably stands opposed to the ideals of his time and is charged with sounding out these ideals for signs of their deterioration into idols as well as with fashioning new ideals. Thinking is an essentially creative, experimental, and also free-spirited activity, one given to adopting a variety of perspectives without becoming dogmatic about any of them. The "new philosophers" or "philosophers of the future" whom Nietzsche believed or hoped to be on the way were "men of experiments," "*attempters*," "*very* free spirits," posers of questions and lovers of masks in addition to being "friends of 'truth.'" Such a philosopher "lives 'unphilosophically' and 'unwisely,' above all *imprudently* . . .—he risks *himself* constantly, he plays the wicked game."[41] Above all, Nietzsche's philosopher of the future is a solitary and inventive spirit, resolute in will and fated invariably to swim against the tide of the present.

Good democrat that he was, Dewey would never describe the philosophical enterprise as a solitary endeavor, yet a singularly demanding one it is. While not without a method, the method of inquiry that he proposed is experimental, informal, and uncertain in its conclusions. Thinking itself Dewey characterized as "the actual transition from the problematic to the secure," an unhurried resolution of an experienced difficulty or doubt involving observation, questioning, hypothesizing, dialogue, and experimentation.[42] Thinking by its nature is contextual, inventive, "an incursion into the novel"; it is content neither to reflect what it sees nor to "leave everything as it is" but works toward resolving the pressing issues of the times in a manner that does not succumb to the "spirit of gravity" against which Nietzsche warned.[43] Philosophical thinking, and beyond this what Dewey described as "the ideal mental condition," is "[t]o be playful and serious at the same time," hence not to fall into humorless scholasticism but to keep the mind open to novel hypotheses and uncertainties.[44] Nietzsche as well characterized philosophical thinking as at the furthest remove from the toil of the technician and as a combination of dialectical rigor and exuberant imagining.

Both figures sought to reconnect thought to life in ways that make philosophy of obvious relevance to the world and to human experience outside of the cloister. Nietzsche's aim in this respect was to reconnect the Apollonian dimension of thought with the Dionysian, a project that required a rehabilitation of the latter in view of its expulsion from philosophy at the hands of the Greeks. It is a comprehensive outlook for which philosophy properly strives, both thinkers maintained, one that transcends the point of view of the specialist and encompasses within itself an ever-increasing number of ideas and points of view. The possibility of attaining what Dewey called "an outlook upon life" in the sense of "a *general attitude* toward it," or in Nietzsche's words "the height for a comprehensive look," belongs to the philosophical nonspecialist alone.[45] The purpose of serious thought in general, as both figures were keenly aware, is not only to clarify concepts but to enhance and often to alter radically the general course of human existence. "Whenever philosophy has been taken seriously," Dewey wrote, "it has always been assumed that it signified achieving a wisdom which would influence the conduct of life."[46]

Clearly, these two thinkers did not hold identical views on the questions that are before us, but what their respective critiques and positive views share is of more than historical significance. A philosophy that understands itself as a quasi-science or technical specialty of any kind, Dewey and Nietzsche likewise warn us, inevitably becomes moribund and disconnected from vital human experience—the only ground from which philosophy properly emerges. That their warnings have gone largely unheeded by later generations of philosophers will, I trust, be evident to all. Their views on the state of philosophy during their lifetimes are strident, uncompromising, and unfashionable by the standards of their time and, still more, our own. Yet few philosophers at present will have difficulty recognizing something of themselves, or at any rate their profession, in Dewey's and Nietzsche's remarks. If not all of us are "scholastics," "herd animals," or some similarly unkind epithet, we nonetheless are all specialists now—technicians or would-be scientists of one kind or another, analysts, critics, scholarly interpreters of some Master Thinker or other, perhaps disciples or heralds. At the worst of times, philosophers are riddlers and solvers of puzzles and micro-puzzles the relevance of which is lost on all but the initiated. This is how graduate students are trained and how the professional ladder is climbed, even while it is no secret that specialization precludes the more comprehensive outlook for which both of these philosophers called and which they and the greatest of philosophers have always sought to articulate. Today, however, a familiar pattern finds students becoming enamored with philosophy at the undergraduate level and proceeding to graduate school only to find blinkers quickly affixed, often for life. From this point forward, specialists are relieved of having to learn of any other field apart from a few preliminaries, or even of the history of their own specialty. It is now common, for instance, for new PhDs in moral or political philosophy not to have read more than bits and pieces of even the most important historical texts in their own field, to have more than a little knowledge only about the latest technical puzzles that are causing a stir in the journals, and to race from conference to conference for the purpose of building a curriculum vitae and competing for employment. It is equally common for specialists not to read the literatures of traditions not their own, for liberals or feminists to take seriously the literature of liberalism or feminism alone, or even a narrow strain of this literature, closing off any possibility of conversation across boundaries of any kind. Specialization and ahistoricism have emerged together and have become difficult to untangle. It is a mystifying proposition that one can be expected to advance the conversation when one lacks more than superficial knowledge of its origins and history and when one is trained to take seriously only one's fellow travelers in liberalism, feminism, or what have you.

While I do not wish to overstate the case, the relevance of these two thinkers' critiques is, I would venture to say, obvious, and my exposition of their critiques here is motivated largely by my agreement with them. Is it possible, however, at a time when philosophy has been so thoroughly absorbed within the university and the academic profession, to take these critiques genuinely to heart? Must philosophy, to attain the more comprehensive outlook on human existence that Dewey, Nietzsche, and many other major figures in the Western tradition thought desirable, bid adieu to the university and to the "dignities and respectabilities" of which Nietzsche spoke with such contempt? Philosophers, of course, have not always been members of the academic profession, and one wonders whether a necessary condition of our field becoming less scholastic and moribund may well be its release from the universities. Is a return of sorts to the philosopher as gadfly of the marketplace, as a writer of dialogues, essays, meditations, and belles-lettres, as Nietzschean wanderer or Deweyan generalist and public intellectual, the antidote to the situation, and quite possibly the malaise, in which philosophy now finds itself? I have no answer to this last question, at least not one for which I could provide a compelling demonstration. I do, however, have a suspicion. This is that if philosophy is to receive a fresh infusion of ideas or undertake a creative change in direction any time soon, one that would render it less vulnerable to the critiques leveled at it by Dewey and Nietzsche, it may well have to be undertaken by outsiders to the academic profession, perhaps the newly emerging class of "independent scholars" who for reasons of choice or necessity exist on the margins of the university. As intellectual history frequently reminds us, it is from the margins and in the realm of the hybrid that creative ideas very often appear, in the writings of free-thinking eccentrics, and not always from the chairs of our venerable universities. A diplomatic formulation of the point is that the professionalization and academization of philosophy has been a mixed blessing. The thorough absorption of philosophy within the university has provided tremendous support for the kind of intellectual work that is called "research," with its institutions of tenure and sabbaticals, conferences and colloquia, research grants and peer review. Whether it has been supportive of what might less technically be called thinking, in the sense of either a Dewey or a Nietzsche, a Heidegger or a Wittgenstein, or for that matter a Thales or a Heraclitus, is an altogether different matter. "Research" (the word itself says much) is meant to be the highest expression of, even to be synonymous with, thought itself, while its institutional accoutrements are widely believed to be necessary conditions of intellectual progress. Whether this or the reverse is so—that such conditions provide only for the outward trappings of thought and for career advancement while on a deeper level constituting a recipe for scholasticism—is a matter on which we might argue for either side with about equal plausibility. While I am not (quite) arguing for the abolition of these institutions, I am recommending that we be mindful of the price that we, or that philosophy itself, has paid for them, including all that which is no longer sayable and publishable—the search for a comprehensive understanding, complete with the "speculation" and "unclarity" that come with it and with which the history of philosophy is so richly replete.

For as long as philosophy retains the self-image of science, it will continue the slide into irrelevance of which students and non-philosophers so often and so rightly complain. The general public largely stopped listening to philosophers long ago, at about the time when the latter began speaking exclusively to and about themselves and within ever smaller circles of insiders and specialists. Were they wrong to do so? Is it a symptom of anti-intellectualism when the general public is perfectly incurious about analytic metaphysics, formal logic, or decision theory? Let me suggest that it is not. Nor are they to be faulted for their failure to make household names of the leading figures in these and many other philosophical subdisciplines. Philosophy as science—meta-, aspiring, handmaid to, quasi-, or pseudo-—is a recipe for the scholasticism and hyperspecialism of which Dewey and Nietzsche warned. Their warnings may have been in vain and far too late, yet it may at least be hoped that conceptions of philosophy reminiscent of their ideals or even of philosophy's original signification will emerge, as a corrective perhaps to the technicist and scientistic excesses of the present.

Existential philosopher Karl Jaspers attributed "the decay of philosophy" in the universities to its disconnection from "the realities of the age," one symptom of which was the lifelong association of virtually all philosophers with the academic world, from their undergraduate years through retirement or beyond. "This is one way, to be sure, but as the only way it lets philosophy dry up, in a manner of speaking. Instead of coming from life, from reality, from science to the flower of philosophizing, instead of nurturing it from the soil in which it grew, the philosophers often deal only with past philosophies and with fine books on everything under the sun. They treat their subject like a herbarium of beautiful plants, with which they operate without arousing new life in them by an infusion of their own blood. One studies philosophy and acquires a virtuosity of intellectual movement, but one does not philosophize in dead earnest, concerned with the truth by which, and with which, we will live."[47] Jaspers's words, echoing those of Dewey and Nietzsche, remain as relevant today as the critiques of philosophy that the latter two figures offered. A philosophy that is sanitized, technicized, and professionalized is not thought "in dead earnest." It does not change one's life or, still less, the world. It "leaves everything as it is" only too well.

Nietzsche's "philosophers of the future" have not arrived, and they do not appear to be on their way. But when he asked, with more than a hint of exasperation, "*Must* there not be such philosophers?" perhaps we can be forgiven for replying in the affirmative.[48]

Notes

1. All references to Dewey's texts are to *The Early Works of John Dewey, 1882–1898*, 5 vols. (*EW*), *The Middle Works of John Dewey, 1899–1924*, 15 vols. (*MW*), or *The Later Works of John Dewey, 1925–1953*, 17 vols. (*LW*), edited by Jo Ann Boydston (Carbondale: Southern Illinois University Press, 1969–90). Dewey, "Modern Philosophy," *LW* 16:411; "Philosophy," *LW* 5:176; "The Liberal College and its Enemies," *MW* 15:208.

2. John Dewey and Arthur F. Bentley, *Knowing and the Known*, *LW* 16:249–50.

3. Ibid., 249.

4. Dewey, "Context and Thought," *LW* 6:5.

5. Dewey, "Has Philosophy a Future?" *LW* 16:361–62.

6. Dewey, *Reconstruction in Philosophy, MW* 12:91.

7. Dewey, *How We Think, LW* 8:172.

8. Dewey, "The Liberal College and Its Enemies," *MW* 15:208.

9. Dewey, *How We Think, LW* 8:162; *Democracy and Education, MW* 9:72.

10. Dewey, *Democracy and Education, MW* 9:71.

11. Dewey, "Bankruptcy of Modern Education," *LW* 3:278; "Academic Freedom," *MW* 2:64.

12. Dewey, *Reconstruction in Philosophy, MW* 12:178.

13. Dewey, "Philosophy's Future in Our Scientific Age: Never Was Its Role More Crucial," *LW* 16:377.

14. Dewey, "The Need for a Recovery of Philosophy," *MW* 10:3–4.

15. Dewey, *Democracy and Education, MW* 9:90.

16. Dewey, "Philosophy and American National Life," *MW* 3:77.

17. Dewey, "Three Contemporary Philosophers," *MW* 12:239–40.

18. Dewey, "Lessons from the War—in Philosophy," *LW* 14:334.

19. Dewey, "The Scholastic and the Speculator," *EW* 3:148–49.

20. Ibid., 150–51.

21. Friedrich Nietzsche, *The Will to Power*, trans. Walter Kaufmann and R. J. Hollingdale, ed. Walter Kaufmann (New York: Vintage, 1968), sec. 439, p. 242.

22. Ibid., sec. 461, p. 253.

23. Friedrich Nietzsche, *Beyond Good and Evil*, trans. Walter Kaufmann (New York: Vintage, 1989), sec. 211, p. 135.

24. Nietzsche, *Will to Power*, sec. 422, p. 226.

25. Nietzsche, *Beyond Good and Evil*, sec. 204, p. 123.

26. Nietzsche, *Thus Spoke Zarathustra*, trans. R. J. Hollingdale (New York: Penguin, 2003), 147.

27. Nietzsche, *Beyond Good and Evil*, sec. 211, p. 136.

28. Nietzsche, *Thus Spoke Zarathustra*, 147.

29. Nietzsche, *Beyond Good and Evil*, sec. 211, p. 136.

30. Nietzsche, *Will to Power*, sec. 420, p. 226.

31. Nietzsche, *Beyond Good and Evil*, sec. 2, p. 10.

32. Friedrich Nietzsche, *Twilight of the Idols*, trans. R. J. Hollingdale (New York: Penguin, 2003), 45; *The Will to Power*, sec. 409, p. 220.

33. Nietzsche, *Beyond Good and Evil*, sec. 204, p. 123.

34. Ibid., sec. 204, p. 121; sec. 206, p. 126, 125.

35. Nietzsche, *Thus Spoke Zarathustra*, 147.

36. Dewey, "The Future of Philosophy," *LW* 17:466–67.

37. Dewey, *Art as Experience, LW* 10:270.

38. Dewey, "Philosophy and American National Life," *MW* 3:73.

39. Dewey, "Philosophy and Civilization," *LW* 3:9.

40. Dewey, "Philosophies of Freedom," *LW* 3:112.

41. Nietzsche, *Beyond Good and Evil*, sec. 212, p. 137; sec. 210, p. 134; sec. 42, p. 52; sec. 44, p. 53; sec. 43, p. 53; sec. 205, p. 125.

42. Dewey, *The Quest for Certainty, LW* 4:181.

43. Dewey, *Democracy and Education*, *MW* 9:165.

44. Dewey, *How We Think*, *LW* 8:347.

45. Dewey, *Democracy and Education*, *MW* 9:334; Nietzsche, *Beyond Good and Evil*, sec. 205, p. 124.

46. Dewey, *Democracy and Education*, *MW* 9:334.

47. Karl Jaspers, *Philosophy and the World*, trans. E. B. Ashton (Washington: Gateway, 1963), 15.

48. Nietzsche, *Beyond Good and Evil*, sec. 211, p. 136.

6] Heidegger: A Pragmatist by Any Means

Joseph Margolis

As early as 1974, Richard Rorty was drawn to a fateful comparison between Martin Heidegger and John Dewey that appeared to confirm the "ontological" superiority of Heidegger's innovations over Dewey's and may therefore have led Rorty to propose his own "pragmatist" version of philosophy—that is, his "postmodernist" dismissal of philosophy—more in the spirit of his reading of Heidegger's having "overcome" the tradition of Western metaphysics than of Dewey's seemingly blander, very different kind of reform.[1] The linkage remains an uneasy one because Rorty misreads Heidegger—deliberately, I would say—misreads Dewey, misreads the similarity between the two, and misjudges the support either might provide for legitimating his own undertaking. None of this would have occasioned much of a correction except for the extraordinary fact that, almost single-handedly and through just such deformations, Rorty revived a badly sagging pragmatism and, because of that, obliged the academy to reconsider a whole nest of redescriptions of what pragmatism (originally) was, is (still), or (from this point on) ought to be.[2]

Of course, Rorty could hardly have proposed a more outrageous or intriguing comparison, since Heidegger was known for his contempt for American pragmatism and a flamboyant commitment to his own brand of transcendental phenomenology. Rorty played his part marvelously well, but he produced a lot of mischief—as we shall see. The problem is to get back to a useful way of reading the convergence between pragmatism and European philosophy, but that concern itself affords an unanticipated, much-needed escape from the parochial habits of academic philosophy.

There is, in fact, no convincing evidence that either Dewey or Heidegger believed that philosophy had exhausted its resources or come to an end. On the contrary, each believed (along the lines of Rorty's charge) that canonical philosophy was profoundly deficient, misguided, in need of a drastic reorientation; but each also believed that he personally had found the essential nerve of the correction required and could present its instruction persuasively. And of course their visions were irreconcilably opposed. In effect, Rorty's double mischief comes to this: first, he deformed both Dewey's and Heidegger's innovations so that they appeared to be little more than ingenious repudiations of philosophy's self-deception—and, in that sense, anticipated his own "postmodernism"; and, second, he read each through the eyes of the other, so that all apparent oppositions between the objectives of each turned out to be little more than variations on the underlying existentialism and pragmatism that they shared.

Dewey's correction of canonical philosophy was thoroughly naturalistic: the whole of the human world, he supposed, arises out of animal sources, which it transforms in sui generis ways but never supersedes; the pragmatist revision was a spare descendant of G. W. F. Hegel's decisive critique of Immanuel Kant's first *Critique*, now cast in Darwinian terms, opposed to every form of cognitive privilege and real fixities, committed existentially in instrumentalist ways in accord with practical interests as they arise in the flux of life, without a priori first principles of any kind, without any telos beyond life itself, guided by pragmatist appraisals of meaning, truth, and value within the confines of nature, shared with other humans with whom we live and who are always in our purview.

Heidegger's correction was very different, though it seemed to favor similar existential themes that it qualified in altogether different ways. Human beings, taken in their natural (or "ontic") guise, exhibiting their characteristic kinds of diversity, might be said (though never more than paradoxically) to be the contingent or historied incarnations of certain "transcendent" (or "ontological") constancies (or "possibilities"), which could never be grasped by the categories we apply in describing the phenomena of the merely natural world. The conceptual relationship between the "ontic" and the "ontological" is never made entirely clear and recedes in Heidegger's later work. On some readings, in fact, Heidegger's well-known concern for the complexities of Being (*Sein*), sans phrase, as opposed to any inquiry into plural beings (*Seiende*)—which could include but would not be primarily addressed to the distinction between the ontic and the ontological—begins to yield in the direction of pondering the very surd of Being, in a sense akin to the unnamable Void of Buddhist and Taoist thought, from which the discourse about Being itself might ultimately arise.[3]

More familiarly, Heidegger cast the human self or subject as a uniquely qualified "onto-ontological being" (*Dasein*), a "being" among similar beings that alone "exist," which Heidegger described as being uniquely occupied ("transcendentally") with the meaning of its own mode of Being and the general question of Being itself. Yet, at its most bewildering, Heidegger's account of *Dasein* and *Dasein*'s concern with Being never fails to signal the conceptual inadequacy of the entire run of "categories" in accord with which we claim to understand the natural world. *Dasein* outstrips all that: hence, Heidegger cannot possibly be a pragmatist.

The description of *Dasein*'s "transcendence" (Heidegger signals, chiefly in *Being and Time*) invokes "existentialia" rather than ordinary "categories" reserved for natural "things": characterized "transcendentally," *Dasein* is said to "exist," as mere "things" do not. All of this is oracularly affirmed (in *Being and Time*), elaborated with great skill and conviction in seemingly self-evident terms, without any apparent need for supporting argument or confirmation (or formal analysis), however paradoxical *Dasein* might then prove to be: *Dasein* is, of course, said to be found (ontically) "in" the world, and (in *Being and Time* at least) it also functions (ontologically) as the unique being to which the being of the world presents itself as the world it is. But, even there, the world thus disclosed *is not* the merely natural world, but "world" that answers to *Dasein*'s unique "ontological" distinction—for instance, the aspect of its "*Temporalität*" or "*In-der-Welt-sein.*" I shall have to allow this sort of extravagance to roam a little freely at first—and I shall need your patience. (The linkage between the ontic and the ontological remains decidedly baffling.) Dewey, I would say, could easily admit the counterparts of such features in entirely naturalistic terms, but that would never satisfy Heidegger's thesis.

That is, to speak more carefully, either the corrective resource from which our evolving concepts are obviously drawn (the ontological source of our ontic categories) requires an enlarged conception of the natural, which applied intelligence accordingly defines—as the "infinite" projections of "finite" understanding according to Hegel, or the reinterpretation of our animal responsiveness according to Dewey, or the confirmation of our abiding "existentialia" under changing circumstances according to Heidegger—or else the alleged resource is to be treated as a privileged gift or a mystery that ordinary discursive intelligence cannot penetrate or master. The second cannot be more than a completely arbitrary scandal, but it clearly collects Heidegger's unyielding animus against pragmatism and every form of naturalism, even where pragmatists have regarded Heidegger with favor.

You may well wonder what's at stake in Heidegger's fixation on the "meaning of Being." What is its bearing on pragmatism's past and future prospects? The answer, roughly, is this: *if* Heidegger is himself a pragmatist, perhaps even a better pragmatist than Dewey (as Rorty rather slyly suggests, though he's also laid down hints that clearly discount such a reading), then it may be that American pragmatism would be considerably strengthened if it could find a way to accommodate Heidegger's alien inquiries. Given Heidegger's dominance in his prime among the strongest forces of continental philosophy, the isolationist tendencies of American philosophy might be outflanked at a stroke by such an adjustment! I'd say that that was as reasonable a reconstruction as can be made out of Rorty's thinking, based on his affirming a distinct philosophical convergence between Dewey and Heidegger, two thinkers about as distant from one another as anyone might imagine.

Rorty was very fond of such juxtapositions: I think he may have set his outlandish traps deliberately, to see how the academy would jump; when he tired of one such tale, he simply substituted another. They all have to do with exposing the confusion of professional philosophy by introducing artifactual confusions the academy had not yet hit on. For example, in a maneuver both brazen and charming, Rorty stoutly affirmed that Donald Davidson was the very best sort of pragmatist, as important as Dewey for orienting the flock—that is, if only Davidson would accept Rorty's pointed instruction about philosophy's exhaustion. In a similar vein, Robert Brandom suggests—Brandom, who had been a student of Rorty's—that Gottlob Frege may be called a pragmatist fairly enough! I don't believe these tricky games would have been possible if American philosophy had not become as unsure of its moorings as Rorty realized must be true. He saw, devilishly well, that he could propose nearly anything he wished, without fear of being called to account: the analysts would never understand; the pragmatists were in disarray; the continentals hardly knew what to make of such a fool.

The upshot, now, is that philosophy still finds itself in a sort of incipient remission. It is emerging from a lengthy conceptual disorder that it needs to have correctly diagnosed, to be able to avoid another such onset of confusion. Heidegger may well be the largest intelligence of twentieth-century continental philosophy, and Rorty is surely the naughtiest, most gifted trickster of the Anglo-American academy—trained as an analyst, drawn to the radical possibilities of pragmatism, willful and wise at the same time about the daring extravagances of continental philosophy, a deliberately self-invented pop entrepreneur who captured at a stroke the unbelievably naive wonder of the fabled rigor of the whole of American thought that dominated for a brief season a considerable part of Eurocentric philosophy. We are of course obliged to exorcise the demons of our own conviction. Hence, we are obliged to begin with Heidegger, even if, in another age, that would have been deemed entirely gratuitous.

Certainly Rorty meant to challenge American academic philosophy and the whole of Western philosophy at its core; and he succeeded for a while. He's been more effective in vivifying philosophy than in demonstrating its supposed exhaustion and self-deception. He's revived pragmatism, though it's hard to say he's provided a convincing new direction. That may be reason enough to hear him out; for if pragmatism has any hope of restoring its own luster, it must surely be able to dispose of Rorty's linkage between Heidegger and Dewey convincingly and in good time. The easy assimilation that Rorty favored between Dewey and a good number of doubtful "pragmatists"—Heidegger, Rorty himself, Ludwig Wittgenstein, Wilfrid Sellars, Donald Davidson, to name the best-remembered candidates—hints at a seriously confused sense of what it was to be a pragmatist in the last quarter of the twentieth century. The contingencies of philosophical history oblige us to review with care what cannot have been more than a joke or a riddle. It has infected honest doubts like a virus of reflective intelligence; but, to be honest, it yields no lesson in its own right.

To return then to the tale involving Heidegger: the "existentials" (or "existentialia") tend to reflect *Dasein*'s essential commitment to the openness of questioning the meaning of Being rather than of affirming the fixed validity of any categorical description of human being itself. Heidegger's later work tends increasingly to challenge the adequacy of any "metaphysics" of the human subject and the world it postulates on the basis of its own primacy. The "ontology" of *Dasein* cannot be captured, for instance, by the metaphysics of Descartes's or Kant's *cogito sum* or of any merely mortally competent *ego*. Heidegger goes so far as to find in Kant a phenomenological anticipation of the deeper ontology of *Dasein* within the first *Critique*, which in effect exposes the error of Kant's entire metaphysics—and with it the metaphysics of the Western world. Increasingly, the primacy of the human subject is displaced by the "mystery" of Being's self-disclosure—moving, for instance, from *Kant and the Problem of Metaphysics* through the "Letter on Humanism," the *Nietzsche* volumes, and late essays like "The Question concerning Technology."

Dewey also challenged, it's true, the static categories of canonical metaphysics (preeminently, Kant) in accord with his sense of the flux of the real world, but he was motivated by a perceived need to avoid the excessive distortions of a vocabulary of rigidly defined individuated things, not any need to escape the constraints of the order of nature itself. Heidegger, by contrast, fastened on how our preoccupation with the way the practical efficiencies of characterizing the world of things threatens to engulf our concept of *Dasein* as well—the point of the primacy of the question of the meaning of Being;

but that question becomes an all-absorbing obsession, a bottomless mystery that eludes every conceivable mode of discursive analysis. Dewey confronted the relative inflexibilities of natural language, which no one can successfully overcome, and Heidegger ultimately yielded to some inexplicable power of Being to call the human voice to its own ineffable source. No partial convergence along pragmatist lines could possibly bridge the difference. Rorty deliberately slights that difference for his own "postmodernist" purpose.

Ulteriorly, we cannot avoid the worry that Heidegger may have fallen into the "seer's disease": that is, he seems to have persuaded himself that he'd fathomed the deepest source of the disorder of the whole of Western thought, which no one else had quite grasped. In any case, I haven't been able to find a single sustained analysis on Heidegger's part (or offered in Heidegger's name) that explains the fatal deflection of Western thought said to center on "the question of Being." I think it very possible that, attracted by the seeming profundity of his Question, he searched for a clue beyond Parmenides and the pre-Socratics—and simply lost his philosophical footing.

In a perfectly obvious sense, therefore, everything that would rightly count as pragmatism's intended correction of the classic metaphysics and epistemology of the Western tradition would be no more than another impoverished manifestation of precisely what Heidegger meant to discard completely! Hence, the most difficult aspect of Rorty's challenge rests with the invention of a vocabulary suited to comparing Dewey and Heidegger as he does—and to facilitating additional heterodox comparisons elsewhere. All this has now become philosophically commonplace, but not for that reason easily fathomed. (Rorty simply ignores the complication or takes advantage of the textual mystery.)

By means of his strategic distinction, Heidegger opposed the adequacy of any naturalistic account of human being. But, unlike Kant, his transcendental conditions are primarily "existential" rather than cognitive, though they are meant to constrain our theory of cognitive competence just as they constrain every ontic dimension of human life: that is, on Heidegger's account, cognition is itself existentially constrained. I find that entirely reasonable, read as a small reminder. It's also perfectly acceptable to pragmatist theory. No doubt, the distinction draws attention as well to the overlapping interests of Dewey and Heidegger in centering the human subject "in-the-world." But, beyond that, there's no sustained or congruent convergence between Heidegger's treatment of *Dasein*'s unique presence according to his own existential ontology and Dewey's naturalistic treatment of a Darwinian continuity between man's animal origins and his uniquely evolved encultured competences. But admitting this much is hardly enough, for instance, to show that transcendental conjectures are *ever* necessary or apodictic or revealed in the way such very different champions as Kant and Edmund Husserl and Heidegger proclaim.

Here, we may usefully remark that Heidegger, though deeply indebted to Husserl's phenomenology, completely eclipsed the transcendental pretensions of Husserl's theory of science and knowledge, just as he did Kant's cognitive transcendentalism—and for cognate reasons. In short, Heidegger rejected the canonical forms of transcendental subjectivism. Nevertheless, he never quite explained in any evidentiarily compelling way how or on what grounds his own transcendental claims arose and were confirmed as defining the existential dispositions, competences, and conditions that qualify *Dasein*'s ontic manifestations. What Heidegger offers (in *Being and Time*) as "existentialia" are certainly intriguing and even reasonable (for instance: *In-der-Welt-sein, Mitsein, Temporalität, Sorge, Befindlichkeit*); but the fact remains that they are easily read in a decidedly un-Heideggerean way as very large, ordinary generalizations, informally affirmed, at times even poetically, without apparent need of rigorous specification or testing. That would be the Deweyan alternative: the "indeterminate" or "problematic situation" of Dewey's *Logic* may be read as a very slim existential version of transcendental thinking, but it could never be reconciled with the versions favored by Kant or Heidegger.

How Heidegger's discoveries are to be judged valid (involving relations between the ontic and the ontological powers of human being) is never made entirely clear. Yet Heidegger begins *Being and Time* in an idiom that is decidedly dependent on the convictions of Husserl's transcendental phenomenology, without ever invoking the *epoché*. Indeed, Heidegger must reject Husserl's characteristic undertaking, because it implicates a "transcendental ego" utterly alien to the a priori "subject" that is *Dasein*. (There is no careful argument to rely on.)

Thus, for instance, Heidegger affirms at an early point in *Being and Time*: "It is true that being-in-the-world is an *a priori* necessary constitution of Da-sein, but it is not at all sufficient to fully determine Da-sein's being. . . . *Being-in is thus the formal existential expression of the being of Da-sein* which has the essential constitution of being-in-the-world." Much later in the same text, Heidegger adds: "The idea of a 'pure ego' and a 'consciousness in general' are so far from including the *a priori* character of 'real' subjectivity that they pass over the ontological character of facticity of Da-sein and its constitution of being, or do not see it at all. Rejection of a 'consciousness in general' does not mean the negation of the *a priori*, any more than the positing of an idealized subject guarantees a factually based *a priori* character of Da-sein."[4]

It seems almost as if "existentialia" are little more than standard *categories* (though such a claim would be profoundly mistaken) raised up to a condition of privileged predication and that, accordingly, *Dasein*'s "ontological" distinction should be easily replaceable by a naturalistic substitute. But though the matter may seem no more than that, existential predicables all involve *Dasein*'s unique and reflexive concern with Being and with its own "temporality," which is not confined to natural time. These conditions identify the "transcendence" of *Dasein*, its manifesting that mode of Being (its "existence") in virtue of which all else encountered-in-the-world is said to be "present" to it alone—*but never in a way* that involves spatial relations or the like between *Dasein* and the "things" of the world: "As an existential, [Heidegger explains,] 'being with' the world never means anything like the being-objectively-present-together of things that occur. There is no such thing as the 'being next to each other' of a being called 'Dasein' with another being called 'world.'"[5] But, of course, if that is so, then it is probably impossible to characterize Heidegger as a pragmatist.

An *existentiale* is rather like a transcendental condition (in Kant's sense) except that it is not a pronouncement implicated in the assertions of *Verstand*, not a category like the Kantian categories, and nowhere legitimated by a priori means ranging over *Verstand*'s own work. It may be said to be phenomenologized along Husserlian lines, except that Heidegger had no use for anything close to Husserl's method of pure phenomenological analysis. There is nothing in Dewey like it, except, as I say, Dewey's "problematic situation"; but Dewey's idea is more of a Darwinian conjecture about how to construe the animal grounding of human understanding, something thoroughly naturalistic, continuous with ordinary analysis, not in any way a clue to high-level discoveries meant to limit our reliance on naturalistic distinctions.

The transcendental standing of Heidegger's account of *Dasein* seems to be implicated in his having contested the specific transcendental pretensions of Kant and Husserl. But his "existentialia," detached from the confrontations just noted, are not easily segregated from naturalistic categories; in fact, Heidegger's discussion of the natural sciences and propositional knowledge (again, in *Being and Time*) is hardly uncongenial to a leaner sort of naturalism.[6] His anti-naturalism (or "extranaturalism") depends entirely, it seems, on the problematic concept of *Dasein*—which suggests the need for a careful review of Rorty's linking Heidegger and Dewey in the way he does. Apart from mere textual quarrels, there is no way to explore the prospect of a rapprochement between pragmatism and continental philosophy that does not pass through Heidegger. But if you concede my worry about Rorty's insouciance, you begin to see that Heidegger's pragmatism may not be the principal issue after all: it has to do, rather, with the compatibility and possible convergence between pragmatism and continental philosophy in general. But that means of course that Rorty's charge has indeed obliged us to review the entire tale of Eurocentric philosophy with greater care than usual—which, though a virtue of sorts, cannot convincingly be said to have been Rorty's purpose at all.

It is worth remarking that when Charles Sanders Peirce replaced Kant's transcendental cognitions by transcendental Hope, he meant to abandon all forms of cognitive privilege: in this, he followed Hegel's critique. My sense is that Heidegger meant to accomplish something not too dissimilar, though he intended to do so by very different means and for a very different purpose. Peirce's transcendental conditions are meant to show us how to gain, a posteriori, a priori conditions adequate for the "possibility" *of an empirically grounded science*, which Kant would have supposed required a determinate source of privileged (in effect privileged) transcendental understanding, whereas Heidegger rejected the entire project of Kant's "metaphysics" and its unearned sources of privileged knowledge—for the sake of *questioning the "meaning of Being"* (which leads ineluctably to its own unacknowledged privilege).

The fact is, Heidegger was respectful of Kant's transcendental attitude, in spite of the fact that he repudiated Kantian metaphysics as misguided and retrograde. The reason for both stands is that he read Kant (in the *Critique of Pure Reason*) as an incipient phenomenologist who *finally* retreats from existential priorities to the arbitrarily detached priorities of the categories of the understanding (and, thus, to various unwelcome paradoxes involving noumena). What is important here, apart from the dialectical appraisal of Kant's own program, is the insuperable informality of Heidegger's transcendentalism, which has itself occasioned a spirited debate as to whether Heidegger is rightly thought to be a transcendentalist at all.[7] The matter also bears on the complete implausibility of Mark Okrent's account of Heidegger's pragmatism.[8] Okrent developed a different account from Rorty's: apparently Okrent's is still the most sustained attempt to establish Heidegger's pragmatism that we have to date. But Okrent is remarkably inattentive to the main themes of Dewey's pragmatism—is in fact terribly insouciant about any pertinent pragmatist's appraisal of such themes as Heidegger's version of transcendentalism, the subjectivist grounds of objective science, verificationism's being subjectivistic *au fond*, and of course *Dasein*'s not being able to be captured naturalistically. These themes deserve a fuller inning, but I cannot spare the space here.

Rorty's comparisons between Dewey and Heidegger begin remarkably early, when you consider that, by the late 1940s and early 1950s, pragmatism seemed to be slipping into a terminal coma. Heidegger, who remained of course the uncontested master of continental philosophy through at least the third quarter of the last century, regularly excoriated American pragmatism as an especially transparent and virulent expression of the barbarism that linked American material culture with the evils of Bolshevism—which, whatever its own "shortcomings," an idealized Nazism sought to defeat! Viewed against *this* history, Rorty's recuperation of Heidegger and Dewey as intellectual mates who, between them, all but invent Rorty's own postmodernism could hardly be more startling or improbable. Rorty is a pragmatist (it seems) because he's followed Dewey and Heidegger and because *they* are pragmatists; but then, *they* are also postmodernists because *he* is a postmodernist, and he has followed them as pragmatists!

Beyond Rorty's gymnastic maneuver, pragmatism's new inning demands a clear sense of what conceptual grounds *it* might, and ought to, attempt to command under the altered circumstances of the turn of the millennium. Heidegger's program seems wildly alien and Rorty's intervention mischievous to a fault. But Rorty's challenge was laid down at a particularly strategic moment. Pragmatism had in any case to examine its then-present needs and dialectical prospects if it was to survive, so that it hardly mattered whether, in appraising Heidegger's and Rorty's (and related) resources, pragmatism finally dismissed the false promise of those new forces: it had to find its new bearings in the middle of that contest.

Rorty commits his philosophical energies to the task of rendering as legible as possible the avant-garde import of the greater "pragmatism" he claims joins Dewey's optimism and Heidegger's drastic conceptual surgery; he views all of this favorably within the terms of his own skeptical rejection of Western philosophy and his enthusiasm for political whiggery, by which I mean an inclination to rebellion within the liberties afforded by a comfortable status quo. (By now, Rorty's rebellion is all but discounted.)

Rorty is probably the earliest postwar figure of importance to attempt this sort of confrontational rereading of two great strands of Eurocentric philosophy: to intend (in doing that) to fill an intellectual void and to ride roughshod over the carefully defined distinctions of an earlier history. Later discussions, for instance those of Hubert Dreyfus and Mark Okrent, tend to be textually more responsible, though not nearly as daring; they are not, for that reason, always accurate or easy to defend, and we cannot read them now except as responding to Rorty's earlier sallies. In short, Rorty has set the main lines of the debate—both the outrageous challenges and the reasons for introducing them at all.

If you allow this way of approaching the comparison between Dewey and Heidegger, you must concede as well that the question is not likely to be confined to textual matters. The interpretation of what to mean by "pragmatism," "transcendental argument," "subjectivism," "intentionality," "mentalism," "metaphysics," "temporality," and the like is bound to be hostage to the partisan arguments actually advanced, so that it's entirely likely that Heidegger *was* a pragmatist *if* you allow Rorty or Okrent to define the term. But if you refuse their definitions (for ample cause), it's just as likely he was not! Also, Rorty and Okrent hold opposed views of what pragmatism entails—and what Heidegger's "pragmatism" requires. Philosophical disputes often proceed this way: a countermeasure must be judged dialectically. Since, however, I discount Rorty's "postmodernism" vis-à-vis Dewey and Heidegger, I read the *agon* in a way that might allow us to assess the larger prospects of Eurocentric philosophy. The limitations and amplitude of naturalism present the obvious touchstone.

Rorty reads Dewey as a kind of lesser Heideggerean: he assumes that the Heidegger he has in mind *is* a superior pragmatist (which I believe is not only false but demonstrably impossible); he assumes that the metaphysical innovations Dewey had in mind *are* really weaker intuitions of what Heidegger had in mind (which is also false and also impossible);[9] *and* he assumes that what he sees as common ground between them *is* simply the "pragmatist" cast of what *they share with him*—another great extravagance. Heidegger's "superiority" refers to Rorty's own postmodernism, which is simply a fiction; Heidegger's deeper critique of philosophy separates him from the pragmatists, since, perhaps because of his indebtedness to Husserl, he favors an idiosyncratic version of transcendentalism, which Dewey would have shunned. Accordingly, Rorty discounts Okrent's reading of Heidegger's pragmatism, since it's cast in more conventional epistemological terms.[10]

Let me remind you, therefore, of one of Rorty's remarks about the point of comparing Heidegger and Dewey: "In what follows, [he says,] I propose to offer sketches of Dewey as he would presumably look to Heidegger and of Heidegger as he would presumably look to Dewey. This exercise will show how an extraordinary amount of agreement on the need for a 'destruction of the history of Western ontology' can be combined with an utterly different notion of what might succeed 'ontology.' It will, I hope, give us some ground on which to stand when trying to 'place' Heidegger, by giving us a sense of how much room is left for maneuver even after one comes to see the philosophical tradition as having exhausted its potentialities."[11]

This is already a large distortion. Rorty plainly means that Dewey and Heidegger were pragmatists in virtue of their being "postmodernists" *avant la lettre*, regardless of their respective views about what should replace "ontology." Heidegger "replaced" metaphysics (Kantian metaphysics) by "ontology" (his own obsession with the "meaning of Being"), by which he meant to undercut the assured objective standing of all determinate categorial systems in Kant's sense; but he did not mean to "replace" ontology as well: as I say, he meant, rather, to abandon the transcendentalist pretensions of any assuredly realist metaphysics, and he meant to strengthen the provisionality of the imputed structures of things characterized in terms of *Dasein*'s passing interests, by emphasizing the *Ereignis* of the disclosedness of Being. Here, there is a genuine comparison with Dewey to be made out, but it cannot strengthen the pragmatist reading of Heidegger: it suggests, rather, the excessive zeal of Heidegger's own extranaturalism.

The compelling evidence stares you in the face: there is no trace of any specifically pragmatist inquiry into the "meaning of Being" that could be shown to fit Heidegger's reflections on his own absorbing question; on the contrary, any such effort would have been instantly dismissed as a sign of our having lost our way completely. Here, the suggestion that Heidegger was drawn increasingly to East Asian themes seems very plausible, though there's also evidence that he avoided naming the sources of his growing interest. In any event, the idea confirms the improbability of Rorty's thesis.

Rorty's account is one of the cleverest false clues we could possibly reclaim from late-twentieth-century philosophy: it's meant to disallow any rapprochement other than a postmodernist's. Also, it's never clear (in Rorty, as in Heidegger) *what* the great "error" is that Heidegger traces from Plato and Aristotle, through Kant and Friedrich Nietzsche, down to its late "oblivion" in pragmatism and modern science and technology, or, for that matter, *what*, precisely, Heidegger's correction comes to. It would be more than difficult to explain Heidegger's treatment of Parmenides if he meant by the question of the meaning of Being anything resembling Dewey's opposition to essentialism and substantive necessity; and if he did mean anything akin to Dewey's view, he would not have needed anything as portentous as the pronouncement on Plato's betrayal of Being—he would surely have been able to interpret our descriptive vocabularies more informally than is usual (as Dewey himself does, in *Experience and Nature*), as less than a validated universal metaphysics in anything like the sense Kant favors. To oppose Rorty this way may appear to slight a genuine contribution, but it need not: it returns us, instead, to the essential comparison between Heidegger and Dewey—in the context of following the interlocking debate among analytic, pragmatist, and continental philosophies.[12] There's the steadier concern.

The phrase "exhausted its potentialities" does indeed capture Rorty's excuse and rationale for what he variously calls "postmodernism," "metaphilosophy," and, of course, "pragmatism." Philosophy's "exhaustion" is the seeming common ground he abstracts from Heidegger and Dewey before they go their separate ways. But if you read what Rorty says about the "nature" of philosophy itself in the introduction to the third volume of his *Philosophical Papers*, which fixes the sense of the divergence between Anglo-American and continental philosophy noted in the passage just cited, you will find that the would-be discovery (the "exhaustion") is no more than an exaggeration of the reasonableness of relativizing, historicizing, pluralizing, provisionalizing—pragmatizing—philosophy's own work (against the stubbornness of the latest "absolutists").[13] If you see that, you are bound to see as well that Rorty takes back the entire extravagance he's launched.

Heidegger, I suggest, is an absolutist of the most attenuated and paradoxical sort: Heidegger poses the unconditional concern for Being as the most distinctive mark of *Dasein* and then permits the question to dissolve into the vacuity of the *Ereignis* of Being out of what can only be called the Void! It might have been promising to argue that Heidegger's own emphasis on such "existentialia" as *In-der-Welt-sein*, *Mitsein*, *Fürsorge*, and the like ultimately signify no more than a sense of *Dasein*'s "ecology" and primary concerns: hence, by swallowing a large dollop of conceptual laxity, we might be persuaded to think of the affinity between Dewey and Heidegger as essentially pragmatist in intent. But it's closer to the truth to say that their paths only appear to converge. Certainly, Heidegger's existential "ecology" has no connection with any Darwinian match at all.[14]

There is no exhaustion looming, no projected "destruction" of metaphysics that the academy anticipates. That is Rorty's pipe dream, which he claims for his own "pragmatism" *and* pragmatism in general and which he happily assigns to Dewey and Heidegger without the least sign that they would ever have accepted the compliment. "It is easier," Rorty says, "to think of [*Experience and Nature,* Dewey's "principal work on metaphysics,"] as an explanation of why nobody needs a metaphysics, rather than as itself a metaphysical system."[15] Well, yes and no—*if* you confine "metaphysics" to the traditional doctrines Dewey thought were bankrupt but could be bettered, or if (with Dewey) you worry that the continued use of the term "metaphysics" may encourage us to fall back to the tired habits of mind Dewey wished to replace, or if you feared that the term "system" signified Kantian-like resources no pragmatist would ever admit. There is nothing in Dewey's labors to support Rorty's subversive verdict.

Notes

1. I refer here to Richard Rorty, "Overcoming the Tradition: Heidegger and Dewey," *Consequences of Pragmatism (Essays: 1972–1980)* (Minneapolis: University of Minnesota Press, 1982). The essay was first published in 1976.

2. I offer a running analysis of the "revival" for which Rorty and Hilary Putnam were responsible in my *Reinventing Pragmatism: American Philosophy at the End of the Twentieth Century* (Ithaca: Cornell University Press, 2002).

3. See, for instance, Reinhard May, *Heidegger's Hidden Sources: East Asian Influences on His Work,* trans. Graham Parkes (London: Routledge, 1996).

4. Here, I have used the translations in Martin Heidegger, *Being and Time,* trans. Joan Stambaugh (Albany: SUNY Press, 1996). Quotes are from pp. 53–54 and 229. I shall use Stambaugh's translation unless otherwise indicated. For a telling impression of Heidegger's philosophical informality, see Stanley Rosen, "Remarks on Heidegger's Plato," in *Heidegger and Plato: Toward Dialogue*, ed. Catalin Partenie and Tom Rockmore (Evanston: Northwestern University Press, 2005). For a sustained sense of Rosen's more fundamental themes, see his *Direction of Being: A Reversal of Heidegger* (South Bend: St. Augustine's Press, 2002). See, further, Heidegger, *Being and Time,* §§7–9.

5. Heidegger, *Being and Time*, 55.

6. For a quick sense of how the claim might be reasonably supported, see Joseph Rouse, "Heidegger on Science and Naturalism," in *Continental Philosophy of Science*, ed. Gary Gutting (Oxford: Blackwell, 2005).

7. On Peirce's fallibilism, which is very distinctly related to Kant's "transcendental truth" shorn of every form of transcendentalism, see my "Rethinking Peirce's Fallibilism," *Transaction of the Charles S. Peirce Society* 43 (2007). On Heidegger's account of Kant, see Béatrice Han-Pile, "Early Heidegger's Appropriation of Kant," in *A Companion to Heidegger*, ed. Hubert L. Dreyfus and Mark A. Wrathall (Oxford: Blackwell, 2005); and Martin Heidegger, *Kant and the Problem of Metaphysics*, trans. R. Taft (Bloomington: Indiana University Press, 1997).

8. See Mark Okrent, *Heidegger's Pragmatism: Understanding, Being, and the Critique of Metaphysics* (Ithaca: Cornell University Press, 1988).

9. On my reading, the quickest way to capture the themes Rorty selects in his comparison between Heidegger and Dewey can be gotten by reading Martin Heidegger, "The Age of the World Picture" (1928), in *The Question Concerning Technology and Other Essays*, trans. William Lovitt (New York: Harper and Row, 1977); and "The End of Philosophy and the Task of Thinking" (1966, 1969), trans. Joan Stambaugh, in *Basic Writings*, ed. David Farrell Krell (New York: Harper and Row, 1977). These are not the papers Rorty favors in his "Overcoming the Tradition," but they collect in an economical way the main thrust of the interval in question. The text by Dewey that Rorty has in mind is of course John Dewey, *Experience and Nature*, 2nd ed. (New York: Dover, 1958 [1929]).

10. For an instructive overview, see Sandra B. Rosenthal, *Time, Continuity, and Indeterminacy: A Pragmatic Engagement with Contemporary Perspectives* (Albany: SUNY Press, 2000), chap. 3.

11. Rorty, "Overcoming the Tradition," 42.

12. I have tried to collect a fair bit of what is needed in ampler detail in my *Reinventing Pragmatism* and in *The Unraveling of Scientism: American Philosophy at the End of the Twentieth Century* (Ithaca: Cornell University Press, 2003). I pursue the issue again in my *Pragmatism's Advantage: American and European Philosophy at the End of the Twentieth Century* (Stanford: Stanford University Press, 2010).

13. Richard Rorty, *Truth and Progress*, vol. 3 of *Philosophical Papers* (Cambridge: Cambridge University Press, 1998).

14. Compare Frederick A. Olafson, *Heidegger and the Ground of Ethics: A Study of Mitsein* (Cambridge: Cambridge University Press, 1998).

15. Richard Rorty, "Dewey's Metaphysics," in *Consequences of Pragmatism*, 72. It is precisely this motivation—which seems to have annoyed Donald Davidson—that colors Rorty's discussion of truth. See Richard Rorty, "Pragmatism, Davidson and Truth," in *Truth and Interpretation: Perspectives on the Philosophy of Donald Davidson*, ed. Ernest Lepore (Oxford: Basil Blackwell, 1986).

7] Science, Nature, and Philosophic Foundations: Dewey and Heidegger

Sandra B. Rosenthal

The reality of the perceived world as well as our mode of access to it has posed problems for philosophy since the rise of modern science, for the modern scientific view of nature gave rise to a reductionism that questioned the objective independent existence of many of the features or qualities of our ordinary experience. This resulted in the tradition of consciousness and object in which a subjective consciousness with its sensory contents was set over against an objective world of scientific properties. The problem then became one of how, or if, knowledge of a world external to mind is possible. On the one hand, the Cartesian answer was a grasp by reason of the features of the world as described by science. On the other hand, this problematic set the stage for the traditional line of empiricism moving from John Locke to George Berkeley and then to David Hume, which incorporated with Locke a causal theory of perception and the separation of primary and secondary qualities, with Berkeley an idealism in which all is reduced to contents of mind, and with Hume a pure phenomenalism and skepticism in which belief in the external world is unjustifiably built up from the association of atomic sensory phenomena. In contemporary philosophy, the debate concerning realism versus phenomenalism, or realism versus idealism, or objectivism versus subjectivism, is to be found, in more updated garb, in the realist-antirealist debate, and it relates as well to the issues of objectivism versus relativism and foundationalism versus antifoundationalism. The positions of John Dewey and Martin Heidegger alike, within their respective frameworks of pragmatism and existential phenomenology, offer a unique approach that undercuts the either-ors of these various alternatives and leads to a more viable understanding of the nature of, and relation between, the abstract claims of science, the deliverances of everyday perceptual awareness, and the speculative claims of metaphysics. Both positions are in agreement with the claims of contemporary postmodernists such as Richard Rorty and Jacques Derrida that our awareness cannot mirror an independent reality and also that our awareness is symbolic in nature; yet Dewey and Heidegger alike definitively reject their claims that as a result we are denied any access to a "hard" independent reality and are instead confined to self-contained conversation or the play of *différance*. Conversely, while agreeing with those who hold that there is an independent reality that enters into our perception, their respective positions deny that this can in any way provide us with a picture of what reality is like independent of our interactions with it. Both avoid the pitfalls of either extreme by turning to human behavior in its primordial, prereflective active engagement with and openness onto a thick natural universe as the holistic context within which the perceived world arises. In undercutting the subject-object split that set the problems of the modern period and focusing on the holistic dimensions of the perceived world, Dewey's position is similar to Heidegger's, but unlike Heidegger he stresses the independent dimension of the perceived world, roots its emergence within perceptual awareness in the dynamics of scientific or experimental method embodied in human behavior, and emphasizes the human as biological organism. It is with the dynamics of scientific or experimental method that the ensuing discussion will first turn.

This may seem like an unlikely way to begin an exploration of the common contours carved within the diverse frameworks of the two philosophers, for the linkage of Dewey's pragmatic position with the method of science as the model for understanding the nature of knowledge has been a key factor in the historical tendency to interpret pragmatism as a type of naturalistic reductionism, which gives an empirical or natural or causal account of cognition based on the findings of science. Given this script, pragmatism becomes the natural enemy of phenomenology, for phenomenology emphatically reacts against these reductionistic tendencies in order to focus on an irreducible field of meanings by which humans constitute their world and on the irreducibility of the qualitative fullness of primary or everyday experience. Indeed, the dominance of reductivistic metaphysics based on the findings of science is directly linked, for Heidegger, with the "blindness and arbitrariness . . . of what is known under the heading 'pragmatism.'"[1]

The tendency to conflate Dewey's focus on scientific method with one or another of the various scientific reductionisms rejected by phenomenology is probably nurtured by the general fact that the method of gaining knowledge that was the backbone of the emergence of modern science was confounded with the results of the first "lasting" modern scientific view—the Newtonian mechanistic universe. An illicit reification of scientific content, resulting from an inadequate understanding of scientific method, led to a worldview that gave rise to a quantitatively characterized natural universe and to either dualistic causal accounts of knowledge in terms of correlations between mental contents and material objects or reductionist accounts in terms of stimulus response, with the complete rejection of mentalistic terms. Heidegger's rejection of the "natural attitude," with its illicit reifications of the objects of science, is in fact a rejection of all remnants of modern worldview frameworks and their evolving variations. However, implicit in Heidegger's criticism of pragmatism is that same conflation of scientific method and scientific content that has plagued the philosophical tradition in one way or another since the rise of modern science but that Dewey emphatically rejects. The radical rejection by Dewey of this conflation, a rejection unrecognized by Heidegger, allows the pragmatic focus on science as method to provide the foundation for Dewey's own criticism, similar to Heidegger's, of the modern worldview understanding of science and its various related frameworks. Thus, while a misunderstanding of the nature of the linkage of his position with scientific method has been a crucial factor in the historical philosophical alienation of the philosophies of Dewey and Heidegger, the clarification of this linkage can provide a key pathway to the exploration of their affinities, helping to illuminate and enrich the significance of their respective attempts to understand, and to establish the proper relation between, abstract thought and concrete experience. It will be seen that Dewey's understanding of scientific method[2] as the model for understanding the dynamics of experience requires a return to the foundations of the everyday world in concrete human existence, the basic features of which are similar to those characterized by Heidegger, while Heidegger's phenomenological account of these foundations incorporates his own understanding, similar to that of pragmatism, of the dynamics of scientific method. The ensuing discussion will first turn to the similar dynamics of scientific method as found in pragmatism and in Heidegger's philosophy and then show how these dynamics reflect and help illuminate the foundational level of experience within which they are rooted.

For Dewey, the beginning phase of scientific method, not as a formalized deductive model, not as a metaphysical enterprise illicitly reifying supposed ultimate truths, not as a causal analysis of humans and their environment but as lived experimental activity, exemplifies human creativity.[3] Such scientific creativity arises out of the matrix of ordinary experience and in turn refers back to this everyday experience. The objects of systematic scientific creativity gain their fullness of meaning from the matrix of ordinary experience. Though the contents of an abstract scientific theory may be far removed from the qualitative aspects of everyday experience, such contents are not the found structures of some "ultimate reality of nature" but rather the possibility of their coming to be as objects of scientific knowledge arise within the context of qualitative experience. As Dewey states, the refined products of scientific inquiry "inherit their full content of meaning within the context of actual experience."[4] This creativity implies a rejection of the "passive-spectator" view of knowledge and an introduction of the active, creative agent, who, through meanings, helps structure objects of knowledge and who cannot be separated from the world in which such objects emerge. Dewey expresses this noetic creativity in science in his claim that "what is known is seen to be a product in which the act of observation plays a necessary role. Knowing is seen to be a participant in what is finally known."[5] As he concludes, both perception and the meaningful backdrop within which it occurs are shot through with the interactional unity between knower and known. Without such a unity, there is no scientific world and there are no scientific objects. Such a creative noetic structuring of a world brings objects into an organizational focus from an indeterminate background and, as constitutive of meanings as dispositional modes of response, yields purposive, teleological, or goal-oriented activity. The system of meanings both sets the context for activity and rigorously limits the direction any activity takes, for such meaning structures are constituted by possibilities of acting toward a world.

In similar fashion, Heidegger holds that the emergence of the scientific object requires what he calls a "working over" of the things in everyday experience, changing them to objects that are decontextualized from the involvements of the everyday world. The abstract objects of science that emerge from the operations of the scientist, operations that work over the concrete things of everyday experience, are not ontologically independent beings but are dependent upon the everyday world of involvements from which they emerge through the creative activity of the scientist.[6] The creative opening of a scientific world, of a region, of a horizon within which a particular type of object can appear is the fundamental event in research.[7] Thus, the projection of a scientific world determines the type of operations that can be used to yield objects within it. It determines the way in which the things of everyday experience are changed to yield the objects that conform to the possibilities allowed within the scientific world.[8] Projection provides the background from which specific types of possibilities emerge and within which particular types of objects can appear. This fundamental event in scientific research secures itself by proceeding rigorously according to its projected possibilities.[9]

Dewey holds that the adequacy of meaning structures in grasping what is there, or in allowing what is there to reveal itself in a significant way, must be tested by consequences in experience. Only if the experiences anticipated by the possibilities of experience contained within the meaning structures are progressively fulfilled—though of course never completely and finally fulfilled—can truth be claimed for the assertions made. Initial feelings of assurance, initial insights, initial common assent, or any other origins of a theory do not determine its truth. Rather, to be counted as true, a claim must stand the test of the anticipated unfolding of experience. Such unfolding of experience in conformity with projected anticipations represents a self-corrective rather than a building-block model of knowledge. The meaning organizations or rules governing the organization of experiences are judged by their ability to turn a potentially indeterminate situation into a resolved or meaningfully experienced one. Heidegger's understanding of methodology as an essential characteristic of research houses Dewey's position here.[10] As Heidegger elaborates on methodology, projection and the rigor it entails can develop as they do because of the characteristic of science that involves rule, law, explanation, and experiment, the various aspects of methodology. Rule and law bring objects into an organizational focus from a background of indeterminate change. "Only within the horizon of the incessant-otherness of change does the plentitude of particularity—of facts—show itself. But the facts must become objective. Hence procedure must represent the changeable in its changing, must bring it to a stand and let the motion be a motion nevertheless."[11] A sphere of objects comes into representation through the establishing and verifying of rule and law. Experiment becomes possible with the laying down of rule and law as a basis, and explanation develops through experimentation. Explanation has a twofold function. "It accounts for an unknown by means of a known, and at the same time it verifies that known by means of that unknown."[12] Further, included in such self-corrective activity is a drive to open up further possibilities for research.[13] Indeed, Heidegger holds that scientific activity becomes "mere business" if it does not constantly remain aware of and open to change of its own projection plan but rather takes its projection plan as an unquestioned given. Science must be continually vigilant against lapsing into mere business, because the essence of scientific research for Heidegger is ongoing activity, and the essential nature of this ongoing activity incorporates the ongoing confirmation or verification of the adequacy of the framework for its accumulated calculation of results.[14]

Thus, the essential features of scientific method, as pure method, involve for both pragmatism and Heidegger the creative opening up in advance of a domain in which only things of a certain kind can show themselves. This world or clearing provides the context within which specific types of possibilities emerge as "there" for our consideration. Only from this backdrop can the scientific endeavor determine which possibilities to utilize as it turns an indeterminate matrix into a realm of meaningful objects. Only through the opening of a world of a particular type can the purposive activity of the scientist proceed rigorously according to projected possibilities, testing explanations by their continuing ability to bring an indeterminate matrix into a network of meaningful objects through rule-guided activity. Finally, scientific method, as self-corrective, ongoing activity, not only collects workable results within its present structure but also should reexamine the justification for the specific possibilities it has chosen for meaningful organization within the world of possibilities it has opened up through its initial projection. Neither Heidegger nor Dewey characterized this latter aspect of ongoing activity as following clearly laid down procedures but rather tended to view it as involving a non-thematic, unarticulated grasp of the way to progress.

In light of this model of scientific method as pure method devoid of any particular type of content, the ensuing discussion will turn to the context of the dynamics of everyday experience in pragmatism and in the philosophy of Heidegger to see what clarifying light this method has to offer. The role of the function of scientific method in understanding everyday experience is evinced by Dewey in several brief but telling remarks. As Dewey observes, awareness, even in its most primordial state, "represents a general trend of scientific inquiry." It means things entering, via directed activity, into a condition of "differential—or additive—change."[15] Or, as he summarizes, "There is no difference in kind between the methods of science and those of the plain man."[16] Dewey's use of the model of scientific activity is in no way an attempt to assert that perceptual experience is really a highly intellectual affair. Rather, the opposite is more the case. Scientific objects are highly sophisticated and intellectualized ways of dealing with experience at a second level, but they are not the product of any isolated intellect. Rather, the total concrete human way of being is involved in the very ordering of any level of awareness, and scientific knowledge partakes of the character of even the most rudimentary aspects by which a world of things emerges within experience. Further, the scientific purpose of manipulation of the environment, and its use of scientific concepts as instruments of such manipulative control, are not technological maneuvers into which human activity is to be absorbed. Rather, again, the opposite is more the case. All activity constitutive of the human way of being, even at its most rudimentary level, is activity guided by direction in light of anticipatory rules that are meaningfully transformative of its environment. At more primordial levels of experience, such rules need not be, in fact are not, explicit or thematic but rather are implicit in the anticipatory nature of the dynamic tendencies or potentialities and possibilities constitutive of the human way of being. Indeed, it was noted earlier that even at the level of scientific knowing, there is an element of unthematic activity. The things of the everyday world, like the objects of science, are unified in terms of their function, not in terms of some underlying essence,[17] and the abstractly manipulative and instrumental purposes attributed to science have their roots at the foundation of the very possibility of human experience in general. All experience incorporates the dynamics of scientific method, not in the sense that it is guided by sophisticated levels of thought but in the sense that the very process that constitutes humans as dynamically developing, both in their way of knowing and their way of being, embodies the features revealed in the examination of scientific method. Scientific endeavor is a more explicit embodiment of the dynamics operative at all levels of experience, and hence the ingredients are easier to distinguish. The pursuit of scientific knowledge, according to Dewey, is an endeavor throughout which are writ large the essential characters of any knowing, and it partakes of the character of even the most rudimentary ways in which human activity involves temporally extended anticipations of future experience to come.

In turning to Heidegger's philosophy, it will be seen, in a similar way, that the difference between the levels of science and the everyday world of active engagement represents not a difference in method but a difference in type of content emerging from a common method. The lived world grounds the possibility of any scientific world. But the explicit, "enlarged version" of the dynamics of experience that emerges in understanding the method of science can in turn help clarify the method by which all contents of awareness emerge in their meaningfulness.

The previous discussion of Heidegger's understanding of scientific method showed that the abstract objects of a particular physical science are revealed in their technical physical structure to a person who is trained in that science, to a person who is operating according to that projection as the opening up of the possibilities of what kind of objects can appear in that physical world, to a person whose purposive activities proceed rigorously according to its laws and rules. For Heidegger, this projective activity of the scientist as scientist is similar to the projective activity of the ontological constitution of the human as human. What differs in science is the nature of the content that its projection allows to emerge, its level of abstraction from,[18] and the degree to which it is "freed" from, the concreteness of everyday experience. For Heidegger, the human being-in-the-world is the clearing where beings can be disclosed and appear as meaningful. The horizon for a certain kind of experience must be projected in advance, must be opened up, before that kind of experience can take place. The objects of science do not disclose some underlying essence. Rather, they are "there" because of their function in a projected world, and this projected world of science can be there only because it and its objects are grounded in the everyday world. This everyday world is in turn grounded in the structural process of the human way of being as being-in-the-world, and within this everyday world the unities of things that emerge into presence lie analogously, for Heidegger, in their functionality, not in some underlying essence.[19] Any interpretive explanation is the development of the possibilities "there" because of an original projection. This original projection opens a realm within which possibilities emerge for consideration as possibilities to be seized upon. Even the most primordial grasp is not a presuppositionless apprehending of something that reveals itself, for the meaning of things is constituted and receives its significant structure from our fore-having, foresight, and fore-conception.[20] Such interpretation may be implicit and concrete in our everyday concernful engagement with things in the world, or explicit and abstract in the scientific grasp of its world of objects. Each manner involves an interpretation of what it is to be, but with the level of science, "what it is to be" results from contents emerging through a narrowing, abstractive projection. In pointing out the blindness of science in mistaking its content as the "absolutely there" for the human as spectator, thus ignoring its world as the meaningful horizon emerging from its own world-founding activity, Heidegger in fact provides an "enlarged explicit" version of the way in which everyday being-in-the-world tends to be oblivious to world as the meaningful horizon and to world-founding as the structure of the human way of being. Thus Heidegger can aptly point out that "where the danger is as the danger, there the saving power is already thriving also."[21]

In retrospect, it should not be surprising that the diverse approaches of Dewey and Heidegger should arrive at a common vantage point. If, as phenomenology holds, there is really a pervasive structure to all knowing, and any one instance can become the initial focal point for the interpretive descriptions that yield its pervasive features, then pragmatism can well begin with the dynamics of scientific knowing as an instance to be analyzed for its pervasive features and, with it as a model, proceed to understand the dynamics of concrete human existence. Conversely, if Dewey was correct in his understanding of the method of science as yielding the pervasive features of all knowing, then such primordial knowing embedded in the dynamics of concrete human existence, as depicted by the descriptive interpretations of phenomenology, should include those features derived from the characteristics of scientific activity. This convergence, from the diverse focal points of Dewey and Heidegger, toward a common understanding of the dynamics of concrete human existence, provides the basis for their common critique of a modern era dominated by the findings of a scientific enterprise that, oblivious to the significance of its method, lost sight of its own foundations. As indicated above, just as science has lost sight of the method by which it obtains its world of objects and, with it, its own foundations as founded in the richer matrix of concrete human existence, the same thing can be said of our everyday world of lived experience for, oblivious to the similar method operative there, we have lost sight of its own foundations in the richer concreteness of a thick, dense reality. The richer context that provides the foundation for our everyday perceptual world can be approached by turning to Dewey's focus on humans as biological organisms.

Dewey's position is a naturalism in that humans are within nature, but it has been seen that this nature cannot be understood as the mechanistic universe of the Newtonian worldview. Rather, the nature into which the human is placed within the pragmatic focus on scientific method contains the qualitative fullness revealed in ordinary experience, and the human grasp of nature within the world is permeated with the irreducible meaning structures by which humans and their world are bound.[22] Only through meanings does that from which humans have arisen reveal itself to them. Such meanings are characterized in terms of possibilities of experience rooted in habits of response. Unfortunately, Dewey's focus on the biological context of meaning as habit, like his focus on experimental method, has tended to lead to far-reaching misinterpretations of the position intended. Dewey's focus on the biological is far removed from the "biologism" that reduces the human to lower levels of existence and to which Heidegger so strongly objected. Dewey's focus on the biological, in its richness, does not lie in opposition to a view of human awareness constitutive of the world that is there as the horizon of meaningful encounter, but rather, when properly understood, it reveals the purposive activity out of which awareness of meanings emerges. For Dewey, the irreducibly meaningful behavior of the human organism in interaction with its natural environment is the foundation of the noetic unity by which humans are bound to their world. Human behavior is meaningful behavior, and it is in behavior that meaning is rooted. There is an inseparable relationship between the human biological organism bound to a natural environment and the perceiver who constitutes a world. There is an interactional unity at a primordial behavioral level that is the context from which a unity at the conscious level emerges. From the context of organic activity and behavioral environment there emerge irreducible meanings that allow objects to come to conscious awareness. Such meanings are irreducible to physical causal conditions or to psychological acts and processes; yet they emerge from the biological, when the biological is properly understood,[23] for the content of human perception is inseparable from the structure of human behavior within its natural setting. Thus, Dewey emphasized that meanings can be expressed both in terms of the ongoing conduct of the biological organism immersed in a natural universe and in terms of the phenomenological description of what appears.[24]

One of the most distinctive and most crucial aspects of Dewey's position is its understanding of experience as a rich ongoing interactional or transactional unity between organism and environment, and only within the context of meanings that incorporate such an interactional unity does what is given emerge for conscious awareness. Such a transactional unity is more than a postulate of abstract thought, for it has experiential dimensions. The interactive ontological unity of organism-environment transaction is reflected in the phenomenologically grasped features of experience. That which intrudes itself inexplicably into experience is not bare datum but rather evidences itself as the over-againstness of a thick reality there for my activity. This thick, ontological interactional unity at the heart of experience is well expressed in his claim that "experience is *of* as well as *in* nature. . . . Things interacting in certain ways *are* experience, they are *what* is experienced. Linked in certain other ways with another natural object—the human organism—they are *how* things are experienced as well." For Dewey, "experience reaches down into nature; it has depth."[25] There is a two-directional openness in experience, such that the pervasive features of experience reflect both the structure of our noetic activity and pervasive features of the independently real. The two-directional openness of experience leads from one pole to the other, from a phenomenology of worldly experience with its temporal dynamics toward a process metaphysics. The temporal structure that belongs to our interpretive processes belongs as well to a universe within which they emerge. Human habits of response, which are for the pragmatist the living embodiment of meaning, are precisely "ontologically thick" dynamic tendencies structuring emerging activities in the context of alternative possibilities for ongoing actualization. The role of human constitutive activity in transforming an indefinitely rich processive, "independently there" matrix into structured things unified in terms of their function within a world is succinctly indicated in Dewey's claim that "structure is constancy of means, of things used for consequences, not of things taken by themselves absolutely."[26] Further, the "isolation of structure from the changes whose stable ordering it is, renders it mysterious—something that is metaphysical in the popular sense of the word, a kind of ghostly queerness."[27] In true pragmatic fashion, its indefinite richness is characterized by Dewey in terms of activity or process.[28] It is this indefinitely rich processive nature that emerges into the structured natural environment of our everyday worldly experience through active interest or intent. The path to the fullness of reality in its indefinite richness for Dewey is not conceptual clarity but a primal attunement to the pulse of existence. This access is represented in Dewey's understanding of primordial experience as a processive unity of activity undifferentiated by any thought distinctions.[29] As Dewey puts it, "experience is double-barreled" in that it recognizes in its primary integrity no division between act and material, subject and object, but contains them both in an unanalyzed totality. Or conversely, as he further points out, "'[t]hing' and 'thought,' as [William] James says in the same connection, are single barreled; they refer to products discriminated by reflection out of primary experience."[30] Here it should perhaps be stressed that such a level does not close one within the subjective but represents the matrix of a primordial interactive unity within the richness of an ontological embeddedness.

Dewey's focus on the "felt" level of experience is not intended as subjectivist but rather is an attempt to capture the qualitative immediacy of experience. It is not a psychological category but a primary level of experiencing. This qualitative immediacy is not the atomic quality of a spectator empiricism but rather is the pervasive qualitative character that distinguishes a situation and the objects that emerge within it, which guides perceptual content but which underlies and overflows any perceptual content. It is not a quality *in* a situation but a quality *of* a situation. Thus, Dewey objects that "the 'fringe' of James seems to me to be a somewhat unfortunate way of expressing the role of the underlying qualitative character that constitutes a situation—unfortunate because the metaphor tends to treat it as an additional element instead of an all-pervasive influence in determining other contents."[31] What Dewey intends here can perhaps be expressed by the word "tonality," the "tone of an experience." It is "an all-pervasive influence determining other contents."

In Dewey's rethinking of the human-nature relation in the return to lived experience, three different senses of nature thus come into focus. First, there is nature as that "thick," dense, independently real that is the foundation for all that is and for all the ways of being, including the uniquely human having of a world as the horizon of meaningful activity. Second, there is nature as our worldly environment, as it emerges within the contours of our world, as it emerges as a network of relations of things used in everyday purposive activity. Finally, there is nature as an object of science, which we theoretically abstract from our everyday natural environment as a second-level reflection upon it. Neither the richness of nature as that from which all, including humans, spring, nor the richness of nature as the human everyday worldly environment, can be confounded with or reduced to the abstract character of the events and objects in the world of science. Nature in its indefinite richness is the foundation for our everyday worldly natural environment; nature as a system of scientific events and objects is a reflective abstraction from it. Further, the first sense of nature is not something "other than" the latter two, but rather the latter two are diverse ways in which this nature enters the openness of human horizons of activity. Thus it founds the latter two. Only because independent nature enters into human purposive activity as the everyday worldly environment can nature as the object of the abstractive focus of the scientific endeavor begin to emerge.

Heidegger almost always speaks of nature in the derived, abstract sense of that which is grasped through the focus of science. Yet Heidegger at times refers to nature not in this derived sense but as that which is discovered in the meaningful network of relations that constitutes the environment as our "closest world." He observes that when nature is defined by science, then "the Nature which 'stirs and strives,' which assails us and enthralls us as landscape, remains hidden."[32] Again, he points out that nature as intraworldly, as that which is discovered within the world, can be thought of as scientifically uncovered in a theoretical, physico-chemical way or as the "'nature out there,' hill, woods, meadow, brook, the field of wheat, the call of the birds."[33] In this latter sense, nature reveals itself within the totality of our involvements with what is ready-to-hand, with what serves as "equipment" within the context of everyday purposive activity. It is precisely this meaningful network of everyday involvements that has been stripped off in the narrow view of nature as grasped by the theoretical gaze. Thus, Heidegger characterizes the nature that makes up the object of physics as the "unworlded world," for it has lost the character of the world in which we dwell.[34] There emerges even in the early Heidegger a third sense of nature. Being-in-the-world belongs to the being of the human as human. However, intraworldliness, as what is within the world, belongs to the being of nature "*not* as a determination of its being but as a *possible* determination . . . one that is necessary for the possibility of the uncoverability of nature."[35] Nature is something "extant," that is, has its being independent of the human,[36] though intraworldliness "devolves upon" it when humans exist.[37] As Heidegger succinctly summarizes, "World is only, if, and as long as a Dasein exists. Nature can also be when no Dasein exists."[38] This nature is not "other than" the nature of our everyday worldly environment but is that which becomes our worldly environment as it enters the domain of the human: "World-entry and its occurrence is solely the presupposition for extant things announcing themselves in their not requiring world-entry regarding their own being."[39] Nor is it "other than" the narrow nature of the scientist; rather, it is that which can enter the world of the scientist through a second-level theoretical, abstractive focus founded upon nature's discoveredness in the everyday environment. At this point, it may be held that though nature is extant for Heidegger, this is not relevant to his fundamental ontology as an uncovering of the existential structure of the human or as the disclosedness of being. It will be seen, however, that the embeddedness of humans in nature is as essential to their being and to the understanding of being as is their being-in-the-world. This claim requires that we move from the earlier to the later Heidegger.

The question of the famous turning in Heidegger's thought, and the debate as to whether or not it constitutes a rupture or a continuity between the earlier and later Heidegger, is by now a well-plowed field.[40] The following discussion both presupposes and illuminates the view that there is no rupture but rather a continuity in which each directional stance helps explain and clarify the other. Because Heidegger so strongly reacted against the recurring understanding of an independent nature in terms of the reification of scientific contents, he never referred to nature in any attempt to characterize this broader being process. Nature in this broadest sense, however, as foundational of all that is and all the ways of being, can gain clarity through the interrelated discussion of two concepts introduced by the later Heidegger: the concepts of region and earth. "Region" represents both the openness and activity of being, and he held that the openness of the region that is the ground of the human's opening must, like the human, be understood as active. To bring this active feature into focus, he called it also "that-which-regions" and at times "regioning."[41] That-which-regions is the dynamic ground that brings forth the essential dimensions of the human.[42] As Heidegger stresses, "The question concerning man's nature is not a question about man."[43] What grounds the human way of being, what lets the horizon be, is not something other than horizon, but rather horizon emerges as this ground enters into the disclosive activity of the human. That-which-regions both reveals and conceals. As the side facing us, as horizon, it reveals, but even as it reveals it conceals, for it is not exhausted in its horizontal relation to the human.[44] It can be named and hence thought about, but it cannot be represented "in so far as representing everything has become an object that stands opposite us within a horizon." It cannot be described, for "any description would reify it."[45] Yet, Heidegger does describe it, but he describes it as that which is not itself an object, which cannot be reified into an object, but which, as the ground for the emergence of the human and hence for the emergence of the possibility of its own world entry, has certain characteristics that flow into, are consonant with, the dynamic, temporal structure of humans and the world in which they dwell. This discussion will gain added significance from, and in turn help reveal the import of, Heidegger's concept of earth.

It has been seen that, for Heidegger, to refer to that which is independent of human disclosive activity as nature would be to employ language in a way which furthered the tendency of past philosophy to illicitly ontologize the contents of science as "ultimate reality." Yet in indicating the interplay between world and that "independently there" from which all springs, including the human way of being as being-in-the-world, Heidegger makes brief but revealing use of the concept of earth. As Heidegger stresses, earth is not to be understood as a mass of matter, or as the astronomical idea of a planet.[46] Rather, his characterizations of earth give to this concept the function of that-which-regions. Earth is essentially the "sheltering agent" for all that arises.[47] The world grounds itself on the earth, and earth juts through the world. The earth cannot dispense with the open region of the world if it itself is to appear, to gain world-entry, while the world in turn "cannot soar out of the earth's sight if, as the governing breadth and path of all essential destiny, it is to ground itself on a resolute foundation," for the earth is that "on which and in which man bases his dwelling."[48]

The earth conceals, but concealment "is not simply and only the limit of knowledge in any given circumstance, but the beginning of the lighting of what is lighted."[49] Thus, like "that-which-regions," earth represents, as "the side facing us," the horizon of the openness of world, which even as it reveals it conceals. Heidegger characterizes the relation between world and earth as one of strife. Such an essential strife, however, is not that of disorder or destruction but rather is a relationship in which the "opponents" allow each other to assert themselves in their essential dimensions, yet to assert themselves as belonging intimately to each other.[50] Though Heidegger usually refers to the strife between world and earth, he once alludes to their "counterplay."[51] This characterization seems more appropriate, and perhaps a better word would be "interplay" or, in Dewey's terms, "interaction" or "transaction," for there is a reciprocal interrelation between the two. Earth roots world, and world lights up earth. Further, earth is as essential to man's nature as is world. To be human is to have a world; being human means being in the world. Yet, being human means, also, "to be on the earth as a mortal. It means to dwell."[52] The earth is that on which and in which the dwelling of man is grounded.[53] To dwell on earth does not mean to use it for technological purposes, nor does it mean to recognize, in reflective or detached manner, one's dependence upon it. Rather, to dwell on earth means to experience the natural embeddedness or earthiness of existence as essential to one's being. Just as the essential feature of the human as world-founding has been concealed, is something essential that has fallen into oblivion, so in losing the import of dwelling on earth something essential has fallen into oblivion, "something decisive is concealed," for the earthiness of dwelling "is not experienced as man's being; dwelling is never thought of as the basic character of human being."[54]

For Dewey and Heidegger alike, our embeddedness in nature is as essential to being human as is the projection of a world as the horizon of meaningful encounter with nature. They demand a return to the pre-scientific horizon of lived experience, and it is their contemporary naturalism—explicit in Dewey, implicit in Heidegger—that makes this experience what it is. The primacy of our natural embeddedness is that from which arises both the distinctively human activity of projecting a world as the horizon of meaningful encounter and the need for any world to accommodate the features of this natural embeddedness, be it the world of everyday purposive activity or the derived abstractions of the world of science.

The above discussion has attempted to show that there is a similar threefold sense of nature operative within the philosophies of Dewey and Heidegger. First, there is the nature from which all, including the human way of being, has arisen, a nature that is rich with processive, generative activity but that cannot be given illicitly reified features read off from our everyday world of commonsense things and their interrelations. Nature, as it enters the horizons of human activity, takes on novel and determinate features through its interaction with human interests and intents. The rich matrix of possibilities for discrimination becomes transformed into discriminated things used within a meaningful context. Nature becomes our meaningful natural world. Finally, there is nature as the objectivities of science, which we reflectively and creatively develop as a second-level understanding of this natural worldly environment but which cannot be reified as the ultimate building blocks of reality. Only by getting beneath the false reifications that have plagued the history of science and philosophy can human existence become attuned to the rich textures of its natural embeddedness.

"Is Metaphysics Possible?" is a much-debated question these days. Announcements of the death of metaphysics pour in from commanding figures such as Rorty and Derrida, among others, while opposing camps proclaim that the announcements themselves are fraught with unexamined metaphysical presuppositions. Debate occurs almost as strongly among advocates of the importance of metaphysics. For many who accept some version of traditional metaphysics, the rejection of the possibility of metaphysics "in the grand tradition" signals the rejection of metaphysics itself. Opposing camps adamantly respond that the rejection of metaphysics traditionally understood nonetheless allows for an understanding of metaphysics as an enterprise that, though changed in nature, yet retains its vital function. This new function is itself understood in widely varying ways. The above position contains important insights for contemporary debates concerning the worth of metaphysics or attempts to reconstruct its nature. It opens a pathway toward a reorientation for uniting the insights of traditional speculative philosophy with some of the contemporary recognitions of its limitations. It has been seen that pervasive textures of experience, which are exemplified in every experience, are at the same time indications of the pervasive textures of the independent universe that, in every experience, gives itself for our responses and provides the touchstone for the workability of our meanings. As attempting to describe the independently real, which provides the concrete basis for all experience, the claims of metaphysics must be "guided through" experience toward it by philosophical extrapolation of the pervasive textures of experience, a process that calls for attunement to the most primal interactive unity of humans with the universe in which they are embedded. According to Heidegger, it is this attunement and its releasement that "calls for" the "foundational thinking" of philosophy.[55] Philosophy, which attempts to articulate this foundational level, is rooted in the experience of attunement, and as Heidegger puts it, only on the basis of attunement does language gain "its tuning."[56] The categories of metaphysics are drawn from attunement to the pervasive textures of experience, and the claims of speculative metaphysics emerge as speculative extrapolations from the pervasive features of experience to the character of that which enters into the texture of every experience. There is a vast difference between this and the illicit reification by past metaphysics of the products of reflective abstraction, products that have lost the concrete foundations that ultimately allow for their own development.

The pervasive textures or tones elicited are not postulated from the structure of a theory but vaguely sensed as the experiential roots for any theory. Their articulation is a development growing from within the features of pre-philosophical lived experience, not an imposition from without. This position does not attempt to ignore, change, or distort the reality of these pre philosophical textures of experience in order to make experience fit within the structures of a closed system imposed from above but rather, in reverse fashion, roots its system in them. Thus, it develops open philosophic system or explanatory structure, giving rise to a view of explanation rooted in, rather than distortive of, the pervasive features of primordial experience and to a view of systematic structure rooted in, rather than opposed to, a history of evolving change. The second-level philosophic reflections must be grounded in lived experience and be constantly fed by such experience. Such an open system is explanation rooted in and verified by lived experience, not direct grasp of "being in itself." Though rooted in the lived level, it is never completely adequate to the lived level. It is open to change and development, just as all second-level interpretations are open to change and development. Indeed, it can be said that this understanding of the metaphysical enterprise reflects the ingredients and dynamics, "writ large," of the understanding of experience as experimental and transactional. One can see in the dynamics of metaphysical method an exaggeration of the experimental method by which we have meaningful everyday experience. There is an exaggeration of the metaphorical, imaginative, creative features of the meanings that arise out of past experience and that legislate for the analysis of future experience. As involving metaphor and interpretation in exaggerated form, these metaphysical meanings are more creative, more like weaving a story, but the compulsive ontological element always intrudes and renders some creations, some stories, more workable than others. Thus, there is concurrently an exaggerated attentiveness to what appears in experience, to its pervasive features or textures, to the sense of ourselves as active beings, an attentiveness that both founds the categories and serves to verify their adequacy. For, that to which we attend opens onto the ontological presence with which we are in constant transaction. This transactional, experimental understanding of the nature of metaphysics has important implications for contemporary attempts to "situate" metaphysics in the context of philosophic inquiry.

In assessing the positive value of metaphysics today, the claim is frequently made that metaphysics provides meaningfulness rather than truth and that it is interpretive rather than cognitive. But, truth involves verification, and it has been seen that for Dewey and Heidegger alike, the creative organization of experience in meaningful ways sets the framework for anticipations of possible experience and verification in experience. Until our world is infused with meanings that contain the conditions for the verification of their application in experience, the concept of truth makes no real sense. Thus, the claims of common sense, science, and metaphysics alike provide meaningfulness, a way of orienting oneself to the world, before the issue of truth can emerge. If one does not confine truth to conformity or correspondence to nonperspectival, unchanging, totally structured reality that we merely "find," then meaningful, creative world orientation and truth as workability go hand in hand. Metaphysics is a cognitive enterprise, but cognition at all levels involves noetic creativity. It includes metaphor and imagination, but so does the most rudimentary perceptual awareness. Cognitive experience is by its very nature interpretive. It is indeed concerned to discern meaning, but not meaning rather than fact, for facts themselves emerge within the contours set by the meaning-bestowing activity of abductions or creative interpretations and hence are partially the results of such activity. Such an understanding of the nature of the metaphysical enterprise offers a positive path for the reconstruction of metaphysics that avoids traditional paradigms and the false dichotomies to which they give rise. In this way, it is more contemporary than much of what is contained in contemporary debates. For, much of contemporary metaphysical criticism, though operating within the seemingly novel paradigm of language or within other seemingly novel paradigms radically restrictive of the nature and limits of metaphysical pursuits, has yet not succeeded in breaking with the alternatives offered by, and hence the possible solutions allowable by, a long philosophical tradition. Though the alternative and possible solutions may take distinctively new turns and though seemingly new alternatives and new limitations emerge, they can too often be seen as new paradigmatic twists to old paradigmatic offerings. For, too often the collapse of spectator absolutes, of closed systems, of indubitable foundations, leads to the claims of the demise of metaphysics and a relativistic, anti-foundationalist turn to conversation or to the play of *differance*. To ignore the novel inroad offered by Dewey and Heidegger is not to distance oneself from metaphysical excesses of the past but to lose an important road map for the future.

For both Dewey and Heidegger, then, there is a primal interactive unity of the noetic creativity of humans and an ontological presence that intrudes within experience that provides an indefinitely rich, thick existential foundation for the levels of everyday perceptual awareness, science, and metaphysics alike. This position offers a shattering attack on dualism, reductionism, atomism, and phenomenalism, at the same time undercutting the alternatives of rationalism or traditional empiricism, idealism or traditional realism, foundationalism-antifoundationalism, objectivism-relativism, or realism-antirealism. In their attempt to draw one toward an awareness of the interactive openness, at the heart of experience, of humans and the natural universe in which they are embedded, Dewey and Heidegger alike provide the path for freeing thinking from premature ontological assertions, from illicit reifications, and from a tradition of philosophy that, in its search for supposed foundations, lost the illusive but pervasive existential foundations of its search. If, as they hold, the pulse of human existence at its very core is creatively intertwined with, and thus attuned to, an indeterminately rich processive universe that reveals itself in various ways both within and among various levels and modes of human activity, then attunement to this sense of human existence can yield at once both a more demanding and more tolerant master than any of the diverse second-level articulations to which it gives rise.

Notes

1. Martin Heidegger, *Basic Writings*, ed. David Krell (New York: Harper and Row, 1977), 231.

2. The term "methodology" in science means something more limited for Heidegger than the present use of the term "method." Methodology, as used by Heidegger, will be seen below to indicate one interrelated set of features of scientific method in general.

3. Causal connections are always expressed as relations among particular types of objects or events, and the nature of the events or objects being connected enter into the very understanding of the nature of the causal relationship sustained. This focus on scientific method as the method of causal analysis is thus still not purified of content and represents a lingering influence of modern worldview thought. This brief sketch of the distinction between scientific method and scientific content within Dewey's philosophy, as well as the ensuing discussion of its understanding of scientific method, is examined and supported in some depth in my book *Speculative Pragmatism* (Amherst: University of Massachusetts Press, 1986).

4. John Dewey, *Experience and Nature*, vol. 1 of *The Middle Works of John Dewey, 1899–1924*, ed. Jo Ann Boydston (Carbondale: Southern Illinois University Press, 1976), 37.

5. John Dewey, *The Quest for Certainty*, in *The Later Works of John Dewey, 1925–1953*, ed. Jo Ann Boydston (Carbondale: Southern Illinois University Press, 1984), 4:163–65. Without the opening of a world of a particular type, there are no scientific objects. Martin Heidegger, "The Age of the World Picture," in *The Question Concerning Technology and Other Essays*, trans. William Lovitt (New York: Harper and Row, 1977), 113–54.

6. It is too easy to get entangled with problems of language at this point. Pragmatists tend to refer to the objects of science as a different kind of object than the objects of common sense. Heidegger, however, distinguished between objects and things, reserving "things" for that which comes to presence within primary experience and "objects"

for the content of the abstract focus of science. Even here, however, there is a possible point of confusion. When Heidegger discusses the thing in his most famous work in this area, *What Is a Thing?* (trans. W. Barton and V. Deutsch [Chicago: Regnery Press, 1967]), he is dealing with the Kantian concept of "thing," which corresponds most closely to his own use of "object." This Kantian concept of "thing" is not appropriated by Heidegger in his own use of "thing." (See, for example, Heidegger, "The Thing," in *Poetry, Language, Thought*, trans. A. Hofstadter [New York: Harper and Row, 1971], 161–84, and "The Turning," in *Question Concerning Technology and Other Essays*, 36–50). This essay will not adhere to technical distinctions between the two terms.

7. Heidegger, *Question Concerning Technology and Other Essays*, 118.

8. It is sometimes held that the concept of the scientific object as "decontextualized," found in the early Heidegger, conflicts with the scientific world characterized by the later Heidegger. However, though the objects of science are decontextualized from the everyday world, they are done so in conformity with the possibilities of a projected scientific world. Thus, Heidegger refers to the world of physics as the "unworlded world." Martin Heidegger, *History of the Concept of Time*, trans. Theodore Kisiel (Bloomington: Indiana University Press, 1985), 217–18.

9. Heidegger, "The Age of the World Picture," in *Question Concerning Technology and Other Essays*, 117–20.

10. Ibid., 120–24. It was indicated earlier that Heidegger's use of "methodology" is more limited than "method" as used in this essay. Scientific method, as used in this essay, is best expressed by Heidegger's use of the term "research," which incorporates projection and its related rigor, methodology, and ongoing activity, with each mutually requiring the other.

11. Heidegger, "Age of the World Picture," 120. This is accomplished through rule and law. Rule allows for the "fixedness of facts and the constantness of their change," while "law" provides "the constancy of change in the necessity of its course." Ibid.

12. Ibid., 121.

13. Ibid., 124.

14. Ibid., appendix 2, 138.

15. John Dewey, "Does Reality Possess Practical Character?" in *The Middle Works of John Dewey, 1899–1924*, ed. Jo Ann Boydston (Carbondale: Southern Illinois University Press, 1977), 4:137–38.

16. John Dewey, *Essays in Experimental Logic* (New York: Dover Publications, 1916), 86.

17. For a good analysis of this point, see Dewey's discussion of "the table" in *Quest for Certainty*, 189–90.

18. Here it should be stressed that in speaking of scientific objects as a reflective abstraction from the everyday world of lived experience, or as a narrow view of the theoretical gaze, neither Dewey nor Heidegger intends this to indicate that the objects of science are merely abstracted from everyday experience by leaving aspects of it behind. There is a radical creativity involved in developing any scientific world, which frequently leads its contents to contradict the sense of lived experience. Yet, however creative and strange to common sense the contents of science may become,

the creativity emerges from the world of everyday experience, and the theoretical content must be verified by a return to the things used in everyday experience, no matter how tenuous this link may become.

19. *Being and Time* still allows for the existence of substances other than the nonsubstantive human way of being, substances that ground the more abstract functional concepts. (See Martin Heidegger, *Being and Time*, trans. John Macquarrie and Edward Robinson [New York: Harper and Row, 1962], 122). However, in the later Heidegger the unity not just of objects but of things lies in their functionality. (See his analysis of the jug in "The Thing," 166–72.) A parallel understanding of this functionality within pragmatic philosophy was given earlier.

20. See, for example, Heidegger, *Being and Time*, 122.

21. In this passage, Heidegger is explicitly referring to the danger of the "enframing" of technology, but it applies equally well, perhaps even more appropriately, in the present context. "The Turning," 42.

22. Heidegger usually reserves the term "nature" for the abstract level of scientific content, but he at times uses it to indicate the realm of "our closest world." Heidegger, "Letter on Humanism," in *Basic Writings*, 213–66. See, for example, Heidegger, *Being and Time*, 100, and *The Basic Problems of Phenomenology*, trans. Albert Hofstadter (Bloomington: Indiana University Press, 1984), 168–69.

23. It must be emphasized that purposive biological activity, as the foundation of meaning, cannot be understood in terms of scientific contents or scientific categories.

24. Dewey, *Quest for Certainty*, 142; "The Experimental Theory of Knowledge," in *Middle Works of John Dewey*, 3:114–15.

25. Dewey, *Experience and Nature*, 12–13. Italics in original.

26. Ibid., 64–65.

27. Ibid., 65.

28. This point is developed by me in some detail in *Speculative Pragmatism*.

29. Dewey, *Quest for Certainty*, 188–89; "Does Reality Possess Practical Character?" 137–38.

30. Dewey, *Experience and Nature*, 18–19.

31. John Dewey, "Qualitative Thought," in *Later Works of John Dewey*, 5:248 n. 1. This view gains support from some of Dewey's writings (see, for example, *Experience and Nature*, 227), while it is contradicted by other of his claims (see, for example, *Experience and Nature*, 236). He never adequately distinguishes quality and fringe, thus allowing for his ambiguity of usage. What Dewey is actually allowing for within perceptual awareness, in addition to focus, is fringe, which is presently vague but which can become an object of another focus, and pervasive qualitative character or tonality, which characterizes a situation in its immediacy but which overflows or eludes any attempt to capture it and render it precise for perceptual awareness. It is irreducibly and irretrievably vague.

32. Heidegger, *Being and Time*, 100.

33. Heidegger, *Basic Problems of Phenomenology*, 168–69.

34. Heidegger, *History of the Concept of Time*, 217–18.

35. Heidegger, *Basic Problems of Phenomenology*, 169.

36. Thus Heidegger can emphasize a certain essential "powerlessness" of the human mode of being. *The Metaphysical Foundations of Logic*, trans. Michael Heim (Bloomington: Indiana University Press, 1984), 215.

37. Ibid.

38. Ibid., 170.

39. Heidegger, *Metaphysical Foundations of Logic*, 195.

40. The early Heidegger is concerned with being as the "total meaningfulness of the world." The coming to pass of being as the luminosity of the world in *Being and Time* occurs through human "care." The later Heidegger focuses on the broader being process in which humans are enmeshed.

41. Martin Heidegger, *Discourse on Thinking*, trans. John M. Anderson and E. Hans Freund (New York: Harper and Row, 1966).

42. What Heidegger here means by "region" is not any one region, or region in general, but "the region of all regions," that which gives rise to particular regions, including the human region. See his *Discourse on Thinking*, 66 n. 1.

43. Ibid., 58.

44. Ibid., 64

45. Ibid., 67.

46. Martin Heidegger, "The Origin of the Work of Art," in *Basic Writings*, 139–212. Elsewhere Heidegger refers to earth as part of the four-fold. There earth, as "under the sky" and as part of the four-fold, is taken in a more limited sense. Heidegger, "Building Dwelling Thinking," in *Basic Writings*, 343–64.

47. Heidegger, "Origin of the Work of Art," 169.

48. Ibid., 169–73.

49. Ibid., 175.

50. Ibid., 173.

51. Ibid., 178.

52. Heidegger, "Building Dwelling Thinking," 325.

53. Heidegger, "Origin of the Work of Art," 169.

54. Heidegger, "Building Dwelling Thinking," 326.

55. Martin Heidegger, *What Is Called Thinking?* (New York: Harper and Row, 1968); see especially 113–18. "What 'calls for' thinking?" is the fourth and decisive way of asking the question "What is called thinking?"

56. Martin Heidegger, *What Is Philosophy?*, trans. William Kluback and Jean Wilde (New Haven, Conn.: College and University Press, 1958), 71.

8] Pragmatism and Hermeneutics

Richard J. Bernstein

At first glance—even at second glance—pragmatism and hermeneutics seem to have little in common. Pragmatism is a philosophical movement that originated in the United States in the latter part of the nineteenth century. It is typically associated with such thinkers as Charles S. Peirce, William James, John Dewey, and George H. Mead. Hermeneutics—on some accounts—can be traced back to the traditions of practical philosophy and rhetoric in Aristotle. In the late nineteenth century, hermeneutics became closely associated with the *Geisteswissenschaften.* And in the twentieth century, it was given an ontological turn in Martin Heidegger. It was Heidegger's student, Hans-Georg Gadamer, who deepened and universalized hermeneutics. The American pragmatic thinkers—for all the sharp differences among them—thought of themselves as extending the spirit of experimental science to philosophical reflection. They were all deeply influenced by the scientist who dominated so much scientific thinking in their time—Charles Darwin. Dewey and Mead were the pragmatic thinkers most concerned with the burgeoning social sciences. But none of the pragmatists thought there was a sharp distinction between the *Naturwissenschaften* and the *Geisteswissenschaften.* It was *continuity* that they stressed—and indeed their mission was to extend the practices of experimental science to dealing with social, political, and ethical issues. This is especially true for Dewey and Mead. They were sharp critics of positivism, materialism, and determinism. But their criticism of these fashionable philosophical doctrines stemmed from their conviction that they were based upon a misunderstanding of the distinctive features of experimental science. The intellectual milieu that shaped and oriented the thinking of Heidegger and Gadamer was totally different. For all their erudition, there is no evidence that either of them ever read the pragmatists or thought of them as worthy of being included in the great philosophic tradition. They shared the prejudice of so many European—especially German—philosophers of their time, that pragmatism was simply an unoriginal variant of a simple-minded positivism and an ideological expression of the most vulgar American materialism. So it might seem to be a "category mistake"—a futile exercise—to even think of comparing these two philosophical orientations. Yet I want to argue that if we stand back and reflect on the contributions of these two movements, there are—despite sharp differences and basic incompatibilities—significant ways in which they overlap and complement each other. More specifically, I want to show that the fundamental insights and concerns of these very different philosophical orientations help correct and overcome some of the limitations and blind spots of each of these movements. I intend to focus primarily on Peirce, Dewey, and Gadamer.

In order to explain and justify my thesis, let me begin with a passage from a famous series of papers that Peirce published in 1868–69.[1] Peirce begins the second paper in this series, "Some Consequences of Four Incapacities," as follows:

> Descartes is the father of modern philosophy, and the spirit of Cartesianism—that which principally distinguishes it from scholasticism which it displaced—may be compendiously stated as follows:
>
> 1. It teaches that philosophy must begin with universal doubt whereas scholasticism had never questioned fundamentals.
> 2. It teaches that the ultimate test of certainty is to be found in individual consciousness, whereas scholasticism had rested on the testimony of sages and of the Catholic Church.
> 3. The multiform argumentation of the middle ages is replaced by a single thread of inference depending often upon inconspicuous premises.
> 4. Scholasticism had its mysteries of faith, but undertook to explain all created things. But there are many facts which Cartesianism not only does not explain, but renders absolutely inexplicable, unless to say that "God makes them so" is to be regarded as an explanation. (28)

Immediately after listing these four points, Peirce comments, "In some, or all of these respects, most modern philosophers have been, in effect, Cartesians" (28). Peirce then sets out to develop a thorough and systematic critique of the "spirit of Cartesianism" that has dominated so much of modern philosophy—and we find variations of this critique in all the pragmatic thinkers. Now what is initially striking is that both Heidegger and Gadamer would endorse Peirce's characterization of modern philosophy—and his critique of the Cartesian spirit. Indeed, we can read Heidegger's *Being and Time* and Gadamer's *Truth and Method* as sustained critiques of Cartesianism (and all that it entails)—and as revealing a new (old) way of understanding of philosophy.

But here we touch upon a significant difference. For Peirce tells us, "Now without wishing to return to scholasticism, it seems to me that *modern science and modern logic* require us to stand upon a very different platform from this" (28, italics added). When Peirce speaks of modern science, he means modern experimental science as illustrated in the natural sciences—not the *Geisteswissenschaften.* But yet, consider the four points that he makes against the spirit of Cartesianism—they all have resonances in Gadamer's version of ontological hermeneutics.

1. Peirce tells us, "We cannot begin with complete doubt. We must begin with all the prejudices which we actually have when we enter upon the study of philosophy. These prejudices are not to be dispelled by a maxim, for they are things which it does not occur to us can be questioned. . . . A person may, it is true, in the course of his studies, find reason to doubt what he began by believing; but in that case he doubts because he has a positive reason for it, and not on account of the Cartesian maxim. Let us not pretend to doubt in philosophy what we do not doubt in our hearts" (28–29). The very use of the word "prejudices" immediately calls to mind Gadamer's own account of the positive role of prejudice and his criticism of the Enlightenment's prejudice against prejudice. It is not simply that Peirce and Gadamer think that we cannot escape from the prejudices and traditions that have shaped us. They both argue that there is something radically mistaken about the very idea that we can rid ourselves of *all* prejudices and prejudgments. It is these very prejudgments—inherited from traditions that have shaped us—that *enable* us to engage in inquiry as well as the "happening" of hermeneutic understanding. They are conditions for the very possibility of knowing. Of course, both Gadamer and Peirce are acutely aware of the need to distinguish between "good" and "bad" prejudices—that is, between *enabling* prejudices and *blinding* prejudices—those unwarranted prejudices that distort our understanding and knowing. They both emphasize that we cannot make this distinction by appealing to an abstract maxim. Distinguishing among prejudices or prejudgments is an *achievement*—one that results from further inquiry and experience. And furthermore, even though we may find reason to doubt what we began by believing, we—as finite human beings—*never* escape from the condition of being shaped by our prejudices and prejudgments. The ramifications of this are extremely consequential. It entails a new way of understanding what is involved in inquiry, knowing, and the role of those traditions that shape us (the source of prejudices and prejudgments). It is only by submitting the results of our inquiries to the criticism and testing of a community of inquirers that

we can sort out what is valid and invalid in these prejudgments. This is why the appeal to a critical community of inquirers is so fundamental for Peirce.[2]

2. Peirce criticizes the Cartesian appeal to certainty of the individual consciousness. He tells us "to make single individuals absolutely judges of truth is most pernicious" (29). He mocks the tendency of metaphysicians who claim that metaphysics has "reached a pitch certainty far beyond that of the physical sciences;—only they can agree upon nothing else" (29). We find here one of Peirce's earliest statements about the importance of a community of inquirers. "We individually cannot reasonably hope to attain the ultimate philosophy which we pursue; we can only seek it, therefore, for the *community* of philosophers" (29). Like Heidegger and Gadamer (and all the pragmatists), Peirce was deeply skeptical and critical of the subject-object distinction that pervades so much of modern philosophy—where typically the *subject* is taken to be an individual consciousness and the *object* is that which this consciousness confronts. It is this epistemological and metaphysical dichotomy of subject and object that has such pernicious consequences for modern philosophy. Furthermore, one of the main targets of the pragmatists is "the quest for certainty" (the title of one of Dewey's most important books). Dewey traced this quest for certainty back to Greek philosophy, although he saw it constantly being reiterated throughout the history of philosophy. It was closely related to a quest for a security that seeks to escape from the contingency, uncertainty, and openness of experience. Positively stated, Peirce and the pragmatists were committed to *fallibilism*. Every knowledge-claim is, in principle, open to further testing, criticism, modification. Certainty does not entail epistemological incorrigibility. What I *take* to be certain may turn out to be mistaken. In the language of Gadamer, our finite being-in-the-world means that we are always open to further experience. For pragmatism and hermeneutics, the very idea of *absolute* first starting points or end points in inquiry and experience is rejected as a misguided illusion. We are always in medias res—in the midst of a journey. Here too we touch on another central theme in pragmatism and hermeneutics. The most fundamental theme in Peirce's comprehensive theory of signs and Gadamer's understanding of language is the intrinsic *openness* of all signs and language to further and novel interpretation. There is no ultimate finality or metaphysical closure to the ongoing process of interpretation. But once again, it is important to emphasize that the basis for Peirce making these points about certainty and the role of the individual subject was his understanding of how the natural experimental sciences actually work. Gadamer, on the other hand, drew his

conclusions about the open horizon of language from his reflections on the understanding and interpretation of texts, art, and history.

3. Peirce, who was a practicing scientist and logician and who described himself as being shaped by a laboratory habit of mind, sought to bring the methods and spirit of experimental science to the practice of philosophy itself. He was critical of the foundation metaphor that had been so seductive in the Cartesianism that he rejected. He states: "Philosophy ought to imitate the successful sciences in its methods, so far as to proceed only from tangible premises which can be subjected to careful scrutiny, and to trust rather to the multitude and variety of its arguments than to the conclusiveness of any one. Its reasoning should not form a chain which is no stronger than its weakest link, but a cable whose fibres may be ever so slender, provided they are sufficiently numerous and intimately connected" (29). We cannot underestimate the importance of this claim for Peirce and the pragmatists. In the first article in this series, "Questions Concerning Certain Faculties Claimed for Man," Peirce criticizes—in a most devastating manner—what Wilfrid Sellars has labeled the "myth of the given." This is the idea that there is a form of immediate (noninferential) knowledge or knowledge by acquaintance of "truths" that can serve as the solid foundation for the edifice of knowledge. The dream (or nightmare) of many modern philosophers has been to discover such basic truths and to construct a chain of reasoning based on the foundation of these immediate premises. This procedure supposedly provides us with a *method* for avoiding error. This has been the "ideal" of *method* shared by all those infected by the "spirit of Cartesianism"—right up to twentieth-century logical positivists. Peirce is making a radical suggestion when he advocates substituting the metaphor of a cable for that of a chain. For in a cable, each fiber may be slender and weak, but collectively they are strong. It is the "multitude and variety of arguments" that is important and not the "conclusiveness of any single one" (29). Sellars, in his now classic paper "Empiricism and the Philosophy of Mind" (written almost a hundred years after Peirce's 1868 paper), epitomizes Peirce's key point. Sellars tells us that "empirical knowledge, like its sophisticated extension science, is rational, not because it has a foundation, but because it is a self-correcting enterprise, which can put any claim in jeopardy, though not *all* at once."[3]

Initially, it appears that the claim that philosophy ought to imitate the successful (natural) sciences in its methods is really foreign to the letter and the spirit of Gadamer's ontological hermeneutics. I certainly do not want to downplay the important differences. But Gadamer is no less relentless in his critique of the doctrine of "immediate knowledge" than is Peirce. Gadamer also thinks that the champions of method are seduced by the foundation metaphor. They believe that reasoning should consist of a tightly linked chain or a set of rigorous deductions. Gadamer's (and Heidegger's) defense of the famous hermeneutic circle is that it is not a vicious circle but a circle—or more properly a spiral—that enlarges, deepens, and enriches our understanding. Peirce's appeal to the cable metaphor has its echoes in Gadamer's insistence on the need for, and the openness of, *multiple* interpretations.

4. Peirce attacks the philosophical supposition of "some absolutely inexplicable, unanalyzable ultimate; in short, something resulting from mediation itself not susceptible of mediation" (29). The very language that Peirce uses reveals his affinity with Gadamer. The language of "mediation" is derived from G. W. F. Hegel—a thinker who had an enormous influence on Gadamer. Hegel seeks to show us—especially in the opening sections of the *Phenomenology of Spirit*—that there is nothing resulting from mediation itself that is not susceptible to mediation. What we *take* to be immediate (noninferential and directly known) is itself "always already" mediated—it always already involves inferential processes. We must be careful not to misinterpret what Peirce and Gadamer are affirming. There is nothing *absolutely* inexplicable in the sense that there is something that is *totally* beyond and "outside" of signs (Peirce) or language (Gadamer). Of course, as finite fallible beings engaged in the open-ended process of interpretation and inquiry, we are *never* is a position to claim that we have achieved *final* comprehension. In this sense, there is always something inexplicable that presents itself as a challenge to further understanding and interpretation—but this does not mean that there is some "unanalyzable ultimate" that is totally beyond all understanding and inquiry.

This last point about mediation opens another perspective for understanding the affinities between pragmatism and hermeneutics. The extent to which German philosophy influenced the nineteenth-century origins of pragmatism (especially the pragmatism of Peirce, Dewey and Mead) has not always been appreciated. Peirce studied Immanuel Kant's *Critique of Pure Reason* so thoroughly that he claimed to know it by heart. Peirce's philosophical reflections began with his attempt to revise the Kantian categories in light of new developments in logic and science. Dewey wrote his doctoral dissertation on Kant under the supervision of G. S. Morris—a thoroughly committed Hegelian. Eventually, Darwin replaced Hegel as a source of inspiration for Dewey, although he acknowledged that Hegel had left a "permanent deposit" on his thinking. Dewey's philosophical development can be seen as a progressive naturalization of this Hegelian legacy. Mead was a student of Josiah Royce, the outstanding American idealist philosopher of his time. And during his studies in Germany, Mead listened to the lectures of Wilhelm Dilthey. In the course of Gadamer's own philosophic development, Hegel came to play an increasingly important role. Gadamer (like Dewey) was always skeptical about some of the grand claims of Hegel concerning Totality, the System, and the Absolute. Sometimes—in an almost humorous manner—Gadamer characterized himself as a "Hegelian of the bad infinite" (which clearly would be an absurdity for any orthodox Hegelian). But the point of this remark is that for hermeneutics, there is no ultimate finality and closure. There is no System in which experience (*Erfahrung*) is ultimately synthesized (*Aufgehoben*). Experience is always and *necessarily* open to further experience. Dewey might also be characterized as a pragmatic Hegelian of the bad infinite who rejects any sense of closure to experience. Dewey would certainly endorse Gadamer's assertion that "the dialectic of experience has its proper fulfillment not in definitive knowledge, but in the openness to experience that is made possible by experience itself."[4] Their affinities go much deeper than this common Hegelian legacy. Let me illustrate this by focusing on three thematic concepts that are central for both Gadamer and Dewey: experience, play, and dialogue.

Earlier I suggested that both hermeneutics and pragmatism reject the subject-object dichotomy that has shaped so much of modern philosophy. One cannot underestimate the extent to which variants of this epistemological and metaphysical dichotomy have dominated—and continue to dominate—philosophical thinking. But if the subject-object dichotomy is rejected, then what is the alternative? Both Gadamer and Dewey appealed to experience, but by experience they meant something that is much closer to what Hegel called *Erfahrung*. Because the subject-object dichotomy (and the closely related mental-physical dichotomy) has become so entrenched in modern thought, it is difficult to avoid the "subjective" and "mental" associations with the word "experience." Experience presumably is something "private," merely "subjective," exclusively "mental." Both Dewey and Gadamer forcefully argued that this is a gross distortion of the concept of experience. Both sought to recover a meaning of experience that was articulated by Hegel but can be traced back to Aristotle.[5] Even today, there are vestiges of *this* sense of experience when we speak of an *experienced* doctor or craftsman. When we use experience in this context, we do not mean something that is subjective and private, but rather we mean a practical know-how or practical wisdom—a cumulative learning process that is achieved from our interactions with our environment. Experience has a temporal and spatial span. Experience changes and develops. *Within* experience there is activity and passivity (undergoing, suffering, pathos). The distinction of subject and object is a dynamic, changing *functional* distinction that arises within experience. It is this organic, fluid, holistic conception of experience that was the source of Dewey's early attraction to Hegel and that became a fundamental theme for him throughout his philosophic development.

There are other important dimensions of Dewey's understanding of experience that he shares with Gadamer. Both Dewey and Gadamer argued that one of the primary reasons why the concept of experience has been distorted in modern philosophy is because of the obsession with epistemology. There has been an almost exclusive concern with experience insofar as it is cognitive, that is, insofar as it does (or does not) contribute to justifying knowledge claims. But experience, conceived in the robust way in which Dewey and Gadamer understood it, is much broader and deeper than knowing. Knowing—or better, inquiry—is one type of experience that is grounded and oriented by experiences that are not primarily cognitive. To illustrate what we learn from experience, Gadamer cites Aeschylus's expression "learning through suffering" (*pathei mathos*). "Experience," Gadamer tells us, "is experience of human finitude. The truly experienced person is one who has taken this to heart, who knows he is master neither of time nor the future."[6] There is another aspect of Dewey's understanding of experience that brings him close to hermeneutics. There is a rhythm within experience. There are moments of disruption and conflict as well as phases of consummation and integration. These consummatory experiences are the key for appreciating the aesthetic dimension experience. Dewey categorically rejected the idea of aesthetic experience as special *type* of experience, just as Gadamer was critical of what he calls "aesthetic consciousness." For Dewey, "aesthetic" names a consummatory phase of *any* experience when it is funded with meaning and emotion.

One of the most illuminating and fertile concepts in Gadamer's philosophy is the concept of play. He seeks to show us how a phenomenological understanding of play deepens our understanding of experience and dialogue. Beginning with reflections on children's play and ordinary games, Gadamer emphasizes the internal buoyancy, the to-and-fro dynamic movement that belongs to play itself. Play is a "happening." There is a distinctive "mode of being" of play. "The players are not the subjects of play; instead play merely reaches presentation [*Darstellung*] through the players."[7] By highlighting the primacy of play itself with its own distinctive to-and-fro rhythms, Gadamer shows us that we misrepresent the phenomenon of play when we attempt to analyze it exclusively in terms of the attitudes of *subjects* toward what is *objective*. The way in which Gadamer understands play as a distinctive "mode of being" is just as applicable to the way in which Dewey understands the dynamic fluidity of experience. One of the reasons why the concept of play is of such fundamental importance for Gadamer is because of its relevance for understanding the character of genuine dialogue: "Now I contend that the basic constitution of the game, to be filled with its spirit—the spirit of buoyancy, freedom, and the joy of success—and to fulfill him who is playing, is structurally related to the dialogue in which language is a reality. When one enters into dialogue with another person and then is carried along by the dialogue, it is no longer the will of an individual person, holding itself back or exposing itself, that is determinative. Rather the law of the subject matter [*die Sache*] is at issue in the dialogue and elicits statement and counter statement and in the end plays them into each other."[8] Dialogue in the most central concept in Gadamer's philosophical hermeneutics. He conceives of the hermeneutic experience on the model of a dialogue. All understanding and interpretation involves application in the sense of our dialogical participation with texts and with the traditions that have shaped us. It is these dialogical encounters that determine our very being—what we are in the process of becoming. The centrality of dialogue in Gadamer's philosophical hermeneutics is comparable to the role of communication for Dewey. Consider how Dewey begins a key chapter in *Experience and Nature*: "Of all affairs, communication is the most wonderful. That things should be able to pass from the plane of external pushing and pulling to that of revealing themselves to men, and thereby to themselves; and that the fruit of communication should be participation, sharing, is a wonder by the side of which transubstantiation pales. When communication occurs, all natural events are subject to reconsideration and revision; they are re-adapted to meet the requirements of conversation, whether it be public discourse or that preliminary discourse termed thinking."[9]

At the beginning of this chapter, I stated that pragmatism and hermeneutics overlap and complement each other. Thus far, I have been focusing on what these philosophic orientations share. But I also claimed that the strengths of each of these philosophic orientations enable us to locate and correct the weaknesses and deficiencies of each other. I now want to clarify and justify this second part of my thesis. I have already begun to show how pragmatic thinkers question the claim that there is a sharp dichotomy between *Naturwissenschaften* and *Geisteswissenschaften*. Insofar as Gadamer plays on the contrast between "method" and "truth," insofar as he leads us to think that hermeneutic understanding is radically different from the type of understanding that is characteristic of the natural sciences, the pragmatists strongly—and in my opinion—correctly object. Like Gadamer, the pragmatists have engaged in a thorough critique of the Cartesianism that has shaped so much of modern thought. But, as we have seen, this critique is based on their understanding of the experimental, self-corrective, intersubjective, fallible character of scientific inquiry. Positively stated, many of the characteristics that Gadamer took to be distinctive of hermeneutic experience have been shown by the pragmatists to be characteristics of experimental science. Where Gadamer suggested that there is a different sense of "knowledge" and "truth" proper to hermeneutics, the pragmatists stress *continuity*. But continuity does not mean the elimination of differences. The pragmatists also reject any form of scientism that claims that the natural sciences *alone* are the measure of knowledge and reality. Ironically, during the decade when Gadamer published *Truth and Method*, philosophers of natural science were engaged in criticizing the canonical conception of science developed by the logical empiricists. They were—as Thomas Kuhn has acknowledged—highlighting the hermeneutic features of the natural sciences. Gadamer himself subsequently came to appreciate these new developments in the philosophy of science—developments that vindicate the pragmatic understanding of experimental science.

At the same time, Gadamer can be read as a warning against some of the excesses in thinking that "scientific method" is sufficient for elucidating the varieties of understanding and interpretation and for guiding us in clarifying complex issues of *praxis*. Sometimes in reading Dewey, one comes away with the impression that nothing more is needed than to extend the methods that have been successful in the experimental sciences in order to confront the issues of moral choice and social reform. One can agree with Dewey that decisions become more informed when we imaginatively think out the consequences of different courses of action. But, at times, Dewey is insufficiently sensitive to the ways in which a narrow instrumental and technological orientation distorts the promise of enlightened *praxis*. Employing the terminology of Jürgen Habermas, Dewey does not always carefully distinguish between the instrumental and communicative dimensions of science and rationality. In this respect, Gadamer can be read as a corrective to the pragmatists. He tells us: "The problem of our society is that the longing of the citizenry for orientation and normative patterns invests the expert with an exaggerated authority. Modern society expects him to provide a substitute for past moral and political orientations. Consequently, the concept of '*praxis*' which was developed in the last two centuries is an awful deformation of what practice really is. In all the debates of the last century practice is understood as application of science to technical tasks. . . . It degrades practical reason to technical control."[10] Dewey would certainly agree that if *praxis* is exclusively understood as technical control or application of expert knowledge, then this is serious deformation of *praxis*. But by blurring the differences between *techne* and *praxis*, between instrumental and communicative action, Dewey does not adequately highlight the real social and political dangers that both Habermas and Gadamer emphasize.

We open up here another area where hermeneutics and pragmatism can be seen as mutually corrective. In his elaboration of philosophical hermeneutics, Gadamer focuses on the interpretation of classic texts, works of art, and history. It is the dialogue with tradition that most concerns him. Questions concerning ethics and politics are not thematized in *Truth and Method*. Nevertheless, Gadamer has had a long and deep interest in the tradition of practical philosophy that has its origins in Plato and Aristotle. The key concept that Gadamer appropriates from Aristotle is the concept of *phronesis* (practical wisdom). And he gives a brilliant analysis of how *phronesis* differs from both *techne* and *episteme*. Gadamer seeks to recover *phronesis* as the most important virtue that is required of citizens today. He gives an eloquent statement of what he takes to be the task of philosophy in our time: "I think, then, that the chief task of philosophy is to justify this way of reason and to defend practical and political reason against the domination of technology based on science. That is the point of philosophic hermeneutics. It corrects the peculiar falsehood of modern consciousness: the idolatry of scientific method and of the anonymous authority of the sciences and it vindicates again the noblest task of the citizen—decision-making according to one's responsibility—instead of conceding that task to the expert. In this respect, hermeneutics philosophy is the heir of the older tradition of practical philosophy."[11]

This passage succinctly brings out the tensions between hermeneutics and pragmatism. Dewey would certainly agree that philosophy ought to defend practical and political reason against "the domination of technology based on science." But he would object to Gadamer's characterization of the "idolatry of scientific method and of the anonymous authority of the sciences." It is essential to distinguish carefully those features of the spirit of experimental scientific inquiry that can enlighten "practical and political reason" for a dogmatic scientism. Dewey would also endorse the importance of vindicating the "noblest task of the citizen—decision-making according to one's responsibility." But if this task is to be taken seriously, then it is not *sufficient* to appeal to *phronesis* and the tradition of practical philosophy. We need a much more comprehensive and robust understanding of the meaning of democracy in our time than we find in hermeneutics. We need to attend to the threats that democracy faces, as well as to what needs to be done to foster what Dewey called creative democracy. Dewey and the other pragmatists emphasize human agency and future consequences far more than does Gadamer. Throughout his long career, Dewey was concerned with the concrete ways of improving the democratic practices of everyday life. Democracy is primarily a normative or moral ideal—a way of life in which we constantly seek to foster those dialogical practices in which all share and all participate. When Dewey speaks of the eclipse of the public in contemporary life, he is expressing the same worry that Gadamer has when he criticizes the technical manipulation of opinion formation. Using Gadamer's language, we might say that if *phronesis* is to flourish, if genuine *dialogue* is to become a living reality, then this can be accomplished only by taking concrete, practical steps to foster democratic participation. I do not think that Gadamer would really disagree with Dewey and the pragmatists, although Gadamer tends to shy away from dealing with concrete issues of social and political reform.

Let me conclude by returning the concept of play to describe what I have attempted to show in this chapter. We noted that it is the mode of being of play—its to-and-fro movement—that enables us to understand what is involved in a genuine dialogue, one in which we listen carefully and respond to the dialogical other. In a genuine dialogue, there are always different voices. There must, of course, be some shared mutual understanding in order for a dialogue to take place. But a dialogue does not necessarily lead to agreement; it may result in a deeper understanding of differences—even irreconcilable differences. But something "happens" in a dialogue when the participants learn from their encounters with others. In this chapter, a play between pragmatism and hermeneutics has been enacted. In this dialogical encounter, we may come away with a subtler understanding of these different voices and the ways in which they at once complement and help to correct each other.

Notes

1. "Questions Concerning Certain Faculties Claimed for Man" (1868); "Some Consequences of Four Incapacities" (1868); "Grounds of Validity of the Laws of Logic (1869). These papers were originally published in the *Journal of Speculative Philosophy*. They are reprinted in *The Essential Peirce*, vol. 1, ed. Nathan Houser and Christian Kloesel (Bloomington: Indiana University Press, 1992). All Peirce quotes in text are from "Some Consequences of Four Incapacities" unless otherwise noted.

2. For a fuller account of the meaning and role of prejudice and prejudgment in Gadamer, see my book *Beyond Objectivism and Relativism* (Philadelphia: University of Pennsylvania Press, 1983).

3. Wilfrid Sellars, "Empiricism and the Philosophy of Mind," in *Minnesota Studies in the Philosophy of Science*, vol. 1, ed. Herbert Feigl and Michael Scriven (Minneapolis: University of Minnesota Press, 1956), 300.

4. Hans-Georg Gadamer, *Truth and Method*, 2nd rev. ed., trans. and rev. Joel Weinsheimer and Donald G. Marshall (New York: Continuum, 1989), 355.

5. See ibid., 312–24.

6. Ibid., 357.

7. Ibid., 103.

8. Hans-Georg Gadamer, "Man and Language," in *Philosophical Hermeneutics*, trans. David E. Linge (Berkeley: University of California Press, 1976), 66.

9. John Dewey, *The Essential Dewey*, vol. 2, ed. Larry A. Hickman and Thomas M. Alexander (Bloomington: Indiana University Press, 1998), 50.

10. Hans-Georg Gadamer, "Hermeneutics and Social Science," *Cultural Hermeneutics* 2 (1975): 312.

11. Ibid., 316.

9] Dewey, Gadamer, and the Status of Poetry among the Arts

David Vessey

When Alcuin argued for the *artes liberales* in the Carolingian court, three things kept poetry from finding a distinctive place: Plato's concerns about the corruptive power of poetry; *poesis*—"making"—suggesting poetry belonged to the mechanical rather than liberal arts; and the Pythagorean mathematicization of music. Through the Middle Ages, the best poetry could hope for was a place under the category of rhetoric; though, since it was then seen as oriented only to pleasure, the medieval church shared Plato's suspicions. When poetry took off in the fourteenth century, it's not surprising that something so connected to both language and music should seem to transcend the split between the *trivium* (grammar, rhetoric, and logic) and *quadrivium* (arithmetic, geometry, astronomy, and music). When Leonardo da Vinci in 1490 argued that painting not only belongs among the liberal arts but is the highest of the arts, it was music and poetry—one the master of invisible things, the other the master of visible things—he sought to dethrone. Poetry was no longer a tool of rhetoric but an art of first rank, and the nature of music lay in its emotional power, not in mathematical relations.

Leonardo's arguments never caught on, but the link between poetry and music has been often repeated, as has been their status as the highest of the arts. In the nineteenth century, G. W. F. Hegel called poetry "the universal art of the mind."[1] It "runs though all the arts" and is art's "highest phase," one phase higher than music. Arthur Schopenhauer inverted the priority: poetry is "the true mirror of the real nature of the world and life,"[2] but music, since it speaks directly to the will unmediated by ideas, is the "most powerful of all the arts."[3] A young John Dewey wrote, "The various fine arts, architecture, sculpture, painting, music and poetry are the successive attempts of the mind to adequately express its own ideal nature, or, more correctly stated, adequately to produce that which will satisfy its own demands for a love of a perfectly harmonious nature, something in which admiration may rest."[4] The ordering of the arts is not accidental; poetry is above music, especially dramatic poetry, as it "consummates . . . the range of fine arts, because in dramatic form we have the highest ideal of self, personality displaying itself in the form of personality. . . . [B]eyond this art cannot go."[5] Forty years later, in *Art as Experience*, Dewey returned to the idea of ranking the arts, but by then his views had changed. He presents the very fact that Schopenhauer even thought to rank the arts as evidence of "a complete failure of philosophy to meet the challenge that art offers reflective thought."[6] By 1931, Dewey was no longer willing to give any art form pride of place among the arts. The question I want to take up is the place of poetry in the arts: specifically, does it hold pride of place either as the telos of art, or as the essence of art, or at least as deserving special consideration among the arts? I will look at Dewey's theory of poetry and how he argues that it does not hold a philosophically distinctive place and contrast it with Hans-Georg Gadamer's theory about "the essential priority of poetry with respect to the other arts."[7] Martin Heidegger may have expressed the view most dramatically when he claimed that "the essence of art is poetry,"[8] but, as in so many other cases, it is Gadamer who fully articulates it and locates it in the history of philosophy. Finally, I will argue with Gadamer that poetry does have a distinctive place among the arts, and poetry is particularly useful for helping us understand the arts in general. The key to this argument is seeing that language, especially poetic language, is not first and foremost a tool, not even, as Dewey writes, the "tool of tools."[9]

Dewey's Understanding of Poetry among the Arts

Of course, what Dewey is known most for is arguing against distinguishing art from other areas of life. In *Art as Experience*, it is the continuity among the arts, and above all the continuity of aesthetic experience and everyday experience, that takes the fore. He argues that were we to understand life as practical through and through, as we should, "then would disappear the separations that trouble present thinking: division of everything into nature *and* experience, of experience in practice *and* theory, art *and* science, or art into useful *and* fine, menial *and* free."[10] Poetry can be analyzed separately from the other arts, but for the Dewey of *Art as Experience*, it holds no special status among the arts. His emphasis is always on the connections between all the arts and experience.

Dewey sees the distinction between fine art and useful art as falling away once we realize the common anthropological roots of the two categories. The role of fine art always arises within the practical needs of life; it does not transcend them. All arts develop in order to emotionally mark significant objects or experiences to enable them to be better communicated across people and over time. Therefore, with respect to poetry, Dewey says, "Words serve their poetic purpose in the degree in which they summon and evoke into active operation the vital responses that are present whenever we experience qualities."[11] The qualities of an experience are those that provide the unity to the experience; poetry becomes a way to communicate these qualities, in the process generating an experience. As a result, poetry brings to attention features of the experience that may be particularly useful for our ongoing adaptation to our environment. It is "the emotional kindling of reality, which is the true province of poetry";[12] poetry "radiates the light that never was on land and sea but that henceforth is an abiding illumination of objects."[13] Of course, this same illuminating and attention-grabbing function might be played by prose as well as poetry; the difference between the two is that "one of them [prose] realizes the power of words to express what is in heaven and earth and under the seas by means of extension; the other [poetry] by intension. The prosaic is an affair of description and narration, of details accumulated and relations elaborated. It spreads as it goes like a legal document or catalogue. The poetic reverses the process. It condenses and abbreviates, thus giving words an energy of expansion that is almost explosive."[14] It is its energy—especially its spontaneous energy—that gives poetry its significant character as art and distinguishes it from prose, but for Dewey it shares that energy with other performance arts: dance, theater, and music.

What Dewey seeks to avoid are two extremes: that poetry is straightforwardly referential and that poetry is wholly unrelated to truth. Poetry, as art, "communicates because it is expressive," not because it is linguistic: "It enables us to share vividly and deeply in meanings to which we had been dumb, or for which we had but the ear that permits what is said to pass through in transit to overt action. For communication is not announcing things, even if they are said with the emphasis of great sonority. Communication is the process of creating participation, of making common what had been isolated and singular; and part of the miracle it achieves is that, in being communicated, the conveyance of meaning gives body and definiteness to the experience of the one who utters as well as to that of those who listen."[15] The emotional qualities of the poem, not the referential properties of the words, create an experience for the reader or listener. Still, Dewey's is not a purely noncognitive account of poetry and art. It is not simply that poetry has its domain of emotions and metaphors, while science and inquiry have their domain of truth. The emotional quality of a poem communicates an experience of an idea or a thing—it communicates the same world that science and inquiry communicate; otherwise, poetry could not connect to action.

In his early, more Hegelian phase, he wrote, "The great power of poetry to stay and to console—a power which neither [Matthew] Arnold nor any other critic can exaggerate one whit—is just because of the truth, the rendering of the reality of affairs, which poetry gives us. The importance and the endurance of poetry, as of all art, [is] in its hold upon reality."[16] As experience is always at the same time emotional and intellectual, often undifferentiably so, its content is never merely a subjective reaction but an active interaction with our environment, revealing things about our environment in the process. "Esthetic and moral experience reveal traits of real things as truly as does intellectual experience, that poetry may have a metaphysical import as well as science, is rarely affirmed, and when it is asserted, the statement is likely to be meant in some mystical or esoteric sense rather than in a straightforward everyday sense."[17] For Dewey, poetry straightforwardly "reveal[s] traits of real things." What makes a poem powerful as a work of art may be its emotional quality, but this is not at the expense of generating insights for inquiry; still, it reveals in a different way than do science or philosophy. Dewey writes: "If the advantage in directness and universality of appeal, in wealth and passionateness of garb, is upon the side of poetry, let us remember that, after all, the advantage upon the side of method and standard are with the side of science and philosophy."[18] Poetry may be able to speak with greater passion and greater universality, but in the end its appeal as art is emotional—in this way, Dewey can bridge the dichotomy between poetry functioning purely intellectually and poetry functioning purely emotionally.[19]

For all this about poetry, we really haven't gone beyond what Dewey says about art in general. At the heart of Dewey's aesthetic theory is "recovering the continuity of aesthetic experience with normal processes of living."[20] All art is created with the goal of generating a single coherent aesthetic experience, and all aesthetic experience includes intellectual, emotional, and practical elements—art generates insights for inquiry, communicates emotions, and guides interaction with our environment. In *Art as Experience*, Dewey is blunt about his focus on the continuity of aesthetic forms and his disdain for distinctions among the arts. He writes, "William James remarked on the tediousness of elaborate classifications of things that merge and vary, as do human emotions. Attempts at precise and systematic classification of fine arts seem to me to share this tediousness. An enumerative classification is convenient and for purposes of easy reference indispensable. But a cataloguing like painting, statuary, poetry, drama, dancing, landscape gardening, architecture, singing, musical instrumentation, etc., etc., makes no pretense to throwing any light on the intrinsic nature of the things listed. It leaves that illumination to come from the only place that it can come from—individual works of art. Rigid classifications are inept (if they are taken seriously) because they distract attention from that which is esthetically basic—the qualitatively unique and integral character of experience of an art product."[21] Distinctions are useful only to the extent they draw our attention to what is aesthetically relevant in the experience of a work of art; but what is most relevant is that "art, in its form, unites the very same relation of doing and undergoing, outgoing and incoming energy, that makes an experience be an experience."[22] Although there are differences between poetry and other arts, they are not differences that make a difference, and no art form assumes an elevated status about others. Poetry is neither the telos of art, nor the essence of art, not even exemplary among the arts.

Gadamer's Elevation of Poetry among the Arts

Gadamer regularly claims that the distinctive feature of poetry is its autonomy. By this he means that poems "interpret themselves insofar as one need no additional information about the occasion and the historical circumstances of their composition."[23] Gadamer is not denying that our interpretation of a poem draws on our particular cultural, historical, and personal backgrounds; all interpretation is shaped by our facticity. Indeed, for Gadamer it is only because we are finite that poems can become intelligible; the claim of autonomy connects three related ideas. First, poetry, like all language and all art, transcends the context of its origins. When we put our thoughts into words, we make open the possibility that the meaningfulness of the words will outlast us and our thoughts. Unlike most prose, though, a poem stands alone as a unitary object to be interpreted in its uniqueness. Any additional information about the author or the context of its creation is a legitimate tool of interpretation to the extent the poem itself bears that interpretation. But even then, additional information provides only clues to the ideality of the poem; it never constitutes the poem's meaning. That the meaning of the poem is not reducible to the intentions of the poet is the second feature of autonomy, for Gadamer. The third is that the poem speaks for itself; the meaning of a poem will not be captured in prose, in other poems, or even, as someone might suggest, through other artistic media. The poem is the best expression of its meaning, and no interpretation will exhaust what it has to say. One way to think of Gadamer's autonomy claim is as a threefold denial of irreducibility: the meaning of the work of art is not reducible to its historical and cultural origin, to its creator's intentions, nor to expression in another medium, including prose.

One extremely significant consequence of the autonomy of poetry is that, for Gadamer and in contrast to Dewey, poetry is not first and foremost a kind of communication. Dewey argues that a poem is successful if there is a connection between the emotions of the artist and the emotions of the reader; at its heart, then, the poem functions as a medium for emotional communication. For Gadamer, the poem stands on its own; its meaning is its own, instead of being a vehicle for its author's meaning. As he puts it, poetry doesn't report, it testifies; it stands on its words.[24]

To flesh out the meaning of poetry's autonomy, Gadamer appropriates Paul Valéry's currency metaphor. Everyday prose is like paper money: it is purely symbolic, and its value comes from its ability to be substituted and exchanged for objects. Poetry is like a gold coin: useful for exchange, of course, but valuable in its own right, even after the images on the coin marking it as currency have worn off.

> [Everyday] language never stands for itself. It stands for something we encounter in the practical activities of life or in scientific experience, and it is in this context that the views we express prove themselves or fail to do so. Words do not "stand" on their own account. Whether they are spoken or written, their meaning is only fully realized in the context of life. Valéry contrasted the poetic word with the everyday use of language in a striking comparison that alludes to the old days of the gold standard: everyday language resembles small change which, like our paper money, does not actually possess the value it symbolizes. The famous gold coins used before the First World War, *on the other hand*, actually possessed as metal the value that was imprinted upon them. In a similar way the language of poetry is not a mere pointer that refers to something else, but, like the gold coin, is what it represents.[25]

Gadamer's point here is that in poetry, the words have an intrinsic value that doesn't vanish in their meaning. Poetry does not lose its textual presence in revealing what it reveals. Whatever insights we may gain from a poem, the poetic words retain their power to reveal and also show the potential for further interpretations. We recognize when reading a poem that it is these words, these sounds, that are producing the effect, and unless the poem is particularly mundane, it is only because of these words that the poem has the effect it has. That the meaning of a poem doesn't leave the words behind is part of its autonomy. Along the same lines, Gadamer points out that no poems are every really translated. What happens instead is new poems are written in a new language that tries to capture the power and meaning of the original poem. This is why the best translators of poems are poets themselves. However, the translation is always a separate poem, autonomous as well.

Finally, to add to Gadamer's account of poetry as autonomous, consider what we do when we interpret a work of art. We seek to make the meaning explicit by finding words that best express what the work expresses. We try to match the subject matter as revealed by the work of art with the subject matter as revealed by our own words. We don't expect perfect success in this project, but we don't let our limitations leave us inarticulate either. In poetry, this situation is changed slightly but significantly. We already have words expressing the subject matter of the work—the poem itself—and we seek new words to express the subject matter in the same way. The activity of interpreting a poem is not one of becoming articulate about what is expressed by the poem but of translating the meaning of the poem into prose. But no translation of the meaning of the poem could express the meaning as well as the poem; the best expression in language of the meaning of the poem is the poem itself. The process of interpreting a poem is not one of finding new words to express the poem's meaning but of finding our way into the meaning of the poem's own words. The words of the poem are irreplaceable in an interpretation; this is the core meaning of Gadamer's claim that poetry is autonomous, and its status as such gives it an "essential priority" with respect to other art forms.

Poetic Language

I think Gadamer is right that poetry deserves special consideration among the arts. I am not going to engage in or endorse the project of ranking the arts, but I do believe that thinking about the uniqueness of poetry helps us to understand general truths about the arts. Something like this is Gadamer's view as well. Let me start by pointing out that both Dewey and Gadamer were "response" theorists in philosophy of art. When discussing what makes art significant, both emphasize the way the work of art is received by the viewer, hearer, or reader. It is in the effects of art that art gets its distinctive character, even if those effects themselves are continuous with other areas of our lives. Artworks are understood not first and foremost in terms of being the outcome of creative acts, nor as being intended to be perceived in a certain way, nor as having certain formal properties, nor as having an appropriate relation to the art world, but as being capable of creating an effect on or with an appreciator—an effect not found in interaction with commonplace objects.[26] In Dewey's case, this effect is an experience; in Gadamer's case, it is the event of truth; but in both cases, the effects are what are relevant.

In addition, Dewey and Gadamer share a naturalistic approach to art; that is, they see art as arising out of our nature and as continuous with our nature. In *Experience as Nature*, Dewey writes, "There are substantially but two alternatives. Either art is a continuation, by means of intelligent selection and arrangement, of natural tendencies of natural events; or art is a peculiar addition to nature springing from something dwelling exclusively within the breast of man, whatever name be given the latter. In the former case, delightfully enhanced perception or esthetic appreciation is of the same nature as enjoyment of any object that is consummatory. It is the outcome of a skilled and intelligent art of dealing with natural things for the sake of intensifying, purifying, prolonging and deepening the satisfactions which they spontaneously afford."[27] Gadamer too thinks that art is "a continuation . . . of natural tendencies of natural events"; the play that reveals truth in the presence of a work of art is but a specific example of the play that models all interaction, and especially dialogical interaction.

The difference between Dewey and Gadamer ultimately falls on the question of the relation between language and experience.[28] On the one hand, their conceptions of language have much in common. Both hold that language is essentially related to conversation, and, accordingly, both would reject the idea there could be a private language; also, both see reflection as an activity that is derivative of, and parallel to, communication with others. We can reflect in words because we can talk to others in words. Both therefore see language as a tool not only of communication but also of thought. Language allows us to keep things present to consciousness even in the thing's absence, and relations among words help us to better understand possible relations among things. On the other hand, they disagree on language's status as a tool—the "tool of tools," in Dewey's words.[29] Dewey grants language special status among tools, yet it is never anything other than a tool. Gadamer joins Heidegger in arguing that although we can and do use language, the mode of being of language is not ready-to-handness; language is not essentially a tool. Heidegger calls it the "house of being" and says we "inhabit" language; Gadamer, not to be out-metaphored, says our relation to language is like a fish's relation to water. We live in and through language, and it is our relation to language that makes it useful as a tool; language's usefulness is derived from its connection to our nature—our "linguisticality."[30] Metaphors aside, the primary function of language, according to Gadamer, is disclosure. A central idea of hermeneutic phenomenology is that phenomena do not first disclose themselves to a subject, only then to be described, but are disclosed through the use of language: "Language always furnishes the fundamental articulations that guide our understanding of the world. It belongs to the nature of familiarity with the world that whenever we exchange words with one another, we share the world. . . . Language gives all of us our access to a world in which certain special forms of human experience arise: the religious tidings that proclaim salvation, the legal judgment that tells us what is right and what is wrong in our society, the poetic word that by being there bears witness to our own being."[31] Working with someone to become articulate about a subject matter—Gadamer's definition of dialogue—is the means by which phenomena become conscious. We articulate things in words and come to understand them in the process. Because language is a medium of shared disclosure, it is a medium for communication.

Compare the difference between Dewey and Gadamer on the tool-nature of language with their views on the usefulness of one's hands—an example dear to both Gadamer and Dewey.[32] Clearly, hands are very useful tools. We do things with them constantly, and were we to lose them—or lose our ability to use them—we'd have to go to great lengths to compensate for the lost functionality. But our hands are not just tools; they are a way in which the world shows itself to us. Not only can we feel and touch things we might not be able to see and not only can properties be disclosed to touch in ways they might not be disclosed to other senses—two obvious ways in which hands might be disclosive—but our hands are integrated with our other senses to guide their disclosive ability. We perceive our environment in the way we do because we have hands with certain functions. Perhaps the clearest presentation of this is by Dewey himself in his essay "The Reflex Arc Concept in Psychology": "[T]he ability of the hand to do its work will depend, either directly or indirectly, upon its control, as well as its stimulation, by the act of vision. If the sight did not inhibit as well as excite the reaching, the latter would be purely indeterminate, it would be for anything or nothing, not for the particular object seen. The reaching, in turn, must both stimulate and control the seeing. The eye must be kept upon the candle if the arm is to do its work; let it wander and the arm takes up another task. In other words, we now have an enlarged and transformed co-ordination; the act is seeing no less than before, but it is now seeing-for-reaching purposes."[33] Although Dewey tends to constrain all attention to occasions of inquiry, for Gadamer the phenomenologist, the at-hand character of experience is ubiquitous, in which case hands are not just tools. They form an essential way the world is disclosed to us. Things reveal themselves to us as something to grasp or to reach for, or as lying within or beyond reach, and it is not a coincidence that "grasping" something is synonymous with understanding something. Hands are useful as tools by virtue of the more fundamental fact that hands disclose.

Language for Gadamer is disclosive of reality in just the same way. Just as things reveal themselves to us the way they do by virtue of our bodily comportment to them, things reveal themselves to us as something or other, and this as-structure of perception is linguistically informed. We see something as a kind of thing because we have words to make sense of it as something. Things disclose themselves to us as objects of conceptual understanding, or as calling for articulation and description, which is to say disclosed as informed by language. This is the sense in which language functions in experience for Gadamer.

It is a short step from the linguisticality of experience to the Gadamerian view that "language preforms thought," that the criteria for successful thinking are the criteria for successful use of language. While Dewey sees language as wholly instrumental, Gadamer sees it as instrumental in virtue of its disclosive power—that difference marks out the differences between their aesthetic theories and their theories of poetry.[34] For Gadamer, poetry has a special status because language has this distinctive role to play in experience. For the most part, we are not aware of the ways in which language is functioning in experience as disclosive; poetry, however, wears its character as disclosive language on its sleeve. It shows language at work—in the process of disclosing—and it is in this sense that Gadamer calls poetry "the highest fulfillment of that revealing which is the achievement of speech."[35] All art connects to experience; because of the distinctively linguistic character of experience, the art of poetry does this most directly and perspicuously.

Moreover, while all aesthetic experience is interactive, poetry reveals this most clearly, since reading poetry is always a performative event. As readers, we are in a position analogous to the musician or the dancer—we are generating the aesthetic experience as well as undergoing it. Since interpreting the work converges with performing it, we can vary the performance—pausing at different points, emphasizing different sounds—in the process varying the interpretation. Now it may be that all art appreciation and interpretation is performative in a similar way; my point here is that in poetry, this fact is most clearly realized, and, accordingly, it places poetry in a privileged position with respect to the other arts. Poetry serves an exemplary role for understanding the nature of art.

Often the small differences are the most illuminating ones. Dewey's and Gadamer's theories of art share much in common; they disagree, however, on the classic question of how the arts should be ranked, or, in Dewey's case, whether they should be ranked at all. It turns out that behind the disagreement lies a significant difference as to how they see our relationship to language, and this difference leads them to competing theories of poetry. Siding with Gadamer that language is not merely a tool but a fundamental way in which the world is disclosed to us, I think Gadamer is right that poetry both holds pride of place among the arts and is exemplary of the disclosive power of all language. "In words we are at home. . . . Especially in the poetic use of language is this clear to all of us."[36]

Notes

1. G. W. F. Hegel, *Hegel's Introduction to Aesthetics*, trans. T. M. Knox (Oxford: Clarendon Press, 1979), 89.

2. Arthur Schopenhauer, *World as Will and Representation* (New York: Dover, 1966), 1:320.

3. Ibid., 2:448.

4. John Dewey, *Psychology* (1970), vol. 2 of *The Early Works of John Dewey, 1882–1898*, ed. Jo Ann Boydston, 5 vols. (Carbondale: Southern Illinois University Press, 1969–72), 274. Hereafter, citations of the *Early Works* will be given as *EW*.

5. Ibid., 2:277.

6. *The Later Works of John Dewey, 1925–1953*, ed. Jo Ann Boydston, 17 vols. (Carbondale: Southern Illinois University Press, 1981–90), 10:295. Hereafter, citations of the *Later Works* will be given as *LW*.

7. Hans-Georg Gadamer, "Poetry and Mimesis," in *The Relevance of the Beautiful and Other Essays* (Cambridge: Cambridge University Press, 1986), 117. Contrasts between Dewey's and Gadamer's work are becoming more prominent in the literature. On just the topic of philosophy of art, see Thomas Jeannot, "A Propaedeutic to the Philosophical Hermeneutics of John Dewey: *Art as Experience* and *Truth and Method*," *Journal of Speculative Philosophy* 15, no. 1 (2001): 1–13; Robert Innis, "Perception, Interpretation, and the Signs of Art," *Journal of Speculative Philosophy* 15, no. 1 (2001): 20–32; Richard Shusterman, "The End of Aesthetic Experience," *Journal of Aesthetics and Art Criticism* 55, no. 1 (1997): 29–41; John Gilmour, "Dewey and Gadamer on the Ontology of Art," *Man and World* 20 (1987): 205–19; Joaquin Zuniga, "An Everyday Aesthetic Impulse: Dewey Revisited," *British Journal of Aesthetics* 29 (1989): 41–46; and Thomas Alexander, "Eros and Understanding: Gadamer's Aesthetic Ontology of the Community," in *The Philosophy of Hans-Georg Gadamer*, ed. Louis Hahn (Chicago: Open Court, 1997), 323–45.

8. Martin Heidegger, "The Origin of the Work of Art," in *Basic Writings*, ed. David Farrell Krell (San Francisco: Harper Collins, 1993), 199.

9. *LW* 1:134.

10. Ibid., 1:269.

11. Ibid., 10:220.

12. *EW* 3:112.

13. *LW* 1:270.

14. Ibid., 10:246.

15. Ibid., 10:248.

16. *EW* 3:122. Compare: "I cannot rid myself of the conviction that the weight and the humanity of the message of the poet are proportionate to the weighty and human ideas which he develops; that these ideas must be capable of verification to the intelligence—must be true in that system of knowledge which is science, in that discussion of the meaning of experience which is philosophy" (ibid., 3:119).

17. *LW* 1:27.

18. *EW* 3:123.

19. Music was often given credit for appealing the more directly and most broadly as music is unmediated by ideas, and Dewey does give music credit for being able to take something otherwise unmalleable and give it rhythmic and melodic meaning. "There are critics who hold that music outrivals poetry in its power to convey a sense of life and phases of life as we should desire them to be. I cannot, however, but think that by the very nature of its medium music is brutally organic: not, of course, in the sense in which 'brutal' signifies 'beastly,' but as we speak of brute facts, of that which is undeniable and unescapable, because so inevitably there. Nor is this view disparaging to music. Its value is precisely that it can take material which is organically assertive and apparently intractable, and make melody and harmony out of it" (*LW* 10:247).

20. *LW* 10:16.

21. Ibid., 10:221.

22. Ibid., 10:54.

23. Hans-Georg Gadamer, "Religious and Poetical Speech," in *Myth, Symbol and Reality*, ed. Alan Olson and Leroy Rouner (Notre Dame, Ind.: University of Notre Dame Press, 1980), 86.

24. "The common aspect in all literature, however, lies obviously in the fact that the writer himself disappears because he has given to the linguistic form such an ideal form that nothing can be added. Everything is in the words of the text exactly as they appear in the text. We call that the art of writing" (Hans-Georg Gadamer, "Philosophy and Literature," *Man and World* 18, no. 2 [1985]: 249).

25. Hans-Georg Gadamer, "Philosophy and Poetry," in *Relevance of the Beautiful*, 132–33, emphasis his.

26. It is no coincidence that Louise Rosenblatt, the American founder of the reception theory of reading, was a Deweyan (see her *The Reader, the Text, the Poem* [Carbondale: Southern Illinois University Press, 1978]) and that Hans-Robert Jauss, the main German proponent of reception theory, did his dissertation under Gadamer (see his *Toward an Aesthetic of Reception*, trans. Timothy Bahti [Minneapolis: University of Minnesota Press, 1982]).

27. *LW* 1:291. He goes on to reject the second alternative.

28. Heidegger had something like this in mind when he wrote: "The linguistic work, poetry in the narrower sense, has a privileged position among the arts as a whole. To see this all we need is the right concept of language. According to the usual account, language is a kind of communication. It serves as a means of discussion and

agreement, in general for achieving understanding. But language is neither merely nor primarily the aural and written expression of what needs to be communicated. The conveying of overt and covert meanings is not what language, in the first instance, does. Rather, it brings beings as beings, for the first time, into the open" ("The Origin of the Work of Art," in *Off the Beaten Track*, ed. and trans. Julian Young and Kenneth Haynes [Cambridge: Cambridge University Press, 2002], 46–47).

29. *LW* 1:134.

30. For Gadamer's account of linguisticality, see especially his "Towards a Phenomenology of Ritual and Language," in *Language and Linguisticality in Gadamer's Hermeneutics*, ed. Lawrence Schmidt (Lanham, Md.: Lexington Books, 2000), 19–50.

31. Hans-Georg Gadamer, "Philosophical Foundations of the Twentieth-Century," in *Philosophical Hermeneutics*, trans. David Linge (Berkeley: University of California Press, 1976), 115.

32. Gadamer writes, "Because the body presents itself as something with which we are intimate and not like an obstacle, it is precisely what sets us free and lets us be open for what is" ("Praise of Theory," in *Praise of Theory: Speeches and Essays*, trans. Chris Dawson [New Haven: Yale University Press, 1998], 30).

33. *EW* 5:98.

34. A version of this argument is made by Bill Blattner in "The Primacy of Practice and Assertoric Truth: Dewey and Heidegger," in *Heidegger, Authenticity and Modernity: Essays in Honor of Hubert L. Dreyfus*, ed. Mark Wrathall and Jeffrey Malpas (Cambridge, Mass.: MIT Press, 2000), 1:231–49.

35. Hans-Georg Gadamer, "On the Contribution of Poetry to the Search for Truth," in *Relevance of the Beautiful*, 112.

36. Hans-Georg Gadamer, "Language and Understanding," in *Theory, Culture and Society* 23, no. 1 (2006): 26.

10] Educating the Self: Dewey and Foucault

C. G. Prado

Richard Rorty once said that John Dewey waited at the end of the road Michel Foucault traveled.[1] Rorty is right with respect to three key ideas which I explore below, but he is wrong about Dewey's and Foucault's respective philosophical positions on science in particular and application of intelligence generally. Dewey's trust in scientific method is very much at odds with Foucault's—and Rorty's own—relativistic construal of science, its methodology, and its self-image. Also, contrary to Foucault, Dewey trusted what I will call the *transparency* of applied intelligence or our ability to determine when we get things right. These differences significantly qualify, if they do not negate, the similarities between Dewey and Foucault.

What I want to focus on in this chapter are the similarities between Dewey's and Foucault's conceptions of *experience*, *habit*, and *the subject*: specifically, the similarities in their views of how experience shapes us by imbuing us with attitude-instilling habits. The similarities between Dewey and Foucault on the subject-shaping roles of habit and experience, as well as on the nature of the subject, are striking. However, as striking are the differences between them regarding whether experience's habit-imbuing results can be controlled and, more generally, on the efficacy and transparency of intellectual endeavor.

In Dewey's optimistic view, experience may be effectively managed for the purpose of educating. In Foucault's pessimistic—one could say nihilistic—view, discipline-imposed experience produces unpredictable and ultimately unmanageable results. Dewey saw planned stimulation of productive experiences as central to the successful imparting and development of positive attitudes and fruitful skills, and he was obviously convinced that stimulation of the right experiences for learners was not only achievable but indeed the main responsibility of enlightened educators. For his part, at least during his genealogical phase, Foucault had a bleak view of how experience's effects are determined by power-relations or "power" and so of how individuals actually are affected by the experiences they undergo. So while Dewey and Foucault traveled the same road for some distance, the question is who traveled farther.

John Dewey's voluminous writings defy adequate summation even with respect to particular areas. Happily, most readers of this collection will be reasonably familiar with Dewey's views, so I will not attempt an inevitably inadequate summary and instead concentrate on the two of Dewey's works most relevant to my comparison of him with Foucault: *Human Nature and Conduct* and *Experience and Education*.[2] With respect to Foucault, my focus is his genealogical work, so I concentrate on *Discipline and Punish* and, indirectly, *The History of Sexuality, Volume 1*.[3] However, the place to begin is not with any of these books but rather with a comment about Dewey that bears importantly on what I want to say.

In his introduction to *The Later Works of John Dewey*, Steven Cahn quotes Charles Frankel as noting "that for Dewey 'all philosophy was at bottom social philosophy implicitly or explicitly.'" Cahn adds, "I would extend this insight and suggest that for Dewey all social philosophy was at bottom philosophy of education implicitly or explicitly."[4] What I think important about Cahn's comment is that, for Dewey, reflection on and positive proposals about education—about the imparting and acquiring of skills and knowledge—were integral to his philosophical thought. Dewey's understanding of the fundamentality of education was as definitive of his general philosophical views as was his pragmatic understanding of truth. Therefore, it is a mistake to read Dewey narrowly as mainly focused on epistemological issues, as so many professional philosophers do, and to think that his interest in education was an interest essentially separable from his concerns with the nature of knowledge and truth and the inadequacies of metaphysics—interests usually thought more philosophically central than educational. Dewey's thought about education manifests his conception of the subject, of how subjects are formed, and so of who or what is educated. These are fundamental philosophical questions, so grounding a comparison of Dewey and Foucault on Dewey's thought about education is hardly a matter of focusing on a peripheral area; it is a matter of focusing on the core of Dewey's philosophizing. As for Foucault, grounding the comparison on his conceptions of power, discipline, and the subject is unquestionably to focus on the essence of his genealogical analytics in particular and of his thinking more generally.

Dewey's consideration of experience in *Experience and Education* is prompted by his endorsement of what he labels the "new" or progressive education over the "old" or traditional education. Most briefly put, the old education prioritizes the conveying of *content*, whereas the new education prioritizes learners' *experiences*. Dewey tells us that "[i]f one attempts to formulate the philosophy of education implicit in the practices of the newer education," one finds that it is defined by a reversal of priorities. In the old education, primacy is assigned to "learning from texts and teachers," whereas in the new education, primacy is assigned to "learning through experience."[5] Most characteristic of the old education is that the role of the learner is *passive* in the reception of imparted knowledge and techniques. In the new education, the learner is *active* in the application and exercise of techniques and knowledge. In the old understanding, "[t]he subject matter of education consists of bodies of information and of skills [and] the chief business of the school is to transmit them to the new generation."[6] Contrary to this, in the new understanding, the focus is on "expression and cultivation of individuality" and on "learning through experience."[7]

In the old understanding, learners' educational experience is simply expected to be attentive receptivity. Little consideration is given to managing learners' experiences beyond ensuring attention and compliance. In the new understanding, managing learners' experiences becomes the central concern of educators because experience is rethought as the means of learning rather than as a condition of learning. However, Dewey's endorsement of the new education is not unreserved. While he agrees with the new education's principles, he is concerned about their proper application; specifically, he is concerned about how experience is understood. Dewey believes that the new experience-focused understanding of education must incorporate an accurate grasp of the nature of experience and of its management, so that implementation of the new understanding will prove productively effective.

In discussing the shift from old to new thinking in education, Dewey recognizes the complexities involved and rejects strict opposition or an either/or way of thinking about the old and new education.[8] He stresses that experience was, of course, an inescapable component of the old education. Therefore, it is not experience per se that is at issue between the old and new understandings; what is at issue is experience's priority and recognition of the decisiveness of its role in educating learners. This is why Dewey dwells on the necessity of educators "having a *correct* idea of experience."[9] He observes that "[e]xperience and education cannot be directly equated to each other. For some experiences are mis-educative."[10] Adoption of the new education cannot be a matter of assuming that it suffices to move away from the conveying of information and to emphasize stimulation of experience. That stimulation must be properly guided by clear understanding of which experiences will prove educative and which would prove mis-educative.

Dewey's pragmatism emerges here: experiences are not educative or mis-educative in themselves. Experiences are mis-educative to the extent that they result in "arresting or distorting the growth of further experience."[11] For instance, a mis-educative experience may "engender callousness; it may produce lack of sensitivity and of responsiveness."[12] Even transiently rewarding experiences may be mis-educative in the long run by fostering carelessness or engendering complacency in learners and in that way distorting learners' future experiences and making those future experiences less productive. There is here implicit recognition, too, that some experiences will affect some learners positively and others negatively, depending on their personal histories and situations, a point central to Foucault's thinking about discipline.

Educators, then, must arrange for learners to have the kind of experiences that "promote having desirable future experiences." This means that "the central problem of an education based upon experience is to select the kind of present experiences that live fruitfully and creatively in subsequent experiences." The difficulty, as Dewey cautions, is that "[t]he *effect* of an experience is not borne on its face."[13] This is why it is crucial that educators have the correct idea of experience. Here we begin to see the similarity between Dewey and Foucault on education and discipline but also get an intimation of what divides them.

With respect to the similarity, Dewey's recognition that experience is integral to both the old and new education, and that therefore issues have to do with the right kind of experience, manifests his understanding of experience's fundamental determining role with respect to the formation of subjects. He makes this understanding explicit by referring to the role of *habit.* What experience does that bears most directly on education is imbue habit. It does so by prompting particular agent-responses to their experiences. In the context of establishing the basic elements of experience's role in education, Dewey articulates the centrality of habit in the formation of subjects in a decidedly Foucaultian way, telling us that "[t]he basic characteristic of habit is that every experience enacted and undergone modifies the one who acts and undergoes [it], while this modification affects, whether we wish it or not, the quality of subsequent experiences. For it is a somewhat different person who enters into them."[14] Experience forms the subject by imbuing habit, and in doing so continuously, it endlessly reshapes the subject.

This is precisely Foucault's view, though he speaks of the imposition of experience and the imbuing of habit in terms of discipline rather than education, given that his initial concern is with the management of inmates in prisons rather than of students in school. For Foucault, subjects are *manufactured* by the attitude-instilling and practice-determining habits that malleable bodies are imbued with in being disciplined—or educated. He insists that "it is . . . one of the prime effects of power that certain bodies, certain gestures, certain discourses, certain desires, come to be identified and constituted as individuals."[15] Foucault's stress on the manufactured nature of subject may go beyond Dewey's conception of the subject, but as I explain below, both conceptions are crucially similar in being anti-Cartesian and *constructivist* in nature. For both Dewey and Foucault, the subject, the self, the person, the individual, is formed by experience and sustained by habit. In a remark that could have been made by Foucault, Dewey tells us that "[w]ere it not for the continued operation of all habits in every act, no such thing as character could exist. . . . Character is the interpenetration of habits."[16] For his part, Foucault maintains that "discipline creates out of the bodies it controls . . . individuality."[17]

Education and discipline work by requiring certain behavior. When pursued, that behavior imbues habits, and those habits form subjects by determining their attitudes: their perspectives, values, priorities, desires, intentions, and self-images. Imbued habit also has a cognitive effect in disposing individuals to more readily accept or reject certain sorts of beliefs. But in talking about habit or habits, Dewey is not talking about simple "fixed way[s] of doing things," like always putting on your right shoe first or reading sections of the newspaper in a certain order. Dewey is talking just as Foucault does about modes of behavior responsible for "the formation of attitudes."[18] Both are talking about experience-imbued habits that by instilling attitudes form the persons that individuals are. And both recognize that the process is a continuous one because experiences change, so their effects on subjects constantly reshape those subjects.

A further similarity in Dewey's and Foucault's thinking is that Dewey anticipates Foucault by arguing that it is not only individual subjects who are changed by educative or mis-educative experiences: "Every genuine experience has an active side which changes in some degree the objective conditions under which experiences are had. . . . In a word, we live from birth to death in a world of persons and things which in large measure is what it is because of what has been done and transmitted from previous human activities."[19] This point is very much in line with Foucault's thinking about power and how actions constrain other actions, as I describe below, but mention of power brings us to what separates Dewey and Foucault.

As noted above, Dewey acknowledges that "[t]he *effect* of an experience is not borne on its face." Both Dewey and Foucault appreciate that experience's effects are not immediately evident. Dewey sees this lack of evidence as calling for diligence in the identification of properly educative experiences; Foucault sees the lack of evidence as signaling the inherently unpredictable and unmanageable nature of experience's power-conditioned influences on individuals. What begins to emerge here is a profound difference between Dewey and Foucault on scientific method and the transparency of applied intelligence.

Dewey is fundamentally optimistic about controlling human activity's effects on ourselves and the world we live in. Experience's "active side," in changing the conditions under which further experiences are had, may improve things for us. For Dewey, human activity can make things *better.* Its inevitable effects on the world we live in can be planned to be positive. This is, at bottom, the point of education and so is basic to Dewey's thinking. However, for Foucault, the consequences of human activity only make things *different.* We may deem the difference better or worse, but that is only our immediate interests-determined reading of the change. This is one of the points driven home in *Discipline and Punish*, where what from one perspective were humanitarian reforms of a brutal penal system are portrayed by Foucault as resulting only in greater control of inmates within and without prison walls.[20]

The disagreement between Dewey and Foucault on the reliability of scientific method and the transparency of applied intelligence is perhaps clearest, on Dewey's side, in the last chapter of *Experience and Education*, where he articulates his optimism regarding the manageability of experience. Dewey tells us that he is "so confident of the potentialities of education when it is treated as intelligently directed development of the possibilities inherent in ordinary experience that I do not feel it necessary to criticize here the other route [imposition of content] nor to advance arguments in favor of taking the route of experience."[21] It is basic to Dewey's understanding of experience's role in education that learners' experiences can be controlled so as to be productively educative rather than mis-educative. Educators must and *are* able to ensure that learners have the kind of experiences that will prove fruitful and creative with respect to their subsequent experiences.

As far as Dewey is concerned, the problems that educators face essentially are methodological rather than axiological; that is, the choices educators need to make have to do less with what is of value in education than with how to achieve what is of value. The value of productive experience is evident; what is less evident is what particular experiences will be most productive for learners and how to go about ensuring that their experiences are positive and enhancing and not mis-educative. Dewey's understanding of experience is commensurate with Foucault's to the extent that both see experience as instilling attitudes by imbuing habits and so to one degree or another forming and changing the subjects who undergo experiences. Moreover, they agree that experience shapes actions and actions in turn shape the contexts in which individual subjects have experiences and in which individual agents do what they do. But problems between Dewey and Foucault emerge with respect to the identification of educative experiences.

For Dewey, it is applied intelligence in the form of scientific method that enables identification of productive experiences and development of techniques that generate those productive experiences in learners as they progress through their education. Dewey makes his faith in scientific method explicit when he maintains that "scientific method is the only authentic means at our command for getting at the significance of our . . . experiences" and adds that "scientific method provides a working pattern of the way in which and the conditions under which experiences are used to lead ever onward and outward." Clearly, Dewey has profound confidence in scientific method or what he describes as "intelligence operating in the best manner."[22]

What makes the difference between Dewey and Foucault more pointed is that obviously Dewey's reliance on scientific method regarding the identification of correct educative experiences is on the *social* sciences. Recourse would not be to physics or chemistry but to psychology, social psychology, educational psychology, and related disciplines. These latter are among the disciplines Foucault thinks lack objectivity and are as much the products of power as are institutional or individual perspectives.[23] Foucault dismisses social-science disciplines as so many more "discourses" and describes them as forms of inquiry "which try to give themselves the status of sciences."[24] His disdain for these disciplines is rooted in the absence of an answer to the deep question he raises about the development and growth of these disciplines, which is how "the human subject took itself as the object of possible knowledge."[25] Foucault sees no obvious answer to the question of how we came to believe and accept that we can be the subject-matter of psychology, sociology, and psychiatry as electrons and tectonic plates are the subject matters of physics and geology. In Foucault's eyes, therefore, employment of scientific method to determine the right experiences to stimulate in learners amounts to no more than more power-determined discursive treatment of imposed theoretical inventions and fabrication of supposedly discerned "facts" about our allegedly essential nature.[26]

Dewey's understanding of habit-imbuing experience and attitude-instilling habit coincides with Foucault's understanding of habit and experience and their effects, but the two part company on the question of whether experience's effects can be controlled. Dewey takes understanding of experience's subject-defining role as realization of the importance of events that can be managed by applying scientific method; Foucault takes understanding of experience's role as realization of the hopeless complexity and uncontrollable nature of the influences that shape us.[27] But to better understand the split between them, we need to say more about the similarity of Dewey's and Foucault's conceptions of the subject, of what or who is educated or mis-educated by undergoing experiences, a similarity that surprises many.

What must be appreciated is that as mentioned above, Dewey had what in today's language would be described as a constructivist understanding of the nature of the subject.[28] Dewey's was a thoroughly un-Cartesian conception of the self or subject. In the context of discussing the importance of habit in the forming of the subject, Dewey tells us that "[t]he doctrine of a single, simple and indissoluble soul was the cause and the effect of failure to recognize that concrete habits are the means of knowledge and thought." Against the Cartesian conception of the subject as a singularity, Dewey contends that "selfhood, subjectivity are eventual functions that emerge with complexly organized interactions, [both] organic and social."[29] Dewey rejects the traditional philosophical "isolation of the ego, the thinking self."[30] He maintains that "habits . . . are the sole agents of observation, recollection, foresight and judgment," adding that "a mind or consciousness or soul . . . which performs these operations is a myth."[31] The mind "is in itself a system of belief, recognitions, and ignorances, of acceptances and rejections, of expectancies and appraisal of meaning which have been instituted under the influence of custom and tradition."[32]

Foucault, of course, also rejects the Cartesian ego-subject. He takes as his central genealogical task "to expose a body totally imprinted by history" and thus to show how the body is "the locus of a dissociated self": a subject that does not recognize itself as emergent and adopts "the illusion of [being] a substantial unity" by creating and identifying with such fictions as the Cartesian ego.[33] In *Power/Knowledge*, Foucault maintains that "the individual is not a pre-given entity" and that we have to produce "an analysis which can account for the subject itself within an historical account."[34]

Subjects for Dewey and Foucault are not self-contained entities that preexist all of their experiences; they are not mental substances as they are for dualists and idealists. Subjects do not *acquire* attitudes and self-images; subjects are constructs *produced* by habit-imbuing experiences. Dewey and Foucault share the understanding that, as Dewey puts it, "habits . . . constitute the self."[35] This is what Foucault means when he tells us that "[d]iscipline 'makes' individuals."[36]

Both are of a mind that, again in Dewey's words, "[t]he dynamic force of habit taken in connection with the continuity of habits with one another explains the unity of character and conduct, or speaking more concretely of motive and act, will and deed."[37] Subjects are what subjects have done and are doing.

With respect to what it is that forms subjects, the basic idea Dewey and Foucault share is at least as old as Aristotle's articulation of it: "A state [of character] arises from [the repetition of] similar activities."[38] Speaking of becoming ethical, Aristotle also tells us that individuals "must keep on observing their regimen and accustoming themselves to it" to become the persons their regimen is designed to form.[39] Whether the conduct is self- or other-imposed, engaging in certain conduct until it becomes habitual makes individuals into what they or others intend them to be because habitual conduct is what individuals do as a matter of course. This understanding of the person-molding nature of habit is evident in abstract psychological treatises, in the reflective practices engaged in by educators and therapists, and in the unreflective practices engaged in by parents. The idea is succinctly captured in the familiar adage, "As the twig is bent, so grows the tree."[40] At base, the idea is that individuals come to be the persons they are, not by thinking but by *doing*, and the idea is as much at the heart of Dewey's view of managed habit-imbuing experience as the essence of education as it is the core of Foucault's understanding of discipline as managed habit-imbuing experience.[41]

The difference between Dewey and Foucault is that while Dewey sees understanding of experience's habit-imbuing role as prompting research into how best to identify and manage educative experiences, Foucault believes that since the *actual* effects of habit-imbuing experience are unpredictable, disciplinary—or educational—habit-imbuing is unmanageable. Foucault's view is that the workings of power unpredictably condition the results of even the most carefully and diligently implemented habit-imbuing plans. Central to Foucault's view is his conception of power as *impersonal* and so as inherently fortuitous in its workings and consequences. Power is so because it is a "set of actions upon other actions."[42] Foucaultian power is not power in the usual sense of the capacity and exercise of dominance or force by individuals or groups on other individuals or groups; it is not persuasion, intimidation, or coercion. Instead, power "is a way in which certain actions modify others." Foucaultian power "is a mode of action which does not act directly and immediately on others. Instead it acts upon their actions." This is because power is "a total structure of actions" that influences "possible actions" in enabling or prompting some acts and inhibiting or precluding others.[43] In this way, power constrains what people actually do and in doing so conditions the habits that are actually imbued in individuals and therefore the precise character of the attitudes instilled in those individuals. These actual attitudes may and often do differ from those educators and disciplinarians intend to imbue in learners or inmates. Most briefly put, power is *the dynamic totality of previous and concurrent actions blindly modifying presently ensuing actions.*[44]

Foucaultian power basically is an *environment*, an environment of blind influences: it is the fluid medium in which individuals act.[45] We are all agents in the medium of power, and what we do or do not do is shaped not only by what we are asked or told to do but also by the complexities of the contexts in which we act or refrain from acting. The result of power's workings is that the attitude-generating habits that actually are instilled in individuals are only some of them or to some degree those intended in the educating and disciplining of protean subjects. Dewey can accommodate a measure of this indeterminacy without abandoning his conviction that the imbuing of attitude-instilling habit can be planned and controlled, but for him such indeterminacy must remain within the scope of the exceptional. For Foucault, on the other hand, indeterminacy of results is the norm.

The indeterminacy of results has to do both with how individual subjects are in fact formed and with what implemented plans actually achieve and, as important, how the results are perceived. Implementation of a plan designed to prompt particular experiences in learners may well succeed in that the learners undergo the intended experiences. But the actual consequences of their doing so may not be as intended. For instance, in an educational setting, the awarding of prizes for academic achievement may well produce pride and elation in those receiving the prizes and envy in others, as planned. But the pride and elation produced may not prove educative. The pride and elation produced may result in fostering arrogance, false self-assurance, or complacency. Again, the envy may not prompt greater effort in other individuals but only festering resentment. Moreover, while these consequences have to do with individuals, they also determine the consequences for the institutions implementing the plan in question. Instead of prompting productive competitiveness, the awarding of prizes may prove unproductively divisive by isolating able learners and discouraging those of more average ability. This is a consequence for the institutions because it is one that significantly affects what their policies systematically achieve. The trouble is that what the institutions' policies achieve may not only be mis-educative but may not be recognized as mis-educative for some time, if at all. The institutions may be perceived as succeeding in their educative objectives despite the introduction of invidious divisions among their learners due to the awarding of prizes.

It is precisely misapprehensions of the actual effects of institutional practices that Foucault's genealogical analytics are intended to expose. *Discipline and Punish* reveals how what was intended and widely perceived as penal reform was in fact development of a series of disciplinary practices that exerted far greater control on prison inmates than the inhumane routines the new practices replaced. Foucault sees this sort of outcome to institutional activity as inevitable; Dewey sees this sort of undesirable and possibly misperceived outcome as avoidable through productive use of scientific method and application of intelligence. Naturally, Dewey's pragmatism precludes his thinking that careful planning and implementation of policy can meet *objective* standards of correctness, but he is profoundly committed to "intelligence operating in the best manner" being able to meet most challenges.[46] Dewey assures us that "[b]ecause intelligence is critical method applied to goods of belief, appreciation and conduct, so as to construct freer and more secure goods . . . it is the reasonable object of our deepest faith and loyalty, the stay and support of all reasonable hopes."[47] Dewey adds that "[t]o claim that intelligence is a better method than its alternatives, authority, imitation, caprice and ignorance, prejudice and passion, is hardly an excessive claim."[48]

Foucault may not find the comparative claim excessive, but what is at issue between him and Dewey does not have to do with the value of intelligence against its alternatives. Foucault can readily grant that applied intelligence is better than recourse to dogmatic authority, for instance, without thereby giving applied intelligence very high marks for efficacy. What is at issue between Dewey and Foucault has to do with applied intelligence's efficacy and especially its transparency. Dewey, being realistic, is not claiming that "intelligence will ever dominate the course of events" or that it necessarily will save us "from ruin and destruction." He freely admits that what "the method of intelligence . . . will accomplish . . . is for the result of trial to determine." His point, though, is that "*some* procedure has to be tried," and given the alternatives, intelligence is our best bet.[49] Though Foucault could not disagree, he does not share Dewey's implicit trust in our ability to know when things work out for the better, to know when trial provides positive or negative determination regarding intended results.

Foucault does not trust us *to know what we are doing or have done.* This mistrust is at the heart of genealogy generally and *Discipline and Punish* in particular. Moreover, his reservations should give us pause. Consider the point of the latter work; the humanitarian reform of penality focused on inmates' subjectivity and abandoned punishment limited to the confinement and persecution of *bodies* as all that were accessible in dealing with lawbreakers. There is an ominous parallel here to the new education's abandonment of teaching as the informing of passively receptive learners, as all that are available to be taught, and to its reconceived focus on learners as subjects of experience. In the case of penal reform, what the reform amounted to was imposition of control of people of an entirely different order than was possible before: imposition of control that was obscured by power's workings.[50] The new education could amount to something similar, especially with regard to what Foucault describes as the invention of the modern *soul.*

The imposition of greatly extended control passing as reform exemplifies how we may not know what we achieve in applying intelligence. This is illustrated in how what enabled the degree of control exercised in the new penal practices was applied intelligence's invention of the soul. The invention of the soul was the reconception of incarceration as rehabilitation of *personae* rather than as retributively punitive treatment of prisoners' physical beings. Foucault claims that the idea of a soul was introduced into penal thinking and practices as part of the reconception of subjectivity.[51] What he means is that a new dimension of personhood was supposedly discerned, a core nature that was perverted by criminality and could be reclaimed or reasserted through training. This invention made possible a kind of control not previously envisaged. But contrary to the implicit assumption made by reformers, the soul did not *antedate* its supposed discernment; it was not something that was there to be discerned: the modern soul was "born . . . out of methods of punishment, supervision and constraint."[52]

Foucault's contentions about the soul show what he distrusts about application of intelligence or scientific method. The adoption of the new rehabilitory practices required an object for those practices to bear on, so through learned discursive treatment a suitable object was produced: a malleable, trainable subject, a supposedly essential self that could be rehabilitated by being imbued with the right habits through discipline. But production of the soul in the process of managing inmates—and for that matter, students, soldiers, factory workers, the sick, the mad, and eventually sexual beings—was perceived as a *discovery.* It was perceived as our learning something crucial about our human nature. Intelligence was certainly used in the production of the soul, but its use led, not to acquisition of new knowledge, but to production of a convenient rationalization for treating certain people in certain ways.

Application of intelligence goes wrong because not only are power's effects unpredictable, but they often go unnoticed or are misperceived because of operant expectations and interpretive inclinations that are themselves products of power. The trouble is that agents do not know the consequences of their actions, whether the agents are acting on their own or corporately in the interests of an institution. Foucault puts the point in this way: "People know what they do; they frequently know why they do what they do; but what they don't know is what what they do does."[53] More important to a comparison of Dewey and Foucault on the efficacy and transparency of applied intelligence is that looking harder at possible and actual consequences will not help because there is "no escaping from power"; power "is always already present, constituting that very thing which one attempts to counter it with."[54] When we try to understand or to resist power's influences, we simply act as the subjects that earlier influences have made us. Our every judgment, construal, and appraisal of the results of trial is produced by a subjectivity shaped by power. Power determines the standards, priorities, relevancies, and values subjects apply in trying to understand themselves and anything else. The application of intelligence is not transparent because its application and assessment of its application's results are always conditioned by power's previous and concurrent effects.

The genealogies Foucault offers "of the different modes by which human beings are made subjects" effectively reduce investigation of and knowledge about ourselves and our social world to power-determined perceptions that may dominate for a time but fluctuate as power-relations change.[55] This is the hard lesson of genealogy and is one Foucault himself learned well, since he sought to change himself, not by self-assessment and willful acts of self-determination, but rather by provoking "limit experiences" or subjectivity-altering radical episodes centering on exploration of the forbidden.[56]

We now see more clearly the pivotal difference between Dewey and Foucault on the efficacy and transparency of applied intelligence. Dewey would reject Foucault's view on the grounds that scientific method enables us to discern significant influences on individuals and to counter them with training, education, and even therapy. He could not accept Foucault's vision of the subject as incapable of usefully delving into its own attitudes and practices. Dewey would insist that psychology, social psychology, psychoanalysis, and related disciplines tell us a great deal about how we are influenced and in doing so enable a significant measure of control over those influences. Dewey would not deny the possibility of individual or collective misperceptions and illusions, but he would reject the holistic scope and impenetrability Foucault attributes to them. Like bad science, such misperceptions and illusions would be exposed, Dewey believed, by further application of intelligence and scientific method. In fact, Dewey no doubt would point to Foucault's own genealogical analyses as confirming the efficacy of applying intelligence and scientific method to our perceptions to enable reexamination of their legitimacy with respect to their grounds or sources.

The trouble is that Foucault's way of thinking is compelling once articulated. Consider that Dewey's own *Experience and Education* lends itself to Foucaultian genealogical analysis. It is possible to argue in a Foucaultian manner that the new education was less progressive than manipulative treatment of learners, despite being perceived as a significant step forward in education. Foucault might have written a book titled *Discipline and Educate.* In it he could have argued that what passed as enlightened realization of the importance of experience in education was the establishment of an extensive system of practices directed less at educating learners than at exercising control over them through the imbuing of normalizing habits. After all, how the new education treated learners is disturbingly comparable to how inmates came to be controlled in the reformation of the penal system. Numerous controlling practices were spawned in that reformation: widely inclusive files were kept on inmates; there was continuous psychological assessment of them; inmates were constantly required to reflect on and voice changes in their attitudes and objectives in a basically confessional manner. Additionally, various areas of special expertise in dealing with inmates' rehabilitory progress emerged and rather self-servingly legitimized and refined the controlling practices.[57] These practices, suitably adjusted, are as much applied in the school as in the prison and, Foucault would argue, to the same effect.

The vulnerability of the new education to Foucaultian analysis brings into sharper focus the difference between Dewey and Foucault regarding applied intelligence in general and scientific method in particular. Dewey is not, and on principle cannot be, committed to application of intelligence or scientific method discerning what is *objectively true* about education or prison reform or anything else. But he is committed to scientific method and applied intelligence discerning what is *better* after suitable testing and evaluation: the success or failure of applied intelligence is "for the result of trial to determine."[58] Against this, as noted earlier, Foucault can only countenance discernment of *difference*, since perception of the results of trial as well as the very structuring of testing and evaluation are as much power-determined as anything else. The key point is that Dewey's stance allows for application of intelligence to achieve *progress*, while Foucault's stance allows it only to achieve *change*.

What needs to be appreciated here is that, in the end, once absolutes are surrendered, whether it is by embracing pragmatism or postmodernism, there is no recourse to objective standards to establish once-and-for-all the correctness of assessments of the success or failure of collective or individual efforts and consequences. Once absolutes are abandoned, we are left in the position Rorty describes as realization that there is "no criterion that we have not created in the course of creating a practice," hence no standard "that is not obedience to our own conventions."[59]

Dewey believes that application of intelligence can achieve progress by devising better conventions and validating the good ones we already have. As *Experience and Education* makes clear, he considers the new education to be progress and firmly believes that further application of intelligence will establish that it is genuine progress and will improve matters by determining which are the most productive sorts of experiences for education to foster. Foucault sees the conventions we obey as not of our own making, much less as correctable by us in any efficaciously self-reflective way. The conventions are products of power. This is why Foucault would treat the new education as he treated penal reform: as power-determined extension of control.

Given the lack of recourse to absolutes, at first glance it may look as if Dewey and Foucault simply have opposed positions on applied intelligence and scientific method and that choosing between them is a matter of either siding with Dewey's optimism about our ability to productively assess and re-direct our intellectual and practical efforts or siding with Foucault about our individual and collective impotence to resist power. However, a closer look at Foucault's position reveals a key weakness and so shows that it was Dewey who traveled farther down the road he shared for a distance with Foucault.

The point has to do with the nature of genealogy. Foucault tells us that genealogies oppose "the institution and functioning of an organized scientific discourse within a society."[60] It is always "against the power of a discourse that is considered to be scientific that . . . genealogy must wage its struggle."[61] But in being always oppositional, genealogy cannot aspire to establishing new orthodoxies. It functions by constant problematization of dominant discourses, not by establishing its own.[62] Problematization is the objective, not a means. Foucault saw intellectuals' mandate as being "[t]o change something in the minds of people." He asked what intellectual activity could consist in "if not in the endeavor to know how and to what extent it might be possible to think differently."[63] Foucault's priority was *novelty*, because *truth* is a fiction; the only truth is what power produces.[64] Truth is "produced . . . by virtue of multiple forms of constraint."[65] We are constantly "subjected to the production of truth through power."[66] And power's production of truth, of "knowledges," is ever more constricting. The dominant discourses that power establishes grow increasingly unaccommodating and rigid, and their employment in the normalization of individuals grows increasingly thorough and unforgiving. Against this, all that genealogy can do is to "separate out, from the contingency that has made us what we are, the possibility of no longer being . . . what we are."[67] Genealogy, then, produces change-provoking *alternative* histories, not error-correcting *true* histories.

This is where the strength of Dewey's pragmatism and reliance on trial becomes evident. As alluded to earlier, the question arises as to why anyone should consider Foucault's genealogical analyses of penality and sexuality as alternatives preferable to the histories he rejects.[68] The question is made more pointed by how Foucault presents his genealogies. He presents *Discipline and Punish* and *The History of Sexuality, Volume 1* in a decidedly instructional mode; neither is presented as only describing an alternative perspective on penality and sexuality. It can be argued, as I myself did, that Foucault has to present his genealogies in a didactic manner to make them convincing.[69] But that just pushes the question back a step: aside from stylistic matters, how are Foucault's genealogies convincing? Foucault's answer essentially is appeal to change and novelty, in line with his conviction that intellectual activity can consist in little or nothing "if not in the endeavor to know how and to what extent it might be possible to think differently."[70] It is not trial that makes a genealogy convincing but rather that it *changes* us. Speaking of books generally and his own in particular, Foucault contends that "what is essential . . . lies . . . in the experience which the book permits us to have."[71] This seems insufficient and prompts agreement with Rorty's dismissal of Foucaultian genealogy as vitiated by the inability to claim to show established histories as power-produced while disavowing hidden realities.[72]

What we have can be summarized in this way: with respect to similarities, both Dewey and Foucault subscribe to an essentially constructivist conception of the subject and its formation. Both reject Cartesian conception of the subject as a preexistent singularity with a continuing essence: a subject that only acquires and discards attitudes. Against this, Dewey and Foucault see attitudes—perspectives, values, inclinations, self-images—as constitutive of subjects. And both understand experience to be the crucial determinant of how subjects are formed because experience is what imbues them with attitude-instilling habits.

With respect to dissimilarities, Dewey has unreserved confidence in the efficacy and transparency of applied intelligence and scientific method; Foucault sees recourse to either or both as thoroughly conditioned by power and so as opaque and yielding results that are always open to displacement through redescription. With respect to development of the new education in particular and innovative ideas more generally, Dewey puts his trust in trial or pragmatic assessment of results. With respect to the cogency of his genealogies of penality and sexuality in particular and of others more generally, Foucault seems to feel that provision of alterity suffices but persists in presenting his alternative histories as if they are truer to events than those they oppose. Ultimately, Foucault seems ambivalent as to whether his genealogies are change-provoking alternative histories or, as Rorty thinks, purport to be correct accounts of what power obscures.[73] In my view, this ambivalence is not resolved by what is available to us in Foucault's writings and interviews, so the question of the nature of genealogies remains open. Given that it does, we must conclude that Rorty's remark about Dewey waiting at the end of the road Foucault traveled is perhaps best interpreted as Foucault never having reached that end.

Notes

1. Richard Rorty, 1982, *The Consequences of Pragmatism* (Minneapolis: University of Minnesota Press), xviii; see also pp. 203–8 and his "Moral Identity and Private Autonomy: The Case of Foucault," in Richard Rorty, 1991, *Essays on Heidegger and Others: Philosophical Papers*, vol. 2 (New York: Cambridge University Press), 193–98.

2. John Dewey, 1930, *Human Nature and Conduct: An Introduction to Social Psychology*, ed. with new introduction by Dewey (New York: Modern Library); John Dewey, 1988, *Experience and Education*, in *The Later Works of John Dewey, 1925–1953*, ed. Jo Ann Boydston, 1988, vol. 13 (Carbondale: Southern Illinois University Press), 1–62.

3. Michel Foucault, 1979, *Discipline and Punish: The Birth of the Prison*, trans. Alan Sheridan (New York: Pantheon); Michel Foucault, 1980a, *The History of Sexuality, Volume 1*, trans. Robert Hurley (New York: Vintage). For my views on Foucault's earlier archaeological and later ethical periods, see C. G. Prado, 2000, *Starting with Foucault: An Introduction to Genealogy*, 2nd ed. (Boulder and San Francisco: Westview Press); also C. G. Prado, 2006, *Searle and Foucault on Truth* (Cambridge and New York: Cambridge University Press).

4. Steven M. Cahn, 1988, "Introduction," in Boydston 1988, ix–xviii, xvii.

5. Dewey 1988, 7.

6. Ibid., 5.

7. Ibid., 7.

8. Ibid., 5.

9. Ibid., 7, my emphasis.

10. Ibid., 11.

11. Ibid.

12. Ibid.

13. Ibid., 13.

14. Ibid., 18.

15. Foucault 1980a, 98.

16. Dewey 1930, 38.

17. Foucault 1979, 167.

18. Dewey 1988, 19.

19. Ibid., 22.

20. There is a major question here about whether Foucault intends his genealogies of penality and sexuality as *different* accounts or as the *correct* accounts of events. I pursue this question later in the text. See Prado 2000, 106–11.

21. Dewey 1988, 61.

22. Ibid., 59.

23. Prado 2006, chs. 4 and 5.

24. Michel Foucault, 1983, "The Subject and Power," afterword to Hubert Dreyfus and Paul Rabinow, 1983, *Michel Foucault: Beyond Structuralism and Hermeneutics* (Brighton, Sussex: Harvester Press), 208–26, 209–9.

25. Michel Foucault, 1988, "Critical Theory/Intellectual History," in *Michel Foucault: Politics, Philosophy, Culture: Interviews and Other Writings 1977–1984*, ed. Lawrence Kritzman, 1988 (New York: Routledge), 30.

26. This form of Foucaultian genealogical argument is clearer in *The History of Sexuality, Volume 1* than in *Discipline and Punish*. Foucault 1980a, 1979.

27. It merits reiteration that in this chapter I am speaking of the genealogical Foucault. In his ethical works, his last two books, Foucault introduces a measure of effective self-governance. See Michel Foucault, 1986, *The Use of Pleasure*, trans. Robert Hurley (New York: Vintage); also Michel Foucault, 1988, *The Care of the Self*, trans. Robert Hurley (New York: Vintage).

28. There was at least one precedent likely familiar to Dewey of what would now be called a constructivist view of the subject. George Herbert Mead offered what might best be described as a precursor constructivist view. What keeps Mead's view from being fully constructivist is that while he regarded the subject as a *product* of cognition rather than as the *condition* of cognition, as the Cartesian tradition held, Mead's was basically still an ontological view of the subject. Charles Taylor comments on the difference between Mead's view and Foucault's constructivist conception of the subject, observing that Mead "does not seem to take account of the constitutive role of language in the definition of self." Charles Taylor, 1989, *Sources of the Self* (Cambridge, Mass.: Harvard University Press), 525 n. 12.

29. John Dewey, 1981, "Nature, Mind and the Subject," in *The Later Works of John Dewey, 1925–1953*, ed. Jo Ann Boydston, vol. 1 (Carbondale: Southern Illinois University Press), 162–90, 162; see also 169–70.

30. Ibid., 173.

31. Dewey 1930, 176.

32. Dewey, 1981, 170; see also 173–74 and 179–80. It merits adding here that Foucault is explicit about something that is implicit in Dewey, namely, that the subject is complex, being both a subject *of* experience and subject *to* social, institutional, and governmental authority.

33. Michel Foucault, 1971, "Nietzsche, Genealogy, History," in *The Foucault Reader*, ed. Paul Rabinow, 1984 (New York: Pantheon), 76–100, 82–83.

34. Michel Foucault, 1980b, *Power/Knowledge: Selected Interviews and Other Writings*, ed. Colin Gordon (New York: Pantheon Books), 73, 117.

35. Dewey 1930, 25.

36. Foucault 1979, 170.

37. Dewey 1930, 43.

38. Aristotle, 1985, *Nicomachean Ethics*, trans. Terence Irwin (Indianapolis: Hackett Publications), 1103b, p. 35.

39. Aristotle, 1976, *Aristotle: Ethics* (London: Penguin Classics), 337.

40. *Oxford Dictionary of Quotations*, 1980, 3rd ed. (Oxford: Oxford University Press), #12, p. 377. The expression is a corruption of Pope's "Just as the twig is bent, the tree's inclin'd."

41. See, for instance, Dewey 1981, 213–15.

42. Foucault, 1983, 219–20.

43. Ibid.

44. Prado 2000, 78.

45. Ibid., ch. 4.

46. John Dewey, 1938, *Logic: The Theory of Inquiry* (New York: Henry Holt), 345n., 535.

47. Dewey 1981, 325.

48. Ibid., 326.

49. Ibid., my emphasis.

50. Here again the question arises of whether or how Foucault can present his genealogical analyses as *better* than the histories and accounts they dismantle.

51. Foucault 1979, 29.

52. Ibid.

53. Dreyfus and Rabinow, 1983, 187.

54. Foucault 1980a, 82.

55. Foucault 1983, 208.

56. James Miller, 1993, *The Passion of Michel Foucault* (New York: Simon and Schuster).

57. Foucault considers five devices used to manage inmates: hierarchical observation, normalizing judgment, examinations, surveillance, and panopticism. This last derives from Jeremy Bentham's design of the ideal prison in which inmates must assume they are constantly watched because of the architecture of the penitentiary. See Foucault 1979 and Prado 2000, 60–61, 63, 95. Foucault observes that these devices can function only in institutional contexts such as industrial plants, prisons, asylums, and, of course, *schools*, because discipline "requires *enclosure*." Foucault 1979, 141.

58. Dewey 1981, 326.

59. Rorty 1982, xlii.

60. Foucault 1980b, 84.

61. Ibid.

62. Michel Foucault, 1989, *Foucault Live*, ed. Sylvère Lotringer, trans. John Johnston (New York: Semiotext[e]), 295. In an interview given not long before his death, Foucault reiterated the point, saying that what is "common to the work I've done since *Madness and Civilization* is the notion of problematization."

63. Foucault 1986, 9.

64. Prado 2000, 85–115 and ch. 6.

65. Foucault 1980b, 131.

66. Ibid., 93.

67. Michel Foucault, 1984, “What Is Enlightenment?” in Rabinow 1984, 46.

68. See notes 20 and 50, above.

69. Prado 2000, 106–11.

70. Foucault 1986, 9.

71. Michel Foucault, 1991, *Remarks on Marx: Conversations with Duccio Trombadori*, trans. James Goldstein and James Cascaito (New York: Semiotext[e]), 36.

72. Richard Rorty, 1986, “Foucault and Epistemology,” in *Foucault: A Critical Reader*, ed. David Couzens Hoy (New York: Basil Blackwell), 41–49.

73. Foucault’s ambivalence between being right and only being provocative is clearer when he moves away from genealogy toward ethics. In his last two books, *The Use of Pleasure* and *The Care of the Self*, he seems to opt for being right to the extent that he introduces—or reintroduces—a measure of reflective self-determination for subjects. It may be a telling point that the first reference to power in *The Use of Pleasure* puts the term in quotation marks. Foucault 1986, 6.

11] The History and Critique of Modernity: Dewey with Foucault against Weber

Colin Koopman

Interpreting and Criticizing Modernity

In bringing the philosophical traditions of pragmatism and genealogy to bear upon contemporary debates regarding modernity, the work of both John Dewey and Michel Foucault has been subjected to misinterpretations that portray both traditions in a way that depletes them of the full force of their critical insight. This is unfortunate in part because it has led to a failure to engage with pragmatism and genealogy in the terms in which they offered themselves. This is further unfortunate because it has led adherents of each tradition to regard the other tradition as a philosophical opponent rather than an unlikely ally.[1] There has been, in short, far too little cross-fertilization between pragmatists and genealogists despite a number of rather obvious philosophical affinities. The philosophical project of a history and critique of modernity is just one area where this lack of cross-fertilization can be discerned. This is particularly notable insofar as the history and critique of modernity is a project that has very much been at the center of both of these traditions of thought. It figures heavily, to concentrate on my exemplary genealogist and pragmatist, in nearly all of Foucault's books, including *Discipline and Punish* and *History of Madness*, and in many of Dewey's most important books, including *The Quest for Certainty* and *Reconstruction in Philosophy.* Foucault and Dewey offer complementary perspectives on a philosophical project that deserves increased attention today.

That this complementary aspect of these two traditions has gone unnoticed in the literature is due at least in part to misinterpretations of each tradition, perpetrated in large part no doubt by adherents of one tradition against the other, though those working out of other lineages (most obviously German critical theory and French postmodernism) have proposed interpretations of both pragmatism and genealogy that would overemphasize their differences. In many cases, the source of these misinterpretations is an attempt to squeeze the philosophical projects of pragmatism and genealogy into the mold that shapes the thought of most other participants on both sides of the modernity debates. This mold can in many instances be traced back to the work of influential sociologist, political economist, and philosopher Max Weber. Weberian concepts dominate contemporary critical thinking about modernity, most notably in the form of Weber's claims that modernity is characterized above all by a grand process of value-sphere differentiation that gives rise to bureaucratized and rationalized separate spheres of society. One unfortunate residue of the subtle dominance of these Weberian concepts in contemporary debates over modernity is that many thinkers who operated largely outside of these concepts cannot be brought into these debates without filtering their thought through this conceptual prism. In the case of Dewey and Foucault, their contributions to our understanding of the history and critique of modernity are widely misunderstood due to being filtered through Weberian concepts that simply were not central in Dewey's or Foucault's thinking.

The extraordinary complexity of Weber's thought helps explain why his interpretation of modernity has proven capacious enough to provide fuel for both pro-modern optimists and anti-modern pessimists. But Weber's interpretation only justifies *either* pro-modernism *or* anti-modernism and yet never both at the same time. Where Dewey and Foucault are interpreted through the Weberian prism, the usual result is to assimilate their critical stances on modernity to either side of this familiar for *or* against debate. Thus, Dewey is often read as a resolutely optimistic modern thinker while Foucault is read from the opposite perspective as a decidedly pessimistic anti-modern. But I want to suggest that Dewey and Foucault were both operating outside of the orbit of Weber's understanding of the basic problems of modernity and that this point of convergence is significant insofar as for both thinkers it enabled an alternative evaluation of modernity that cuts across all of the familiar *either* for *or* against positions that have left the current debates rather vacuous. Dewey and Foucault were complexly *both* for *and* against modernity. This more complex view leads in turn to a more effective critical stance than that mounted by Weber's approach. My claim is not that Weber's work on modernity is burdened by a cognitive defect that Dewey and Foucault could help us to repair but rather that Weber's work is burdened by a critical deficit that Dewey and Foucault enable us to overcome. Weber did not get modernity wrong so much as he left us without any effective means to develop the better aspects of modernity while also resisting its worse parts.

The argument and exposition I develop here can be summarized as follows. Weber's well-known portrait of modernity is a sociologist's portrait in which the differentiation of various social spheres (for example, science, politics, art) is the major thrust of modernity. In this view, what is distinctive about modernity is the way in which we parcel out our practices into the distinctive spheres in a way that enables us to develop bureaucratic forms of rationality immanent to each. Those working within Weber's interpretation of modernity either celebrate the basic modern project of *differentiation* or mourn the lost unity and hope for some future *reunification*. Dewey and Foucault, by contrast, offered an intellectual historical portrait of modernity that focused not on the differentiation of sociological spheres but on the purification of separate modes of thinking. Dewey and Foucault should be read as offering a less sociological and more historical portrait of modernity in which the basic contrast is that between two paradigmatic currents of modern thought, namely utilitarianism and romanticism.[2] While present throughout modernity, utilitarianism and romanticism ascended to prominence over the course of the nineteenth century such that today we might refer to each as indispensable for modernity. It follows from their indispensability that any historical-philosophical evaluation of modernity must be able to accommodate both. Dewey and Foucault painstakingly labored to show that modernity has thus far accommodated both by means of what I shall call *purification*—referring to our tendency to hold apart utility and romance, reason and imagination, sociality and individuality, public and private. Dewey and Foucault sought to elaborate an alternative means of accommodating these two currents of thought, which I call *experimentation*—in this model, utility and romance would no longer be opposed currents of thought but would rather be alternative tendencies whose internal tensions it is our task as moderns to explore.

Weber on Modernity

Max Weber was an enormously complex and extraordinarily difficult thinker. Perhaps this is why wide swaths of contemporary philosophers remain ignorant of his work despite the influence of his concepts and theories on much of what goes on in certain branches of philosophy today. Weber's influence outside of philosophy is well noted by the sociologists, anthropologists, historians, and others who generously borrow from his work. It is well known that Weber was one of the founding figures of modern sociology. As he conceived it, the study of society should be a rigorous inquiry both empirical and conceptual, less positivistic and more hermeneutical in orientation. The goal of such inquiries should be explanatory accounts of the present explaining the forms of our scientific, political, religious, and economic lives. Part of what stands out in Weber's work is a severe focus on that which conditions our modern religions as religion or our modern capitalisms as capitalism, that is, how these various parts of our lives have come to appear parceled out and divided off from one another. These are heavy questions at the heart of our modernity. In being one of the first to help us understand how we might even ask these questions of ourselves, Weber bequeathed an embarrassment of riches to modern thought as modern. I cannot here put this full wealth of riches on display. I shall only focus on one fairly standard reading of a core theme in Weber's thought, for it is this core theme on this standard reading that continues to hold dominance over contemporary theories of modernity in contexts as diverse as philosophy, history, anthropology, macro-sociology, and more.[3]

The common Weberian denominator found across so many of these contemporary theories of modernity is that of social differentiation, with its attendant processes of rationalization and bureaucratization. Weber once referred to social differentiation with a striking image of modernity as a "parceling-out of the soul."[4] In sum, this parceling-out refers to that modern tendency to splinter off from one another various value-spheres or social spaces such as science and politics.[5] As value-spheres get increasingly differentiated, powerful modes of thought are opened up whereby each domain can push its immanent logic to its furthest limits. This enables an unprecedented development of rationality in all spheres at the seemingly small cost of the isolation of each mode of practice from every other. It is this fact of autonomous internal development that Weber above all else marked as distinctive of modernity: scientific technicization and political emancipation are disconnected in a way that seems to promise an unprecedented development of each. This essentially modern process of value-sphere differentiation-cum-autonomization can be grasped in its broader form in terms of the two-sided process whose external face is bureaucratization and whose internal logic is that of rationalization.[6] Social value-spheres differentiate themselves by developing their own autonomous rationalities and their own autonomous bureaucratic systems.

There remains a basic ambiguity in this theory of modernity. Weber thought that differentiation presents us with precarious opportunities and alluring dangers: "The fate of an epoch which has eaten of the tree of knowledge is that it must know that we cannot learn the meaning of the world from the results of its analysis, be it ever so perfect; it must rather be in a position to create this meaning itself."[7] So although our modernity is an "iron cage" of obedience, it is also a cage in which we might learn to freely remake the meaning of ourselves.[8] In short, the conceptual constellation revolving around differentiation contains both an idea of the proliferation of instrumental rationality and an idea of the expansion of self-assertive freethinking, as commentators have not been lax to point out.[9] At the bottom of both estimations is a separation between a certain picture of scientific technicization and a certain picture of political emancipation, that is, a separation between the categories, practices, and social spaces of "objective control" from those of "subjective freedom."[10] Herein lies a central tension in Weber's work.

This generative ambiguity (generative because of the sheer power of Weber's categories) has enabled both pro-moderns and anti-moderns to use Weber's interpretation of modernity as a basis upon which to articulate conflicting sets of evaluations of modernity. While some witness differentiation as a legitimate move that today requires only piecemeal adjustment, others regard it as signaling the demise of emancipation as modernity is increasingly swept up by promises of systemic technicization. The common Weberian core behind both positions suggests that pro-moderns and anti-moderns embrace all the same dualisms: reason versus imagination, intellect versus will, sameness versus difference, social versus individual, technicization versus emancipation. Which is the real meaning of our modernity? It is difficult to say. But perhaps it is not as important to determine which interpretation better reflects the facts as it is to recognize the underlying presuppositions that animate both interpretations. As Bruno Latour urges, "Except for the plus or minus sign, moderns and antimoderns share all the same convictions."[11] The basic contrasts framing both sides, contrasts that are so easily and so often inflated into dichotomies, should be the focal point of attempts to evaluate the viability of Weber's interpretation of modernity. The central question concerns whether or not Weber's interpretation of modernity as an era of differentiation locks us into these contrasts or provides a means for thinking beyond them. My argument is that Weber's theory forces us to leave modernity more or less where he finds it. It is, in other words, critically debilitating.

The opposition between Jürgen Habermas and Jacques Derrida, for example, reflects the Weberian assumptions that typically separate pro-moderns from anti-moderns.[12] If Derrida is concerned to blur the very lines between philosophy and literature that Habermas strives to sharpen, then already both positions are framed in Weberian terms of differentiation, which Derrida is very much against and Habermas is very much in favor of. In working from a Weberian starting point, whether consciously or not, such critics of modernity risk descending into reductive interpretations of modernity that can yield only simplistic for-or-against evaluations. This shows not that the work of Habermas and Derrida is essentially incorrect. It shows rather that thought that is so fecund can be rendered so barren by hewing to an interpretation of modernity that is all too often unquestioningly accepted. In order to adopt a properly critical relationship to modernity, we must first adopt a critical relationship to modernity's interpretation of itself—which means getting away from a certain picture of modernity for which Weber is representative.

A Deweyan-Foucaultian Alternative to Weberian Sociology of Modernity

In focusing on modernity, pragmatism and genealogy have together departed from the sociological style of interpretation of which Weber is representative in favor of a more intellectual historical style of interpretation. This difference emerges as crucial if we see as our goal the project of developing *critical evaluations* of modernity on the basis of our *descriptive interpretations* of modernity. Those working with Weber's interpretation tend to evaluate modernity in terms of sociological categories such as science, politics, religion, and art. This too often leads to generalizing evaluations such as "science is good" or "religion is dangerous." Such views are rarely helpful insofar as scientific and religious practices are often too complex for canonical sociological boxes. Those working with Dewey's and Foucault's interpretation would do better to focus instead on currents of thought that cut across familiar sociological distinctions. In turning from interpretation to evaluation, focusing on currents of thought enables us to distinguish what we like in scientific and religious practices from what we find troublesome. This means we can stop worshiping and castigating sociologically defined categories such as science and religion in favor of a more complex argument to the effect that scientists and religions ought to play up some parts of their practices while playing down other parts. To see how we might learn to evaluate modernity on these alternative terms, I would like to concentrate on the Deweyan and Foucaultian grounds for such an approach as provided by their interpretations of modernity. Before doing so, allow me to first clear up some interpretive difficulties looming large in the literature.

Countless commentators have suggested that Foucault intensifies all of the key problems formulated by Weber. The standard line is that whereas Weber saw modern rationalization as an "iron cage," Foucault saw it as a something like an "iron cave" that we cannot even see we are in, let alone see our way out of. Indeed, it is difficult not to hear the retroactive echo of *Discipline and Punish* when reading the passages on discipline in *Economy and Society*.[13] Such echoes have led a number of otherwise insightful commentators to suggest that Foucault's work builds on Weber's core concern with rationalization and differentiation.[14] This common interpretation of Foucault reflects just how pervasive the Weberian framework is for contemporary historical interpretations and critical evaluations of modernity.

There are at least two difficulties yielded by such a reading. First, it is tough to square Weber's image of value-sphere differentiation with Foucault's presentation of the increasing interlacing of power and knowledge in modernity. Reading Foucault's work on the entwinement of power and knowledge through Weberian concepts would in fact expose Foucault's thought to many of the traps that it was designed to point out. One of Foucault's most enduring points was that the core problems of our day should not be described in terms of reunifying the differentiated modes of knowledge and power, because this would merely be a call for more of the same. A second difficulty for reading Foucault as a Weberian is that it makes Foucault seem far less exceptional than he really is. Is Foucault really just one more protester in a long line of intellectuals chanting the familiar mantras of anti-modernity? Foucault was certainly critical of modernity, but at the same time he positively embraced what he saw as its most valuable tendencies. Foucault was both for and against modernity. Paul Rabinow claims that Foucault did not proceed "by opposing modernity to post-modernity, but by opposing modernity to counter-modernity," such that his parrhesiastic practice was simultaneously modern and counter-modern.[15] What I am suggesting is that Rabinow is right to see Foucault as both modern and counter-modern and that this sort of complex critical evaluation of modernity simply cannot be made sense of within the usual Weberian frame that so thoroughly dominates contemporary thought about modernity, counter-modernity, and post-modernity.

Turning now to pragmatism, the interpretive situation is a little different, but no better for it. When pragmatism is not altogether neglected by those engaged in the modernity debates, it is usually denounced as either a celebratory philosophy proclaiming all the benefits of the modern age or as a profoundly relativistic doctrine out of step with modern progress. Both of these caricatures borrow much from Weber and gather relatively little from Dewey. In the only important comparative study of Weber and Dewey yet undertaken, James Kloppenberg discerns an important point of overlap in Dewey's and Weber's shared view that differentiating rationalization is the central problem of modernity.[16] Though not wishing to discount other points of overlap concerning ethics and epistemology that Kloppenberg has explicated,[17] I wish to call into question his claim for a more basic point of convergence in terms of their supposedly shared interpretation of modernity.

Weber saw modernity as haunted by a series of divisions that Dewey may indeed have found troubling had he not confronted modern culture as problematized by a more basic dichotomy. If Weber saw modernity as split between science and morality, then Dewey saw it as split between utilitarian rationality and romantic pathos. Dewey's pragmatism is best seen as attempting to develop a conscious integration of utilitarian and romantic styles of thought. He championed an experimentalism that he thought captured what is best in certain early modern scientists but also in certain artists, politicians, novelists, and everyday people. This bears important consequences for Dewey's frequently cited, but also frequently derided, praise of science.[18] Dewey never thought that modernity had parsed itself out into a healthy science over here and a deficient morality over there. His view was rather that the attitude of experimentalism had not sufficiently taken hold throughout the great variety of our modern practices, including our modern scientific practices. Dewey was not interested in praising a differentiated bureaucracy of science but rather an "experimentalism" for which science had provided many, but certainly not the only, exemplars. Only in this view can we understand why in addition to certain scientific practices, Dewey also championed certain aesthetic, religious, political, and ethical practices. Dewey found in each of these the seeds of an experimentalism that he hoped could flower forth practically anywhere. Dewey's view thus enabled him to move beyond many of those critically debilitating categories that have haunted so much of modern thought, including Weber's. This helps explain why Weber retained many of the dichotomies that Dewey thoroughly rejected (for instance, that between facts and values).[19]

Neither Dewey nor Foucault should be read through the prism of Weberian concepts. Dewey and Foucault never argued that power and knowledge, expressions of the supposedly differentiated value-spheres of politics and science, ought to be reunited. They argued that the two had never been separated. Modernity as Weber described it had never taken place. As such, Dewey and Foucault never urged a reunification of the various modalities of experience split off into various differentiated value-spheres. Rather, they responded by urging the adoption of a critical attitude that both of them often referred to as "experimentalism." This much helps us negatively clear away any Weberian remnants inflecting our interpretations of Dewey and Foucault. But what, positively, can those interpretations contribute to contemporary work on modernity?

Dewey on Modernity

My approach to pragmatism thus far takes as one of its points of departure Richard Rorty's fertile suggestion that we think of pragmatism as "romantic utilitarianism."[20] Rorty's image of pragmatism as an experimentalism that integrates romantic and utilitarian currents of thought captures what is best in the work of John Dewey. Seen in this way, the tradition of pragmatism should be understood as an attempt to further that experimental project of forging productive new relations among modernity's utilitarian and romantic tendencies.

In books such as *The Quest for Certainty* and *Reconstruction in Philosophy*, Dewey describes modernity as held captive by a process of purification that rigorously divides reason from its others.[21] Dewey here and elsewhere details the philosophical quest for certainty that emerged during the seventeenth and eighteenth centuries as truth was increasingly identified with the condition of subjective certainty. Although this quest is unique to modernity, it is central to Dewey's argument that it institutes no deep breaks from the ambition for transcendence that has characterized philosophy since its beginnings. In ancient thought, purity was figured in various conceptions of eternity. In medieval philosophy, the purity standard was similarly articulated as a divine force to which human reason and imagination should chain themselves. In modern thought, purity is relocated in the unassailability of mental certainty. The ongoing quest for certainty simply revamped the ancient and medieval quests for purity in the light of the subjectivism of the modern age. Going forward into the nineteenth century, the full and final solidification of the quest for certainty was witnessed as the currents of utilitarianism and romanticism assumed cultural ascendance. What the simultaneous ascendance of these two opposed currents of thought signals is the meticulous purification of two modes of direct contact with truth. Certainty is enthroned as both a form of reason and a form of intuition or imagination. Utilitarianism crowns certainty in the form of reason, efficiency, discipline, and order while romanticism crowns it in the form of imagination, will, striving, and genius. Dewey aptly summarized this picture of modernity in his description of Immanuel Kant as simultaneously striving for "cognitive certainty in the region of phenomena, practical certainty in the realm of moral authority."[22]

The quest for certainty thus entails a separation of pure reason from its others. This separation is the specific problem situation to which Dewey addressed his pragmatism. Without this historical interpretation of the central problem of modernity as its backdrop, much of Dewey's thought remains difficult to understand. But with this backdrop in place, many of his most central concepts can be clarified—meliorism in politics, fallibilism in epistemology, growth as the only moral end. These central concepts can be read as responding to a modernity in which the central problem we face is the separation not between two sociological spheres of experience but between two moods of prosaic utilitarianism and poetic romanticism. From this separation, there follows a whole train of invidious philosophical distinctions that Dewey found misguided: reason versus imagination, sociality versus individuality, public versus private. It is above all against this philosophical thematic, and the modern figure of certainty that has been its outward face, that Dewey's pragmatism was written.

Richard Rorty is better than perhaps any other contemporary pragmatist in advancing Dewey's quintessential skepticism toward the idea that there exists extra-human powers that we mere humans ought to try and get in touch with: "The problem with both universalist metaphors of grandeur and romantic metaphors of depth is that they suggest that a practical proposal, whether conservative or radical in character, can gain strength by being tied in with something not merely human—something like the intrinsic nature of reality or the uttermost depths of the human soul."[23] The promises of grandeur and depth have been exciting for both romantics and utilitarians—the spirit of purity pervades modern thought in both of its major currents, and the further each is pursued, the more refined is its purification. It follows from all of this, however, that the category most central to Dewey's own experimentalism, uncertainty, has been widely absent from most forms of utilitarianism and romanticism. Dewey's experimentalism should thus be seen as an alternative that negotiates around both utility and romance, which is to say that pragmatism is, to borrow from Rorty once again, "an alternative to both universalism and romanticism."[24]

The charges of scientism and aestheticism imputed to various pragmatists by their most hostile critics fail to capture crucial elements of pragmatist experimentalism. These crucial elements, I have argued, are likely to be misunderstood if one understands pragmatism as attempting to come to terms with the kind of modernity described by Weber. Pragmatists regard the various value-spheres such as politics and science as reciprocal rather than differentiated. For the pragmatist, fact and value or knowledge and power travel together, not separately. Pragmatist experimentalism, just like the utilitarianism and romanticism it is meant to replace, is operative not only in science (the scientism imputed to Dewey) or only in literature (the aestheticism imputed to Rorty and sometimes William James) but throughout modern culture. Once we start experimenting on any broad scale, it turns out that science, aesthetics, and politics grow increasingly indistinguishable. Pragmatist experimentalism must therefore work across supposed differentiated social spheres as a quality operative throughout culture. Indeed, the purest forms of utilitarianism and romanticism have rooted themselves in just this way. Ideals of utilitarian order and romantic organicism have been operative simultaneously in our epistemic and political practices. Pragmatists interpret modernity as a series of decisive transformations reverberating throughout all of culture—the purification of utilitarian reason and romantic imagination that empties from each the corruptions of the other is a culture-wide project occurring in legislatures and laboratories simultaneously and with reciprocal benefit to both. The response to such a modernity bent on purification cannot be the expansion of an experimentalism thus far developed in only one of science or politics (thus replacing a monistic totalization for a purifying totalization) but rather must be an experimentalism that will increasingly pervade both simultaneously. Pragmatists thus urge a reconstruction of modern culture along paths worn by particular cultural moods (an experimentalism about knowledge and politics) rather than by others (utilitarianism or romanticism about knowledge and politics). For this, the Weberian theory of modernity as differentiated social spheres can only be a hindrance.

This is an important point of connection linking pragmatism to genealogy. For in his attempt to develop an experimental alternative to prevailing cultural tendencies, Dewey makes much the same point as Foucault did when he envisioned practices of experimentation and transgression that could carry us beyond the dominant confines of modern thought. Both Dewey and Foucault looked forward to a culture that would sustain itself by simply trying things out as an alternative to that cultural self-containment implicit in the modern will to purify.

Foucault on Modernity

The following remark of Foucault's might be read as an index to his entire work: "In every culture there exists a coherent series of gestures of division. . . . [But] the moment they mark a limit, they create the space of a possible transgression."[25] Across the long span of his career, Foucault returns again and again to his central theme of two moments of modernity: division and transgression, or as I prefer to call them, purification and experimentation. On the basis of these two themes, I offer an interpretation of Foucault's history and critique of modernity that, like my interpretation of Dewey, amounts on some points to a significant revision of the standard reception of his work.

Appropriating from Foucault a concept that he used only once and never further developed, I propose a rereading of the histories of modernity developed in *History of Madness* and *Discipline and Punish* as characterized by what Foucault once called a "reciprocal incompatibility."[26] The idea of reciprocal incompatibility helps us conceptualize Foucault's points in these texts about the relations between pairs like madness and reason or power and freedom, pairs that are, in his view, at the very heart of modernity itself. Foucault's view was that these pairs are simultaneously reciprocal and incompatible, which is to say that they can neither be fully liberated from nor totally assimilated to one another. There is nothing in this story of the differentiation of these pairs through a process of social bureaucratization and rationalization. To complain that Foucault failed to liberate either side of these oppositional terms from the total repression of the other, as so many critics have, is thus to miss his point entirely. When Derrida insisted that Foucault's work on modern madness and reason was a lament of the domination of madness by reason, and when Habermas insisted that Foucault's theory of modern power and freedom left us devoid of autonomy and totally oppressed by discipline, they were reading Foucault through a Weberian lens that was not really Foucault's.[27] Their influence on subsequent Foucault reflection cannot be overstated, nor can the deleterious effects of this influence.

Take those passages at the end of *History of Madness* where Foucault seems to issue a lament for Friedrich Nietzsche and other marginalized figures of modern culture. Contrary to the standard reading of these passages, the Nietzsche in these pages is not for Foucault a forgotten madman. What Foucault laments in invoking Nietzsche, rather, is the philosopher capable of reinvigorating a forgotten dialogue between a romanticized madness and a utilitarian rationality.[28] Foucault laments the fact that a new Nietzsche can no longer be "on the border of reason and unreason," since that border is forever banished by modern purification.[29] In such a reading, Foucault's history of modernity does not chart reason's subjugation of madness so much as a more insidious separation of reason from madness. It is not that some former reality of madness is held at bay by the production of reason; it is rather that madness and reason in their modern form are simultaneously produced as incoherent with one another. Only this sort of reading can sustain Foucault's remark that the study of madness and rationality must "go back toward the decision that simultaneously links and separates reason and madness; it must aim to uncover the perpetual exchange, the obscure common root, the original confrontation that gives meaning to the unity, as well as to the opposition, of sense and non-sense."[30] We must, in other words, aim to restore that broken interaction where madness and rationality are interactive with one another. It was in this spirit that Foucault, in an early essay written only a few years after this book, was eager to celebrate "the possibility of the mad philosopher."[31] The mad philosopher would be the kind of experimentalist who could at once be mad and be philosophical and in so doing transgress the separation of reason and madness that forms a core problem of our modernity. In praising the mad philosopher, Foucault does not mourn a banished madman but rather that forgotten space of interaction between madman and philosopher. He finds Nietzsche, the paradigm of the mad philosopher, waiting for us there.

There is an important symmetry in these matters between Foucault's earlier work on modern reason and his later work on modern power. Just as madness can be neither totally subject to nor totally liberated from reason, freedom and power are similarly bound to one another. Seen in this light, Foucault's point in his work on power and knowledge was never that we are trapped in power. Foucault, rather, sought to elaborate the difficulty we moderns face in our task of simultaneously negotiating freedom and power. The complex idea that Foucault was striving to articulate and that so many of his critics misunderstood was that freedom and power can neither be dissociated nor assimilated. They must be deployed simultaneously so that we can work within the internal tensions of their relationships. Foucault therefore found himself working as an experimentalist at the interstices where freedom and power connect.

As Foucault elaborated this version of his history and critique of modernity in *Discipline and Punish*, the problematization at the heart of our modernity is the production of autonomous freedom and disciplinary power as two reciprocal but incompatible aspects of our political existence. These two presuppose one another but are at the same time incoherent with one another. So it is not that disciplinary power eliminates autonomous freedom, just as it is not that modern rationality eliminates madness. There is no pure freedom to be emancipated just as there is no pure power to repress it. It is rather that disciplinary power and autonomous freedom are simultaneously produced so as to render the latter ineffective as a force pitted against the former. As Foucault succinctly puts it: "The 'Enlightenment,' which discovered the liberties, also invented the disciplines."[32] And so just as madness finds itself in no position to question reason, freedom understood on the modern model of autonomy finds itself hardly equipped to oppose power in the model of discipline. But it was never Foucault's point that we need regard modernity as a trap. His more modest point was simply that the modern conception of an autonomous freedom totally liberated from power is but a corollary of a disciplinary power that totally cages up freedom. Autonomous individuality is one of the intended effects of disciplinary power rather than a predisciplinary capacity for freedom that might seek revenge on power.[33] This understanding of the problematization of modern freedom and power helps explain why Foucault held that the freedom of resistance must be sought elsewhere than in the romantic ideals of autonomy and liberation. Foucault's late work on ethics never sought to rehabilitate the autonomous form of freedom that Foucault's middle work on power had ruled out.[34] Foucault's late work on ethical freedom is in fact better understood as elaborating the possibility for a modern form of experimental liberty on the basis of the study of premodern practices in which freedom and power were not yet purified as they were to become in modernity. Foucault did not in his late work abandon his earlier theses about modern power in order to elaborate a theory of modern freedom, which these theses had explicitly invalidated.[35] On the contrary, Foucault's late work elaborates a conception of experimental freedom that specifically aims to address the very problem established by our reciprocal but incompatible practices of modern disciplinary power and modern autonomous freedom.[36]

Foucault's emphases on experimental transgression and his concern with the pernicious effects of much that has marched under the banner of modernity simply would not make sense if interpreted through the Weberian picture of modernity. Foucault did not witness the increasing differentiation of the vocations of science and politics. What he witnessed, rather, was the increasing purification, the reciprocal incompatibility, of two great cultural imperatives: emancipatory freedom on the one side and disciplinary control on the other. So it would not make sense to understand Foucault as having rallied against rationalization in the name of enchantment or mysticism or revolt or any other favorite of romanticism. Foucault was never against reason and simply for passion, madness, and freedom. He is better seen as having explored the long and slow formation of those great divisions, those formidable reciprocal incompatibilities, through which we moderns have attempted to erect high walls separating our reasons from our passions, our sociality from our individuality, our utility from our romance. It was these walls that he found debilitating, not the concepts and practices (instrumental rationality, romantic passion) located on either side of them. If Foucault's critical histories have any positive upshot, then it consists in his articulation of practices of experimental transgression that would aim to scale these walls. These transgressions would not demonstrate that reason and its others are really the same but would open up the possibility of a new phase of modernity in which these two aspects of modern culture are not as rigorously purified as they were in previous phases of modernity. This new phase was envisioned by Foucault not as a reunification of power and knowledge (for that is what modernity has deployed all along) but rather as an intensification of experimental tensions resulting from the blending of powers and freedoms and the dialogue between rationalities and madnesses. That is why Foucault should be read as neither pro-modern nor anti-modern but as complexly modern in the interests of a future phase of modernity.[37]

Toward a Genealogical Pragmatist Critique of Modernity

Foucault and Dewey can be read as picking up on a crucial but underdeveloped aspect of Kant's legacy to modernity. Weber, and all those in his train, located Kant's legacy in a modern tendency toward differentiation by which we have carved ourselves up into separate spheres according to the critical limits located in the first two of Kant's *Critiques*. But Foucault and Dewey located Kant's legacy elsewhere. According to their view, we do not find ourselves divided into the two worlds of experience discerned by a standard quasi-sociological interpretation of Kant's critical philosophy. We find ourselves instead divided into two currents of thought, or two different standpoints for thinking, which Kant's critical system was an attempt to do simultaneous justice to.[38]

Dewey and Foucault stood together in seeing our modernity as divided from itself above all by this purifying impulse to pry apart our utilitarian selves from our romantic selves. In this they offer a challenging alternative to the more comfortable Weberian model of seeing our selves as riven only insofar as we are here a scientist and there an artist, or here a churchgoer and there a citizen. Utility and romance, along with processes of their purification, cut across these familiar sociological divides. This purification cannot be overcome by reunifying supposedly divided spheres of experience but rather only by experimentally testing the divisions between utilitarian rationality and romantic autonomy that we impose on ourselves. These are two very different orientations toward our present. It might be thought that a great deal depends on which we use to orient our ongoing critical efforts.

The important details of Dewey's and Foucault's conceptions of an experimental critique of ourselves will have to be elaborated on another occasion. What I have sought to focus attention on here is only an important overlap between Deweyan pragmatism and Foucaultian genealogy in their interpretations of the basic problems of modern culture. In closing, I point out that from the point of view of both traditions, this is no small similarity. Both traditions hold that processes such as modernity gain their coherence from the problems they are formulated as responses to, such as the inheritance of utilitarian disciplinary imperatives and romantic emancipatory dreams. Gaining a view of the problems we face is, for both genealogy and pragmatism, a crucial task for thought. In Dewey's view, this is expressed in terms of his account of inquiry as beginning with and aiming at the resolution of a problem situation.[39] In Foucault's view, this is expressed in his articulation of a historiography focused around problematizations, or the ways in which accepted truths come to be problematized over time and as a result propel the new truths achieved by the resolution of these problems.[40] This shared focus on problems suggests an important elective affinity among pragmatism and genealogy that those working in both traditions have thus far failed to take seriously enough.[41]

Despite these similarities concerning their shared focus on thought as addressed to problems, an important difference is that Foucault was largely focused on the creation of problems and Dewey on their resolution. This difference has given rise to the familiar caricatures of Foucault as somewhat too pessimistic and Dewey as somewhat too optimistic, caricatures that are ultimately unfair but nevertheless rooted in obvious predilections of both thinkers. Fortunately, this seeming disjunction is easily overcome. All we need to do is to recognize that, from a robustly philosophical rather than a merely scholarly point of view, pragmatist problem-solving and genealogical problem-specifying are two activities that require one another. Problems that do not invite solutions are as worthless as solutions that do not respond to problems. The prospective orientation of pragmatism is blind without the retrospective orientation of genealogy—genealogy without pragmatism is likewise an empty exercise.

By bringing genealogy and pragmatism into intimate dialogue with one another, we are finally able to realize the important promise that lay at the heart of both traditions: that we moderns can look forward with hope when we face up to the endless uncertainty that threatens continually to undo everything that we have in our history struggled to create. We can characterize both traditions as oriented simultaneously toward problematization and solution, toward past and future, and toward history and philosophy. This characterization fits with what is best in both Dewey's pragmatism and Foucault's genealogy: the practice of a criticism that is simultaneously philosophical and historical.[42]

Notes

1. The most important work treating pragmatism and genealogy as largely oppositional is that of Richard Rorty (1981a), but see also discussions by Cornel West (1989), Thomas McCarthy in Hoy and McCarthy (1994), John Patrick Diggins (1999), James Marshall (1994), Jim Garrison (1998), Todd May (2004), and Carlos Prado (this volume).

2. This is best seen as a version of the more familiar contrast between Enlightenment and romanticism given central place by many important intellectual historians. Exemplary for their approach (and certainly influential on my own) are Isaiah Berlin (1960; 1965; 1975) and Arthur Lovejoy (1936). See also Maurice Mandelbaum (1971), Hayden White (1973), Charles Taylor (1989), and, taking a much longer view, Harold Bloom's description (2004) of Homeric cognitivism and Hebraic spiritualism as the two great forces of Western wisdom.

3. Recent revisionist scholarship notwithstanding, the best of which is Lawrence Scaff (1989) and Wilhelm Hennis (1987), most theorists continue to interpret Weber's theory of modernity according to the classic terms of rationalizing differentiation-cum-bureaucratization established by Karl Löwith (1932), Reinhard Bendix (1960), and above all Talcott Parsons (1937). See Richard Swedberg (2003; 2005) on the current state of Weber scholarship. My presentation of Weber here is not so much an attempt at fine-grained Weber scholarship as it is an attempt to dispute the central Weberian theses that continue to exert tremendous influence on political philosophy and intellectual history. I leave it to others to show how the thought of Weber can today be reinterpreted so as to yield better results—my project is merely to cast doubt on a certain *Weberianism* dominant in contemporary histories and critiques of modernity.

4. On the complicated textual context of this metaphor, see Sica 2000, 53.

5. Weber 1917; 1919.

6. I am here paraphrasing a formulation given by David Owen and Tracy Strong (2004, lvi).

7. Weber 1904, 57.

8. Weber 1905, 181.

9. James Kloppenberg (1986, 345) explicates Weber's concept of disenchantment as featuring both decline and opportunity. Alan Sica (2000, 56) notes a "Faustian bargain" in Weber. Fritz Ringer (2004, 220) describes the "two faces" of Weber's evaluation of modernity. Lastly, Raymond Aron (1959, 360–72) offered many useful remarks on the multiple valences of Weber's pluralism.

10. On this contrast, see Lawrence Scaff 2000, 103.

11. Latour 1991, 123.

12. While the Derrida-Habermas debates have been much discussed, two particularly helpful evaluations are those of Richard Bernstein (1991) and David Hoy (1989).

13. See Foucault 1975 and Weber 1964, 1148–56.

14. See work by John O'Neill (1986), Peter Dews (1987), Colin Gordon (1991), Bryan Turner (1987), David Owen (1994), and Arpád Szakolczai (1998). While few comparative analyses of Weber and Foucault emphasize the differences separating the two, an excellent book by Mitchell Dean (1994) casts doubt on the claim that Weber's rationalization thesis can be meaningfully articulated to Foucault's work on modernity—Dean's argument anticipates aspects of mine insofar as he finds Weberian rationalization too totalizing for Foucaultian purposes and then goes on to use this difference to distance Foucault from the Weber-inspired work of the anti-modernism of Adorno and the pro-modernism of Habermas. Also worth noting is that some com-

mentators have emphasized the affinities between Foucault and Weber on the basis of an interpretation of the latter that abandons the familiar "iron cage" view of Weber in favor of a more nuanced interpretation of Weber emphasizing his self-formation as a problematic thinker attempting to grasp the core problems of modernity—this, for example, is the basis for Paul Rabinow's claims (2003; Rabinow and Dreyfus 1982) on behalf of a Foucault and Weber alliance.

15. Rabinow 1994, 197; cf. Rabinow and Dreyfus 1986.

16. Kloppenberg 1986, 349–94. In the only other comparative works on Dewey and Weber of which I am aware, Mustafa Emirbayer (2005) rather loosely argues the point I am offering, Christopher Roederer (2000) concedes my point within an account that explicitly aims to build on Kloppenberg, and John Patrick Diggins (1999) compares Dewey and Weber very quickly in only summary terms. See also Martin Jay (2005) for an interesting reading of Dewey through somewhat Weberian lenses.

17. Kloppenberg 1994, 82–99.

18. Helpful discussions of the charge of scientism in Dewey include those by H. S. Thayer (1968, 165), David Hollinger (1980, 29), and Kloppenberg (1986, 383).

19. In the two other comparative works on Dewey and Weber of which I am aware, Emirbayer (2005) rather loosely argues my point while Roederer (2000) concedes my point within an account that explicitly aims to build on Kloppenberg; Diggins (1999) compares Dewey and Weber only but only summarily.

20. See numerous works by Rorty (1998a; 1998b; 2004). Similar interpretations of pragmatism as between romanticism and utilitarian positivism have been offered by James Livingston (1994; 2001), Thelma Lavine (1991; 1995), and H. S. Thayer (1968). Notable is George Herbert Mead's view in his impressive intellectual history *Movements of Thought in the Nineteenth Century*, where he explicitly contrasts pragmatism to the conception of inquiry common to "the Romantic idealists and the rationalists" according to which "knowledge is a simple getting of the nature of the world" (1936, 344).

21. Dewey 1929; 1920.

22. Dewey 1929, 49.

23. Rorty 2004, 137.

24. Ibid., 136.

25. Foucault, quoted in Miller 1993, 115, from "Les déviations religieuses et la savoir medical" (1962, 19).

26. Foucault quoted in Eribon 1989, 97; this passage is from the longer version of *Histoire de la Folie* only recently translated into English.

27. See Derrida (1963) and Habermas (1981; 1985). For a more convincing version of the sort of worry expressed in Derrida's critique, see Gary Gutting (1989) and James Bernauer (1990). Habermas borrowed much of his argument from Nancy Fraser (1981), but see also related criticisms by Richard Rorty (1981b), Michael Walzer (1983), Charles Taylor (1984), Thomas McCarthy (1990), and Béatrice Han (1998).

28. Clare O'Farrell (1989, 74–78) develops a similar reading.

29. Foucault 1961, 287.

30. Foucault 1961 quoted in Derrida 1963, 43; from the longer version of *Histoire de la Folie.*

31. Foucault 1963, 80.

32. Foucault 1975, 222; see also a different version of this view as developed in Foucault's 1978 course lectures: "Freedom is nothing else but the correlative of the deployment of apparatuses of security" (1978, 48).

33. Foucault 1975, 184; cf. Foucault 1979 and Colin Gordon 1991.

34. See Foucault 1984a and, for helpful discussion, John Rajchman 1985, 92, 115, and David Hoy 2004, 100.

35. Among those arguing for a basic incoherence between the so-called middle and late works are Peter Dews (1989), Thomas McCarthy (1990), Béatrice Han (1998), and Eric Paras (2006).

36. Among those arguing for important continuities between the so-called middle and late works are Ladelle McWhorter (1999, 189); Timothy O'Leary (2002, 107); Johanna Oksala (2005, 157); Benda Hofmeyr (2006); and Amy Allen (2008, 45).

37. See the interpretations offered by Rabinow and Dreyfus (1986), Hoy (1988), and Rabinow (1994). I further build on the reading of Foucault developed in this section in my forthcoming "Genealogy as Problematization."

38. On these well-known differing interpretations of Kant, see Christine Korsgaard 1996, x.

39. Dewey 1938.

40. Foucault 1984b.

41. Overlaps between Dewey and Foucault along these lines have thus far been very much unexplored, although an important comparison in similar terms is given by Rabinow (2003; 2008) and John Stuhr (1997, 2003). For other important comparative work, see Randall Auxier (2002), Carlos Prado (this volume), James Livingston (2001), and my own work (Koopman 2009, ch. 7; cf. 2007). For a nearly complete survey of the literature on genealogy and pragmatism, see my on-line reference paper (Koopman forthcoming-b).

42. For helpful comments on earlier versions of this paper, I thank Barry Allen and David Hoy. In addition, I also extend thanks to Martin Jay for extensive help on the sections on Weber in his reading of a much longer version of this argument, to Paul Rabinow for insightful discussions of both Weber and Foucault, and to Amy Allen for generosity in offering comments on a longer version of the portions on Foucault. I also thank Paul Fairfield for helpful thoughts on how to improve my arguments and explications. Lastly, I gratefully acknowledge a postdoctoral research grant from the Social Sciences and Humanities Research Council of Canada, which provided me with the opportunity to undertake this work in the context of the larger research project of which it is a part.

References

Allen, Amy. 2008. *The Politics of Our Selves.* New York: Columbia University.

Aron, Raymond. 1959. "Max Weber and Modern Social Science." In *History, Truth, and Liberty*, ed. Franciszek Draus Aron, trans. Charles Krance. Chicago: University of Chicago, 1985. 335–73.

Auxier, Randall. 2002. "Foucault, Dewey, and the History of the Present." *Journal of Speculative Philosophy* 16, no. 2 (Summer): 75–102.

Bendix, Reinhard. 1960. *Max Weber: An Intellectual Portrait.* London: Methuen, 1966.

Berlin, Isaiah. 1960. "The Romantic Revolution: A Crisis in the History of Modern Thought." In *The Sense of Reality*, ed. Henry Hardy Berlin. New York: Farrar, Strauss, and Giroux, 1996. 168–93.

———. 1965. *The Roots of Romanticism.* Ed. Henry Hardy. Princeton: Princeton University, 1999.

———. 1975. "The Apotheosis of the Romantic Will." In *The Crooked Timber of Humanity*, ed. Henry Hardy. Princeton: Princeton University Press, 1990. 217–37.

Bernauer, James. 1990. *Michel Foucault's Force of Flight.* Atlantic Highlands, N.J.: Humanities Press.

Bernstein, Richard. 1991. "An Allegory of Modernity/Postmodernity: Habermas and Derrida." In *The New Constellation.* Oxford: Polity Press. 199–229.

Bloom, Harold. 2004. *Where Shall Wisdom Be Found?* New York: Penguin.

Dean, Mitchell. 1994. *Critical and Effective Histories: Foucault's Methods and Historical Sociology.* New York: Routledge.

Derrida, Jacques. 1963. "Cogito and the History of Madness." In *Writing and Difference*, trans. Alan Bass. Chicago: University of Chicago Press, 1978. 31–63.

Dewey, John. 1920. *Reconstruction in Philosophy.* In Dewey *MW*12.

———. 1929. *The Quest for Certainty.* In Dewey *LW*4.

———. 1938. *Logic: The Theory of Inquiry.* In Dewey *LW*12.

———. 1969–90. *The Early Works of John Dewey, 1882–1898*, 5 vols. (*EW*1–5), *The Middle Works of John Dewey, 1899–1924*, 15 vols. (*MW*1–15), and *The Later Works of John Dewey, 1925–1953*, 17 vols. (*LW*1–17). Ed. Jo Ann Boydston. Carbondale: Southern Illinois University Press.

Dews, Peter. 1987. *Logics of Disintegration: Post-structuralist Thought and the Claims of Critical Theory.* London: Verso.

———. 1989. "The Return of the Subject in Late Foucault." *Radical Philosophy* 51 (Spring): 37–41.

Diggins, John Patrick. 1999. *Max Weber: Politics and the Spirit of Tragedy.* New York: Basic Books.

Emirbayer, Mustafa. 2005. "Beyond Weberian Action Theory." In *Max Weber's Economy and Society*, ed. Charles Camic et al. Stanford: Stanford University Press. 185–203.

Eribon, Didier. 1989. *Michel Foucault.* Trans. Betsy Wing. Cambridge: Harvard University Press, 1991.

Foucault, Michel. 1961. *History of Madness* or *Madness and Civilization: A History of Insanity in the Age of Reason.* Trans. Richard Howard. New York: Vintage Books, 1965.

———. 1963. "A Preface to Transgression." In Foucault *EW*2:69–87.

———. 1975. *Discipline and Punish: The Birth of the Prison*. Trans. Alan Sheridan. New York: Vintage Books, 1995.

———. 1978. *Security, Territory, Population: Lectures at the Collège de France, 1977–1978*. Ed. Arnold Davidson. New York: Picador, 2007.

———. 1979. "'Omnes et Singulatim': Toward a Critique of Political Reason." In Foucault *EW*3:298–325.

———. 1984a. "What Is Enlightenment?" In Foucault *EW*1:303–20.

———. 1984b. "Polemics, Politics and Problematizations." Interview by Paul Rabinow. In Foucault *EW*1:111–20.

———. 1997–2000. *Essential Works, Volumes 1–3* (*EW*1–3). Ed. Paul Rabinow and James D. Faubion. New York: New Press.

Fraser, Nancy. 1981. "Foucault on Modern Power: Empirical Insights and Normative Confusions." In *Unruly Practices*. Minneapolis: University of Minnesota Press, 1989. 17–34.

Garrison, Jim. 1998. "Dewey, Foucault, and Self-Creation." *Educational Philosophy and Theory* 30, no. 2: 111–34.

Gordon, Colin. 1991. "Governmental Rationality: An Introduction." In *The Foucault Effect: Studies in Governmentality*, ed. Graham Burchell, Colin Gordon, and Peter Miller. Chicago: University of Chicago Press. 1–51.

Gutting, Gary. 1989. *Michel Foucault's Archaeology of Scientific Reason*. Cambridge: Cambridge University.

Habermas, Jürgen. 1981. "Modernity versus Postmodernity." Trans. Seyla Benhabib. *New German Critique* 22 (Winter): 3–14.

———. 1985. *The Philosophical Discourse of Modernity*. Trans. Frederick Lawrence. Cambridge: MIT Press, 1987.

Han, Béatrice. 1998. *Foucault's Critical Project*. Trans. Edward Pile. Stanford: Stanford University Press, 2002.

Hennis, Wilhelm. 1987. *Max Weber: Essays in Reconstruction*. Trans. Keith Tribe. London: Allen and Unwin, 1988.

Hofmeyr, Benda. 2006. "The Power Not to Be (What We Are): The Politics and Ethics of Self-Creation in Foucault." *Journal of Moral Philosophy* 3, no. 2 (July): 215–30.

Hollinger, David. 1980. "The Problem of Pragmatism in American History." In *In the American Province: Studies in the History and Historiography of Ideas*. Baltimore: Johns Hopkins University Press, 1989. 23–43.

———. 2001. "The Enlightenment and the Genealogy of Cultural Conflict in the United States." In *What's Left of Enlightenment? A Postmodern Question*, ed. Keith Michael Baker and Peter Hanns Reill. Stanford: Stanford University Press, 2001. 7–18.

Hoy, David Couzens, ed. 1986. *Foucault: A Critical Reader*. Cambridge: Basil Blackwell.

———. 1988. "Foucault: Modern or Postmodern?" In *After Foucault*, ed. Jonathan Arac. New Brunswick: Rutgers University Press. 12–41.

———. 1989. "Splitting the Difference: Habermas's Critique of Derrida." In *Working Through Derrida*, ed. G. B. Madison. Evanston: Northwestern University Press, 1993. 230–51.

———. 2004. *Critical Resistance*. Cambridge: MIT Press.

Hoy, David Couzens, and Thomas McCarthy. 1994. *Critical Theory*. Oxford: Blackwell.

Jay, Martin. 2005. *Songs of Experience: Modern American and European Variations on a Universal Theme*. Berkeley: University of California Press.

Kloppenberg, James T. 1986. *Uncertain Victory: Social Democracy and Progressivism in European and American Thought: 1870–1920*. Oxford: Oxford University Press.

———. 1994. "Democracy and Disenchantment: From Weber and Dewey to Habermas and Rorty." In *The Virtues of Liberalism*. Oxford: Oxford University Press, 1998. 82–99.

Koopman, Colin. 2007. "A New Foucault: The Coming Revisions in Foucault Studies" (review essay). *Symposium: Canadian Journal of Continental Philosophy* 11, no. 1 (Spring): 167–77.

———. 2009. *Pragmatism as Transition: Historicity and Hope in James, Dewey, and Rorty*. New York: Columbia University Press.

———. Forthcoming-a. "Genealogy as Problematization." Manuscript.

———. Forthcoming-b. "Pragmatism and Genealogy: An Overview of the Literature." Available on-line at SSRN, http://papers.ssrn.com/so13/papers.cfm?abstract_id=1011513 (accessed February 5, 2010).

Korsgaard, Christine. 1996. *Creating the Kingdom of Ends*. Cambridge: Cambridge University Press.

Latour, Bruno. 1991. *We Have Never Been Modern*. Trans. Catherine Porter. Cambridge: Harvard University Press, 1993.

Lavine, Thelma Z. 1991. "Modernity and the Spirit of Naturalism." *Proceedings and Addresses of the American Philosophical Association* 65, no. 3 (Nov.): 73–83.

———. 1995. "America and the Contestations of Modernity: Bentley, Dewey, Rorty." In *Rorty and Pragmatism: The Philosopher Responds to His Critics*, ed. Herman Saatkamp. Nashville: Vanderbilt University Press. 37–49.

Livingston, James. 1994. *Pragmatism and the Political Economy of Cultural Revolution, 1850–1940*. Chapel Hill: University of North Carolina Press, 1997.

———. 2001. *Pragmatism, Feminism, and Democracy: Rethinking the Politics of American History*. New York: Routledge.

Lovejoy, Arthur O. 1936. *The Great Chain of Being: A Study of the History of an Idea*. Cambridge: Harvard University Press, 1964.

Löwith, Karl. 1932. *Max Weber and Karl Marx*. Ed. Tom Bottomore and William Outhwaite. London: Routledge, 1993.

Mandelbaum, Maurice. 1971. *History, Man, and Reason: A Study in Nineteenth-Century Thought*. Baltimore: Johns Hopkins University Press.

Marshall, James D. 1994. "On What We May Hope: Rorty on Dewey and Foucault." *Studies in Philosophy and Education* 13:307–23.

May, Todd. 2004. "Michel Foucault: Nietzschean Pragmatist." *International Studies in Philosophy* 36, no. 3:63–75.

McCarthy, Thomas. 1990. "The Critique of Impure Reason: Foucault and the Frankfurt School." *Political Theory,* 18, no. 3 (Aug.): 437–69.

McWhorter, Ladelle. 1999. *Bodies and Pleasures: Foucault and the Politics of Sexual Normalization.* Bloomington: Indiana University Press.

Mead, George Herbert. 1936. *Movements of Thought in the Nineteenth Century.* Ed. Merrit Moore. Chicago: University of Chicago Press.

Miller, James. 1993. *The Passion of Michel Foucault.* New York: Simon and Schuster.

O'Farrell, Clare. 1989. *Michel Foucault: Historian or Philosopher?* London: Macmillan.

Oksala, Johanna. 2005. *Foucault on Freedom.* Cambridge: Cambridge University Press.

O'Leary, Timothy. 2002. *Foucault and the Art of Ethics.* London: Continuum.

O'Neill, John. 1986. "The Disciplinary Society: From Weber to Foucault." *British Journal of Sociology* 37, no. 1 (Mar.): 42–60.

Owen, David. 1994. *Maturity and Modernity: Nietzsche, Weber, Foucault and the Ambivalence of Reason.* New York: Routledge.

Owen, David, and Tracy Strong. 2004. "Max Weber's Calling to Knowledge and Action." In Weber 2004, ix–lxii.

Paras, Eric. 2006. *Foucault 2.0: Beyond Power and Knowledge.* New York: Other Press.

Parsons, Talcott. 1937. *The Structure of Social Action.* New York: Free Press, 1968.

Rabinow, Paul. 1994. "Modern and Counter-Modern: Ethos and Epoch in Heidegger and Foucault." In *The Cambridge Companion to Foucault*, ed. Gary Gutting. Cambridge: Cambridge University Press. 197–214.

———. 2003. *Anthropos Today: Reflections on Modern Equipment.* Princeton: Princeton University Press.

———. 2008. *Marking Time: On the Anthropology of the Contemporary.* Princeton: Princeton University Press.

Rabinow, Paul, and Hubert Dreyfus. 1982. *Michel Foucault: Beyond Structuralism and Hermeneutics.* Chicago: University of Chicago Press.

———. 1986. "What Is Maturity? Habermas and Foucault on 'What Is Enlightenment.'" In Hoy 1986, 109–22.

Rajchman, John. 1985. *Michel Foucault: The Freedom of Philosophy.* New York: Columbia University Press.

Ringer, Fritz. 2004. *Max Weber: An Intellectual Biography.* Chicago: University of Chicago Press.

Roederer, Christopher. 2000. "Ethics and Meaningful Action in the Modern/Postmodern Age: A Comparative Analysis of John Dewey and Max Weber." *South African Journal of Philosophy* 19, no. 2:75–94.

Rorty, Richard. 1981a. "Method, Social Science, and Social Hope." In *Consequences of Pragmatism.* Minneapolis: University of Minnesota Press, 1982. 191–210.

———. 1981b. "Beyond Nietzsche and Marx." *London Review of Books* 19 (February): 5–6.

———. 1998a. "Afterword: Pragmatism, Pluralism and Postmodernism." In *Philosophy and Social Hope.* New York: Penguin, 1999. 262–77.

———. 1998b. "Pragmatism as Romantic Polytheism." In *The Revival of Pragmatism,* ed. Morris Dickstein. Durham: Duke University Press. 21–36.

———. 2004. "Universalist Grandeur, Romantic Depth, Pragmatist Cunning." *Diogenes* 51, no. 202 (Summer): 129–40.

Scaff, Lawrence A. 1989. *Fleeing the Iron Cage: Culture, Politics, and Modernity in the Thought of Max Weber.* Berkeley: University of California Press, 1991.

———. 2000. "Weber on the Cultural Situation of the Modern Age." In *The Cambridge Companion to Weber,* ed. Stephen Turner. Cambridge: Cambridge University Press. 99–116.

Sica, Alan. 2000. "Rationalization and Culture." In *The Cambridge Companion to Weber,* ed. Stephen Turner. Cambridge: Cambridge University Press. 42–58.

Stuhr, John. 1997. *Genealogical Pragmatism: Philosophy, Experience, and Community.* Albany: SUNY Press.

———. 2003. *Pragmatism, Postmodernism, and the Future of Philosophy.* New York: Routledge, 2003.

Swedberg, Richard. 2003. "The Changing Picture of Max Weber's Sociology." *Annual Review of Sociology* 29 (Aug.): 283–306.

———. 2005. *The Max Weber Dictionary.* Stanford: Stanford University Press, 2005.

Szakolczai, Arpád. 1998. *Max Weber and Michel Foucault: Parallel Life-Works.* New York: Routledge.

Taylor, Charles. 1984. "Foucault on Freedom and Truth." In Hoy 1986, 69–102.

———. 1989. *Sources of the Self: The Making of the Modern Identity.* Cambridge: Harvard University Press.

Thayer, H. S. 1968. *Meaning and Action: A Critical History of Pragmatism.* 2nd ed. Indianapolis: Hackett, 1981.

Turner, Bryan. 1987. "The Rationalisation of the Body: Reflections on Modernity and Discipline." In *Max Weber, Rationality and Modernity,* ed. S. Whimster and S. Lash. London: Allen and Unwin.

Walzer, Michael. 1983. "The Politics of Michel Foucault." In Hoy 1986.

Weber, Max. 1904. "'Objectivity' in Social Science and Social Policy." In *The Methodology of the Social Sciences,* ed. Max Weber, Edward Shils, and Harry Finch. New York: Free Press, 1949. 50–112.

———. 1905. *The Protestant Ethic and the Spirit of Capitalism.* Trans. Talcott Parsons. New York: Dover, 2003.

———. 1917. "Science as a Vocation." In Weber 2004, 1–31.

———. 1919. "Politics as a Vocation." In Weber 2004, 32–94.

———. 1923. *General Economic History.* Trans. Frank Knight. Ed. S. Hellman and M. Palyi. New York: Dover, 2003.

———. 1964. *Economy and Society.* Ed. and trans. Guenter Roth, Claus Wittich et al. Berkeley: University of California Press, 1978.

———. 2004. *The Vocation Lectures.* Ed. David and Owen and Tracy Strong. Trans. Rodney Livingstone. Indianapolis: Hackett.

West, Cornel. 1989. *The American Evasion of Philosophy.* Madison: University of Wisconsin Press.

White, Hayden. 1973. *Metahistory: The Historical Imagination in Nineteenth-Century Europe.* Baltimore: Johns Hopkins University Press.

12] Meanings, Communication, and Politics: Dewey and Derrida

Antonio Calcagno

The literature devoted to the connection between poststructuralism, deconstruction, and pragmatism is as rich as it is divided.[1] Richard Rorty claims that John Dewey and Jacques Derrida share hope and optimism for changing humanity, but whereas the former provides concrete pragmatic solutions, the latter is more of a conversant, fashioning a private self. Rorty remarks, "In my own writing about Derrida I have urged that we see him as sharing Dewey's utopian hopes, but not treat his work as contributing in any clear or direct way to the realization of those hopes."[2] Derrida responds to Rorty's challenge by maintaining that his work is politically relevant. He argues, "Deconstruction is hyper-politicizing in following paths and codes which are clearly not traditional, and I believe it awakens politicization in the way I mentioned above, that is, it permits us to think the political and think the democratic by granting us the space necessary in order not to be enclosed in the latter. In order to continue to pose the question of the political, it is necessary to withdraw something from the political and the same thing for democracy, which, of course, makes democracy a very paradoxical concept."[3]

John Stuhr points out that the traditional discourse between pragmatism and poststructuralist and postmodern thought in general can be divided along two lines.[4] First, there are those pragmatists who bring the two schools of thought together, seeing in them a relevant dialogue. The second line is dismissive and is critical of the attempt to bring the schools together. Stuhr maintains that thinkers like Vincent Colapietro, Kai Nielsen, and John Ryder have made remarkable advances, showing how both pragmatists and postmodern thinkers converge but also displaying how the significant differences between them open a potent philosophical discussion. Stuhr, however, believes that the debate has been too one-sided. The focus has been on the pragmatists, that is, on what the pragmatists can offer the poststructuralists. More work needs to be done, so claims Stuhr, in the opposite direction, namely, what can the postmoderns and poststructuralists offer pragmatists? Rereading Michel Foucault and Dewey, Stuhr argues that the thinkers like Foucault challenge pragmatist politics; Stuhr ultimately calls for a genealogical pragmatism:

> Instead, the real challenge of postmodernism to pragmatism is the challenge to recognize and critically consider the differences, distances, destructions, violence, interests, agonies and foreignness at work in pragmatism's own will to intimacy. This is the challenge to make explicit the exclusions, oppositionalities, and single-mindedness embedded in pragmatism's own notions of community, inquiry and pluralism. It is the challenge to pragmatists to recognize the delimitations and violence of all ideals even as they engage in the reconstruction of those ideals. It is the challenge to recognize the formations of subjects, the discourses of rationalization, and the perspectival political differences at work in pragmatism's own will to intimacy. Finally, it is the challenge to refrain from privileging in a final or closed manner this intimacy, association and community among subjects.[5]

Given Stuhr's insight, this chapter takes up this very same challenge, albeit not from a Foucaultian genealogical perspective; rather, I will focus on the Derridean challenge to Dewey.

In particular, I wish to focus on the relation between language and politics. Both Dewey and Derrida maintain that language, understood here in its broader context as communication as opposed to a merely logical analysis of linguistic meaning, signs, and reference, is critical for understanding and acting. Derrida and Dewey recognize that philosophy in its attempt to communicate universally and make metaphysically present realities, especially political ones, has caused violent and deplorable situations. Dewey remarks, "The difficulty is that philosophy, even when professing catholicity, has often been suborned. Instead of being a free messenger of communication it has been a diplomatic agent of some special partial interest; insincere, because in the name of peace it has fostered divisions that lead to strife, and in the name of loyalty has promoted unholy alliances and secret understandings. One might say that the profuseness of attestations to supreme devotion to truth on the part of philosophy is a matter to arouse suspicion."[6] The democracy to come is Derrida's political response to Dewey's insight. The democracy to come entails a double bind of possibility and impossibility; a true democratic state is simultaneously possible and impossible as outlined in *Voyous*, where Derrida explicitly lists the five constituent elements of the democracy to come. They include: (1) a militant political critique without end, (2) an advent that will never come to show itself fully (read promise), (3) moving beyond borders and citizenship to an international notion of sovereignty that continues to differentiate itself and share new things (*nouveaux partages*), (4) justice, (5) and unconditional injunction.[7] In *Experience and Nature* and *Democracy and Education*, Dewey argues that communication fosters community and stems from a communal life. One of its chief tasks is to build community.

For Derrida, there is nothing outside of the text; all is text. But, the text is another way of expressing what Derrida means by reality and experience. His analysis of *différance* is an analysis of how we actually experience and "read," speak, and think in the world. Derrida believes that meanings shift and change and that there is no absolute, fixed identity between an object and an ascribed meaning. Politically, the differentiation and deferral of *différance* play themselves out as the democracy to come. Communication and politics are "conditioned" by the double bind of impossibility and possibility of *différance* or the democracy to come. Politics is not merely about action but about thinking, experiencing, and communicating as well. Like Dewey, Derrida believes we must consider our actions and their political meanings. Indeed, Derrida sees his philosophy as a political thinking that conditions the way we judge, experience, perceive, read, and enact politics; it is a critical account or a "militant political critique," to borrow from *Voyous*, of events and ideas past, present, and future.

Recalling Dewey's claim that philosophy is criticism, albeit with an empirical and objective, social end, one can certainly see a parallel between the two thinkers. Furthermore, Dewey also believes that communication is essential in understanding and experiencing the world, including politics. Like Derrida, he believes meanings shift and change depending on various contexts, events, and circumstances. Politics for Dewey, however, serves the purpose of advancing human well-being. Given this parallel concerning meaning, I wish to argue that though both philosophers believe that meanings shift while still being communicable and intelligible,[8] Dewey inevitably does not recognize the extent to which meanings shift and alter their sense, especially when thinking about the meaning of political events. His liberal democratic vision, for example, can be read as too fixed in terms of its end and shape. Derrida shows Dewey that thinking politics must account for a radical differentiation of meaning that not only changes the senses of thoughts, giving new meanings to them, but also concomitantly makes meaning absent, leaving what Derrida calls a supplement and a trace. Dewey's views of a liberal democracy resulting in well-being, community, and an advanced and economically prosperous society, therefore, may be read or "communicated" as metaphysically present or, in Dewey's language, a "diplomatic agent of some special partial interest."

Dewey on Communication and Politics

Dewey views communication as both wonderful and revelatory. Language as a form of communication is an important bridge that serves to connect, express, and give meaning to the relation between ourselves and the external world.[9] Unlike Derrida, Dewey maintains that language has as one of its chief ends "enjoyment": "Language is similarly not a mere agency for economizing energy in the interaction of human beings. It is a release and amplification of energies that enter into it, conferring upon them the added quality of meaning. The quality of meaning thus introduced is extended and transferred, actually and potentially, from sounds, gestures and marks, to all things in nature. Natural events become messages to be enjoyed and administered, precisely as song, fiction, oratory, the giving of advice and instruction. These events come to possess characters: they are demarcated, and noted."[10] Derrida never speaks of enjoyment in such definitive terms. He often will refer to *jouissance*, but this kind of orgasmic, psychological pleasure is never pure, for it always contains *la petite mort* or "a small death," as Jacques Lacan and others rightly point out. What is striking, though, in Dewey's account is his insight into how meaning through language transforms the world; the world becomes a series of communicable and communicated messages, denoted and marked. Here, one thinks of Derrida's claim that there is no outside of the text; all is text.

For Dewey, like for Derrida, the interaction of meanings achieves two things. First, it can transform, shift, or change meanings. Second, it can also create new meanings. The interaction and connection between words can shift because of a new event or a new interaction between words in various circumstances. So, A may have intended X, but B had a different sense of what A had understood by X. Meaning shifts or is transformed. Likewise, an event or a change in circumstance or an invention may occur where new meanings arise. The example that quickly comes to mind is the computer or the Internet. These words certainly did not exist a hundred years ago in the sense we understand them today, and it should be noted that their meanings are constantly shifting with the development of new technologies. Ultimately, Dewey wishes to undermine the notion that signs have meaning only because they refer to fixed essences (*EN* 167–68).

Though both thinkers share this desire to move us away from a fixed notion of language based on an identity or correspondence between sign and signified, there are also some profound differences. First, Dewey believes that one can still fix meaning, albeit not in any fixed Platonic sense. One can refer to a singular meaning that we can all understand at a certain time. In *How We*

Think, Dewey sets out to find a definition for thought. "No words are oftener on our lips than *thinking* and *thought*. So profuse and varied, indeed, is our use of these words that it is not easy to define just what we mean by them. The aim of this chapter is to find a single consistent meaning."[11] The search for a "singular consistent meaning" is impossible for Derrida. Meanings are traceable to some extent, but they are never the same; this is due to the irreducible arch-structuring of *différance*.

Dewey says that there are two tools we can use that aid us in retaining meaning. First, there are words that are written down, preserved for future common memory. We can make lists of possible meaning and refer to these lists or words. Second, there is education. We can teach and learn about words and their variegated and varying senses: "Things come and go; or we come and go, and either way things escape our notice. Our direct sensible relation to things is very limited. The suggestion of meanings by natural signs is limited to occasions of direct contact or vision. But a meaning fixed by a linguistic sign is conserved for future use. Even if the thing is not there to represent the meaning, the word may be produced to evoke the meaning. Since intellectual life depends on possession of a store of meanings, the importance of language as a toll of preserving meanings cannot be overstated. To be sure, the method of storage is not wholly aseptic; words often corrupt and modify the meanings they are supposed to keep intact, but liability of infection is a price paid by every living thing for the privilege of living" (*HWT* 174). Dewey's image of asepsis and infection reminds one of Derrida's later image of autoimmunity. More than liable to infection, Derrida would claim that we are already infected as we live. One could read Derrida's notion of *héritage* or legacy as accomplishing what Dewey says. Recall that deconstruction is para(c)scitical. It draws from the legacy that has been preserved in common memory, but it simultaneously cites "around it" (*para*), showing the hidden, absent, and profuse meanings that can constantly merge in the reading of a text; meanings alter and shift.

Concerning education and instruction, Dewey believes that one should learn not only certain meanings but also an awareness of how meanings and signs operate. "Learning, in the proper sense, is not learning things, but the *meanings* of things, and this process involves the use of signs, or language in its generic sense" (*HWT* 176). Learning gives to students the practical skills, always employing human reason, to handle any situation and to make meaningful sense of anything they experience. They must also be taught that meanings shift and alter and that new meanings will emerge. The non-absolute nature of meanings should not come as any surprise. Education assists in preserving this knowledge and is seen as a process that helps "discipline the mind" in order that it can assist one in living a meaningful, productive, and enjoyable life.

If it is true that both Derrida and Dewey argue that fixed meanings are both impossible and possible, what exactly is the difference between the two? In my view, it is timing. Dewey has a chronological view of time that unfolds in his understanding of the playing out of linguistic meaning. Derrida, however, has a simultaneous view of linguistic time. Dewey believes that meanings shift, alter, and preserve their meaning in time that flows rectolinearly from speaker A to speaker B. Derrida believes that the double bind of possibility and impossibility simultaneously conditions and structures all meanings. Concretely, Dewey believes that X may mean X for a certain amount of time. As time flows, X may change its meaning and become Y because of event D: "Primarily meaning is intent and intent is not personal in a private and exclusive sense. A proposes the consummatory possession of the flower through the medium or means of B's actions; B proposes to cooperate—or act adversely—in the fulfillment of A's proposal. Secondarily, meaning is the acquisition of significance by things in their status in making possible and fulfilling shared cooperation. In the first place, it is the *motion and sounds* of A which have meaning, or are signs. Similarly, the movements of B, while they are immediate to him, are signs to A or B's cooperation or refusal. But secondarily the *thing* pointed out by A to B gains meaning. It ceases to be just what it brutely is at the moment, and is responded to in its potentiality, as a means to remoter circumstances" (*EN* 180). For Derrida, X *ab initio* or "originally" was never ever only X. It may have been simultaneously X, B, F, G, and so on. The more we read X, the more its meanings alter, become absent, and shift, although they leave traces of themselves; this is the heritage of "X."

If we pay attention to Dewey's description of what happens in linguistic communication, we note that there is a flow that moves according to a cause-effect logic. First, something happens, which causes something else to happen. For Derrida, a sign or meaning can never fully or wholly refer to its preceding sign, as it has been altered and is therefore not identically repeatable. Moreover, there is a delay, and so both the origin and the effect become deferred or absent, thereby rendering meaning both possible and impossible at the same time. How does Derrida justify the aforementioned claim?

Derrida expands his treatment of writing by showing how speech operates like writing. In making this shift, Derrida demonstrates how his treatment of absence conditions speech and all communication in general.[12] In order to expand his treatment of writing to speech, Derrida examines Edmund Husserl and John Austin. Derrida begins his treatment by claiming that speech, like writing, can communicate as a unified speech or discourse when there is repetition. Each of the elements must be repeatable or sayable again if we are to have a communicative chain of speech. But, though iterability is necessary, the specific referent of the speech need not be present, and neither need a speaker be present—for example, when we watch "repeated" clips of famous speeches of known people who are dead. Other speakers can repeat the same speech just as other hearers can hear the speech again, each repetition creating new differentiated meanings. Moreover, the speech is a delay or defers the originally present origin of the speech, which is not only delayed by the repetition but deferred because the speech itself makes use of phonetic signs (phonemes).[13] The repeated speech pronounced by others, then, is twice deferred and will continue to be deferred with each repetition. That speech need not have "present" a speaker or referent for it to be meaningful is significant, for it shows that meaning transcends the relationship of speaker-hearer, writer-recipient, and so on. Meaning needs the absence in order for it to be meaningful, but meanings will always be deferred and differentiated because of the repetition and the intervalling that happens between the elements in speech and writing. If there is a constant delay and differentiation *(différance)* and if absence is necessary for there to be any communication, then meanings of speech are not determined by context or by the referent or by the speaker.[14]

Derrida claims that all marks—that is, all graphemes or phonemes of whatever kind—in and of themselves have no fixed meaning and are not determined by context, speaker/writer/experiencer or hearer/recipient/experienced object. Derrida turns to Husserl to elaborate his point. Following the deconstructive method, Derrida draws on Husserl only to subvert the latter's claims. Husserl concedes in the *First Logical Investigation* that any utterance whose object is possible and not impossible can be understood without its referent or object actually being present. So when we hear the utterance "The sky is blue," we can understand the meaning of the utterance, even though the sky is not actually blue today or possibly will not be blue tomorrow. Husserl also acknowledges the absence of the signified as being inferior in that it could potentially lead to unfulfilled meaning intentions, which have to be fulfilled if we are to have anything like Husserlian notion of self-evidence and truth as described in the *Sixth Logical Investigation*. In fact, the absence of the signified can open up the possibility of the crisis of meaning.

There are certain Husserlian utterances that need not have objects or referents but that are very problematic for Husserl: statements that are *widersinnig* ("contradictory," for example, "the square circle") or statements that are *sinnlos* ("without meaning," for example, "the green is either"). But it is these statements that are pivotal for Derrida, for he finds in such statements the possibility of disengagement and the possibility of being grafted onto other contexts. For example, the sentence "The green is either (*oder*)" in German has no sense, but when you graft (translate) the French *où* onto the German *oder* ("either" or "or"), the sentence can have meaning—but only if spoken because the sound of the French *où* and *ou* are indistinguishable. The "green is where (*où*)" can become the French equivalent of "Where is the green?," that is, "*Le vert est où?*" The green can refer to many things or to the color itself. There is an ambiguity as to the referent, to the absent referent. But even such translations and various contextual positionings do not go far enough. The fact is that one can continually cite with quotations the utterance "The green is either." This quotation can be grafted on to any context, "before and outside of every horizon of semio-linguistic horizon." Rather than the Husserlian crisis of meaning as represented by the utterance being *widersinnig oder sinnlos*, Derrida sees in this absence of the referent/object a transcending of context, meaning, and the regular speaker-hearer-context relation, which traditionally we assume to be present in order for communication to occur.[15]

Why is undecidability (ensuing from the double bind) present in Derrida's account of speech and writing? First, there is the undecidability of using the texts of Husserl and Austin, which are central to making Derrida's point while simultaneously claiming that such texts are inadequate because they reveal a deeper arch-structure at play. Derrida does not reject outright such texts, even though they are inadequate. One cannot say, methodologically speaking, that the texts employed are neither absolutely inadequate nor adequate, for the texts themselves display the force of the double bind of possibility and impossibility. Second, if we take seriously what Derrida has to say about a plethora of contexts and the notion of grafting citations, along with the absence and differentiation and deferral of writer/speaker and recipient/addressee, then the meanings of texts are ultimately undecidable, as is all human experience, including politics. They become undecidable in that what is originary can never come to presence, and what comes to presence is simultaneously erased by the intervalling that is difference and iterability. If what we experience politically is constantly differentiating itself and constantly deferring itself, then all political action and all political decision-making becomes colored by the undecidability that the arch-structure called *différance* brings to the fore. We are never able to bring political decisions, processes, conventions, laws, movements, and, above all, their meanings to any kind of full presence.

Dewey could reply to Derrida's view of communication and meaning by arguing that though signs and meanings may defer and differentiate themselves as they are being experienced, this is not what necessarily guarantees some kind of fixed meaning in a rectolinear sequence. Dewey admits that there is both community and participation in the flow of linguistic meaning. Fixing a meaning is ensured by the fact that both speakers and hearers have the same idea or understand the same thing at the same time. There is a meaning held in common by individuals; this is what guarantees a common understanding of meaning. This community may fix meanings in time, but they may also change them. Dewey remarks, "The significant consideration is that assemblage of organic human beings transforms sequence and coexistence into participation" (*EN* 175). More explicitly, he says, "Such is the essence and import of communication, signs and meaning. Something is literally made common in at least two different centers of behavior. To understand is to anticipate together; it is to make a cross-reference which, when acted upon, brings about a partaking in common, inclusive, undertaking" (*EN* 179).

In a very profound way, language is a pragmatic tool that enables us to communicate experiences and relations between individuals and things. Dewey cleverly lodges "fixed" meanings—in Derrida's language, "possible" meanings—not in the playing out of linguistic signifiers but in the human community itself. That we can share together a common understanding and that we can respond to one another practically and socially is what guarantees some kind of fixed meanings, especially through education and various techniques of preserving meanings (for example, dictionaries, computer programs, and the like). In fact, Dewey is convinced that language can build cooperation, which is necessary for societies to thrive. He notes, "The heart of language . . . is communication; the establishment of cooperation in an activity in which there are partners, and in which the activity of each is modified and regulated by partnership. To fail to understand is to come into agreement in action; to misunderstand is to set up actions at cross-purposes" (*EN* 179). Dewey appeals to something outside of language itself to ground fixed and common meanings, namely, human community and sociality. Meaning is only communicable and shared insofar as we have the same meaning in common. Here, the connection between language and the social-political world becomes central. Action becomes possible only when we have shared meanings and common understanding of these meanings. It is this point that Derrida would challenge.

Linguistic Meanings and Politics

If all is text for Derrida, the divide between language and community is not tenable. We can understand something as common only insofar as it is communicated. We need signs and linguistic communication to do so. If Dewey and Derrida are right about the shifting of meanings, then there is nothing to prevent the very meaning of a common understanding, community, and participation from actively being misunderstood and misread in the first place. That is, our very understanding of what is "common" may be skewed by the shifting meanings of things and language. Furthermore, do we need common understanding to have action? Could we not have action when meanings are both understood and not understood, when they are both possible and impossible? I believe Derrida would say that Dewey has not gone far enough.

We do not need participatory communities where there is a common understanding in order for action to be carried out. When Dewey calls a meaning an "essence," and this does not mean an absolutely fixed essence, he ascribes a certain clarity and accessibility to meanings. And, though he acknowledges with Derrida the flux of meanings, he ascribes value to fixed meanings in concrete and pragmatic situations, forgetting the flux and shifting he also discusses. We can see this when Dewey describes how to think of the value of certain political ideas for a renewed liberal democracy in chapter 7 of *Democracy and Education.* Dewey emphasizes the need for a measure to judge the worth of any given model of social life; in seeking this measure, he says we have to avoid two extremes: (1) we must base our conception upon societies that actually exist, not ideal societies; and (2) we must extract the desirable traits of forms of community life that actually exist and employ them to criticize undesirable features and suggest improvement. Furthermore, he lays out two important considerations about society. First, in order to have a large number of values in common, all the members of the group must have equitable opportunity to receive and to take from others. There must be a large variety of shared undertakings and experiences. Otherwise, there arise influences that educate some into masters and others into slaves. Second, there must be a lack of free and equitable intercourse, which springs from a variety of shared interests. Diversity of stimulation means novelty, and novelty means challenging thought. Dewey feels that a democratic ideal can make people more social toward an awareness of good and concrete participation; it can also stem isolation. Why? He argues that, first, in democracy you get more numerous and more varied points of shared common interest but also greater reliance upon the recognition of mutual interests as a factor in social control. Second, there is a freer interaction between groups (once isolated so far as intention could keep up a separation) but change in social habit—its continuous readjustment through meeting the new situations provided by varied intercourse. And these two traits are precisely what constitute the democratically constituted society, says Dewey.

Notice Dewey's language; he has attached a singular significance to liberal democracy. He says it provides for participation and advances the "good." Such a society must have an education system that gives individuals a personal interest in social relationships, control, and the good habits of mind that secure such change without lapsing into chaos and disorder. He even shows us how to read past theories of education. For example, he reads Plato, Jean-Jacques Rousseau, and G. W. F. Hegel as making positive contributions but failing to deliver the goods when it comes to a liberal democratic society that emphasizes individual rights and freedoms within a communal setting. Plato was too aristocratic, scorning democracy and privileging the *aristoi* while most of the population were slaves. Rousseau emphasized a solitary individual with no real social links, and the idealists collapsed everything into some Absolute, thereby negating the relationship between individual and communities. Dewey's speeches, thinking, and writing about a renewed liberal democratic society communicate an expression of a concrete desire or end. He critically, and therefore philosophically, examines other philosophical visions of politics and rejects them as insufficient for their favoring either the individual or the state, ultimately neglecting the fine balance between them.

Dewey sorts through what he feels are unnecessary and deleterious, but it is this very discarded information that Derrida believes is absent but communicated in any political assessment—hence, Derrida's discussion of the intimate relationship between friends and enemies in *Politics of Friendship*. A friend does not stand in opposition to an enemy, as is traditionally conceived. In Derrida's account, a friend can be a friend only insofar as he or she "is not" an enemy; the "is not" is not a pure negation or opposition. There is a trace of the enemy within the friend; the enemy is constantly deferring in its absence, although it is constitutive of what it is to be a friend. Also, this is why borders and ethnic identities are to be both preserved and broken down in *Voyous*. One could ask whether Dewey is committing the famous selective error he thinks many philosophers of the past have committed. Derrida reminds us that what is discarded or even critically rejected never disappears. It is constitutive of all that which is positively chosen and acted upon to build a better society. If this discarded material is not given a place or does not allow itself to play itself out as constitutive for meaning, then we have lapsed into a metaphysics of presence; we become blind to that which was part of the problem or perplexity, to borrow an expression from Dewey, in the first place. Derrida's double bind tempers Dewey's critical enthusiasm. In Dewey's desire for a concrete society based on individual and communal ends, firmly rooted in invigorated liberal democracy, Dewey has dismissed what Derrida sees as constitutive of this claim, namely, the totalitarianism and despotism that Dewey saw as disordered and of which he was so critical. In many ways, Derrida reminds us to keep such despotism and totalitarianism in mind. More important, he shows us that Dewey's wish for a liberal democracy has as one of its sources a reaction against the rise of National Socialism and Communism. If liberal democracy is not achieved, one runs the risk of lapsing into either one of these totalitarian forms of government. Liberal democracy can be democratic and liberal only insofar as it does not become despotic and totalitarian. The despotism and totalitarianism are always there, simultaneously creating limits of possibility and impossibility in and against which liberal democracy must articulate itself. These limits are the double bind of possibility and impossibility. Liberal democracy, in Dewey's account, must not simply stand in a vis-à-vis relationship with anti-liberal, totalitarian visions of politics. We must think and speak about them, following Derrida, as co-constitutive. They are a meaningful internal negative limit that must condition liberal democracy insofar as its survival depends on its not lapsing into despotic or totalitarian rule.

Furthermore, and I think this could be Derrida's main critique of Dewey's democratic liberal vision, Dewey presupposes that his notions of liberal democracy are clear and have a pragmatic political "cash value." But, the very articulation of the expression "Dewey's liberal democracy" is rife with ambiguity. What Dewey meant by such a term, as an author, is inaccessible today. Dewey is no longer; he is an absent or dead author. His writing is a fragment or a trace of who he was; there is a heritage and trace of Dewey the thinker. Moreover, what he understood by a liberal democracy, which is essentially defined in opposition to Communism and National Socialism, as well as the America of the two wars and the Cold War, is not the same as liberal democracy today, even though we use the same term, especially as it is understood by thinkers like Rorty and Martha Nussbaum. The massive shifts brought on by globalization, a more racially and ethnically diverse and urbanized population ("legal" and "illegal"), the great change in women's social and political roles—all of these have meant that liberalism had to be redefined. Derrida's question remains: Whose democracy? Which liberalism? Can one even be faithful to Dewey given the changes and iterability of what has happened in the last thirty years, especially after 9/11? It is hard to refer to liberal democracy, both in terms of its starting point but also as a term, whether it be in thought or even pragmatic politics. There is an ambiguity that operates in all language and expression, but there is also a trace or a legacy that we can point to that allows us to be able to at least "recognize" a concept or expression. Dewey's life-long advocacy of liberal democracy, and Dewey knows that there are abuses and misuses of liberal democratic policy and rhetoric, wishes to achieve good ends for humanity. Derrida too was tireless in his fight for justice, but he also recognized that every attempt at justice was laced with some kind of internal limit or shifting meaning, resulting in a double bind, a simultaneity of possibility and impossibility. Part of the "militant" internal critique of any political position is not only to recognize the short-term external consequences or disadvantages of a given political situation but to mine the very political position itself to see its own inherent contradictions precisely as a communicative idea or expression. In the case of Dewey, Derrida would argue that democratic liberalism is to be judged as good or bad not only by its pragmatic consequences but also by its own inherent double bind, which includes the very struggle to even name (read define) what liberal democracy is for Dewey. Can one invoke Dewey in today's political context without the risk of never quite accessing what Dewey was saying or meant? Does not liberal democracy contain an inherent contradiction, as pointed out in Derrida's *L'autre cap*? On one hand, democracy wants freedom for all individuals, but, on the other hand, it has to legislate such freedom with the consequence of freedom becoming a legislative necessity. Those reading Dewey today and invoking his political ideas must face Derrida's challenge, for he urges us not to dismiss Dewey but to read him more closely, always with an eye to his age and our present day and the shifts that have occurred in the meanings of political words and expressions that we use to communicate certain political desiderata and ends. Meanings continue to accrue and shift as time flows, which means our political decisions and ideas are subject to this very same differentiating time flow. This is why for Derrida, democracy is always to come, because it is never completely capable of being articulated fully; its meaning is open.

Notes

1. J. Garrison, "Dewey, Derrida, and the 'Double Bind,'" *Educational Philosophy and Theory* 35, no. 3 (2003): 349–62; J. Steinnes, "Paralyses or Battlefields: Pedagogy and Proposed Parricide," *Educational Philosophy and Theory* 38, no. 2 (2006): 185–200; L. A. Hickman, ed., *Reading Dewey: Interpretations for a Postmodern Generation* (Bloomington, Ind.: Indiana University Press, 1998); J. P. Diggins, *The Promise of Pragmatism: Modernism and the Crisis of Knowledge and Authority* (Chicago:

University of Chicago Press, 1994); C. Mouffe, ed., *Deconstruction and Pragmatism* (New York: Routledge, 1996); J. Stuhr, *Genealogical Pragmatism: Philosophy, Experience, and Community* (Albany. N.Y.: SUNY Press, 1997).

2. Richard Rorty, "Remarks on Deconstruction and Pragmatism," in *Deconstruction and Pragmatism*, ed. Chantal Mouffe (New York: Routledge, 1996), 16.

3. Jacques Derrida, "Remarks on Deconstruction and Pragmatism," in *Deconstruction and Pragmatism*, 85.

4. Stuhr, *Genealogical Pragmatism*, 88–89.

5. Ibid., 110.

6. From *Experience and Nature*, in *The Later Works of John Dewey, 1925–1953*, ed. Jo Ann Boydston (Carbondale: Southern Illinois University Press, 1981), 1:306.

7. J. Derrida, *Voyous* (Paris: Galilée, 2003), 126–35.

8. For Derrida, this is what he refers to as *héritage*, literally a legacy that he can draw upon and shape and reshape again and again through his own analyses. Though shifting in meaning, its "sense" or "meaning" is communicable precisely as conditioned by the double bind of *différance*. See my article "On the Rates of Differentiation: Derrida on Political Timing," *Symposium: Canadian Journal for Continental Philosophy* 11, no. 1 (Spring 2007): 15–31.

9. J. Dewey, *Experience and Nature* (Mineola, N.Y.: Dover Publications, 1958), 166. Hereafter referred to as *EN*.

10. Ibid., 174. Dewey also notes, "Communication is also an immediate enhancement of life, enjoyed for its own sake." Ibid., 183.

11. J. Dewey, *How We Think* (Mineola, N.Y.: Dover Publications, 1997). Hereafter referred to as *HWT*.

12. Jacques Derrida, "Signature Event Context," trans. S. Weber and J. Mehlman, in *Limited Inc.*, trans. Samuel Weber (Evanston, Ill.: Northwestern University Press, 1988), 1–23. Originally published as "Signature Événement Contexte" in *Marges de la philosophie* (Paris: Galilée, 1972). English translation will be used in this article.

13. That is, "the nonpresent *remainder* of a differential mark cut off from its putative 'production' or origin." Derrida, "Signature Event Context," 9.

14. Derrida, "Signature Événement Contexte," 378–79.

15. Ibid., 381.

13] Eagerness for Experience: Dewey and Deleuze on the Problematic of Thinking and Learning

Inna Semetsky

Richard Rorty, in his *Consequences of Pragmatism*, acknowledging the pragmatic direction taken by both modern and postmodern philosophy, declared that "James and Dewey were not only waiting at the end of the dialectical road which analytic philosophy traveled, but are waiting at the end of the road which, for example, Foucault and Deleuze are currently traveling."[1] Gilles Deleuze, a French poststructuralist philosopher, never cited John Dewey; however, he was familiar with Charles Sanders Peirce, whose unorthodox logic or triadic semiotics Deleuze used in a number of his original works.[2] This chapter does not aim to establish who traveled the farthest along the road posited by Rorty. Instead, its purpose is to trace a common direction as a sort of pragmatic trajectory that will map a territory constituting both philosophers' anti-Cartesian image of thought, which encompasses, contra static factual knowledge, a dynamic process of experimental learning from experience.

The approach of positioning the philosophical figure of Gilles Deleuze as a Deweyan counterpart does not aim to compare or contrast the two philosophers or to pick up any of the postmodern trends lurking in the background of the modern epoch. Rather, this chapter is based on the idea of freely juxtaposing—following Richard Bernstein's methodological model—two thought processes so as to be able to construct a commonly shared plane between the two.[3] Bernstein addressed the possible intersections of continental and pragmatic traditions from both substantive and methodological perspectives.[4] He specifically acknowledged the importance and value of "experimental knowing" advocated by both traditions.[5] This chapter employs the cartographic method of Deleuze's philosophy, which—instead of following analytic philosophy's narrow path of reasoning solely—employs the contemporary cultural studies' format of diverse and broad forms of mapping. Such a geographical metaphor was prominent in the process-oriented metaphysics of both Dewey and Deleuze.[6]

Experimental knowing is embedded in human experience per se. This method of inquiry is not reduced to the knowledge of facts but encompasses practical understanding of meanings "located" in real life, in the middle of experiential events. Stressing the difference between a pragmatic inquiry and traditional epistemology, the former focusing on "*the relation to one another of different successive states of things*," Dewey considers such a relation to be a powerful substitute for the eternal question of "how one sort of existence, purely mental . . . immaterial . . . can get beyond itself and have valid reference to a totally different kind of existence—spatial and extended."[7] Reorganization of experience must include "a threshold (. . . or plateau), . . . waxings and wanings of intensity," therefore constituting a continuous process of experimental, practical adaptation and readaptation when "the old self is put off and the new self is only forming."[8] All thinking and learning—or "reaching the absent from present"—involves a particular dynamics described as "a jump, a leap, a going beyond what is surely known to something else accepted on its warrant. . . . The very inevitableness of the jump, the leap, to something unknown, only emphasizes the necessity of attention to the conditions under which it occurs."[9] It is the conditions of the experiential problematic situation that "calls up something not present to the senses," which would otherwise guarantee and determine the direct action-reaction or cause-effect link.[10]

What Dewey in his analysis of thinking described as a pre-reflective state of mind is a necessary condition arising from a disturbed and perplexed situation that calls for the momentous state of suspense,[11] which is an affective state filled with desire and uncertainty and open to imagination. Imagination functions so as to create a vision of realities "that cannot be exhibited under existing conditions of sense-perception"; instead, they constitute an uncertain reality that may be called virtual in the sense of it being "the remote, the absent, [and] the obscure."[12] Still, these realities are not imaginary but totally real and potentially amenable to a "clear insight."[13] Such an "eagerness for experience" contains in itself—in the shared and social world—"the germ of intellectual curiosity," because "to the open mind, nature and social experiences are full of varied and subtle challenges to look further."[14] Experience exceeds its confinement to a private Cartesian mind; in Dewey's experiential reality, things are had prior to becoming known. It cannot be otherwise, because experience is not shut off from nature in the manner of the dualistic split that has haunted us since the days of antiquity but "is of as well as in nature."[15] Conscious decision-making is deferred for a moment; the state of mind is pre-reflective yet: "we de-fer conclusion in order to in-fer more thoroughly" so as to create a more refined inference and more complex meaning.[16] The key word for Dewey is "suggestion," leading in all probability to a solution that would be merely possible, and such "propriety . . . cannot be absolutely warranted in advance, no matter what precautions be taken."[17] Consciousness, the very stuff of human subjectivity, thus acquires a derivative status as a result and an outcome, "an eventual function"[18] and not the reason behind the total process: mind as a whole must be greater than the sum of its solely *cogito* parts.

How is a similar eagerness for experience approached in Deleuze's philosophy? His philosophical stance was best addressed in the two works of the late 1960s, *Difference and Repetition* and *The Logic of Sense*, and then defined and reconstructed two decades later in *What Is Philosophy?*, coauthored with Felix Guattari, a practicing social psychologist and psychoanalyst. The latter project gives philosophy, the task of which is the creation and invention of new concepts, its instrumental, tool-like—pragmatic—flavor. It invites the philosopher (whose intellectual practice therefore becomes one of a constructive pragmatist in the tradition of Dewey's philosophy) to think the unthinkable, envisaging something that is yet to come. Deleuze identified the realm of unthinkable as the problem of the Outside, which represents inquiry that is not solely based on background knowledge but is forward-looking and future-oriented in terms of evaluating present conditions under which new concepts, "for unknown lands," would have been produced.[19] Deleuze considered himself to be a pluralist and empiricist, yet not in the reductive, tabula rasa–like, passive sense reminiscent of traditional British empiricism. Experience is that milieu that provides capacity to affect and be affected; it is a-subjective and impersonal. The Deweyan waxings and wanings of intensity constitute the folds of experience; in fact, the ontological Being itself is folded: "Being as Fold."[20] Experience is not an individual property; rather, subjects are constituted in relations within experience itself, that is, by means of individuation in the here-and-now of the Deweyan disturbed, perplexed, and problematic situation.

Experience is rendered meaningful not by grounding empirical particulars in abstract universals but by experimentation on ourselves. Something in the experiential "world forces us to think. This something is an object not of recognition but a fundamental 'encounter.' . . . It may be grasped in a range of affective tones."[21] The affective capacity is that which describes the body in action, and it is practically impossible to know ahead of time "the affects [one] is capable of, funded in what is . . . called ethology [as] the study . . . of the capacities for affecting and being affected."[22] The exploration of affects becomes a long experimental and experiential affair that would have required practical wisdom in a Spinozian sense. Contrary to the assumptions of the reductive classical empiricism, human experience does have an affective dimension that has been stripped away by traditional dualistic logic. Deleuze's transcendental empiricism is as irreducible to given sense-data as Dewey's naturalistic pragmatism: "one never has a tabula rasa; one slips in, enters in the middle; one takes up or lays down rhythms" enfolded in the real-life experiential situation.[23] Experience is enfolded or inclusive; it includes "a draft, a wind, a day, a time of day, a stream, a place, a battle, an illness":[24] thus, an experiential event is subject-less or a-personal, and human subjectivity, contrary to the Cartesian maxim, is produced or constructed in experience. We are made up of relations, says Deleuze, and experience makes sense to us only if we understand the relations in practice between conflicting schemes of the said experience.[25]

Deleuze asserts that "problems must be considered not as 'givens,'" that is, requiring the Cartesian method as "the search for the clear and distinct" solution.[26] If givens are reconceptualized as takens, then all data become "discriminated for a purpose:—that, namely, of affording signs or evidence to define and locate a problem, and thus give a clue to its resolution."[27] It is "the problematic and confused" that the reflective thinking starts with, thereby leading to our learning from experience.[28] Learning is "infinite [and] of a different nature to knowledge,"[29] but that of the nature of a creative process as a method of invention. A problem in question is always constituted by differential relations "between what is done and what is undergone. . . . To apprehend such relations is to think."[30] The difference embedded in real experience makes thought encounter a shock or crisis, which is embedded in the objective structure of an event per se. There is perplexity there that thereby transcends the faculties of perception beyond the supposedly given data of sense-impressions. Going beyond the recognition of the old toward the creation of the new, thinking necessarily becomes a model of learning, and not at all "fall[ing] back, as upon a stereotype, upon some previously formed scheme."[31]

Both Dewey and Deleuze continued the legacy of Charles Sanders Peirce's philosophy. In the pragmatic tradition of Peirce, Dewey acknowledged the continuity in nature, describing it as being "the intimate, delicate and subtle interdependence of all organic structures and processes with one another."[32] According to Dewey's naturalistic logic, there is no breach of continuity between the operations of inquiry and biological and physical operations; that is, cognitive operations grow out of organic activities without, however, being identical to that from which they emerge.[33] As inquiry into inquiry, Dewey's naturalistic logic is recursive; that is, its function does not depend on anything extraneous to inquiry. Instead, it establishes continuity between the less complex and the more complex activities and forms that make up the multiplicity of heterogeneous levels constituting "an" experience. Dewey considered the reorganization of experience to have its origin in real-life problematic situations. It is the perplexity of a particular situation that demands a constructive process based on reflective thinking grounded in "superpropositional" logic, that is, logic irreducible to linear syllogistic inference; instead, it becomes the "creative logic of artistic construction."[34]

Interactions are being established between, as Dewey was saying, what is done and what is undergone, and it is by means of apprehending these connections and interrelations that "an organism increases in complexity"—in other words, learns.[35] As for Deleuze, he too emphasized an "extra-propositional or subrepresentative" quality of learning: "Learning to swim or learning a foreign language means composing the singular points of one's own body or one's own language with those of another shape or element, which tears us apart but also propels us into a hitherto unknown and unheard-of world of problems. . . . '[L]earning' express that extra-propositional or subrepresentative problematic instance: the presentation of the unconscious, not the representation of consciousness."[36]

In the pragmatic tradition of overcoming the dualistic split between the sensible and the intelligible, between thought and experience, between ideas and sensations, Deleuze posits an experimental and experiential logic of social practice as not reducible to the logic of identity, to the logical copula "is." Deleuze suggests: "Substitute the AND for IS. A *and* B. The AND is . . . the path of all relations."[37] This remarkable additive or relational change was indeed noted by Dewey, who posited the question of whether reality possesses practical character half a century earlier than Deleuze. Dewey noticed the existence of "a peculiar condition of differential—or additive—change,"[38] the peculiarity appearing because of the present condition both having emerged from the prior state and having been related to the consequent, yet absent, state of affairs as its own constituent part, a condition of possibility. The additive change is by necessity in-between the old and the new: "it marks the assumption of a new relationship" that might lead to new properties appearing as a consequence of the said relationship.[39]

The curiosity, or eagerness, for experience is described by Dewey as being of interest, which is equivalent to being "'between' the agent and his end";[40] Dewey emphasized the richness of the metaphor involved in this concept by deliberately putting the word "between" in quotation marks. One way of arousing interest is by bringing about a sense of connection so that "what a person gets and gives as a human being, a being with desires, emotions and ideas, is not external possessions but a widening and deepening of conscious life—a more intense, disciplined, and expanding realization of meanings."[41] To be full of desire is as important for Dewey as it is for Deleuze: desire—or affect—is a qualitative element of experience constituting Deweyan affective thought. As for Deleuze, his practical philosophy is accomplished by the method of transcendental empiricism. According to transcendental empiricism, thinking cannot be considered a natural a priori faculty of mind. It is not a primary exercise but always a secondary power of thought, called forth from the depth of the unconscious, and born under the constraints of real experience as a material, almost physical, force. What inspires thinking is the complexity of life itself, or what Dewey identified as a necessity "to cope with the emergence of new modes of life—of experiences that demand new modes of expression."[42]

The intensity of difference is embedded in experiential events and is a function of implicit desire, or affect, situated in the midst of the very experience because its object is "the entire surrounding which it traverses" or transcends: hence, empiricism is transcendental.[43] The relational (additive or differential) logic defies the whole dualistic split haunting us since modernity, it being either between thought and world, or the inside and the outside, or private and public. The relational logic is the logic of experimentation not "subordinate to the verb to be," to the boring logic of identity.[44] For Dewey, too, it is not that "identity works and then reinstates differences by contiguity. . . . 'Identity' seems to be the result rather than the antecedent of the association," "identity" itself being a vague term that Dewey deliberately puts in quotation marks because identity—by virtue of itself being a function of the dynamics of experience—is bound to be different depending on its own spatio-temporal distribution in real experience.[45] Thinking, enriched with desire, is experimental and experiential: experience therefore is future-oriented, lengthened, and enfolded, representing an experiment with what is new or coming into being. Experience constitutes a complex place, and it is our experimentation on ourselves that becomes, for Deleuze, our very identity. This identity is paradoxical; it is not sameness but the Deleuzian becoming-other in experience. Identity, therefore, is always different because it is embedded in the dynamics of the process when, as I said earlier citing Dewey, the old self is being put off while the new self is forming!

By virtue of experimentation, the future-oriented thought flies away along the line of becoming, called by Deleuze a "line of flight," along which our thinking escapes the old frame of reference within which this flight seems like a sort of immaterial vanishing through some imaginary event-horizon. Instead, it is our practical learning from experience that creates its own terms of actualization, thereby leading to the "intensification of life" by means of evaluation and re-valuation—reorganization—of experience.[46] The practical logic of experimentation is inspired by radical, nonreductive empiricism because, sure enough, "only empiricism knows how to transcend the experiential dimension of the visible" without a sole recourse to the universal ideas: universals and particulars are interrelated, enfolded.[47] Respectively, the supposed intentionality of the Cartesian cognizing subject "is surpassed by the fold of Being, Being as Fold."[48] The fold is encompassed by the aforementioned Deweyan "between," an intermezzo, as Deleuze says, that would have been located not within the private world of a Cartesian subject but precisely, as Dewey points out, "'between' the agent and his end."[49]

This in-between-ness of the fold positions it as "the inside of the outside," where the outside is virtual yet real by virtue of its pragmatics.[50] It unfolds in an unpredictable manner, and it is impossible to know ahead of time what the body (both physical and mental) can do. As affective, experience is as yet a-conceptual, and Deleuze emphasizes the passionate quality of such an experience: "perhaps passion, the state of passion, is actually what folding the line outside [and] making it endurable . . . is about."[51] An intellectual understanding gives way to "intensity, resonance, musical harmony."[52] Such an intensive object of experience, being as yet un-thought, is presented only in its tendency to exist, or rather to subsist, in a virtual, subrepresentative state. It actualizes itself through multiple different/ciations. Experience, in contrast to direct unmediated sense-data, is not limited to what is immediately perceived: the line of flight or becoming is real as embedded in real experience even if it appears inaccessible and imperceptible; we remember Dewey's emphasis on this particular dimension of experience as "something not present to the senses"![53] Deleuze would have agreed: "[W]e don't see it, because it's the least perceptible of things," even as it is embedded in experience despite the fact that we cannot see or hear it directly.[54]

Yet, "in the end what is unseen decides what happens in the seen."[55] The dynamic, mediated understanding of meanings is different from direct knowledge of facts. If the "conception of the role of experience within nature means that 'human affairs, associative and personal, are projections, continuations, complications of nature which exists in the physical and prehuman world,' [as] Dewey writes," then the Deweyan "means of detour" is paramount for evaluating and understanding such an experience.[56] For Deleuze and Guattari, it is the dynamic understanding of experience that constitutes a transformational pragmatics within which our deeply ingrained habits can themselves be transformed and changed, therefore leading to self-becoming-other in experience. The method of intelligent, pragmatic inquiry as dynamic understanding differs in principle from predictability and knowledge of facts. It is "the striving to make stability of meanings prevail over the instability of events" that remains a driving force behind the reorganization of experience.[57] Perception itself is capable of differentiating between, as Dewey says, what may be and is not, so that both human actions and their consequences become joined in perception.

Dewey defined the art of perception as an ability to acknowledge many unattained possibilities so as to be able to "refer the present to consequences." Such a thought experiment is capable of containing in its present phase also "affairs remote in space and in time."[58] Functioning in the mode of an imaginary excursion into some possible future, an inquiry assumes the function of deliberation. Deliberation has been defined by Dewey as "a dramatic rehearsal (in imagination) of various competing possible lines of action. . . . Deliberation is an experiment in finding out what the various lines of possible action are really like."[59] An expanded perception enables one—in an unprecedented, as Dewey says, response to conditions—to creatively reorganize the change in a given direction. This creativity ensures novelty. Novelty, for Dewey, may be created precisely at a critical point where the human mind "comes in contact with the world. . . . When the new is created, the far and strange become the most natural, inevitable things in the world."[60]

It is the background of organized meanings that is capable of converting the problematic situation from being obscure into being clear and determined. The human mind existing in contact with the world is not just an attractive metaphor but literally acquires an almost physical reality in the capacity of being a possible catalyst that would have contributed to overcoming the dualistic split between the knower and the known by expanding the boundaries of a total organism-environment system. As described by Dewey, what we call "habit" is a mode of organization that both commands an action but also has "a hold upon us because we are the habit."[61] Sinking toward the very bottom of consciousness, habits wear the cloth of Deleuzian desire or Eros, especially considering that symbolic Eros tends to sometimes embody its own alter ego, carrying the "traits of a bad habit" in the guise of some quite undesirable qualities of Trickster in itself.[62] Habits "perpetuate themselves, by acting unremittingly upon the native stock of activities. They stimulate, inhibit, intensify, weaken, select, concentrate and organize the latter into its own likeness."[63]

Similar to the powerful Deleuzian affects, habits are "active means, means that project themselves, energetic and dominating ways of acting."[64]

Habits are forces that are dynamic and projective, yet by being unconscious they may continuously manifest in human behaviors by means of "routine, unintelligent habit[s]."[65] The reorganization of habits then becomes a mode of inquiry so as to make a habit enter consciousness as perceived and subsequently "intelligently controlled."[66] Such a mode of organization effectuated by "cooperating with external materials and energies" is potentially capable of reaching "our perception and thought," thus, sure enough, blending affect together with both percept and concept in accord with Deleuze's triadic structure of experience.[67] Deleuze specifically emphasized the triadic relationship based on the inseparability of percepts, affects, and concepts in one's experience: we "need all three to get things moving."[68] These dynamic moving forces, "whether perceived or presented in imagination," breathe real life into philosophical thinking.[69] The transformation of an unconscious, and unintelligent, habit into the conscious and intelligent is possible by means of connections via the movement along the Deleuzian line of flight as the means to traverse some of our old and outlived habits.

Because "any habit is a way or manner of action," such a movement along what Deleuze called the transversal line would necessarily bring forth changes and transformations in ourselves by means of "new percepts and new affects."[70] This dynamic process contributes to the creation of new concepts as new modes of not only our thinking but also feeling, perceiving, and acting in the world enfolded in the meaningful understanding of experience. Because the experience always has its affective quality, novel concepts are to be invented or created in order to make sense out of singular experiences and, ultimately, to affirm it in practice, to realize its meaning. For Deleuze, the creation of concepts is impossible without "the laying out of a plane."[71] To think means to construct a plane so that, pragmatically, to "find one's bearings in thought"[72] comes by means of stretching, folding, unfolding, infolding, that is, by multiple movements of this plane's diagrammatic features that may, or may not, traverse the plane as a result of potential interactions so that concepts appear as intensive features of the said plane.

The plane, elaborated upon by Deleuze, can also be translated from French as *plan*, its meaning thus moving closer to what Dewey prophetically called "the drawing of a ground-plan of human experience."[73] The novel concepts that will have been laid down on the plane are forever fuzzy and never completely determined: they are born from intuitions and impulses that subsist at the precognitive level "as a substratum in the depth of the subconsciousness, the basic pattern of the relations of the live creature to his environment."[74] This level is foundational for the Deleuzian plane of immanence, and "immanence is the unconscious itself."[75] Dewey described the "unconscious activities [as] realities . . . of the kind to re-shape natural objects. . . . Hence [their] liberating, expansive power."[76] Affects are qualities that, according to Dewey, are "attached to events and objects in their movement [as belonging] to the self that is concerned in the movement of events toward an issue that is desired or disliked. . . . They . . . are not . . . private."[77] They constitute the qualitative whole of an enduring situation, the whole that is being held together by the Deleuzian rhizomatic multiplicities. Deleuze borrows the rhizome from biology as the metaphor for unlimited growth due to multiple transformations; the rhizome's underground sprout does not have a traditional root but a stem, the oldest part of which dies off while simultaneously rejuvenating itself at the tip, analogous to the Deweyan process of growth during which indeed "the old self is put off and the new self is only forming."[78]

This transformation from the old to the new can be expressed in terms of "the focal culmination of the continuity of an ordered temporal experience in a sudden discrete instant of climax."[79] What Dewey called tension is the Deleuzian difference embedded in conflicting and perplexing experiences and representing the necessary presence of instability or uncertainty that serves as a climactic precursor for the reorganization of experience. All reflective thinking demands turning upon its own as yet unexpressed unconscious assumptions so as to be able to express them explicitly: "The im-plicit is made ex-plicit; what was unconsciously assumed is exposed to the light of the day" when it becomes unfolded in practice.[80] In French, *le pli* means "the fold," which therefore is a concept of utmost significance for Dewey and Deleuze alike. For Dewey, the optimal relation between the unconscious and the conscious is nothing less than the test that determines the success of education! Education as our continuous learning from experience is our practical life itself that becomes full of realized meanings, hence fulfilled. As Dewey points out, "Education is not a mere means to such a life. Education is such a life."[81]

Yet, there are no preexisting equations that would sufficiently describe the relation between the precognitive phase and reflexive thinking or, for that matter, establish a precise line between the old and the new. The singular character of concepts makes it impossible to establish the general rule of where the unconscious attitude or habitual thinking stops and the analytic phase begins. Therefore, for Dewey, the task of learning and education in general consists of nurturing a particular "type of mind competent to maintain an economical balance of the unconscious and the conscious" that should include, besides intellectual seriousness, an element of free play as well.[82] It is the unconscious that "gives spontaneity and freshness; [but] consciousness, conviction and control."[83] Deleuze called the unconscious ideas "'differentials' of thought . . . related not to a Cogito . . . but to the fractured I of a dissolved Cogito."[84] To put the fractured pieces together means to learn, to integrate, to connect, to be a living rhizome, to actualize the virtual, to construct the plane of immanent consistency in the process that becomes "the conquest of the unconscious." How to maintain a Deweyan economic balance of the unconscious and consciousness? For Deleuze, the unconscious should be conquered, that is, made conscious or integrated into consciousness, by means of a *double* process: differenciation and differentiation.[85]

It is the philosopher as a creative artist who can read and interpret various signs enfolded or implicated in experience that make the very situation problematic and, by being able to differentiate between them, can transform this disturbed situation into a new one, in which disjointed fragments ultimately form a unified integrated whole. The Deweyan qualitative whole, as embodying aesthetic and emotional qualities exceeding a solely "intellectual activity,"[86] accords with Deleuze's describing a concept in terms of a cinematic image, or a musical composition, or an artistic creation rather than a statement or a proposition: "A painter is someone who creates in the domain of lines and colors. . . . Likewise a philosopher is someone who creates in the domain of concepts, someone who invents new concepts. . . . Concepts are singularities which react with ordinary life, with ordinary or everyday fluxes of thought."[87]

The lines constituting the Deleuzian rhizome serve as diverse artistic means to enrich the aforementioned intellectual understanding with its aesthetic and ethical dimensions and, in Dewey's words, to "express the ways in which things act upon one another and upon us; the ways in which, when objects act together, they reinforce and interfere. For this reason, lines are wavering, upright, oblique, crooked, majestic; for this reason they seem in direct perception to have even moral expressiveness. They are earth-bound and aspiring; intimate and coldly aloof; enticing and repellent. They carry with them the properties of objects."[88]

The rhizomatic lines intersect and branch out; they curve and close into areas, creating multiple topological surfaces as a precondition for the creation of concepts on the plane of immanence. The newly created concepts, the meanings of which would have been altered, impose new sets of evaluation on the aforementioned fluxes of life, and for Deleuze, as for Dewey, no thinking is value-free. A thinker becomes the thinker by virtue of his or her being "lured and rewarded by total integral experiences that are intrinsically worth while."[89] Because every concept must embody the situation as a whole—otherwise no concept, as a "fragmentary whole," would have been created—it "speaks the event, not the essence or the thing—pure Event."[90] Concepts, albeit belonging to individual minds, make mind per se a processual affair, a verb, an infinitive, an active event, notwithstanding that "belonging is always a matter of . . . distributive assignment," a nomad.[91] Deleuze's nomad metaphor carries a dynamic, topological nuance as a spatio-temporal function of a problematic situation. Nomad is always in-between, always in the process of becoming; "the life of nomad is the intermezzo," distributed at once between here and there, between now and then, "always the day before and the day after."[92] Therefore, when humankind discovered the method of fire-making, or, in Dewey's words, "when men come to the point of *making* fire, fire is not an essence, but a mode of natural phenomena, an order in change, a 'how' of a historic sequence," an event in a series.[93]

The becoming "divides itself infinitely in past and future and always eludes the present" because what is called thinking contains in its "'present' phase, affairs remote in space and in time."[94] Becoming is always in the present, but the present per se is elusive, making the self-becoming-other all the more difficult and challenging. Because one never knows in advance, there are only explorations and experimentations. Only then the flight along the rhizomatic lines of becoming is toward life: life itself becomes a work of art, a process of self-creation by realizing the meaning of experience. Real events embody an ethical dimension, the different values being the "intrinsic qualities of events,"[95] and the ethical theme of an event's having an intrinsic value is as paramount for Deleuze's philosophy as for Dewey's. For Dewey, an individual experience is never "some person's; it [is] nature's, localized in a body as that body happened to exist by nature."[96] One—in whose body an event is localized—is to be worthy of this event: the totality of experience is, for Dewey and Deleuze alike, intrinsically worthwhile. For this purpose, one has to attain an ethical responsibility or, as Deleuze says, "this will that the event creates in us," as if ourselves become a quasi-cause of "what is produced within us."[97] Deleuze too is firm on the question of the impersonality of event: as a multiplicity, an event is profoundly social and collective and therefore "irreducible to individual states of affairs, particular images, [or] personal beliefs."[98] It is an event that produces subjective will, the meaning of this Deleuzian statement leaning toward Dewey's addressing the central factor in responsibility as being "the possibility of a . . . modification of character and the selection of the course of action which would make this possibility a reality."[99]

Responsibility is a by-product of learning, but learning is a feature of responsibility, and both operate recursively by means of reorganization of experience, making the issue of responsibility all the more crucial: "a creator who isn't grabbed around the throat by a set of impossibilities is no creator."[100] Responsibility arises from "[t]he fact that each act tends to form, through habit, a self which will perform a certain kind of acts."[101] For Dewey and Deleuze alike, habits are material forces that are simply had at the bodily, affective level. They constrain experience by imposing impulses that compel one to think—and "where there is thought, things present act as signs or tokens of things not yet experienced."[102] In this respect, a newly created concept will always contain in itself an affective quality acting in the manner of intuitions or impulses in its vague and only potential form. Importantly, impulses are, for Dewey, the very pivots or turning points for the reorganization of experience. Defining impulses as "agencies of deviation, for giving new directions to old habits," Dewey indeed implies the Deleuzian becoming-other in the process of individuation as the formation of the self in practice and experience.[103] Deleuze says that "directions . . . are fractal in nature," using the image of crossing and zigzagging "interacting lines" to describe intuitions populating the plane.[104]

The implications are far-reaching because the concepts are never simply deduced but are created by means of multiple and constructive connections against the qualitative background of Deweyan affective thought. An immediate experience needs mediation, and "bringing these connections . . . to consciousness embraces the meaning of the experience. Any experience, however trivial in its first appearance, is capable of assuming an indefinite richness of significance by extending its range of perceived connections," creating the very depth of experience that thus becomes meaningful and significant.[105] Dewey used the term "depth" "with respect to the plane upon which it occurs—the intrinsic quality of the [intellectual] response" of different people, asserting that "one man's thought is profound while another's is superficial. . . . This phase of thinking is perhaps the most untaught of all."[106] For Deleuze, too, his conceptualizations of the unconscious include the dimension of depth in the sense of the unconscious of thought, which is "as profound as the unknown of the body."[107] For Deleuze, the thinking process reflects "an adimensional *profondeur* (depth or depths)" of one's creative and intensive potential, and "to think is to create," or to invent concepts in practice.[108]

The immediate qualities, for Dewey, are inscribed in "the 'subconscious' of human thinking" and have the flavor of the Deleuzian affect, or becoming, that jump-starts all cognitive reflection, while by themselves they would be staying out of one's awareness.[109] Despite the fact that we may not be consciously aware of these qualities, they effect "an immense multitude" of immediate organic acts. As feelings, that is the affective qualities, they effectively direct one's behavior, having an organic "efficiency of operation which it is impossible for thought to match." Dewey asserts that these qualities are indeed "the stuff of 'intuitions.'"[110] As intuitions, they play the role of "the dynamic or motivational factors influencing intellectual activity" and, by implication, human habitual behaviors.[111] As immediate qualities, they belong to a single plateau represented by an affective dimension of that complex plane, which Deleuze called the "plane of immanence." Without affects' entering what Deleuze called a zone of indiscernability with percepts, a percept per se would never undergo a deterritorialization (Deleuze's term) into a dynamic line of flight in order to reterritorialize, that is, enter a new territory, the one of a concept, so that, in Dewey's words, "feelings are no longer just felt. They have and they make sense," thus contributing to the realization of meanings in practice.[112]

For Dewey, the immediate being and having as primarily experienced are preconditions for reflective knowledge. Human experience based on empirical facts points to nature itself as saturated with "hidden possibilities [and] novelties." The multitude of things are experiential objects of emotions and desires, joy and pain, happiness and suffering, acted upon and acted by—in short, they are "things had before they are things cognized," the two predicates, "had" and "cognized," constituting two different dimensions of otherwise the same things.[113] Dewey positioned habits as constituting the self in a way of forming its desires and ruling its thoughts. "They are will," says Dewey, but in the affective sense of being an "immensely more intimate and fundamental part of ourselves than are vague, general, conscious choices."[114] All logical reasoning must be preceded by "more unconscious and tentative methods" because any object of primary experience contains potentialities that are not yet actualized or factors "which are not explicit; any object that is overt is charged with possible consequences that are hidden."[115] In a pragmatic sense, the number of possible consequences can never be fully exhausted. So the methods of inference necessarily are "more or less speculative, adventurous,"[116] or, as Deleuze says, nomadic. Nomadic thinking implies the significance of a direction but simultaneously affirms the multiplicity of paths that nomadic tribes wander along in their movement in the unpredictable "smooth space," the structure of which cannot be reduced to a simple description in terms of Cartesian analytical geometry.[117]

Such a smooth space cannot be described by the universal equation of "motion as F=ma," which would have reduced it to what Deleuze called a striated, gridded space, but is likely to be "probabilistic, semialeatory, quantum" and hence dependent on "the frequency distributions . . . and redistributions of what existed before."[118] Deleuze uses the word "polyvocality," stressing the very physicality of the embedded in experience signs and their affective (Deweyan) quality. In order to find one's way, one's bearings or whereabouts in the smooth space, one must feel as much as see or listen. Those are genuine nomads who, in Dewey's words, will "act on the basis of the absent and the future. . . . [For them,] nature speaks a language which may be interpreted. To a being who thinks, things are records of their past, as fossils tell of the prior history of the earth, and are prophetic of their future."[119] The nomad's way is an immanent trajectory and not a fixed ideal or transcendental end, a deviant footpath and not the royal road. As a symbol for future-oriented becoming, nomads always "transmute and reappear in the lines of flight of some social field," exceeding any individual experience.[120] Deleuze's method of nomadic—pragmatic—inquiry is compatible with Henri Bergson's intuition; it enables the reading of signs, symbols, and symptoms that lay down the dynamic structure of experience.

As did Deleuze after him, Dewey indeed acknowledged Bergson's positing the primacy of intuition: "[I]ntuition precedes conception and goes deeper. . . . Reflection and rational elaboration spring forth and make explicit a prior intuition. . . . [R]eflection about affairs of life and mind consists in an ideational and conceptual transformation of what begins as an intuition."[121] Such is the living process of learning from experience because life itself contains lessons to be learned in practice. The learning process, by its very definition, "reaches down into nature. . . . [I]t has breadth . . . to an indefinitely elastic extent. It stretches."[122] This stretch expands the horizon of meaningful experience and contributes to overcoming the limitations of perceptible reality by fine-tuning the perception per se. Perception merges into inference because "[t]hat stretch constitutes inference," and for pragmatists, perception differs not in kind but only in degree from such forms of human knowledge as cognition.[123]

Among the conflicting experiences situated in the midst of "critical junctures" embedded in a problematic situation, the enriched and perceptive thinking represents a potential "tendency to form a new [habit]"; as such, it necessarily "cuts across some old habit."[124] Cuttings and cross-cuttings establish multiple becomings as "a new threshold, a new direction of zigzagging line, a new course for the border" together with the "emergence of unexpected and unpredictable combinations" functioning as ideas along many experiential lines of flight.[125] Ideas—which are as yet simply potential tendencies—are nonetheless capable of generating ever new ideas as embedded in the active dynamic process that Peirce called semiosis. Every new actualized idea becomes therefore none other than the created possible, potentially capable of a new meaning. Thinking embedded in experience tends to cut continuously across old habits so that the concept has no reference outside itself. It becomes self-referential, that is, at the moment of creation, it posits itself and its object simultaneously. Concepts are invented, or created, as if reborn in experience. The peculiar "feeling of the direction and end of various lines of behavior [as] . . . the feeling of habits working below direct consciousness" leads eventually to the transformation of old habits and creation of new ones.[126]

The functioning of our habits, when described in terms of Deleuze's post-structuralist conceptualizations, takes place through a diagram, an abstract and informal yet powerful and intensive multiplicity that itself is positioned along the via media between discursive and nondiscursive formations, yet "makes others see and speak."[127] What Deleuze and Guattari called the "abstract machine" always operates "within concrete assemblages" taking the form of human behaviors and actions that embody habits.[128] Thinking is oriented toward evaluation of one's current, here-and-now mode of existence, and "beneath the generalities of habit in moral life we rediscover singular processes of learning," solving the problematic situations in practice, in the living process of our very experience, hence learning our moral lessons.[129] The process-metaphysics implicit in both Dewey's and Deleuze's philosophies defies experience as merely consisting of separate atomistic parts. Nature is much broader than the physical world alone and includes its own virtual (as yet, imperceptible) dimension, which is of utmost significance for Dewey and Deleuze alike. The dualistic split between experience and the world dissolves because mind is not confined to brain alone.

Experience that has been taken out of the head, so to speak, but instead put back into the world (where it originally "resides" in its virtual, potential form) means that the causes operate not intrinsically but relationally, meanwhile defying the habitual fact-value distinction. Values are not just subjective feelings but do reside in the world: the start of any inquiry and acquiring knowledge (facts) is motivated by us experiencing the world of values that make us strive for certain goals; these goals and purposes, reciprocally, shape our experience and inform new values. Experience by necessity has both logical and bio-logical character, and values cannot be represented by a fixed set but, in their functional role, are dynamic and depend on the evolving meanings of experience. The folds of experience transcend the split between private and public, individual and collective, the inside and the outside. As an ontological category, what Deleuze called the Outside is a virtual space that nevertheless "possesses a full reality by itself. . . . [I]t is on the basis of its reality that existence is produced."[130] However, "in order for the virtual to become actual it must create its own terms of actualization. The difference between the virtual and the actual is what requires that the process of actualization be a creation. . . . The actualization of the virtual . . . presents a dynamic multiplicity . . . the multiplicity of organization. . . . Without the blueprint of order, the creative process of organization is always an art."[131]

In a pragmatic sense, what is defined as potentiality (the virtual) represents a departure from the classical Aristotelian telos that, unless thwarted by the interference of some unforeseeable accidents, asserts success in actualization and assigns to matter the status of being just a passive receptacle for essences. As Dewey emphasized, "potentialities must be thought of in terms of consequences of interactions with other things. Hence potentialities cannot be known till after the interactions have occurred."[132] The Deweyan experiential transaction is a fundamental, triadic unit of analysis exceeding the role of an individual agent or Cartesian *cogito*. Such mutual exchange, a transaction, is described by Dewey as a situation whenever "response to another's act involves contemporaneous response to a thing as entering into other's behavior, and this upon both sides."[133]

Contrary to the spectator theory of knowledge, transaction is an "unfractured observation," which may seem a contradiction in terms if not for realizing that it represents a spatio-temporal event encompassing a triad of "the observer, the observing, and the observed."[134] An experiential event per se is as yet subject-less: yet such a virtual subject of experience still speaks (or thinks, or acts) by means of using a specific poetic language that appears to exist "in the form of undetermined infinitive. . . . It is poetry itself. As it expresses in language all events in one, the infinitive expresses the event of language—language being a unique event which merges now with that which renders it possible."[135] Deleuze has stressed the a-personal and collective nature of subjectivity by introducing his novel concept of the fourth person singular as a specific language expressing the singularity of an event embedded in a Deweyan problematic situation. For Dewey, too, "language [is] considered as an experienced event."[136]

As if speaking in the fourth person singular, the subject is not an a priori given intentional and speaking subject. As becoming, developing, and learning by means of multiple interactions embedded in experience, it is a collective subject whose thinking is enriched with both affect and percept. It is the perception of a creative artist or a poet that allows one to prophetically envisage the difference between "what may be and is not" so that eventually "the action and its consequence . . . [become] joined in perception."[137] Because "to perceive is to acknowledge unattained possibilities . . . to refer the present to consequences," such an expanded perception enables one creatively—that is, "in an unprecedented response to conditions"—to reorganize the "change in a given direction," hence to invent concepts in practice as the goal of experimental knowing contra-traditional epistemology.[138] The dynamics of the process is cooperative as the "response to another's act involves contemporaneous response to a thing as entering into the other's behavior, and this upon both sides. It constitutes the intelligibility of acts and things. Possession of the capacity to engage in such activity is intelligence."[139]

At the ontological level, this intelligibility belongs to what Deleuze asserts as the univocity of Being, when matter and mind meet each other along the line of creative becoming and humans and nature appear to be speaking in one voice. Being is univocal; however, "because the diagrammatic multiplicity can be realized only and the differential of forces integrated only by taking diverging paths," Being necessarily becomes plurivocal when, due to the immanent difference, it becomes diversified, articulated, and enacted in its actual manifestations.[140] The natural world is broader than its solely mechanical aspect and includes its own virtual, or as yet unrealized, dimension similar to experience as exceeding one's blind action and reaction: using Dewey's example, being burned is not yet "an" experience but merely a physical change. Learning from experience takes time and self-reflection. Importantly, understanding and mind denote "responsiveness to meanings . . . not response to direct physical stimuli."[141] In his analysis of human conduct, Dewey assigned the subjective element to the problem of agency, that is, determining how a particular individual functions, but the social element as embedded in what Dewey called "larger life" must by necessity relate to the very content of what an individual needs to do. We repeat that "an" experience represents collective, non-atomistic, but what Deleuze called smooth, space.

For Dewey, experience is not just the knowledge of facts: an experienced person does not just possess knowledge; rather, he or she makes connections between perceived facts and the multiplicity of goals, aspirations, purposes, and so on in order to construct a meaning for a singular experience, that is, to reconstruct it, to revaluate, to create the value anew. The ethical task as a revaluation, or reconstruction, of experience is what Deleuze called the clinical dimension of experience: it is clinical not only by virtue of its implying a diagnosis of a particular mode of existence by means of assessing the latter's symptoms—that is, reading them as the signs of the present—but also because of, as Dewey says, "a look into the future . . . an anticipation, or a prediction of some possible future experiences."[142] Dewey and Deleuze both speak of values that are yet to come, to be created in practice: Dewey brings in a clinical metaphor by comparing reflective thinking with the task of a physician who has to make "a prognosis, a forecast of the probable future course of the disease. And not only is his treatment a verification—or the reverse—of the idea . . . but the result also affects his treatment of future patients," that is, the greater community, or society, or even civilization (as invoked by Friedrich Nietzsche).[143] The critical, as the art of combination, amounts to constructing the Deleuzian immanent plane of consistency as such; the clinical, as the art of declension, demands the evaluation and outlining of the rhizomatic lines, each one capable of being potentially connected with any other line: "which are dead-ended or blocked, which cross voids . . . and most importantly the line of the steepest gradient, how it draws in the rest, towards what destination."[144]

For Dewey and Deleuze alike, the evaluation of experience—the interpretation of signs—is meaningless without the relation between signs and the corresponding apprenticeship in practice. Deleuze elaborates on the complexity in the dynamics of meaning-making in his work *Proust and Signs*, noticing the dynamic character of signs, that is, their having an "increasingly intimate" relation with their enfolded meanings so that truth becomes contingent and subordinate to interpretation.[145] Meanings are not given but depend on signs entering "into the surface organization which ensures the resonance of two series," the latter converging on a paradoxical differentiator, which becomes "both word and object at once."[146]

Coincidentally, R. D. Boisvert, addressing the reconstruction of experience as advanced by Dewey, points to the affinity between Dewey's articulation of experience as qualitative, multidimensional, and inclusive and Proust's famous madeleine that becomes "a nexus of meaning far surpassing—'infinitely other' as Dewey puts it—the description in terms of sense-data" but including an affective, qualitative aspect.[147] Deleuze, in *The Logic of Sense*, points out that a personal uncertainty cannot be reduced to the doubt of Cartesian subject but is derived from the objective structure of an event itself, insofar as the latter moves in two directions at once and insofar as it fragments the subject following this double direction. Concepts cannot be limited to the concepts of something, which would have been defined strictly by reference to some external object. Instead, they are artistic creations like sounds in music and colors in painting or like cinematic, futuristic images. They accord with Dewey's describing the realm of thinking traditionally represented "in terms of symbols, verbal and mathematical . . . [to being expanded to] thinking effectively in terms of the relational qualities,"[148] the latter appearing to comprise what Deleuze has later called qualitative multiplicities.

Dewey's pragmatic theory of experimental inquiry accords with the logic of relations embedded in Deleuze's growing rhizome. Naturalistic (bio)logic is immanent: as Dewey pointed out in his *Logic: The Theory of Inquiry*, such a logic does not depend on anything extraneous to inquiry. Instead it establishes continuity between many heterogeneous levels making up the Deleuzian multiplicity, because naturalistic inquiry is open-ended and grows like a real-life rhizome. The rhizome's life is not separate from its environment: for Dewey, "the logical [is] connected with the biological in the process of continuous development."[149] The rhizome's growth is an active process: in fact, in Dewey's words, "it does not live in the environment; it lives by means of its environment [and] with every differentiation of structure the environment expands."[150] Because such an expansive process is effectuated by an encounter with the unknown, therefore at the present moment unthinkable, it is future-oriented, tending toward "the limit of a lengthened and unfolded experience."[151] Dewey's example in this respect describes common, real-life experiential situations that nonetheless have an untimely dimension: "A thinking agent will perceive that certain given facts are probable signs of a future rain, and will take steps in the light of this anticipated future. To plant seeds, to cultivate the soil, to harvest grain, are intentional acts, possible only to a being who has learned to subordinate the immediately felt elements of an experience to those values which these hint at and prophesy."[152]

Dewey was adamant that the more an organism learns, the more it still has to learn. The system keeps itself going by means of continuously reorganizing itself to achieve a series of unsteady temporary equilibria from initial disequilibria; "otherwise death and catastrophe" would result.[153] For Dewey, there exists a peculiar "feeling of the direction and end of various lines of behavior"; he distinguished between the realm of thinking traditionally represented in terms of symbols and an expanded thinking in terms of relations of qualities.[154] The dynamic process of growth comprises "the past [that] is carried into the present so as to expand and deepen the content of the latter" but also involves a sense of anticipation of future consequences.[155] The creative "will is thus not something opposed to consequences or severed from them. It is a cause of consequences," which is capable of creating novelty.[156] The newly created concept would be an end-in-view that, by virtue of it also being the means, may open new possibilities. Each decision-making represents a change described by a novel distribution of parts acting within the overall dynamics of the total system. Dewey considered a part as always "already a part-of-a-whole . . . conditioned by the contingent, although itself a condition of the full determination of the latter."[157]

For Dewey, growth is possible only through participation in the dynamic process enacted in the rhythmic fluctuations between disequilibrations and the restoration of equilibrium at the new level. The notion of rhythm is poignant. The constant rhythms are created by virtue of the tension represented first by the loss of integration with the environment and second by the recovery of a new union.[158] These rhythmic fluctuations enable human evolution and growth as a function of the continuous reconstruction of experience based on the "integration of organic-environmental connections."[159] Analogously, what Deleuze called his new image of thought manifests itself in "new connections, new pathways, new synapses . . . produced not through any external determinism but through a becoming that carries the problems themselves along with it."[160] The concept of immanent becoming thus agrees with Dewey's asserting that the energy enabling the process "is not forced in from without"; rather, human evolution and growth by means of continuous inquiry, which is necessary for the reconstruction of experience, is based on the rhizomatic "integration of organic-environmental connections" depending on an initial tension, or difference.[161] It is a Deweyan tension, or Deleuzian difference, that enables an import of energy or information from an organism's environment under the necessary "condition of tensional distribution of energies."[162] Thereby the total organism-environment system restructures itself. Indeed, what takes place is the system's growth in terms of it expanding its own boundaries: the reorganization of experience, the realization of meanings, and the invention of novel concepts.

In his *Difference and Repetition*, Deleuze describes the creation of novel concepts as a nomadic, dynamic inquiry, a far cry from the foundational epistemology of analytic philosophy: "I make, remake and unmake my concepts along a moving horizon, from an always decentered centre, from an always displaced periphery which repeats and differentiates them."[163] For Dewey, we give way in our mind to some impulse; we try, in our mind, some plan. Following its development through various steps, we find ourselves in imagination in the presence of the consequences that would follow. Imagination functions by providing the opportunities to see what is possible in the actual, and "deliberation has the power of genesis"; it is dramatic and active.[164] It results in a modification, as Dewey says, of the whole objective order and involves dissolution of old objects together with a creative and unpredictable "suddenness of emergence" of new objects, among which the self, as emerging subject, is just one.[165] Hence the anti-Cartesian subject-less-ness of a problematic situation, the transformation of which inherently leads to self-making in practice.

For Dewey, human emotions, desires, wishes, purposes—as ends-in-view—are "informed . . . when . . . spent indirectly in search of material and in giving it order," hence participating in the reorganization of experience.[166] The fact that, as Dewey says, order itself develops means that the system's dynamics is such that its evolution tends toward greater organization and learning. Order can develop only providing a system is open, that is, it exists by means of a continuous network of relations that demonstrate themselves as interactions with the environment. The world threatened with disorder constitutes an objective uncertainty, which cannot be reduced to the personal uncertainty of a Cartesian subject. We repeat that a problematic situation, an event, would be as yet subject-less; and subject or self is constituted relationally. What is customarily called the self becomes an outcome of the whole series of experiential events: indeed, "among and within these occurrences, not outside of them nor underlying them are those events which are denominated selves."[167] An individual experience, for Dewey, is never exclusively personal: "[I]t [is] nature's, localized in a body as that body happened to exist by nature."[168] It is a transaction that, itself being an event in the dynamic time-series, culminates in the intercourse when, for Dewey, the human mind virtually comes in contact with the world because human attitudes, dispositions, and habits are always relational in character and should never be taken as "separate existences. They are always of, from, toward, situations and things."[169]

The reorganization of experience involves both organism and its environment. Significantly, in such a "continuum . . . there is no attempt to tell exactly where one begins and the other ends": the transaction between both is what constitutes "the intercourse of the live creature with his surroundings."[170] Transaction ensures the operational closure of the system open at large, making each end-in-view a temporary means for a new end, thereby correcting and ordering the course of events. Dewey emphasized that it is "processes [that] are self-maintaining" and not at all any individual components of a system.[171] Dewey envisaged that "personality, selfhood, subjectivity [become] eventual functions that emerge with complexly organized interactions."[172] The reorganization of experience embedded in pragmatic inquiry ensures "a continual beginning afresh," that is, the emergence of new experiences and novel meanings.[173] As for Deleuze, he specifically indicated that "there is no other truth than the creation of the New: creativity, emergence."[174] The emphasis on the creative process of organization makes a philosopher a creative artist for Dewey and Deleuze alike. Philosophical concepts, for Deleuze, are artistic and by necessity involve "two other dimensions, percepts and affects. Affects, percepts, and concepts are three inseparable forces, running from art to philosophy and from philosophy into art."[175] As created, new concepts acquire life; they are, as Deleuze says, vitalistic, and as embodied in meaningful and transformed experience, they must bring forward the desired "reward of [the] transformation" of the initially problematic situation.[176]

The realization of new meanings in experience demonstrates "efficiency in action . . . capacity to change the course of action, to experience novelties. . . . [I]t signifies the power of desire and choice to be factors in events."[177] The creative process is marked by "a release and amplification of energies that enter into it, conferring upon [human beings] the added quality of meaning. The quality of meaning thus introduced is extended and transferred, actually and potentially, from sounds, gestures and marks, to all other things in nature. Natural events become messages to be enjoyed and administered," therefore empowering the as yet subject-less subject with a newly acquired feeling of the Self and the awareness of creating new opportunities in life by means of continuously becoming-other in experience.[178] Subjectivity becomes manifest by one's being capable of expressing oneself passionately and freely in order "to bring something to life, to free life from where it's trapped, to trace lines of flight," to break down old methods and to break out into new territories.[179] Deleuze uses the French *savoir,* that is, "knowing-how," to emphasize the difference of such a vital experiential construction of subjectivity from the epistemic Cartesian subject. A subject-less subject is a philosopher par excellence who reads, interprets, and invents signs that "imply ways of living, possibilities of existence. . . . [Signs are] the symptoms of life gushing forth or draining away. . . . There is a profound link between signs, events, life and vitalism."[180] What inspires the ways of thinking—hence, the production of subjectivity—is the complexity of life itself. Thought thinks "by virtue of the forces that are exercised on it in order to constrain it to think. . . . Thinking, like activity, is always a second power of thought, [and] not the natural exercise of a faculty. . . . A power, the force of thinking, must throw it into a becoming-active," thus producing new modes of existence.[181] For Deleuze, indeed, it is "experimentation on ourselves [that] is our only identity, our single chance for all the combinations which inhabit us," constituting the process of continuously becoming-other, becoming-self.[182]

We encounter the tension (or difference) as embedded in experience; we cannot understand or recognize it as definite "something" yet; still this "something" inevitably motivates us to think, grasping the immediate affects in terms of "wonder, love, hatred, suffering," all the attributes that belong to the Deweyan qualitative and affective thought.[183] Despite the fact that we may not be consciously aware of these qualities, they effect "an immense multitude" of immediate organic acts, but an immediate experience needs mediation in order to make the unconscious affects and feelings conscious.[184] Thinking, enriched with its affective dimension, "is always experiencing, experimenting . . . and what we experience, experiment with, is . . . what's coming into being, what's new, what's taking shape" in the mind of a philosopher as if in the hands of a creative artist.[185] J. J. Holder, addressing the conception of creativity and Dewey's logic as a theory of inquiry, presents a powerful example in "the instance of a great work of art—for example, the thinking that coordinates the emergence of Michelangelo's David from a hunk of marble—[this is] a degree of discontinuity that epitomizes the kind of thinking that is called creative."[186] For Dewey and Deleuze alike, the production of the self in experience is a creative art: "subjectification is an artistic activity."[187]

Ethics is inherent in the production of subjectivity, and subject-formation is "ethical and aesthetic, as opposed to morality," if morality is understood as an a priori given code of behavior.[188] It cannot be otherwise in a world filled with conflicting experiences situated in the midst of critical junctures embedded in Dewey's problematic situations. An ethical dimension is complemented by an affective one: the experience would satisfy the conditions of being an experience, that is, "an integral event," when permeated through and through with affects or becomings that alone enable "genuine initiations and conclusions" versus just "things happen[ing]" without their making any sense.[189] There is always an affect exceeding and spilling over any preconceived thinking conforming to a prescribed course of action. As a quality manifesting in a "feeling of the direction and end of various lines of behavior [as] . . . the feeling of habits working below direct consciousness," it becomes an impulse for the transformation of old routine habits and the creation of new, intelligent habits that would have embodied new meanings and values as a function of the reorganization of experience.[190] It is the philosophical method as creative, artistic, and cooperative "that would affirm life instead of a knowledge that is opposed to life. Thinking would then mean . . . inventing new possibilities of life" akin to Dewey's task of the reconstruction of experience.[191]

Philosophical practice, for both Dewey and Deleuze, focuses on both critical and ethical dimensions. The purpose of Deleuze's philosophical method is, apart from creating novel concepts, radically ethical in the manner of being worthy of what is to come into existence, to become. Novel concepts are invented so as to make sense out of experiential events and, ultimately, to affirm this sense. For Deleuze and Guattari, the major message of their philosophy is "to become worthy of the event."[192] Critical and ethical aspects reciprocally presuppose each other. The critical aspect of Dewey's pragmatic philosophy functions as the criticism of criticisms and emphasizes the "wide awake" thought capable of self-refection.[193] Thinking and learning originate in real practical life full of tensions, differences, and perplexities. What is there left to learn if the difference refers back to some primary identity rather than moves forward to further differences? For Dewey, one only "excels in complexity and minuteness of differentiations."[194] Importantly, we learn "nothing from those who say: 'Do as I do.'"[195] Those who insist on such an a priori established identity betray the new image of a creative thought; and the one "who executes the wish of others [is] doomed to act along lines predetermined to regularity."[196] What follows is the conformity to "the law of reflection" solely, thus eliminating the creative power of difference when a thought encounters perplexity, similar to a novice athlete who is thrown into water.[197] Says Dewey: "I am told that there is a swimming school in a certain city where youth are taught to swim without going into water, being repeatedly drilled in the various movements which are necessary for swimming. When one of the young men so trained was asked what he did when he got into water, he laconically replied, 'Sunk.'"[198]

For the youths who find themselves in a novel situation, there is no solid foundation under their feet, and the world that they have to face loses its reassuring power of familiar representations but demands a practical realization of what it means to swim. Deleuze's example is remarkably similar: he reconstructs a powerful story, based on the classic example used by Gottfried Leibniz in his idea of the sea as a system of differential relations, of a novice athlete who learns to swim through a literal becoming when she struggles against the waves because she is facing the unknown and unthinkable. The swimmer is learning "by grasping [the movement of the wave] in practice as signs."[199] Deleuze emphasizes the "sensory-motivity" of the genuine learner who, exemplified in the image of the swimmer, tries to coordinate her own sensor-motor activity—that is, at every moment evaluate her mode of existence—with an intense, as if opposite, force of water. The swimmer begins by being within the totality of a situation and not at all by repeating movements that have been imposed upon her outside the qualitative whole: her environment is, as Dewey puts it, unified and capable of "vital contact."[200]

The swimmer has to emerge and not sink as if assuming a role of a docile body overwhelmed by the power of water. Many turbulent waves exist in the "precarious and perilous" world, and one must cut through them when either making "suggestions reaching out and being broken in a clash, or being carried onward by a cooperative wave."[201] Only then the athlete and the water, as an image of the perplexity, even hostility, of the world outside, may undergo a shared deterritorialization, leading eventually to "a growing progressive self-disclosure of nature itself."[202] The specifics of a local problematic situation indicate the extent of the "interpenetration of the self with objective conditions. . . . The unique, unduplicated character of experienced events . . . impregnates the emotion that is evoked."[203] The future-oriented, somewhat untimely epistemology makes an object, in effect, a consequence or a limit-case of the inquiry: it is becoming that is the very condition of being.

A novel concept is derived in its uniqueness, as a singularity, from the multiplicity of its rhizomatic components and connections as a datum, as yet "the big, buzzing, blooming confusion of which James wrote" and as such the only entity that may be given to senses in the full complexity of its "underlying and pervasive quality."[204] What must be taken, however, is its meaning, what Deleuze called the logic of sense, or the evaluation depending on "the context of every experience."[205] Although "a concept . . . has the truth that falls to it as a function of the conditions of its creation," the very singularity of conditions embedded in the experiential situation turns some abstract final knowledge into Dewey's warranted assertion.[206]

As in the case of the athlete who can learn how to swim only if and when immersed in the water and actively moving together and within this milieu, the thinking process for Dewey amounts to the interplay of signs embedded within both an inquirer and an inquiry. The swimmer's preconceived knowledge of what swimming is, the knowing that, would be of little help under the circumstances of the real-life experience as compared to knowing how. "A moving force" of the water, as if signifying the hazardous and "uncertain character of the world" in general, "includes the self within it."[207] The athlete, sure enough, has to emerge and not sink: her newly acquired knowledge becomes an emergent property contingent on ever-changing local conditions with which she must interact in order to learn. Genuine learning, as encompassing the Deleuzian triangle of percepts, affects, and concepts, amounts to "novelty in action, greater range and depth of insight and increase in poignancy of feeling."[208]

The swimmer cannot be a passive spectator maintaining an indifferent gaze with the a priori given certainty. An active participation, that is, a "unity of the self and its acts" and not a set of logical propositions, is what produces thinking.[209] The athlete is moving together with water, the total movement comprising "desire . . . integrated with an object . . . completely" so as to learn, to literally assert and warrant life and not death.[210] Multiple becomings are relational entities that function "as clues to and of something still to be reached, they are intermediate, not ultimate; means not finalities."[211]

A life itself—with an indefinite article, as in an experience—is full of entangled lines and "tangled scenes," and for Deleuze, as for Dewey, thinking is a practical art.[212] Thinking is "not just a theoretical matter. It [is] to do with vital problems. To do with life itself."[213] The athlete is learning how to swim because the means she uses are intrinsic to the whole situation, and the very "activity of learning is completely one with what results from it. . . . Means and ends coalesce."[214] Dewey was adamant that what a person "gets and gives as a human being, a being with desires, emotions and ideas, is . . . a widening and deepening of conscious life—a more intense, disciplined, and expanding realization of meanings."[215] Experience as a site of learning is the focal point for Dewey and Deleuze alike. It is through organic resonances in experience that the Deweyan continuity is carried further toward the ultimate "unity of sense and impulse, of brain and eye and ear" overcoming the apparent dualisms in the process of the "integration of the shifting scenes of the world."[216]

To make a concluding remark, this chapter has constructed the new constellation between Dewey's and Deleuze's respective philosophies in the context of experimental thinking and learning from experience.[217] Rather than reducing their thoughts to a single common denominator, the chapter has demonstrated similar premises, as well as ethical commitments and insights, shared by these two philosophers who not only never met physically but were separated by time, place, and culture. The convergence of Dewey's and Deleuze's philosophical positions was thus established. If in this process the Deweyan thought itself went through changes and transformations, it only confirms the fact that Dewey himself, in accord with his philosophical project, would have welcomed the novel reconstruction of his own ideas so as "to better respond to the vicissitudes of new times and contexts," having been interpreted creatively and pragmatically, thus producing something which is not just "an illustration of something familiar."[218]

Notes

1. R. Rorty, *Consequences of Pragmatism: Essays, 1972–1980* (Minneapolis: University of Minnesota Press, 1982), xviii.

2. E.g., G. Deleuze, *Cinema 1: The Movement-Image* (Minneapolis: University of Minnesota Press, 1986); and *Cinema 2: The Time-Image* (Minneapolis: University of Minnesota Press, 1989).

3. R. J. Bernstein, *The New Constellation: The Ethical-Political Horizons of Modernity/Postmodernity* (Cambridge, Mass.: MIT Press, 1995).

4. R. J. Bernstein, *Praxis and Action: Contemporary Philosophies of Human Activity* (Philadelphia: University of Pennsylvania Press, 1971); *Beyond Objectivism and Relativism: Science, Hermeneutics, and Praxis* (Philadelphia: University of Pennsylvania Press, 1983); and *New Constellation.*

5. Bernstein, *Praxis and Action*, 219.

6. Compare L. A. Hickman, *Reading Dewey: Interpretations for a Postmodern Generation* (Bloomington: Indiana University Press, 1998); G. Deleuze, *The Logic of Sense* (New York: Columbia University Press, 1990); and G. Deleuze and F. Guattari, *What Is Philosophy?* (New York: Columbia University Press, 1994).

7. J. Dewey, *Does Reality Possess Practical Character?* in *The Essential Dewey*, ed. L. A. Hickman and T. M. Alexander (Bloomington: Indiana University Press, 1988), 133. Dewey's italics.

8. J. Dewey, *Experience and Nature* (New York: Dover Publications, 1925), 313, 245.

9. J. Dewey, *How We Think* (Buffalo, N.Y.: Prometheus Books, 1991), 26.

10. Ibid., 75.

11. Compare I. Semetsky, "The Adventures of a Postmodern Fool, or the Semiotics of Learning," in *Trickster and Ambivalence: The Dance of Differentiation*, ed. C. W. Spinks (Madison, Wis.: Atwood, 2001), 55–70.

12. Dewey, *How We Think*, 224.

13. Ibid.

14. Ibid., 30, 32, 33.

15. Dewey, *Experience and Nature*, 4.

16. Dewey, *How We Think*, 108.

17. Ibid., 75.

18. Dewey, *Experience and Nature*, 308.

19. G. Deleuze, *Negotiations, 1972–1990* (New York: Columbia University Press, 1995), 103.

20. G. Deleuze and S. Hand, *Foucault* (Minneapolis: University of Minnesota Press, 1988), 110.

21. G. Deleuze, *Difference and Repetition* (New York: Columbia University Press, 1994), 139.

22. G. Deleuze, *Spinoza: Practical Philosophy* (San Francisco: City Lights Books, 1988), 125.

23. Ibid., 123.

24. Deleuze, *Negotiations*, 141.

25. G. Deleuze, *Proust and Signs: The Complete Text*. Vol. 17, *Theory Out of Bounds* (Minneapolis: University of Minnesota Press, 2000).

26. Deleuze, *Difference and Repetition*, 159, 161.

27. J. Dewey, *The Quest for Certainty* (New York: Minton, Balch and Company, 1929), 143.

28. Dewey, *Experience and Nature*, 65.

29. Deleuze, *Difference and Repetition*, 192.

30. J. Dewey, *Art as Experience* (New York: Minton, 1934), 45.

31. Ibid., 52.

32. Dewey, *Experience and Nature*, 295.

33. J. Dewey, *Logic: The Theory of Inquiry* (New York: H. Holt and Company, 1938).

34. Dewey, *Art as Experience*, 85; J. Dewey, *Qualitative Thought*, in *Philosophers of Process*, ed. D. Browning and W. T. Myers (New York: Fordham University Press, 1998), 199.

35. Dewey, *Art as Experience*, 23.

36. Deleuze, *Difference and Repetition*, 192.

37. G. Deleuze and C. Parnet, *Dialogues* (New York: Columbia University Press, 1987), 57.

38. Dewey, *Does Reality Possess Practical Character?* 131.

39. Dewey, *Experience and Nature*, 222.

40. J. Dewey, *Democracy and Education: An Introduction to the Philosophy of Education*, Text-book Series in Education (New York: Macmillan, 1916), 149–50.

41. Ibid., 417.

42. Dewey, *Art as Experience*, 303.

43. G. Deleuze and F. Guattari, *A Thousand Plateaus: Capitalism and Schizophrenia* (Minneapolis: University of Minnesota Press, 1987), 30.

44. Deleuze and Parnet, *Dialogues*, 57.

45. Dewey, *Qualitative Thought*, 206–7.

46. Deleuze and Guattari, *What Is Philosophy?* 74.

47. Deleuze, *Logic of Sense*, 20.

48. Deleuze and Hand, *Foucault*, 110.

49. Dewey, *Democracy and Education*.

50. Deleuze and Hand, *Foucault*, 96.

51. Deleuze, *Negotiations*, 116.

52. Ibid., 86.

53. Dewey, *How We Think*, 75.

54. Deleuze, *Negotiations*, 45.

55. J. Dewey, *Time and Individuality*, in *Philosophers of Process*, 229.

56. J. Campbell, *Understanding John Dewey: Nature and Cooperative Intelligence* (Chicago: Open Court, 1995), 77; Dewey, *Art as Experience*, 4.

57. Dewey, *Experience and Nature*, 50.

58. Ibid., 182, 279.

59. J. Dewey, *Human Nature and Conduct: An Introduction to Social Psychology* (Carbondale: Southern Illinois University Press, 1988), 132.

60. Dewey, *Art as Experience*, 267.

61. Dewey, *Human Nature and Conduct*, 21.

62. Ibid.

63. Ibid., 88.

64. Ibid., 22.

65. Ibid., 55.

66. Ibid., 23.

67. Ibid., 22, 26.
68. Deleuze, *Negotiations*, 165.
69. Dewey, *Democracy and Education*, 153.
70. Dewey, *Logic*, 163; Deleuze, *Negotiations*, 164.
71. Deleuze and Guattari, *What Is Philosophy?* 36.
72. Ibid., 37.
73. Dewey, *Art as Experience*, 22.
74. Ibid., 150.
75. Deleuze, *Spinoza*, 29.
76. J. Dewey and R. D. Archambault, *John Dewey on Education: Selected Writings* (New York: Modern Library, 1964), 145.
77. Dewey, *Art as Experience*, 42.
78. Dewey, *Experience and Nature*, 245.
79. Dewey, *Art as Experience*, 24.
80. Dewey, *How We Think*, 214.
81. Dewey, *Democracy and Education*, 417.
82. Dewey, *How We Think*, 215–16.
83. Ibid., 217.
84. Deleuze, *Difference and Repetition*, 194.
85. Deleuze, *Spinoza*, 29; Dewey, *Art as Experience*, 118.
86. Ibid., 38.
87. Deleuze, original French, quoted in R. Bogue, *Deleuze and Guattari* (New York: Routledge, 1989), 155.
88. Dewey, *Art as Experience*, 100–101.
89. Ibid., 37.
90. Deleuze and Guattari, *What Is Philosophy?* 16, 21.
91. Dewey, *Experience and Nature*, 234.
92. Deleuze and Guattari, *Thousand Plateaus*, 380; Deleuze, *Negotiations*, 77.
93. Dewey, *Experience and Nature*, 235.
94. Deleuze, *Logic of Sense*, 5; Dewey, *Experience and Nature*, 279.
95. Dewey, *Experience and Nature*, xvi.
96. Ibid., 231.
97. Deleuze, *Logic of Sense*, 148.
98. Ibid., 19.
99. J. Dewey, *The Moral Self*, in *The Essential Dewey*, 351.
100. Deleuze, *Negotiations*, 133.
101. Dewey, *Moral Self*, 351.
102. Dewey, *How We Think*, 14.
103. Dewey, *Human Nature and Conduct*, 94.
104. Deleuze and Guattari, *What is Philosophy?* 40; Deleuze, *Negotiations*, 33.
105. Dewey, *Democracy and Education*, 255.
106. Dewey, *How We Think*, 37.
107. Deleuze, *Spinoza*, 19.
108. Bogue, *Deleuze and Guattari*, 53; Deleuze, *Difference and Repetition*, 94.

109. Dewey, *Experience and Nature*, 299.

110. Ibid., 299, 300.

111. N. Noddings and P. J. Shore, *Awakening the Inner Eye: Intuition in Education* (New York: Teachers College, Columbia University, 1984), 51.

112. Dewey, *Experience and Nature*, 258.

113. Ibid., 21.

114. Dewey, *Human Nature and Conduct*, 21.

115. Dewey, *How We Think*, 113; Dewey, *Experience and Nature*, 20–21.

116. Dewey, *How We Think*, 75.

117. Deleuze and Guattari, *Thousand Plateaus*, 371.

118. Dewey, *Qualitative Thought*, 192; Deleuze, *Negotiations*, 149; Dewey, *Time and Individuality*, 220–21.

119. Dewey, *How We Think*, 14–15.

120. Deleuze, *Negotiations*, 153.

121. Dewey, *Qualitative Thought*, 198.

122. Dewey, *Experience and Nature*, 1.

123. Ibid.

124. Dewey, *Time and Individuality*, 223; Dewey, *Experience and Nature*, 281.

125. Deleuze, *Negotiations*, 45; Dewey, *Experience and Nature*, 281.

126. Dewey, *Human Nature and Conduct*, 26.

127. Deleuze and Hand, *Foucault*, 34.

128. Deleuze and Guattari, *Thousand Plateaus*, 510.

129. Deleuze, *Difference and Repetition*, 25.

130. Ibid., 211.

131. M. Hardt, *Gilles Deleuze: An Apprenticeship in Philosophy* (Minneapolis: University of Minnesota Press, 1993), 18.

132. Dewey, *Time and Individuality*, 222.

133. Dewey, *Experience and Nature*, 178.

134. J. Dewey, *Knowing and the Known* (with Arthur F. Bentley), in *The Later Works of John Dewey, 1925–1953*, ed. J. A. Boydston (Carbondale: Southern Illinois University Press, 1991), 16:97.

135. Deleuze, *Negotiations*, 185.

136. Dewey, *Experience and Nature*, 173.

137. Dewey, *Time and Individuality*, 225; Dewey, *Art as Experience*, 44.

138. Dewey, *Experience and Nature*, 182; Dewey, *Time and Individuality*, 225.

139. Dewey, *Experience and Nature*, 179–80.

140. Deleuze and Hand, *Foucault*, 38.

141. Dewey, *Democracy and Education*, 315.

142. J. Dewey, *Analysis of Reflective Thinking* (from *How We Think*), in *The Essential Dewey*, 143.

143. Ibid.

144. Deleuze and Parnet, *Dialogues*, 120.

145. Deleuze, *Proust and Signs*, 88.

146. Deleuze, *Logic of Sense*, 104, 51.

147. R. D. Boisvert, *John Dewey: Rethinking Our Time* (Albany, N.Y.: SUNY Press, 1998), 15.

148. Dewey, *Art as Experience*, 46.

149. Dewey, *Logic*, 25.

150. Ibid.

151. Deleuze, *Logic of Sense*, 20.

152. Dewey, *How We Think*, 15.

153. Dewey, *Experience and Nature*, 281.

154. Dewey, *Human Nature and Conduct*, 26.

155. Dewey, *Art as Experience*, 24.

156. Dewey, *Human Nature and Conduct*, 33.

157. Dewey, *Experience and Nature*, 65.

158. See Dewey, *Art as Experience*, 15.

159. Dewey, *Experience and Nature*, 279.

160. Deleuze, *Negotiations*, 149.

161. Dewey, *Logic*, 25; Dewey, *Experience and Nature*, 279.

162. Dewey, *Experience and Nature*, 253.

163. Deleuze, *Difference and Repetition*, xxi.

164. J. W. Garrison, "Introduction: Education and the New Scholarship on John Dewey," in *The New Scholarship on Dewey*, ed. J. W. Garrison (Boston: Kluwer Academic, 1995), 121.

165. Dewey, *Art as Experience*, 75.

166. Ibid., 70.

167. Dewey, *Experience and Nature*, 232.

168. Ibid., 231.

169. Ibid., 238.

170. Dewey, *Art as Experience*, 227, 22.

171. Dewey, *Logic*, 26.

172. Dewey, *Experience and Nature*, 108.

173. Dewey, *Democracy and Education*, 417.

174. Deleuze, *Cinema 2*, 146–47.

175. Deleuze, *Negotiations*, 127.

176. Dewey, *Art as Experience*, 22.

177. Dewey, *Human Nature and Conduct*, 209.

178. Dewey, *Experience and Nature*, 174.

179. Deleuze, *Negotiations*, 141.

180. Ibid., 143.

181. G. Deleuze, *The Fold: Leibniz and the Baroque* (Minneapolis: University of Minnesota Press, 1993), 108.

182. Deleuze and Parnet, *Dialogues*, 11.

183. Deleuze, *Difference and Repetition*, 139.

184. Dewey, *Experience and Nature*, 299.

185. Deleuze, *Negotiations*, 104.

186. J. J. Holder, "An Epistemological Foundation for Thinking: A Deweyan Approach," in *The New Scholarship on Dewey*, 186.

187. Deleuze, *Negotiations*, 114.

188. Ibid.

189. Dewey, *Art as Experience*, 38, 40.

190. Dewey, *Human Nature and Conduct*, 26.

191. Compare Campbell, *Understanding John Dewey*; Deleuze, *The Fold*, 101.

192. Deleuze and Guattari, *What Is Philosophy?* 160.

193. Dewey, *How We Think*, 57.

194. Dewey, *Art as Experience*, 23.

195. Deleuze, *Difference and Repetition*, 23.

196. Dewey, *Human Nature and Conduct*, 208.

197. Deleuze and Guattari, *Thousand Plateaus*, 5.

198. Dewey and Archambault, *John Dewey on Education*, 116.

199. Deleuze, *Difference and Repetition*, 23.

200. Ibid.; Dewey and Archambault, *John Dewey on Education*, 116.

201. Dewey, *Experience and Nature*, 41; Dewey, *Art as Experience*, 38.

202. Dewey, *Experience and Nature*, x.

203. Dewey, *Art as Experience*, 67.

204. Dewey, *Qualitative Thought*, 203, 195.

205. Dewey, *Art as Experience*, 198.

206. Deleuze and Guattari, *What Is Philosophy?* 27.

207. Dewey, *Moral Self*, 345; J. Dewey, *Existence as Precarious and Stable*, in *Philosophers of Process*, 229; Dewey, *Moral Self*, 345.

208. Dewey, *Art as Experience*, 23.

209. Dewey, *Moral Self*, 343.

210. Ibid., 344.

211. Dewey, *Quest for Certainty*, 80.

212. Dewey, *Art as Experience*, 290.

213. Deleuze, *Negotiations*, 105.

214. Dewey, *Art as Experience*, 198.

215. Dewey, *Democracy and Education*, 417.

216. Dewey, *Art as Experience*, 22–23; Dewey, *Analysis of Reflective Thinking*, 407.

217. Compare Bernstein, *New Constellation*; and I. Semetsky, *Deleuze, Education and Becoming* (Rotterdam: Sense Publishers, 2006).

218. Garrison, "Introduction," 1; Dewey, *Art as Experience*, 75.

Contributors
Index

Contributors

Barry Allen teaches philosophy at McMaster University and is an associate editor of the interdisciplinary journal *Common Knowledge*. He is author of *Truth in Philosophy* (1993), *Knowledge and Civilization* (2004), and *Artifice and Design* (2008).

Richard J. Bernstein is Vera List Professor of Philosophy at the New School for Social Research. He has authored numerous books, most recently *Radical Evil* (2002) and *The Pragmatic Turn* (forthcoming).

Antonio Calcagno is associate professor of philosophy at King's University College at the University of Western Ontario. He has published in continental and Renaissance philosophy. His latest book is *Badiou and Derrida: Politics, Events and Their Time* (2007). He serves as editor of *Symposium: Canadian Journal of Continental Philosophy.*

Paul Fairfield is associate professor of philosophy at Queen's University. His recent books include *Education After Dewey* (2009), *Why Democracy?* (2008), and *Public/Private* (2005). He is former editor of *Symposium: Canadian Journal of Continental Philosophy.*

Jim Garrison is professor of philosophy of education at Virginia Tech University. He is a past president of the Philosophy of Education Society and the John Dewey Society. His most recent edited book is *Reconstructing Democracy, Recontextualizing Dewey* (2008), and his latest coauthored book is *John Dewey at 150: Reflections for a New Century* (2009).

James A. Good is chair of the department of social sciences and professor of history at Lone Star College–North Harris. He is author of *A Search for Unity in Diversity: The "Permanent Hegelian Deposit" in the Philosophy of John Dewey* (2006) as well as numerous essays on pragmatism and on the American reception of German idealism.

James Scott Johnston is assistant professor in the faculty of education at Queen's University. He is author of several books, including *Inquiry in Education* (2006) and *Deweyan Inquiry* (2009). His latest (coauthored) book is *Democracy and the Intersection of Religion and Tradition* (2010).

Colin Koopman is visiting assistant professor of philosophy at the University of Oregon. He is author of *Pragmatism as Transition* (2009) and is presently at work on a book on Michel Foucault's project of genealogical critique. He has published several articles on pragmatism, genealogy, and political philosophy.

Joseph Margolis is Laura H. Carnell Professor of Philosophy at Temple University. He has authored numerous books in the fields of American philosophy, philosophy of the human sciences, aesthetics, and epistemology. Recent titles include *The Arts and the Definition of the Human* (2008), *Pragmatism without Foundations* (2007), and *The Unraveling of Scientism* (2003).

C. G. Prado is professor emeritus of philosophy at Queen's University. His most recent books are *Starting with Descartes* (2009), *Choosing to Die* (2008), and *Searle and Foucault on Truth* (2006). His most recent coauthored book is *The Best Laid Plans* (2002); his latest edited anthology is *Foucault's Legacy* (2009).

Tom Rockmore is McAnulty College Distinguished Professor and professor of philosophy at Duquesne University. He is author of many books, most recently *Kant and Idealism* (2007) and *In Kant's Wake: Philosophy in the Twentieth Century* (2006).

Sandra B. Rosenthal is Provost Distinguished Professor of Philosophy at Loyola University. She has published twelve books and over 250 articles on pragmatism and its relation to other areas of philosophy. Her publications include *Speculative Pragmatism* (2000), *Charles Peirce's Pragmatic Pluralism* (1994), *Time, Continuity, and Indeterminacy* (2000), and *C. I. Lewis in Focus* (2007).

Inna Semetsky is research academic in the School of Education at the University of Newcastle. Her latest books are *Deleuze, Education, and Becoming* (2006), *Nomadic Education: Variations on the Theme by Deleuze and Guattari* (2008), and *Resymbolization of the Self: Human Development and Tarot Hermeneutic* (forthcoming). She is on the editorial board of several journals, including the *European Legacy*.

David Vessey is assistant professor of philosophy at Grand Valley State University. He has published a number of articles on philosophical hermeneutics, especially as it compares to other philosophical traditions.

Index